PENGUIN CLASSICS

AUGUSTAN CRITICAL WRITING

DAVID WOMERSLEY is a Fellow and Tutor in English Literature at
Jesus College, Oxford. His book *The Transformation of the Decline and Fall
of the Roman Empire* was published by Cambridge University Press in
1988. He has also edited Gibbon's *The History of the Decline and Fall of
the Roman Empire* in three volumes for Penguin Classics.

AUGUSTAN
CRITICAL WRITING

Edited with an introduction and notes by
DAVID WOMERSLEY

PENGUIN BOOKS

PENGUIN BOOKS

Published by the Penguin Group
Penguin Books Ltd, 27 Wrights Lane, London w8 5TZ, England
Penguin Books USA Inc., 375 Hudson Street, New York, New York 10014, USA
Penguin Books Australia Ltd, Ringwood, Victoria, Australia
Penguin Books Canada Ltd, 10 Alcorn Avenue, Toronto, Ontario, Canada M4V 3B2
Penguin Books (NZ) Ltd, 182–190 Wairau Road, Auckland 10, New Zealand

Penguin Books Ltd, Registered Offices: Harmondsworth, Middlesex, England

First published 1997
1 3 5 7 9 10 8 6 4 2

Set in 10/12.5 pt Monotype Baskerville
Typeset by Rowland Phototypesetting Ltd, Bury St Edmunds, Suffolk
Printed in England by Clays Ltd, St Ives plc

for Howard Erskine-Hill
teacher, colleague and friend

CONTENTS

IV Introducing Shakespeare, 1725–1744

V Editing Milton, 1732–1734

ACKNOWLEDGEMENTS

A generous grant of sabbatical leave from my college and university allowed me to complete this anthology in circumstances of comparative leisure. My colleague Don Fowler gave invaluable help in the tracking down of Latin quotations, and Leofranc Holford-Strevens provided reassurance when it proved impossible to track down quotations. Roger Lonsdale was generous and prompt in sharing with me his unrivalled familiarity with eighteenth-century poetry: *bis dat qui cito dat.*

The dedication indicates an academic and personal debt extending back over many years, and still increasing. It is perhaps maladroit to dedicate an anthology so preoccupied with literary Whiggism to a great scholar of Jacobitism. But even Whigs, after their fashion, were not unacquainted with loyalty and gratitude.

Jesus College, Oxford, 1996

ABBREVIATIONS

ALC   D. A. Russell and M. Winterbottom (eds.), *Ancient Literary Criticism* (Oxford: Oxford University Press, 1972)

Jonson   C. H. Herford and P. and E. Simpson (eds.), *Ben Jonson*, 11 vols. (Oxford: Oxford University Press, 1925–52)

Parker   W. R. Parker, *Milton: A Biography*, 2 vols. (Oxford: Oxford University Press, 1968)

Prose Works   *The Complete Prose Works of John Milton*, 8 vols. (New Haven: Yale University Press, 1953–82)

Sherburn   George Sherburn (ed.), *The Correspondence of Alexander Pope*, 5 vols. (Oxford: Oxford University Press, 1956)

Smith   D. Nichol Smith (ed.), *Eighteenth Century Essays on Shakespeare* (Oxford: Clarendon Press, 2nd edn, 1963)

INTRODUCTION

In Book II of the *Critique of Judgement* (1790), Kant illustrated his contention that *a priori* rules are impotent to coerce judgements of taste by imagining a confrontation with a poetaster:

> If any one reads me his poem . . . which, all said and done, fails to commend itself to my taste, then let him adduce *Batteux* or *Lessing*, or still older and more famous critics of taste, with all the host of rules laid down by them, as a proof of the beauty of his poem; let certain passages particularly displeasing to me accord completely with the rules of beauty, (as set out by these critics and universally recognized): I stop my ears: I do not want to hear any reasons or arguments about the matter. I would prefer to suppose that those rules of the critics were at fault, or at least have no application, than to allow my judgement to be determined by *a priori* proofs.[1]

Kant's stopping of his ears marked a change of direction in the European conversation about the nature, the reception and the valuing of the work of art. Finding the province of the aesthetic in the grip of vicious confusions of words and ideas, Kant sought to cleanse our aesthetic judgements (thus his disagreement with the poetaster is offered to us at one level as a conflict between old sophistry and new honesty). Having defined the beautiful as the form of finality in an object, which pleases necessarily and universally, Kant asserted that both the work of art and our appreciation of it were therefore disinterested.[2] The consequences of so conceiving the realm of the aesthetic were profound. In respect of the work of art, it implied that the forms of the beautiful could not be inferred from our notions of fitness or propriety in any other area of life, such as the social, the political or the moral. The work of art was made independent of such consider-ations.[3] In respect of our reception of the work of art, the implication was that, if we are honest, our aesthetic judgements are uninfluenced by the allegiances we happen to have formed in other areas of our lives. And when Kant had his imaginary poetaster cite Batteux and Lessing to shore up his position, it was clear his philosophy required its adherents to shun even the greatest and most systematic of the earlier generation of critics.[4]

English literary criticism of the period 1660–1750 was everything Kant thought criticism should not be. Literary art, and men's responses to it, were openly and deliberately coordinated with other areas of their lives, in particular with their political lives. Yet the book which remains the most recent attempt to write the history of criticism in this period is framed as the story of a quest to wade through the treacherous quicksands of neoclassicism and reach the firm shore of romanticism.[5] It applauds critics where they seem to anticipate the early nineteenth century and rebukes them where they persist in holding to their own, unreformed, views. Whatever one may think about the methodology of such a teleological narrative, it is necessarily condemned to seeing some of the most characteristic aspects of late-seventeenth- and eighteenth-century English criticism as mere errors.[6] It therefore cannot lead to a truly historical understanding of the nature and purpose of the body of work it takes for its subject.

The dominant consideration in this earlier tradition of commentary was the question of aesthetics, and this in two senses. First, works of pure aesthetic inquiry loomed disproportionately large in the map of the subject. Second, works which are varied and flexible in their interrogation of literature were pillaged for their imputed core of aesthetic doctrine.[7] It is, however, one of the principles of the present anthology that *how* people wrote about literature is of interest, as well as the propositional content of *what* they were saying about it. There-fore works such as Samuel Cobb's *A Discourse on Criticism and the Liberty of Writing* (1707) and the anonymous *Milton Restor'd and Bentley Depos'd* (1732) have been included. These are not, and do not claim to be, works of high intellectual seriousness. But they are far from unintelligent. Moreover, their satiric tonalities and conversational freedom can sensitize us to similar exuberances in more celebrated works with which they are in dialogue but which have tended to be handled with a well-intentioned but unfortunate reverence, thereby occasionally obscuring their flexibility of idiom and register.[8] Jonathan Richardson's attack on Bentley's edition of Milton has therefore a double claim on its place in the anthology. In the first place, its strictures on how Milton should be edited inform us about how poems as literary objects could be conceived of in the 1730s. But equally, in its eccentricity of procedure and the startling dynamics of tone which result from its passing so easily from piety to satire to the informality of anecdote and personal revelation, it speaks to us from a time before literary criticism had become codified and professionalized. Such modalities have a central place in the study of literary criticism.

The end result of the scholarly tradition dealing with critical writing between the Restoration and the French Revolution is therefore a complicated misrepresentation, arising from both the selection of which works to foreground and the approach to the selected works. The importance and interest of some writers has not been acknowledged because the field was conceptualized such that they were either excluded or obscured. At the same time, the discussion of some included works has been skewed by the need to fit them into a narrative which was committed to depicting their authors struggling blindly towards positions of which they had no knowledge, and which they might have rejected with a frown or a laugh had they been proposed to them. Rule; line; regularity; authority; decorum; correctness; law; restoration; reformation; plot: the vocabulary of these critics was remarkable for the extent and the insistence of its metaphorical reach outside the domain of art. The resulting possibilities were exploited consciously and unapologetically in the period between the accession of Charles II and that of George III. Those critics would in their turn have stopped their ears if told that they should eschew the powerful polemical effects those metaphors placed within their grasp out of deference to an incomprehensible doctrine insisting that art envisaged no end beyond itself.

If the study of literary criticism during the reigns of the later Stuarts and early Hanoverians has been distorted by misguided attempts to construct a genealogy for romanticism, it has also been misled by the stridency of some of the voices within that period to which it was bound to lend an ear. After the Restoration, judgements on individual works first began to be voiced within a broader vision of the sequences of English literary history. For instance, Fleckno's *A Short Discourse of the English Stage* (1664) and Dryden's *Of Dramatick Poesie, An Essay* (1668) connected the revival of English literary achievement to the return of the monarchy in 1660. Thus the phases of literary achievement or decline were linked to political events, such as the interregnum and Restoration. At the same time the language of dullness, which was originally an idiom of literary lampooning, began to be transformed into the framework for a much broader critical vision: nothing less than a mythologizing of the contemporary literary scene, which attained its most memorable form in Pope's *The Dunciad* (1728).[9] This myth was in essence Tory. Forged during the long hegemony of the Whigs under Sir Robert Walpole, it claimed to deplore modern English culture and the writing it had fostered. Estranged from the best in both the classical and the native traditions, this writing was presented as the work of tradesmen in words rather than artists. It was consequently imprisoned within mediocrity. The heroes of this vision were the Scriblerians and those they claimed for their ancestors: Pope, Swift and Gay; behind them, Dryden, Waller, Roscommon and Jonson; and behind them, Virgil, Horace and Homer.[10] Its villains were contemporary Whig writers such as John Dennis, Sir Richard Blackmore, Charles Gildon, Leonard Welsted and John Oldmixon.

However, this Tory version of the English literary past has enjoyed a hegemony with posterity which it was unable to secure when first promulgated. We have tended to take it at its own self-estimate, as a superb dismissal of a disreputable crew of literary chancers. In fact it was a response to a self-consciously modern programme for English poetry propounded in the 1690s and 1700s by Whig writers concerned to identify the literary forms and models appropriate to a nation which, with the Glorious Revolution of 1688, had grasped its political liberty and entered into possession of itself. A more detailed discussion, concentrating on the works reprinted in Part III of this anthology, 'Criticism and the War of the Spanish Succession, 1704–1711', and alluding to works contained in other sections of the anthology where appropriate, will suggest something of the interest of this neglected Whig vision, which it is one of the aims of this anthology to exemplify and reintroduce to critical discussion.

The Tory interpretation of literary history was founded on a distinctive view of the English political past, and particularly of English experience in the seventeenth century, taken over in its outline if not its detail from an earlier generation of writers and critics such as Dryden, Roscommon, Buckingham and Atterbury, all of whom were committed and acknowledged Stuart loyalists. The key issue can be formulated as a simple question: When did English literature become polite, and the English language reach maturity? The answer given by this group of Stuart writers was: In 1660. As Atterbury put it in his 'Preface' of 1690 to the Second Part of Waller's *Poems*:

[Waller] undoubtedly stands first in the List of Refiners, and for ought I know, last too; for I question whether in *Charles* the Second's Reign, *English* did not come to its full perfection; and whether it has not had its *Augustan Age*, as well as the *Latin*.[11]

In this he was echoing Dryden, who as early as 1668 had written that:

And though the fury of a Civil War, and Power, for twenty years together, abandon'd to a barbarous race of men, Enemies of all good Learning, had buried the Muses under the ruines of Monarchy; yet with the restoration of our happiness, we see reviv'd Poesie lifting up its head, & already shaking off the rubbish which lay so heavy on it.[12]

There is a family (and a political) relationship between this group of writers. They emplot the English literary past so that the advent of the refinement necessary for English literature to make good its claim to challenge comparison with any other comes hand in hand with the return of a Stuart monarch to the English throne.

As their posing to themselves of this question about the period of English literature's maturity suggests, these writers were preoccupied with the standing of English literature in comparison with the literatures of other modern European nations, and with the literatures of classical

Greece and Rome. Yet they tended to see the quality of English literature as arising out of its relation to the classical literatures, rather than separately from them. The classics were a storehouse of achievement by which, to be sure, the modern English writer should not be confined in a client relationship of imitative dependency, but which equally he should not ignore, and by which he should be happy to be guided. In *Of Dramatick Poesie, An Essay* Dryden had Neander triumphantly vindicate the quality of English drama through an analysis of Ben Jonson's *Epicœne*, prefaced by an account of Jonson's character as a playwright in which it was claimed, 'He was deeply conversant in the Ancients, both Greek and Latine, and he borrow'd boldly from them.'[13] Roscommon, determined, in the midst of what he represents as a climate of hostile criticism of English literary achievement, that he would 'to the few virtues that we have, be just', asked:

> For who have long'd, or who have labour'd more
> To search the Treasures of the *Roman* store;
> Or dig in *Grecian Mines* for *purer Oar*;

He then compared the English achievement favourably with the French:

> When *France* had breath'd, after intestine *B*roils,
> And Peace, and Conquest crown'd her forreign Toils,
> There (cultivated by a Royal Hand)
> Learning grew fast, and spread, and blest the Land;
> The choicest *B*ooks, that *Rome*, or *Greece* have known,
> Her excellent *Translators* made her own:
> And *Europe* still considerably gains,
> *B*oth by their good *Example* and their *Pains*.
> From hence our gen'rous Emulation came,
> We undertook, and we perform'd the same.
> But now, *We* shew the world a nobler way,
> And in *Translated Verse*, do more than *They*.[14]

The implication was clear. The present pre-eminence of English letters was to be secured by means of an unrivalled familiarity with, and appropriation of, the achievements of classical literature. In that way the strengths of the ancient Greeks and Romans could be made our own.[15]

This view of English literary history and of the models appropriate for English writers to follow did not go unchallenged. Against it arose what we may properly call a Whig interpretation of literary history: properly, because not only were its advocates to a man known and declared Whigs, but its values and emphases were an extension into the realm of literature of the Whig principles emerging in the realm of political action. Indeed, some of the advocates and practitioners of this Whig literary vision were the very men who, in Parliament or at court, were pushing forward Whig measures in foreign and domestic policy. What was the content of this rival Whig vision of English literature?

The Whig interpretation of English literature offered, in the first place, a different periodization of the English literary past. For the Whigs, the moment of literary maturity was not 1660, but 1688. Leonard Welsted's *Dissertation on the English Language*, which served as the preface to the volume of his poetry published in 1714, made plain that the Revolution was glorious for the Englishman's literature as well as for his religion and liberty. The accession of the Stuarts had but prepared the way for the flourishing of letters which followed the gift of political freedom at the hands of William of Orange:

It is not . . . much more than a century, since England first recovered out of something like barbarism, with respect to its state of letters and politeness. . . . at the Restoration it was, that Poetry and Polite Arts began to spring up. In the reign of William the Third, the founder of English Liberty, they acquired great strength and vigour, and have continued to thrive, gradually, down almost to our times.[16]

Joseph Addison's poem of 1694, '*An* ACCOUNT *of the Greatest* ENGLISH POETS', is striking in its coordination of the political and literary spheres. Waller, admired for the dubious skill to 'make the vanquish'd great, the coward strong', was offered condolences on the prematurity of his arrival:

> Oh had thy Muse not come an age too soon,
> But seen great *Nassau* on the *British* throne!
> How had his triumphs glitter'd in thy page,
> And warm'd thee to a more exalted rage!
> What scenes of death and horror had we view'd,
> And how had *Boin*'s wide current reek'd in blood!

But the climax of this short but fascinating poem was reserved for Charles Montagu, pre-eminent Whig politician, but lesser poet,[17] to whom Addison nevertheless offered this extravagant praise:

> How negligently graceful he unreins
> His verse, and writes in loose familiar strains;
> How *Nassau*'s godlike acts adorn his lines,
> And all the Heroe in full glory shines.
> We see his army set in just array,
> And *Boin*'s dy'd waves run purple to the sea.
> Nor *Simois* choak'd with men, and arms, and blood;
> Nor rapid *Xanthus*' celebrated flood,
> Shall longer be the Poet's highest themes,
> Tho' gods and heroes fought promiscuous in their streams.
> But now, to *Nassau*'s secret councils rais'd,
> He aids the Heroe, whom before he prais'd.

Four emphases deserve comment here. First, Addison gives us the sketch of a Whig aesthetic for poetry, in which negligence, grace, looseness and familiarity are prized. This is patrician, assured, and unconcerned about classical models. Second, there is the explicit relegation of classical poetry, embodied in Homer and evoked through the names of the rivers of the *Iliad*:

> Nor *Simois* choak'd with men, and arms, and blood;
> Nor rapid *Xanthus*' celebrated flood,
> Shall longer be the Poet's highest themes,
> Tho' gods and heroes fought promiscuous in their streams.

Third, there is the identification of the reign of William III – 'great *Nassau*', victor over James II at the Battle of the Boyne (or '*Boin*') – as an apogee of achievement in both literature and affairs of state. Fourth, and perhaps most interestingly, there is the implication that political and military events create the substantive content of the poetical agenda; this is importantly different from the parallel Tory contention that affairs of state create the conditions within which literature either flourishes or declines.

This vision of English literary history was not peculiar to Addison. It was the common property of a group of writers and politicians particularly active in the reign of Queen Anne, many of whom were members of the Kit-Cat Club, which functioned at this time almost as a Whig literary academy. It was a vision coherent in its principles and ambitious in its scope. However, its values and its personnel were pilloried and derided by that rival grouping of writers and politicians, the Scriblerians.[18] And today we still approach the literature of this period in accordance with the habits of reading, the principles of judgement, and the hierarchizing oppositions disseminated by Pope and his lieutenants. To rectify this state of affairs, let us concentrate on two poems: first, Sir Richard Blackmore's *Advice to the Poets*, the poem he wrote in 1706 to commemorate Marlborough's victory at Ramillies, and, second, Pope's *An Essay on Criticism* of 1711, a poem which engaged polemically with the political and cultural situation which obtained at the moment of its publication. And let us approach these poems by way of a cursory account of the European war during which they were composed and published, and of the significance of that war for the literary world.

The War of the Spanish Succession had ramifications in areas of national life remote from foreign policy and military adventuring. During the decade preceding the outbreak of war William III had transformed the military and financial institutions of England in a way which led to a political transformation.[19] These political events in their turn generated an intense cultural conflict, commonly called 'the rage of party', in which the broadest questions of national identity were fought over. What were the transformations effected by William III, and to what did they give rise?

In 1688 William III had been welcomed in England as the defender of the national Church and the champion of the Englishman's liberty, but there is little reason to imagine that this was how he saw himself. His outlook was European, not nationalistic, and religion troubled him little. His extraction, like that of his favourites Bentinck and Keppel, was from the aristocratic cadres of the old duchy of Burgundy: it would be hard to imagine men less sympathetic either to the urban republicanism of the Low Countries which they had just left or to the ancient constitutionalism of their new subjects.[20] William saw in England a vast source of money to help him fight his wars with France, and for most of the 1690s fight with France was precisely what he did. By the time of the signing of the Peace of Ryswick in September 1697, a national debt of £13.5 million had been run up.

English governments had, of course, borrowed money before, but not on this scale. It was, however, not the size of the debt William had created which was pregnant with political consequences. What so alarmed the majority of MPs, who sat in the 'Country' interest and who already harboured profound suspicions of the Dutch, was the policy – devised by the very Charles Montagu whom, as we have seen, Addison had flatteringly placed at the summit of Parnassus – of never repaying the loan, but instead of using the revenue from taxation to service the interest on it.[21] The results were complex, and far-reaching. In the first place, members of the House were quick to appreciate that government borrowing was merely deferred taxation, and that the resolution never to liquidate the principal of the national debt therefore extended the costs of war into peacetime. Those costs, for 'Country' members, were ruinously high. In 1692 Parliament had been obliged to reintroduce the Land Tax, and therefore the burden of the war fell with disproportionate weight on those who held land, since there was no parallel tax on liquid assets. The natural and traditional way for Parliament to show its displeasure at this would have been to refuse to pass measures to raise taxes. But here the new permanence of the national debt disclosed its most revolutionary implication. To refuse taxation to service the debt would not have applied pressure to the King and his advisers: it would have produced a wholesale financial crisis. The costs of effective opposition were suddenly too high to be contemplated. As a result, parliamentary opposition to the measures of government was inhibited, and William was thus able for the most part to conduct the war with France in consultation with a small group of mainly Dutch advisers, none of whom held Cabinet posts.

It was the opposition's sense of practical disablement which ensured that the factional propaganda war, which arose in the 1690s and spilled over into the early years of the eighteenth century, was fought with such virulence. It also influenced the language in which opposition was carried forward. The customary language of the 'Country' interest was the Harringtonian idiom of civic humanism, of which the roots lay in classical republicanism.[22] The developments of the 1690s meant that, not only were the exponents of this idiom restricted in their political effectiveness, but the very applicability of their habitual political language to a society so remodelled in its financial and political life was suddenly questionable.

William did not live to fight the War of the Spanish Succession: war was declared in the May following his death in March 1702. But the foundations of the war had been laid in his reign, and it was his Continental policy which had dictated England's involvement in this latest European conflict. In one of the articles of the Peace of Ryswick it had been agreed that, on the death of the childless Charles II of Spain, the bulk of his territories (including Spain itself and the Indies) would go to the 'neutral' Elector of Bavaria. On the untimely death of the Elector, William and Louis XIV had in 1699 negotiated the Second Partition Treaty, which provided for the division of the Spanish territories between the French and Austrian claimants. By these measures William had sought to prevent the unification of the Spanish and French crowns – a unification which would have struck fatally at his policy of resisting the French drive towards hegemony in Europe. But in the summer of 1700 Charles died, and bequeathed his dominions in their entirety to Philip of Anjou, the French claimant. William's response was to make some sacrifices to Parliament at home, the better to allow him to put together an alliance (the so-called 'Grand Alliance') to resist Louis abroad. This he achieved in the summer of 1701, with the assistance of his captain-general, John Churchill, then Earl of Marlborough.

The Alliance was held together by three war aims. The neutrality of the Emperor was to be secured by the surrender to him of some minor Italian territories and the Spanish Netherlands; the Indies trade was to be thrown open; and the union of the French and Spanish crowns was to be prevented. All these war aims were achieved by the 'Preliminary Articles' of 1711, the document which was later embodied in the Treaty of Utrecht of 1713, concluding the war. The War of the Spanish Succession was therefore, from the English point of view, an astonishingly successful conflict. Despite the railing of Tory satirists such as Swift, for the first time since the fourteenth century England had demonstrated a capacity to wage and win Continental wars on the largest scale. As we shall see, Whig writers responded with alacrity and enthusiasm to the prospect of enlarged, even imperial, influence and prosperity.

In summary, the broader domestic consequences of the War of the Spanish Succession were two. On the one hand, the remodelling of the financial and political life of the nation had called into question the currency of certain idioms within the language of politics, in particular a civic humanist idiom. On the other hand, national self-identity had acquired a new gloss from military victory. Taken together, these developments imparted a new urgency to a question which had been in the minds of prominent Whigs since before the War of the Spanish Succession had begun: namely, What are the appropriate cultural models and exemplars for this nation? In 1700 Sir Richard Blackmore had published his *A Paraphrase on the Book of Job*, and in the 'Preface' to this work he had reflected in Whiggish vein on how the '*Liberty* of *Poetry*' had been infringed by the unwarranted influence exerted by classical poets, particularly Homer and Virgil, over their modern successors. Their dominion was nothing less than an affront:

But upon what Authority is this imposed on the *World*? What *Commission* had these two *Poets* [Homer and Virgil] to *settle* the *limits* and *extent* of *Epick Poetry*, or who can prove they ever intended to do so?

Their influence was either tyranny or conspiracy. Either way, it was high time it was overthrown, and the 'revolution principles' of 1688 extended to the realm of poetry:

'Tis therefore to be wish'd that some *good Genius, qualify'd* for such an *Undertaking*, would break the *Ice*, assert the *Liberty* of *Poetry*, and set up for an *Original* in *Writing* in a way accommodated to the *Religion, Manners*, and other *Circumstances* we are now under.

This new way of writing, accommodated to the circumstances of eighteenth-century Britain, would partly involve the abandonment of machinery derived from pagan mythology (' 'tis *high time* to leave out our *Allusions* to the *Pagan Divinity*') and its replacement by a machinery derived from Christianity. It was an argument promptly seconded by John Dennis's *The Grounds of Criticism in Poetry* (1704). When Dennis contrasted 'Antient and Modern Policy' towards the stage, and compared them with 'Antient and Modern Extent of Empire', he implied that the dawning imperial destiny of Britain required her statesmen to take care that the nation's literature would be a match for her political and military grandeur. Dennis's work was a blueprint for how this might be done. His project to restore poetry 'to all its Greatness, and to all its Innocence' implied nothing less than an emulation and eventual surpassing of 'the happiest of *Grecian* and *Roman* Ages'.[23] Blackmore offered his paraphrase of the Book of Job as a pattern for such Christianized epic.[24] But that was not all that such a remodelled poetry might comprise, and in *Advice to the Poets*, the poem Blackmore wrote in 1706 to commemorate Marlborough's victory at Ramillies, we are given a fuller insight into what Whig epic might look like.

Advice to the Poets falls into a genre which was initiated by Charles Montagu's poem on the Boyne (so extravagantly admired by Addison), 'An Epistle to . . . Charles Earl of Dorset . . . Occasion'd by His Majesty's Victory in Ireland'. The genre was continued in Addison's own poem on Blenheim, 'The Campaign', and Blackmore's later 'Instructions to Vander Bank' of 1709. It is a genre we might call Battle Hymns of the Junto Whigs, and, as we shall see, it is a genre unified by a certain feature of poetic structure, as well as by a similarity of subject matter. *Advice to the Poets* immediately attracted scornful ripostes, such as the anonymous *A Panegyrick Epistle . . . to Sir R— B— on his most incomparable incomprehensible poem, call'd Advice to the poets* (1706). It certainly possesses a grandiloquence which can perplex the unattuned reader. But my concern is less with the quality of Blackmore's actual performance than with the project of which the poem is a (perhaps flawed) embodiment. The project of Whig epic which we can discern within and behind the poem is coherent in its own terms, and profoundly exciting. Moreover, it is difficult for us to assess how good a performance *Advice to the Poets* in fact is, so thoroughly have our ideas of the poetry of this period been saturated with the inimical values and preferences of the Scriblerians. If we are to arrive at a genuinely historical understanding of the literature and the criticism of this period, we have to discover a way of reading Blackmore's poetry which has not already, by virtue of the unspoken aesthetic assumptions buried within it, dismissed it as unmeaning bluster.[25]

In the *Paraphrase on the Book of Job* Blackmore had argued that the classical epics of Homer and Virgil were no longer useful models for English poets because English mores, and in particular English religious mores, were so changed. In *Advice to the Poets*, however, the discarding of classical poetic precedent was justified on different grounds. The poem takes the form of advice to poets who would commemorate Marlborough's military triumphs. It thus moves backwards and forwards between, on the one hand, reflecting on poetic practice and, on the other, providing a heroically mythologized narrative of Marlborough's campaigns in the Low Countries.[26] Blackmore is convinced that the magnitude of Marlborough's achievement exceeds what could be expressed by the imitation of Virgil and Homer. On the field he has surpassed the heroes of antiquity: 'The *Briton*'s Course of Glory does out-shine / Thy progress, *Cæsar* . . .'; 'Thus *Marlbro*'s Arms excel ev'n *Cæsar*'s Fame, / Conqu'ring before he saw, before he came.'[27] As a result, he has conquered not only the French, but the poets of his own country:

> His Conquests are so sudden, so compleat,
> He does so oft his Miracles repeat,
> The Muse exhausted pants, and hangs the Wing,
> Has no more Strength to rise, and no more Breath to sing.
> He Danger seeks, he asks unequal Fight,
> He Conquers faster, than our Bards can Write.

> So thick Illustrious Victories on them throng,
> That half his Triumphs must be left unsung.[28]

In writing about Blenheim, Blackmore suggests, the British bards 'did their Stock exhaust, / They spent their Genius, and their Vigor lost'.[29] Yet the achievements of Marlborough in the sphere of war nevertheless create a poetic imperative. The European dominance of English armies in the field must be reflected by a dominance on the page:

> . . . *Cam* and *Ouze*, which, from the *Gaul*'s Alarms,
> And thine, O *Rome*, preserv'd by *Marlbro*'s Arms,
> Do Peace enjoy, and gently murmuring flow,
> Should tell the World, what they to *Marlbro'* owe.
> And since superior in the Field, 'tis fit
> We should assert the Empire too of Wit,
> And make the haughty *Gaul* in both submit.
> To sing *Ramillia*'s Field, ye Bards, awake,
> The tuneful Lyre let none but Masters take.[30]

Yet how is this to be done? Where should the poet turn for an answerable style and serviceable model? To appreciate how Blackmore answered those questions, we need for a moment to place the poem within its genre.

For the first three-quarters of its length, *Advice to the Poets* continues in the way I have described, tacking between military narrative and poetic guidance, the constant refrain of which is that an adequate poeticizing of the campaign is hard enough to envisage, let alone perform. However, at this point the poem suddenly changes direction:

> 'Tis done. I've compass'd my ambitious Aim,
> The Hero's Fire restores the Poet's Flame.
> The Inspiration comes, my Bosom glows,
> I strive with strong Enthusiastic Throws.
> Oh! I am all in Rapture, all on Fire,
> Give me, to ease the Muse's Pangs, the Lyre.
> How can a Muse, that *Albion* loves, forbear
> To sing the Wonders of the glorious War?

> I rise, O whither am I caught away?
> I mount, I must the tow'ring Muse obey.
> I cut the Space immense, and reach the Realms of Day.
> Where will the Flight, where will the Labour end?
> Thro' the steep Gulph I to the Stars ascend.[31]

Blackmore has become inspired by his own poetry to reach for the appropriately sublime style the lack of which he has just been deploring:

> While I so near, so long the Hero view,
> And Hints suggest to be improv'd by you,
> My fading Flame does in my Veins renew.
> I feel an inward Impulse not unknown,
> Urging your Muse, I have provok'd my own.[32]

It was passages such as these which allowed Pope to write Blackmore's poetry off as mere bombast:

> What? like Sir Richard, rumbling, rough and fierce,
> With ARMS, and GEORGE, and BRUNSWICK crowd the Verse?
> Rend with tremendous Sound your ears asunder,
> With Gun, Drum, Trumpet, Blunderbuss & Thunder?[33]

But this is a deliberately unsophisticated reading of such moments of afflatus in Blackmore's verse. We should consider these moments not so much as attempts actually to compose verse of this loftiness but, more knowingly, as the dramatization of a moment of great significance in Whig poetic. Charles Montagu's poem on the Boyne has a structure exactly parallel to that of *Advice to the Poets*, pivoting about a moment when the poem suddenly becomes what it has been describing and calling for: 'Oh, DORSET! I am rais'd! I'm all on fire!'[34] This moment of afflatus is not, therefore, peculiar to Blackmore: it is a generic element in this class of poetry. And its importance is that it dramatizes an enthusiastic moment of poetic inspiration free from any trace of imitation. It therefore connects very directly with the Whiggish rejection of classical models for modern British epic. With this rupture from a conversational tone, and explicit movement into the register of the sublime, the poem becomes its own model. At that moment it takes on the completeness and self-sufficiency which, within the poem, is the characteristic of transcendent achievement.[35]

Advice to the Poets, then, emerged from a critical position to which it gave voice within itself. It enacted the independence and 'liberty' of modern British poetry by becoming its own exemplar, thereby embodying the ideology of Whig epic. In so doing, it also revealed the aesthetic principles of this new poetic form. *Advice to the Poets* is built around a principle of recursiveness. The initial long section of advice is followed by the moment of afflatus and Blackmore's movement into a more inspired mode, and this is itself succeeded by a divine poem sung by an angel, 'the bless'd Poet of the glorious Choir'.[36] Each of these two latter sections marks an advance on its predecessor, moving a notch up the ratchet of sublimity. Equally, however, since each is devoted to praising Marlborough's achievements, each duplicates its predecessor, covering the same ground in a different poetic register. This repetition is one of the ways in which the poem moves as the respectful shadow of its subject, since Marlborough's campaigns themselves are images of each other, the later ones both duplicating and surpassing their predecessors by yielding yet greater triumphs from the same campaigning country:

> Fair Liberty, and Right, and ancient Laws,
> And *Anna*'s, which is Human Nature's Cause,
> Invite the Chief, his Labours to repeat,
> *Europa*, thy Redemption to compleat.
>
> He yields; he undertakes the Pious Toil;
> Laden with Trophies, and with *Gallic* Spoil,
> With Laurels sprung from *Danaw*'s Banks adorn'd,
> His rapid Course of Glory back he turn'd.[37]

The redoubling which marked Marlborough's military career was echoed in the structure of Blackmore's poem. Indeed, as the polyphony of praise builds, echo itself becomes the mode of Whig epic:

> Good Heav'ns! – but hark, I hear an ecchoing Sound,
> It does from Sphere to Sphere, from World to World rebound.
> The Noise augments; attend, it seems to rise

From *Belgia*'s Land; hark, how it fills the Skies?
This mighty Noise is Triumph, 'tis Applause,
'Tis loud Rejoycing for some Victor Cause.
'Tis known. I hear, I hear these Accents plain,
Arms, Anna, Malbro', Dyle, Ramillia's Plain. . . .

   Hark! now I hear the Shouts of Joy around,
I hear the Triumph's multiplying Sound.
Th'Angelic Acclamation grows, it fills
All the blue Plains, and all the crystal Hills.
They shew by this, repeated loud Applause,
Those fight in Heav'n's, who fight in *Anna*'s Cause.[38]

The echo is created by the harmonious coincidence of all the various tributes to Marlborough's conquests. Such multiplicity is proper to the scale of Marlborough's triumph. But it also picks up an emphasis from the earlier part of the poem, in which Blackmore has been dispensing advice to his fellow poets. Blenheim, according to Blackmore (perhaps momentarily unmindful, perhaps deliberately negligent, of Addison's 'The Campaign'), had received no adequate poetic celebration:

> For *Blenheim* was a Theme too bright, too strong
> For any Rapture, any master Song.
> In this Attempt, they did their Stock exhaust,
> They spent their Genius, and their Vigor lost.[39]

The same fate cannot be allowed to befall the yet-greater victory (as Blackmore sees it) of Ramillies. Therefore:

> Let none, betray'd by generous Thirst of Fame,
> Adventure singly on this Mighty Theme:
> Lest crush'd beneath th'unsufferable Weight,
> He curse th'ambitious Flame, that caus'd his Fate,
> And learn his Error in his Fall too late.
> Let many Master Bards their Force unite,
> And with Confederate Fire a Song Heroic write.[40]

   The idea of a poem written by committee is not one to excite the

reader of perhaps any age, but one must be careful not to abstract
suggestions such as this from the poem before one has considered how
they operate in what we might call the poem's aesthetic economy.
This is particularly important in the case of this notion of a collaborative
poetic effort, because it offers us some direct avenues to an appreciation
of the distinctively Whig character of Blackmore's poetics. The first
point to appreciate is that the idea of a poetic confederacy was
connected in Blackmore's scheme of things with the surpassing of
classical models:

> Tho' any one unvulgar Bard might raise
> The *Briton*'s Triumphs, in superior Lays,
> To my unfinish'd songs, and crude Essays;
> Yet a distinguish'd, and consummate Piece,
> Excelling that of *Mantua*, that of *Greece*,
> A wond'rous, unexampled *Epick* Song,
> Where all is just, and beautiful, and strong,
> Worthy of *Anna*'s Arms, or *Marlbro*'s Fire,
> Does our best Bards united Strength require.[41]

This poetic alliance (a parallel in the realm of letters to the Grand
Alliance which fought the actual war) holds out the hope of realizing
an 'unexampled *Epick* Song', exceeding Homer and Virgil in quality
while differing from them in kind by rejecting pagan machinery for
Christian, and making more appropriate historical comparisons (as
when Blackmore himself twice compared Marlborough with Constantine, a martial, imperial and Christian hero).[42] But it also prompted
him to imagine a poetic parliament, a 'Sovereign Court of Sense and
Wit' in which such schemes would be properly conceived and carried
forward:

> For this great Task, let all these Sons of Art,
> Their utmost Skill and Energy exert;
> Let each his Genius know, each take his proper Part.
> Let *Summers*, and let *Montague* preside,
> Correct their Labours, and their Progress guide.
> One is with all politer Science grac'd,

Of Thought refin'd, and delicate of Taste.
All to his Judgment, as decisive fly,
By that just Standard all their Notions try;
Like the fam'd *Grecian*'s chief Intelligence,
He sits sublime, in the first Sphere of Sense:
He rules the rest by his superior Force,
Puts them in Motion, and directs their Course.
And one, like *Rome*'s Immortal *Angelo*,
Does rich and universal Genius show.
This Master, this Poetic Architect,
Can stately Domes and Palaces erect:
The Painter too, and Sculptor in his Turn,
He can the Building, which he rears, adorn.
Let these sustain the chief Surveyors Care;
By these directed, can the Poets err?
The Age in Taste, grown curious to a Vice;
(O, that it were as delicate, as nice!)
And all contending Parties will submit
To such a Sovereign Court of Sense and Wit.
Let those employ'd the Building to erect,
Some Hero worthy of the Song elect,
Whose conquering Arms in *Albion*'s Annals shine,
And let the Action suit the Great Design.[43]

Again, the likely practical results here are less interesting than the concept itself. The two presiding geniuses, Somers and Montagu, were both leading Whigs of the 1690s and 1710s.[44] Both had played important parts in the events leading up to the accession of William III and in the Convention parliament of 1689 – the parliament which had inquired into, debated, formulated and resolved upon the new model of British monarchy. Blackmore's 'Sovereign Court of Sense and Wit', also to be dominated by Somers and Montagu, looks very like a poetic version of that momentous and Whiggish assembly, which had been bold enough to dismiss the past and strike out resolutely for the future.[45]

It is clear, then, that *Advice to the Poets* sought to draw together the world of actions and the world of poems. The linking of these worlds was expressed by Blackmore in a verbal touch of some delicacy, when he spoke of 'the Bards, whose Laurels spring and thrive / By *Marlbro*'s'.[46] The interest of this phrase centres on the ambiguity of 'by': does it mean 'alongside' or – a stronger claim, which links poetic and military laurels less accidentally because more functionally – 'because of' or 'through'? The poem progressively inclines towards the stronger claim, the eventual status of the poet as simulacrum of the warrior enforced through a repetition of a verbal detail redolent of sublimity. Marlborough's return to the Continent is figured through his mastery of its rivers:

> He yields; he undertakes the Pious Toil;
> Laden with Trophies, and with *Gallic* Spoil,
> With Laurels sprung from *Danaw*'s Banks adorn'd,
> His rapid Course of Glory back he turn'd.
> Bless'd by the numerous States to Peace restor'd,
> And Princes rescu'd by his conquering Sword,
> The Great Deliv'rer marches to the *Rhine*,
> To break his Chains, and drive encroaching *Sein*.
> 'Tis done. The *Sein*'s ambitious Waves subside,
> Reluctant roar, and backward roll their Tyde.[47]

The immediate imposition of will evoked by ' 'Tis done' is repeated later at the poem's crux when Blackmore is struck with inspiration:

> 'Tis done. I've compass'd my ambitious Aim,
> The Hero's Fire restores the Poet's Flame.[48]

It is through such details of organization, which show a poetic imagination for which he does not often receive credit, that Blackmore reached towards the unexampled epic style which might match the unexampled times through which he lived.

This account of *Advice to the Poets* encourages us to examine Pope's *An Essay on Criticism* (1711) from an angle neglected since John Dennis's attack on the poem in its year of publication. Dennis justified his hostility towards the poem by stigmatizing it as the work of a man with Jacobite sympathies who looked forward eagerly to the restoration of Stuart monarchy. Such a prospect, we know, alarmed Dennis profoundly. A French landing bruited, he went to the now Duke of Marlborough to inquire how he, Dennis, such a known foe of France, might be safe, only to be told by the victor of Blenheim that he believed Dennis to be no more ungrateful to the French than himself, and that he, the Duke, proposed to take no special measures. Dennis's attack on Pope's poem, when it has been considered at all, has tended to be interpreted in the light of such anecdotes as a product of Dennis's imbalanced outlook. This is partly because scholarly exegesis of *An Essay on Criticism* has examined the poem as a statement of aesthetic principle which, although it may have been constructed to some extent out of the views of Pope's contemporaries and predecessors, nevertheless did not engage primarily with those views but is most fruitfully to be considered either as a blueprint for the poems Pope was later to write or as a poem whose intrinsic profundity and coherence as a piece of literary critical argument and exposition are what should most preoccupy the critic. There is, however, a third approach, which obliges us to consider *An Essay on Criticism* in the context of the politicized poetics generated by the debates arising from international conflict during the reign of Queen Anne.

The interest of such an approach is suggested by the fact that Pope seems to have tried to guard against it. The text of the *Essay* is no more stable than that of many of Pope's other poems. The MS shows clear signs of second thoughts and correction, despite the fact that the ornateness of the first page suggests that it was begun as a final, good copy.[49] In the second edition, of 1713, Pope refashioned a number of lines which had caused controversy.[50] But the revision by way of which we shall enter the poem was not made until much later. In the first edition of the poem, and in every reprinting thereafter up to and including that published in 1732, Pope's attack on the religious integrity of the reign of William III read as follows:

> The following Licence of a Foreign Reign
> Did all the Dregs of bold *Socinus* drain;
> Then *first* the *Belgian Morals* were extoll'd;
> We their *Religion* had, and they our *Gold*:
> Then Unbelieving Priests reform'd the Nation,

> And taught more *Pleasant* Methods of Salvation;
> Where Heav'ns Free Subjects might their *Rights* dispute,
> Lest God himself shou'd seem too *Absolute*.[51]

But in the octavo edition of his *Works* published in 1736 Pope deleted the epigrammatic couplet figuring the reign of William III as a bad bargain exchanging gold for irreligion:

> Then *first* the *Belgian Morals* were extoll'd;
> We their *Religion* had, and they our *Gold*:

And he inserted the following footnote: '*The Author has omitted two lines which stood here, as containing a* National Reflection, *which in his stricter judgment he could not but disapprove, on any People whatever.*'

The anti-Dutch content of the deleted couplet is redolent of the 'Country' opposition to William carried on by Tory MPs in the 1690s, while its epigrammatic form recalls the compacted wit which Whig critics such as William Coward had censured as typical of earlier satirists such as the Stuart loyalists Cleveland and Cowley.[52] And the timing of its revocation is revealing. At the earliest opportunity after he had enlisted (however tentatively, and with whatever mental reservations) in the Patriot opposition to Walpole of the 1730s, Pope repudiated this couplet, which might have been hard to digest for the Whig members of that opposition, whose antipathy to Walpole implied no disenchantment with 1688.[53] The revision suggests that, when first published, *An Essay on Criticism* was a poem which engaged with the political circumstances of its time in a way which Pope, in deference to changes in those political circumstances, later decided to disown.

Where can we see Pope's politics influencing the aesthetic positions canvassed within the poem? There are at least three areas where the poem mounts resistance to a suddenly vigorous Whig poetic. First, there is the poem's contention that the classical poets mark the bounds and heights of poetic attainment. Virgil serves Pope as an embodiment of temerity chastised. At first Virgil scorns to be influenced by past poetic practice and instead seeks to draw from only '*Nature's Fountains*', until he discovers, 'amaz'd', that '*Nature* and *Homer* were . . . the *same*'. His discomfiture served as an implicit reproof to all those in Pope's own day (such as Blackmore, Addison and William Coward) who had sought to emancipate British heroic poetry from its traditional deference to the ancients:

> Convinc'd, amaz'd, he checkt the bold Design, ⎫
> And did his Work to Rules as strict confine, ⎬
> As if the *Stagyrite* o'erlook'd each Line. ⎭
> Learn hence for Ancient *Rules* a just Esteem;
> To copy Nature is to copy *Them*.[54]

This thread in the poem's argument culminates in a passage of great interest. Having rejected the common saying that even Homer nods, by arguing instead that it is we who dream, Pope inflected the tone of his verse towards rapture:

> Still green with Bays each *ancient* Altar stands,
> Above the reach of *Sacrilegious* Hands,
> Secure from *Flames*, from *Envy*'s fiercer Rage,
> Destructive *War*, and all-devouring *Age*.
> See, from *each Clime* the Learn'd their Incense bring;
> Hear, in *all Tongues* Triumphant *Pæans* ring!
> In Praise so just, let ev'ry Voice be join'd,
> And fill the *Gen'ral Chorus* of *Mankind* !
> Hail *Bards Triumphant*! born in *happier Days*;
> *Immortal* Heirs of *Universal* Praise!
> Whose Honours with Increase of Ages *grow*,
> As Streams roll down, *enlarging* as they flow!
> Nations *unborn* your mighty Names shall sound,
> And Worlds applaud that must not yet be *found*!
> Oh may some Spark of *your* Cœlestial Fire
> The last, the meanest of your Sons inspire,
> (That with weak Wings, from far, pursues your Flights;
> *Glows* while he *reads*, but *trembles* as he *writes*)
> To teach vain Wits that Science *little known*,
> *T'admire* Superior Sense, and *doubt* their own![55]

With that final couplet, and its chastisement of modern Whiggish confidence, we have encountered Pope's hostility to the very different notions disseminated by Blackmore about both the standing of Homer and Virgil and the directions to be taken by modern British poetry. Compare William Coward's impatience with such reverence for the classics, published two years before Pope's poem but at the moment of its composition:

I think not Modern English Poetry without Blemish . . . but my endeavour is to justifie our own Nation from the aspersion and calumny of some Bigots to *Ancient Poetry*, who are of Opinion, that nothing can be done well, but what must have *Their* Stamp, and *Authority* to support it, else they condemn it.[56]

The second area in which *An Essay on Criticism* took issue with contemporary Whig positions was in its posture towards the Whig project to enlarge discussion on literary matters beyond the circles of (in Coward's phrase) 'some Bigots to *Ancient Poetry*'. Pope's rebuke to modern self-confidence is perhaps unexpected, given the conversational, Horatian, form in which the poem is cast. But this gap between form and doctrine is calculated to set the doctrine off with more vividness when it finally emerges. Pope's poem was opposed to Addison's project in *The Spectator*, of reinforcing critical confidence in a general readership, and to Blackmore's intentions in the 'Preface' to *A Paraphrase on the Book of Job*, of separating modern heroic poetry from its classical forebears, and thereby encouraging modern British writers and readers to reflect independently on the form and idiom appropriate to heroic poetry composed to be read in the 1700s. Pope's intention was to disable such unfounded confidence, and in the *Essay* he set about this task through dissimulation. The tone and form of the poem are conversational and informal, and so create the expectation that criticism might be open to contributions from all sides. After all, 'Most have the *Seeds* of Judgment in their Mind.'[57] But, as the poem moves forward, the intimidating difficulty of the critical art is insisted upon with steadily increasing gravity. In part this arises through Pope's proffering of critical 'rules' which are in conflict with each other. For example, we are invited to censure flexibility of judgement in this couplet:

> Some praise at Morning what they blame at Night;
> But always think the *last* Opinion *right.*

and to admire it in these:

> Some positive persisting Fops we know,
> That, if *once wrong*, will needs be *always so*;
> But you, with Pleasure own your Errors past,
> And make each Day a *Critick* on the last.[58]

Reticence is enjoined at one moment:

> Be *silent* always when you *doubt* your Sense;
> *Speak* when you're *sure*, yet speak with *Diffidence*;

and deplored the next:

> Be Niggards of Advice on no Pretence;
> For the *worst Avarice* is that of *Sense*:[59]

Of course, different kinds of flexibility and reticence are at stake in each of these passages. Nevertheless, the newcomer, seeking initiation into the principles of criticism and reading Pope with attention, is more likely to sense exclusion than to receive enlightenment from this clash of precepts.

The picture of the ideal critic is also intimidating:

> But where's the Man, who Counsel *can* bestow,
> Still *pleas'd* to *teach*, and yet not *proud* to *know*?
> Unbiass'd, or by *Favour* or by *Spite*;
> Not *dully prepossest*, or *blindly right*;
> Tho' Learn'd, well-bred; and tho' well-bred, sincere;
> Modestly bold, and Humanly severe?
> Who to a *Friend* his Faults can freely show,
> And gladly praise the Merit of a *Foe*?
> Blest with a *Taste* exact, yet unconfin'd;
> A *Knowledge* both of *Books* and *Humankind*;
> *Gen'rous Converse*; a *Soul* exempt from *Pride*;
> And *Love to Praise*, with *Reason* on his Side?[60]

The chiastic organization of the couplets creates the image of a critic both dauntingly complete and almost the embodiment of paradox in his incorporation of commonly antagonistic qualities. It would be a bold reader who saw in these lines his own reflection.

Pope implied, then, that the modern age was inimical to true criticism: 'Such once were *Criticks*, such the Happy *Few*, / *Athens* and *Rome* in better Ages knew.'[61] This estrangement between modernity and true critical judgement was reinforced by the third area in which Pope countered Whiggish notions of poetry: namely, the *Essay*'s revival of the critical judgements and principles of an earlier generation of Tory writers, notably Roscommon, Buckingham, Dryden and Atterbury. Three years later, Welsted would find little profit in the poetical treatises of these men: 'they do but hackney the same thoughts over again, making them still more trite; most of these pieces are nothing but a pert insipid heap of common-place'.[62] William Coward also censured this group of critics, and contrasted his own work with theirs: 'For I conceive there ought to be something *more observable* in our Poetry to make it *please*, than what has been already taken notice of by former Writers.'[63] But Pope gave these critics a renewed currency by allusively weaving their judgements and principles into the fabric of his own poem.

Where, for instance, Atterbury had written '[Waller] had a fine Ear, and knew how quickly that Sense was cloy'd by the same round of chiming Words still returning upon it,' Pope echoed with:

> While they ring round the same *unvary'd Chimes*,
> With sure *Returns* of still *expected Rhymes*.

Where Roscommon had epitomized truth as light:

> *Truth* still is *One*: *Truth* is Divinely *bright*,
> No cloudy *Doubts* obscure her *Native light*,

Pope borrowed the phrasing and the rhyme, and applied it to Nature:

> *Unerring Nature*, still divinely bright,
> One *clear*, *unchang'd*, and *Universal* Light,

Where Dryden, addressing artistic drabness in political language, had censured the 'Leveller in Poetry' who 'creeps along with ten little words in every line, and helps out his Numbers with *For to*, and *Unto*, and all the pretty Expletives he can find, till he draggs them to the end of another line; while the Sense is left tir'd half way behind it', Pope attacked the depraved taste of his own day by means of a similar confusion of social and artistic lowness:

> These *Equal Syllables* alone require,
> Tho' oft the Ear the *open Vowels* tire,
> While *Expletives* their feeble Aid *do* join,
> And ten low Words oft creep in one dull Line,

Where Buckingham had compared wit to the sun:

> True Wit is everlasting, like the Sun;
> Which though sometimes beneath a cloud retir'd,
> Breaks out again, and is by all admir'd.

Pope adopted and elaborated the comparison, as John Dennis was quick to spot:

> For envy'd Wit, like *Sol* Eclips'd, makes known
> Th' *opposing Body's* Grossness, not its *own*.
> When first that Sun too powerful Beams displays,
> It draws up Vapours which obscure its Rays;
> But ev'n those Clouds at last adorn its Way,
> Reflect new Glories, and augment the Day.[64]

Part of Pope's intention in the *Essay*, as his first readers noticed, was thus to restate in a form of unimpeachable modernity the substance of an older, Tory, view of poetry then in danger of being overwhelmed by more recent, Whiggish, attitudes. So readily do we accord Pope the status of the poetical arbiter of his age that it is surprising to see him, as we must do here, on the back foot. However, it may be that our appreciation for the brilliance of the *Essay* will be deepened as well as complicated once we have understood that it was an eloquent rearguard action, rather than an unthreatened display of platitudes.

The views Pope articulated in the *Essay* eventually contributed to the much more elaborate vision of *The Dunciad*. The immediate origins of this poem lay in the quarrel over the editing of Shakespeare which was carried on in the prefaces to the editions by Pope and Theobald and which, as David Mallet's *Of Verbal Criticism* (1733) and the references to Bentley in Theobald's 'Preface' (1733) show, was linked to contemporary quarrels over the editing of Milton. But this was only the most recent battle in a cultural war going back to the later seventeenth century and consistently overlaid with the assumptions and language of the pungently dynastic politics of the period. As Pope asserted, there were '*Parties*, both in Wit and State',[65] and a title such as *Milton Restor'd and Bentley Depos'd* addressed them equally in a language which resonated powerfully in both spheres. So, too, did the myths of textual corruption which are so prominent in both Pope's 'Preface' to Shakespeare (1725) and Bentley's 'Preface' to Milton (1732): the substitution of the genuine for the spurious was, after the accession of George I in 1714, a pattern for political as well as literary conspiracies. And the various roles played by the urban populace in these works also show how the political outlook of a critic might condition his writing. The populace were the source of textual contamination for Pope; the vile antithesis of Hanmer's genteel and amicable recension of Shakespeare's text by himself and 'other Gentlemen equally fond of the Author'; but also the tribunal before whom Theobald was proud to lay his work.[66]

When the dynastic question began to wane in national politics, as it did after the failure of the Jacobite rebellion of 1745, and particularly once it had been extinguished as a viable political option after the accession of George III in 1760, so literary criticism and the nature of critical argument also changed.[67] The political life of the nation and the languages within which literature was discussed entered a new phase together. On 26 August 1762 Thomas Percy wrote to Thomas Warton, encouraging him to write a continuation to Chaucer's Squire's Tale: 'The novelty of such a performance would be a means of recovering to poesy that attention, which it seems in great measure to have lost. The appetite is so palled with all the common forms of poetry, that some new Species seems wanting to quicken & revive it.' And Warton replied just over a week later to endorse his friend's reading of the public taste: 'You are certainly right in thinking that the Public ought to have their Attention called to Poetry in new forms; to Poetry endued with new Manners & new Images.'[68]

The nature of the ensuing changes of taste, the arguments by which they were defended and assailed, the critical languages to which they gave rise: these are the province of another anthology.

Jesus College, Oxford, 1996

NOTES TO THE INTRODUCTION

1. Immanuel Kant, *The Critique of Judgement*, tr. J. C. Meredith (Oxford: Oxford University Press, 1952), p. 140.

2. Ibid., pp. 80, 85, 60 and 50.

3. In English criticism of the decades following the publication of Kant's *Critique* the most striking expression of this principle is Coleridge's dictum that the work of art contains within 'itself the reason why it is so, and not otherwise' (S. T. Coleridge, *Biographia Literaria*, ed. J. Engell and W. Jackson Bate, 2 vols. (Princeton: Princeton University Press, 1983), ii. 12).

4. Charles Batteux (1713–80); French philosopher and aesthetician. His major publications were *Les Beaux-Arts réduits à un même principe* (1746); a translation of Horace (1750); *Cours de belles lettres* (1765); *Principes de la littérature* (1774). His work was for the most part a narrow and pedantic working out of his doctrines that art consisted in the faithful imitation of the beautiful in nature, and that the beauty of poetry consisted in the felicity of individual expressions.

Gotthold Ephraim Lessing (1729–81); German critic and dramatist. In his most celebrated work, *Laokoön* (1766), he had explored the limitations of poetry and the plastic arts, and had tried to specify the peculiar aptitude of each separate art. In *Zerstreute Anmerkungen über das Epigramm* (1771) he had explored the rules for epigrammatic verse.

5. J. W. H. Atkins, *English Literary Criticism: Seventeenth and Eighteenth Centuries* (London: Methuen, 1951).

6. Atkins himself cites Benedetto Croce's dictum that 'the only true history, the history which is philosophy, is that which sees the past as pressing towards a goal and consummation in the future' (p. 356). For the most powerful recent ripostes to such a conception of how the project of intellectual history should be framed, see the early theoretical essays of Quentin Skinner, conveniently republished in the first section of J. Tully (ed.), *Meaning and Context: Quentin Skinner and His Critics* (Oxford: Polity Press, 1988).

7. Pope's *An Essay on Criticism* has been a particular beneficiary – or victim – of this approach, which is of course not confined to Atkins's study. Virtually all the criticism inspired by this poem has been devoted to isolating its aesthetic doctrine. No critic since Dennis has tried to relate the poem's positions on art to its political and religious orientation.

8. This could be a process in which authors themselves collaborated. For instance, Pope's revisions to *An Essay on Criticism* steadily eroded the engagement with politics and religion which had been so vivid to some of the poem's first readers, while also gradually thickening the crust of notes and prefatory matter which surrounded the poem. In its final form – and this is the form reprinted in all modern editions of Pope – *An Essay on Criticism* looks much more like a formal treatise on aesthetics than the brilliant, at times unguarded, essay which had been published in 1711. (The addition of the analytic table of contents in 1736 was particularly powerful in changing the ostensible character of the poem.)

9. One can see this process taking place within the *œuvre* of Pope if one considers how *The Dunciad* was in part compiled out of fragments from the early years of the century, such as the lines added to Wycherley's *Poems*, and 'To the Author of a Poem, intitled, Successio'.

10. The secondary literature on this subject has recently been strengthened by the publication of Christine Gerrard's detailed and thoughtful study *The Patriot Opposition to Walpole: Politics, Poetry and National Myth, 1725–1742* (Oxford: Oxford University Press, 1994). See also I. Kramnick, *Bolingbroke and His Circle: The Politics of Nostalgia in the Age of Walpole* (Cambridge, Mass.: Harvard University Press, 1968) and B. Goldgar, *Walpole and the Wits: The Relation of Politics to Literature, 1722–1742* (Lincoln, Nebr.: University of Nebraska Press, 1976). Pope's 'For One Who Would Not be Buried in Westminster Abbey' shows that the Scriblerian allegiance to Virgil and Horace was not unconditional.

11. See below, p. 121.

12. See below, p. 64. Compare also Thomas Brown's *Essay Upon English Satyr*: '*Poetry* has had its *Crisis* in these Nations, as well as in other Countries. It was during the Reign of King *Charles* the II. that Learning in general flourish'd, and the Muses like other fair Ladies, met with the Civillest sort of Entertainment' (*The Works of Thomas Brown*, 4 vols. (1707–9), i, 34). Brown was famous for his burlesques of the poetry of Blackmore.

13. See below, p. 59.

14. See below, pp. 108–9, ll. 11–13 and 29–40.

15. For a characteristically Whig alternative to this admiration for Louis XIV's cultural imperialism, see William Coward's *Licentia Poetica* (1709). Coward sees the French eagerness for translation as an attempt to make their language 'a Kind of Universal Language; This Attempt is suitable to the Character of their Great Master, who wou'd perhaps be Universal Monarch' (p. 78). In his *A Discourse to Sir Robert Walpole* (1727) Leonard Welsted would note that the French language became 'the key to all literature, and, as it were, a compendium of all other tongues' by virtue of the industry of its translators (*Works*, ed. J. Nichols (1787), p. 164).

16. Welsted, *Works*, p. 121.

17. Charles Montagu, Earl of Halifax (1661–1715) (not to be confused with Charles Montagu, first Duke of Manchester (1660?–1722)). One of the signatories of the letter of invitation to William of Orange. Prime architect, with John Somers, of William III's financial policy in the 1690s. Founder of the Bank of England. Out of favour during the reign of Anne. Immediately rewarded and ennobled on the accession of George I. A posthumous volume of his literary works, including his poem on the Battle of the Boyne and his burlesque of Dryden's *The Hind and the Panther*, supplemented with an account of his life and a selection of his parliamentary speeches, was published in 1715 as *The Works and Life of . . . Charles, late Earl of Halifax*.

18. The Whigs, at least in the field of literature, have never recovered from the mauling they received at the hands of Pope and Swift, as the patronizing tone of *DNB* articles on important figures such as Welsted and Dennis shows.

19. On financial matters, see P. G. M. Dickson, *The Financial Revolution in England: A Study in the Development of Public Credit, 1688–1756* (London: Macmillan, 1967) and E. A. Reitan, 'From Revenue to Civil List 1689–1702', *Historical Journal*, 13 (1970). On political parties in the period, see B. W. Hill, *The Growth of Parliamentary Parties 1689–1742* (London: Allen & Unwin, 1976).

20. For a succinct account of the character and measures of William's reign, on which I have relied, see J. P. Kenyon, *Stuart England* (Harmondsworth: Penguin, 1978), pp. 268–97.

21. The measures which betrayed that such was the intention of William and his advisers were Montagu's Act of 1693, and the creation of the Bank of England in 1694.

22. On this see J. G. A. Pocock, *The Machiavellian Moment: Florentine Political Thought and the Atlantic Republican Tradition* (Princeton: Princeton University Press, 1975), and 'The Varieties of Whiggism from Exclusion to Reform: A History of Ideology and Discourse' in his *Virtue, Commerce and History* (Cambridge: Cambridge University Press, 1985), pp. 215–310.

23. See below, pp. 139 and 175.

24. Sir Richard Blackmore, *A Paraphrase on the Book of Job* (1700), sigs. b^r, c2^r and b^r. Blackmore returned to these topics in his essay on 'Epick Poetry', in

Essays upon Several Subjects, 2 vols. (1716 and 1717). See also his *A Collection of Poems on Various Subjects* (1718), pp. vii–ix. The notion of replacing machinery drawn from pagan mythology with that drawn from Christianity was picked up by Addison in *The Spectator*, no. 523 (30 October 1712).

25. It is worth noting that the charge of vacuous grandiloquence was also levelled by Whigs at Tory poets such as Dryden. See, for example, Coward's *Licentia Poetica*, p. 9.

26. This heroic mythologizing is partly the result of Blackmore's handling of proper names, translating them into vaguely Latinate forms such as 'Ramillia', 'Gallia', 'Lovania', 'Brussella', 'Mechlinia' and 'Brabantia'.

27. See below, pp. 191 and 193, ll. 497–8 and 547–8.

28. See below, p. 177, ll. 7–14.

29. See below, p. 179, ll. 62–3.

30. See below, p. 182, ll. 176–84.

31. See below, p. 194, ll. 571–83.

32. See below, p. 193, ll. 556–60.

33. Pope, 'The First Satire of the Second Book of Horace Imitated', ll. 23–6.

34. *The Works and Life of . . . Charles, late Earl of Halifax* (1715), p. 23.

35. Consider the sketch of Marlborough's self-possession in victory: 'Describe him ent'ring high *Brussella*'s Gate, / 'Midst loud Applauses, in triumphant State. / Express his God-like unelated Air; / Oh! who can conquer so? who Conquest so can bear?' (below, p. 192, ll. 517–20).

36. See below, p. 195, l. 636.

37. See below, p. 180, ll. 93–100.

38. See below, pp. 194 and 195, ll. 594–601 and 628–33.

39. See below, p. 179, ll. 60–63.

40. See below, p. 183, ll. 215–21.

41. See below, pp. 183–4, ll. 228–36.

42. See below, pp. 189 and 190, ll. 415–29 and 441–60.

43. See below, pp. 184–5, ll. 249–77.

44. For Montagu, see above, n. 17. John, Lord Somers (1651–1716). Lord Chancellor of England. Junior counsel for the seven bishops accused of resisting indulgence of Catholicism, 1688. Legal and political adviser to William III. Head of the Whig Junto during the reign of Anne.

45. I paraphrase here the significance of this parliament in Whig mythology. Modern historians have discovered it to have been a far more mixed and in some respects conservative parliament. See J. P. Kenyon, *Revolution Principles* (Cambridge: Cambridge University Press, 1977), pp. 7–9.

46. See below, p. 182, ll. 172–3.

47. See below, p. 180, ll. 97–106.

48. See below, p. 194, ll. 571–2.

49. Bod. MS Eng. poet. c. 1.

50. For the details of these revisions, see the headnote to the text of the *Essay* in the appropriate volume of the Twickenham edition, and R. H. Griffith, 'Pope Editing Pope', *University of Texas Studies in English* (1944), pp. 37–49.

51. See below, p. 224, ll. 545–52.

52. Coward, *Licentia Poetica*, p. 9. We should not forget that Pope had cut his teeth as a poet on imitations of his seventeenth-century predecessors.

53. On the literature surrounding this political grouping, see Gerrard, *The Patriot Opposition to Walpole*. The collection of British worthies assembled in the grounds of Viscount Cobham's house, Stowe, indicates clearly his high estimation of Whigs of William III's reign such as Locke and Newton.

54. See below, p. 212, ll. 134–41.

55. See below, pp. 213–14, ll. 184–203.

56. Coward, *Licentia Poetica*, sig. B2^r. The MS of *An Essay on Criticism* is inscribed by Pope with the phrase 'Written 1709' (Bod. MS Eng. Poet. c. 1 f.1^r), but this does not solve the problem of the date of the poem's composition: see the headnote to the poem in the Twickenham edition.

57. See below, p. 208, l. 20.

58. See below, pp. 221 and 224–5, ll. 431–2 and 571–4.

59. See below, pp. 224–5, ll. 569–70 and 581–2.

60. See below, pp. 226–7, ll. 634–45.

61. See below, p. 227, ll. 646–7.

62. Welsted, *Works*, pp. 128–9.

63. Coward, *Licentia Poetica*, sig. A3^r.

64. For these quotations, see below, pp. 123, 218, 114, 210, 21, 218, 97 and 222. Further borrowings are recorded in the notes to Pope's poem: below, pp. 378–86. For Dennis's alertness to this aspect of Pope's poem, see below, pp. 237 and 387, n. 11.

65. See below, p. 272.

66. See below, pp. 267, 303 and 302.

67. For this periodization of the restoration of the Stuarts as a political reality, see J. C. D. Clark, *English Society 1688–1832* (Cambridge: Cambridge University Press, 1985), especially pp. 119–98.

68. *The Correspondence of Thomas Warton*, ed. D. Fairer (Athens, Ga.: University of Georgia Press, 1995), pp. 124 and 126.

FURTHER READING

A: ANTHOLOGIES OF CRITICISM

Adams, H. H., and Hathaway, B. (eds.), *Dramatic Essays of the Neoclassical Age* (New York: Columbia University Press, 1950).

Chapman, G. W. (ed.), *Literary Criticism in England, 1660–1800* (New York: Alfred A. Knopf, 1966).

Durham, W. H. (ed.), *Critical Essays of the Eighteenth Century, 1700–1725* (New Haven, Conn.: Yale University Press, 1915).

Elledge, S. (ed.), *Eighteenth-Century Critical Essays*, 2 vols. (Ithaca, N.Y.: Cornell University Press, 1961).

Hynes, S. (ed.), *English Literary Criticism, Restoration and Eighteenth Century* (London: Peter Owen, 1966).

Smith, D. Nichol (ed.), *Eighteenth Century Essays on Shakespeare* (Oxford: Clarendon Press, 1963).

Spingarn, J. E. (ed.), *Critical Essays of the Seventeenth Century*, 3 vols. (Oxford: Clarendon Press, 1908–9).

Vickers, B. (ed.), *Shakespeare: The Critical Heritage, Vol. 2 1693–1733* (London and Boston: Routledge and Kegan Paul, 1974).

B: HISTORIES OF CRITICISM

Atkins, J. W. H., *English Literary Criticism: Seventeenth and Eighteenth Centuries* (London: Methuen, 1951).

Blamires, H., *A History of Literary Criticism* (London: Macmillan, 1991).

Saintsbury, G., *A History of English Criticism* (Edinburgh and London: William Blackwood & Sons, 1911).

Watson, G., *The Literary Critics: A Study of English Descriptive Criticism* (London: Chatto & Windus, 1964).

Wellek, R., *A History of Modern Criticism 1750–1950*, 4 vols. (London: Cape, 1955–66).

Wimsatt, W. K., and Brooks, Cleanth, *Literary Criticism: A Short History*, 4 vols. (London: Routledge & Kegan Paul, 1970).

C: SCHOLARLY STUDIES

Bate, W. J., *From Classic to Romantic: Premises of Taste in Eighteenth-Century England* (Cambridge, Mass.: Harvard University Press, 1946).

Bosker, A., *Literary Criticism in the Age of Johnson* (New York: Hafner Publishing Company, rev. edn, 1953).

Crane, R. S., 'English Neo-Classical Criticism: an Outline Sketch', in R. S. Crane (ed.), *Critics and Criticism Ancient and Modern* (Chicago: University of Chicago Press, 1952).

— 'On Writing the History of English Criticism, 1650–1800', *University of Toronto Quarterly*, 22 (1953).

De Bolla, P., *The Discourse of the Sublime: Readings in History, Aesthetics and the Subject* (Oxford: Basic Blackwell, 1989).

Engell, James, *Forming the Critical Mind: Dryden to Coleridge* (Cambridge, Mass.: Harvard University Press, 1989).

Galaway, F., *Reason, Rule, and Revolt in English Classicism* (New York: Charles Scribner's Sons, 1940).

Hipple, W. J., *The Beautiful, the Sublime, and the Picturesque in Eighteenth-Century British Aesthetic Theory* (Carbondale: Southern Illinois University Press, 1957).

Jones, T. Burnley, and Nicol, B. de Bear, *Neo-Classical Dramatic Criticism 1560–1770* (Cambridge: Cambridge University Press, 1976).

McKenzie, G., *Critical Responsiveness: A Study of the Psychological Current in later Eighteenth-Century Criticism* (Berkeley: University of California Press, 1949).

Monk, S. H., *The Sublime: A Study of Critical Theories in XVIII-Century England* (New York: Modern Language Association, 1935).

Robertson, J. G., *Studies in the Genesis of Romantic Theory in the Eighteenth Century* (Cambridge: Bowes, 1925).

A NOTE ON THE TEXTS

Precise bibliographical information will be found in the headnote which prefaces the explanatory annotation for each text, but in general I have transcribed the texts without change. Punctuation and orthography correspond to the cited copy-text, and therefore often flout modern usage. Evident slips, however, have been silently corrected.

Where a text was significantly revised, a selection of the more interesting or important variants is provided in the notes. Needless to say, in no case does this amount to a full collation.

The logic of the principle adopted in this anthology, of presenting criticism in its dialectical context, has dictated that some well-known works appear in unfamiliar versions; for instance, Pope's *An Essay on Criticism* is represented by the first edition of 1711 and Dryden's *Of Dramatick Poesie, An Essay* by the first edition of 1668. While the main reason for such preferences is one of rigour, I also hope that readers will be interested to see how these celebrated works first came before the public.

I
Nationalism and the Stage,
1664–1671

Richard Fleckno,
A Short Discourse of the English Stage
(1664)

To his Excellency, the Lord Marquess of
NEWCASTLE.

My Noble Lord,

I SEND your Excellency here a short Discourse of the *English Stage*, (which if you pleas'd you could far better treat of then my self) but before I begin it, I will speak a word or two of those of other Countreys.

About the midst of the last Century, Playes, after a long discontinuance, and civil death in a manner, began to be reviv'd again, first in *Italy* by *Guarino*, *Tasso*, *de Porta*, and others; and afterwards in *Spain* by *Lopes de Vega*; the French beginning later by reason of their Civil Wars, Cardinal *Richlieu* being the first that brought them into Vouge and Esteem as now they are; well knowing how much the Acting noble and heroick Playes, conferr'd to the instilling a noble and heroick Spirit into the Nation. For us, we began before them, and if since they seem to have out-stript us, 'tis because our Stage ha's stood at a stand this many years; nor may we doubt, but now we shall soon out-strip them again, if we hold on but as we begin. Of the Dutch I speak nothing, because they are but slow, and follow other Nations onely afar off. But to return unto our present subject.

Playes (which so flourisht amongst the Greeks, and afterwards amongst the Romans) were almost wholly abolished when their Empire was first eonverted to Christianity, and their Theaters, together with their Temples, for the most part, demolished as Reliques of Paganisme, some few onely reserved and dedicate to the service of the True God, as they had been to their false gods before; from which time to the last Age, they Acted nothing here, but Playes of the holy

Scripture, or Saints Lives; and that without any certain Theaters or set Companies, till about the beginning of Queen *Elizabeths* Reign, they began here to assemble into Companies, and set up Theaters, first in the City, (as in the Inn-yards of the *Cross-Keyes*, and *Bull* in *Grace* and *Bishops-Gate Street* at this day is to be seen) till that Fanatick Spirit which then began with the Stage, and after ended with the Throne, banisht them thence into the Suburbs, as after they did the Kingdom, in the beginning of our Civil Wars. In which time, Playes were so little incompatible with Religion, and the Theater with the Church, as on Weekdayes after Vespers, both the Children of the Chappel and St. *Pauls*, Acted Playes, the one in *White-Friers*, the other behinde the Convocation-house in *Pauls*, till people growing more precise, and Playes more licentious, the Theatre of *Pauls* was quite supprest, and that of the Children of the Chappel, converted to the use of the Children of the Revels.

In this time were Poets and Actors in their greatest flourish, *Johnson*, *Shakespear*, with *Beaumont* and *Fletcher* their Poets, and *Field* and *Burbidge* their Actors.

For Playes, *Shakespear* was one of the first, who inverted the Dramatick Stile, from dull History to quick Comedy, upon whom *Johnson* refin'd; as *Beaumont* and *Fletcher* first writ in the Heroick way, upon whom *Suckling* and others endeavoured to refine agen; one saying wittily of his *Aglaura*, that 'twas full of fine flowers, but they seem'd rather stuck, then growing there; as another of *Shakespear*'s writings, that 'twas a fine Garden, but it wanted weeding.

There are few of our English Playes (excepting onely some few of *Johnsons*) without some faults or other; and if the French have fewer then our English, 'tis because they confine themselves to narrower limits, and consequently have less liberty to erre.

The chief faults of ours, are our huddling too much matter together, and making them too long and intricate; we imagining we never have intrigue enough, till we lose our selves and Auditors, who shu'd be led in a Maze, but not a Mist; and through turning and winding wayes, but so still, as they may finde their way at last.

A good Play shu'd be like a good stuff, closely and evenly wrought, without any breakes, thrums, or loose ends in 'um, or like a good

Picture well painted and designed; the Plot or Contrivement, the Design, the Writing, the Coloris, and Counterplot, the Shaddowings, with other Embellishments: or finally, it shu'd be like a well contriv'd Garden, cast into its Walks and Counterwalks, betwixt an Alley and a Wilderness, neither too plain, nor too confus'd. Of all Arts, that of the Dramatick Poet is the most difficult and most subject to censure; for in all others, they write onely of some particular subject, as the Mathematician of Mathematicks, or Philosopher of Philosophy; but in that, the Poet must write of every thing, and every one undertakes to judge of it.

A Dramatick Poet is to the Stage as a Pilot to the Ship; and to the Actors, as an Architect to the Builders, or Master to his Schollars: he is to be a good moral Philosopher, but yet more learned in Men then Books. He is to be a wise, as well as a witty Man, and a good man, as well as a good Poet; and I'de allow him to be so far a good fellow too, to take a chearful cup to whet his wits, so he take not so much to dull 'um, and whet 'um quite away.

To compare our English Dramatick Poets together (without taxing them) *Shakespear* excelled in a natural Vein, *Fletcher* in Wit, and *Johnson* in Gravity and ponderousness of Style; whose onely fault was, he was too elaborate, and had he mixt less erudition with his Playes, they had been more pleasant and delightful then they are. Comparing him with *Shakespear*, you shall see the difference betwixt Nature and Art; and with *Fletcher*, the difference betwixt Wit and Judgement: Wit being an exuberant thing, like *Nilus*, never more commendable then when it overflowes; but Judgement a stayed and reposed thing, alwayes containing it self within its bounds and limits.

Beaumont and *Fletcher* were excellent in their kinde, but they often err'd against *Decorum*, seldom representing a valiant man without somewhat of the *Braggadoccio*, nor an honourable woman without somewhat of *Dol Common*[1] in her: to say nothing of their irreverent representing Kings persons on the Stage, who shu'd never be represented, but with Reverence. Besides, *Fletcher* was the first who introduc't that witty obscenity in his Playes, which like poison infused in pleasant liquor, is alwayes the more dangerous the more delightful. And here to speak a word or two of Wit, it is the spirit and quintessence

5

of speech, extracted out of the substance of the thing we speak of, having nothing of the superfice, or dross of words (as clenches, quibbles, gingles, and such like trifles have) it is that, in pleasant and facetious discourse, as Eloquence is in grave and serious; not learnt by Art and Precept, but Nature and Company. 'Tis in vain to say any more of it; for if I could tell you what it were, it would not be what it is; being somewhat above expression, and such a volatil thing, as 'tis altogether as volatil to describe.

It was the happiness of the Actors of those Times to have such Poets as these to instruct them, and write for them; and no less of those Poets to have such docile and excellent Actors to Act their Playes, as a *Field* and *Burbidge*; of whom we may say, that he was a delightful *Proteus*, so wholly transforming himself into his Part, and putting off himself with his Cloathes, as he never (not so much as in the Tyring-house) assum'd himself again until the Play was done: there being as much difference betwixt him and one of our common Actors, as between a Balladsinger who onely mouths it, and an excellent singer, who knows all his Graces, and can artfully vary and modulate his Voice, even to know how much breath he is to give to every syllable. He had all the parts of an excellent Orator, (animating his words with speaking, and Speech with Action) his Auditors being never more delighted then when he spake, nor more sorry then when he held his peace; yet even then, he was an excellent Actor still, never falling in his Part when he had done speaking; but with his looks and gesture, maintaining it still unto the heighth, he imagining *Age quod agis*, onely spoke to him: so as those who call him a Player do him wrong, no man being less idle then he, whose whole life is nothing else but action; with only this difference from other mens, that as what is but a Play to them, is his Business; so their business is but a play to him.

Now, for the difference betwixt our Theatres and those of former times, they were but plain and simple, with no other Scenes, nor Decorations of the Stage, but onely old Tapestry, and the Stage strew'd with Rushes, (with their Habits accordingly) whereas ours now for cost and ornament are arriv'd to the heighth of Magnificence; but that which makes our Stage the better, makes our Playes the worse perhaps, they striving now to make them more for sight, then hearing, whence that solid joy of the interior is lost, and that benefit which men formerly receiv'd from Playes, from which they seldom or never went away, but far better and wiser then they came.

The Stage being a harmless and innocent Recreation; where the minde is recreated and delighted, and that *Ludus Literarum*, or School of good Language and Behaviour, that makes Youth soonest Man, and man soonest good and vertuous, by joyning example to precept, and the pleasure of seeing to that of hearing. Its chiefest end is, to render Folly ridiculous, Vice odious, and Vertue and Noblenesse so amiable and lovely, as, every one shu'd be delighted and enamoured with it; from which when it deflects; as, *corruptio optimi pessima*: of the best it becomes the worst of Recreations. And this his Majesty well understood, when after his happy Restauration, he took such care to purge it from all vice and obscenity; and would to God he had found all bodies and humours as apt and easie to be purg'd and reform'd as that.

For Scenes and Machines they are no new invention, our Masks and some of our Playes in former times (though not so ordinary) having had as good or rather better then any we have now.

They are excellent helps of imagination, most grateful deceptions of the sight, and graceful and becoming Ornaments of the Stage, transporting you easily without lassitude from one place to another; or rather by a kinde of delightful Magick, whilst you sit still, does bring the place to you. Of this curious Art the *Italians* (this latter age) are the greatest masters,[2] the *French* good proficients, and we in *England* onely Schollars and Learners yet, having proceeded no further then to bare painting, and not arriv'd to the stupendious wonders of your great Ingeniers, especially not knowing yet how to place our Lights, for the more advantage and illuminating of the Scenes.

And thus much suffices it briefly to have said of all that concerns our Modern Stage, onely to give others occasion to say more.

Sir Robert Howard,
'Preface' to *Four New Plays*
(1665)

To The
READER.

THERE is none more sensible than I am, how great a Charity the most Ingenious may need, that expose their private Wit to a publique Judgment; since the same Phansie from whence the Thoughts proceed, must probably be kind to its own Issue: This renders Men no perfecter Judges of their own Writings, than Fathers are of their own Children, who find out that Wit in them which another discerns not, and see not those Errors which are evident to the unconcern'd. Nor is this self-kindness more fatal to Men in their Writings, than in their Actions; every Man being a greater Flatterer to himself than he knows how to be to another; otherwise it were impossible that things of such distant Natures shou'd find their own Authors so equally kind in their affections to them, and Men so different in Parts and Virtues, should rest equally contented in their own Opinions.

This Apprehension, added to that greater which I have of my own Weakness, may I hope incline the Reader to believe me, when I assure him that these Follies were made publique as much against my Inclination as Judgment: But being pursu'd with so many Sollicitations of *Mr Herringman*'s, and having received Civilities from him if it were possible exceeding his Importunities; I at last yielded to prefer that which he believed his Interest, before that which I apprehended my own Disadvantage: Considering withal, That he might pretend it would be a real Loss to him, and could be but an imaginary Prejudice to me; since things of this nature, though never so excellent, or never

8

so mean, have seldom prov'd the Foundation of Mens new-built Fortunes, or the Ruine of their old; it being the Fate of Poetry, though of no other good Parts, to be wholly separated from Interest; and there are few that know me but will easily believe I am not much concern'd in an unprofitable Reputation. This clear account I have given the Reader of this seeming Contradiction, to offer that to the World which I dislike my self; and in all things I have no greater an ambition than to be believ'd a Person that would rather be unkind to my self, than ungrateful to others.

I have made this excuse for my self; I offer none for my Writings, but freely leave the Reader to condemn that which has receiv'd my Sentence already. Yet I shall presume to say somthing in the justification of our Nations Plays, though not of my own; since in my Judgment, without being partial to my Country, I do really prefer our Plays as much before any other Nations, as I do the best of ours before my own.

The manner of the Stage-Entertainments have differ'd in all Ages; and as it has encreas'd in use, it has enlarg'd it self in business: The general manner of Plays among the Ancients we find in *Seneca*'s Tragedies for serious Subjects, and in *Terence* and *Plautus* for the Comical; in which latter we see some pretences to Plots, though certainly short of what we have seen in some of M *Johnson*'s Plays; and for their Wit, especially *Plautus*, I suppose it suited much better in those days than it would do in ours; for were their Plays strictly Translated, and Presented on our Stage, they would hardly bring as many Audiences as they have now Admirers.

The serious Plays were anciently compos'd of *Speeches* and *Choruses*, where all things are related, but no matter of Fact presented on the Stage: This Pattern the *French* do at this time neerly follow, only leaving out the *Chorus*, making up their Plays with almost entire and discoursive Scenes, presenting the business in Relations: This way has very much affected some of our Nation, who possibly believe well of it more upon the account that what the *French* do ought to be a Fashion, than upon the Reason of the thing.

It is first necessary to consider why probably the Compositions of the Ancients, especially in their serious Plays, were after this manner;

and it will be found, that the Subjects they commonly chose drove them upon the necessity, which were usually the most known Stories and Fables: Accordingly, *Seneca* making choice of *Medea*, *Hyppolitus*, and *Hercules Oetus*, it was impossible to shew *Medea* throwing old mangled *Æson* into her Age-renewing Caldron, or to present the scattered Limbs of *Hyppolitus* upon the Stage, or shew *Hercules* burning upon his own Funeral Pyle: And this the judicious *Horace* clearly speaks of in his *Arte Poetica*, where he says,

> *non tamen intus*
> *Digna geri, promes in Scenam: multaque tolles*
> *Ex oculis, quæ mox narret facundia præsens.*
> *Nec pueros coram populo* Medea *trucidet:*
> *Aut humana palam coquat exta nefarius* Atreus,
> *Aut in avem* Progne *vertatur,* Cadmus *in anguem.*
> *Quodcunque ostendis mihi sic, incredulus odi.*[1]

So that it appears a fault to chuse such Subjects for the Stage, but much greater to affect that Method which those Subjects enforce; and therefore the *French* seem much mistaken, who without the necessity somtimes commit the Error; and this is as plainly decided by the same Author in his preceding words;

> *Aut agitur res in Scenis aut acta refertur:*
> *Segnius irritant animos demissa per aurem,*
> *Quam quæ sunt oculis subjecta fidelibus, & quæ*
> *Ipse sibi tradit spectator.* —[2]

By which he directly declares his Judgment, That every thing makes more impression Presented than Related: Nor indeed can any one rationally assert the contrary; for if they affirm otherwise, they do by consequence maintain, That a whole Play might be as well Related as Acted: Therefore whoever chuses a Subject that inforces him to Relations is to blame; and he that does it without the necessity of the Subject, is much more.

If these Premises be granted, 'tis no partiality to conclude, That our *English* Plays justly challenge the Preheminence; yet I shall as candidly acknowledg, That our best Poets have differed from other

Nations (though not so happily) in usually mingling and interweaving Mirth and Sadness through the whole Course of their Plays, *Ben. Johnson* only excepted, who keeps himself entire to one Argument; and I confess I am now convinc'd in my own Judgment, That it is most proper to keep the Audience in one entire disposition both of Concern and Attention; for when Scenes of so different Natures immediately succeed one another, 'tis probable the Audience may not so suddenly recollect themselves, as to start into an enjoyment of the Mirth, or into a concern for the Sadness: Yet I dispute not but the variety of this World may afford pursuing Accidents of such different Natures; but yet though possible in themselves to be, they may not be so proper to be Presented; an entire Connexion being the natural Beauty of all Plays, and Language the Ornament to dress them in, which in serious Subjects ought to be great and easie, like a high-born Person that expresses Greatness without pride or affectation; the easier dictates of Nature ought to flow in Comedy, yet separated from obsceneness, there being nothing more impudent than the immodesty of Words: Wit should be chaste; and those that have it can only write well. –

Si modo —
Scimus in Urbanum Lepido seponere dicto.[3]

Another way of the Ancients which the *French* follow, and our Stage has now lately practis'd, is to write in Rhime; and this is the dispute betwixt many ingenious Persons, Whether Verse in Rhime, or Verse without the sound, which may be call'd Blank Verse, (though a hard Expression) is to be preferr'd?[4] But take the Question largely, and it is never to be decided, but by right application I suppose it may; for in the general they are both proper, that is, one for a Play, the other for a Poem or Copy of Verses; a Blank Verse being as much too low for one as Rhime is unnatural for the other: A Poem being a premeditated form of Thoughts upon design'd Occasions, ought not to be unfurnish'd of any harmony in Words or Sound: The other is presented as the present Effect of Accidents not thought of; so that 'tis impossible it should be equally proper to both these, unless it were possible that all Persons were born so much more than Poets, that Verses were not to be compos'd by them, but already made in them.

Some may object, That this Argument is trivial, because, whatever is shew'd, 'tis known still to be but a Play; but such may as well excuse an ill Scene, that is not naturally painted, because they know 'tis only a Scene, and not really a City or Country.

But there is yet another thing which makes Verse upon the Stage appear more unnatural; that is, when a Piece of a Verse is made up by one that knew not what the other meant to say, and the former Verse answered as perfectly in Sound as the last is suppli'd in Measure; so that the smartness of a Reply, which has it's beauty by coming from sudden Thoughts, seems lost by that which rather looks like a Design of two, than the Answer of one. It may be said, That Rhime is such a confinement to a quick and luxuriant Phansie, that it gives a stop to its speed, till slow Judgment comes in to assist it; but this is no Argument for the Question in hand; for the dispute is not which way a Man may write best in, but which is most proper for the Subject he writes upon; and if this were let pass, the Argument is yet unsolv'd in it self, for he that wants Judgment in the liberty of his Phancy, may as well shew the defect of it in its Confinement; and to say truth, he that has Judgment will avoid the errors, and he that wants it will commit them both. It may be objected, 'Tis improbable that any should speak *ex tempore* as well as *Beaumont* and *Fletcher* makes them, though in Blank Verse; I do not only acknowledg that, but that 'tis also improbable any will write so well that way; but if that may be allow'd improbable, I believe it may be concluded impossible that any should speak as good Verses in Rhime as the best Poets have writ; and therefore that which seems neerest to what it intends, is ever to be prefer'd: Nor is great Thoughts more adorned by Verse, than Verse unbeautifi'd by mean ones; so that Verse seems not only unfit in the best use of it, but much more in the worse, when a Servant is call'd, or a Door bid to be shut in Rhime. Verses (I mean good ones) do in their height of Phancy declare the labour that brought them forth, like Majesty that grows with care; and Nature that made the Poet capable, seems to retire, and leave its offers to be made perfect by Pains and Judgment: Against this I can raise no Argument but my Lord of *Orory*'s[5] Writings, in whose Verse the greatness of the Majesty seems unsullied with the Cares, and his unimitable Phancy descends to us in such easie Expressions, that they seem as if neither had ever been added to the other, but both together flowing from a height; like Birds got so high, that use no labouring Wings, but only with an easie care preserve a steadiness in motion: But this particular Happiness, among those multitudes which that excellent Person is Owner of, does not convince my Reason, but employ my Wonder: Yet I am glad such Verse has been writ for our Stage, since it has so happily exceeded those whom we seem'd to imitate. But while I give these Arguments against Verse, I may seem faulty that I have not only writ ill ones, but writ any; but since it was the fashion, I was resolv'd, as in all indifferent things, not to appear singular, the danger of the vanity being greater than the error; and therefore I follow'd it as a Fashion, though very far off.

For the *Italian* Plays I have seen some of them which have been given me as the best; but they are so inconsiderable, that the Particulars of them are not at all worthy to entertain the Reader; but as much as they are short of others in this, they exceed in their other performances on the Stage; I mean their *Opera*'s, which consisting of Musique and Painting, there's none but will believe it is much harder to equal them in that way, than 'tis to excel them in the other.

The *Spanish* Plays pretend to more, but indeed are not much, being nothing but so many Novels put into Acts and Scenes, without the least attempt or design of making the Reader more concern'd than a well-told Tale might do; whereas a Poet that endeavours not to heighten the Accidents which Fortune seems to scatter in a well-knit Design, had better have told his tale by a Fire-side, than presented it on a Stage.

For these Times wherein we write, I admire to hear the Poets so often cry out upon, and wittily (as they believe) threaten their Judges, since the effects of their Mercy has so much exceeded their Justice, that others with me cannot but remember how many favourable Audiences some of our ill Plays have had; and when I consider how severe the former Age has been to some of the best of *Mr Johnson*'s never to be equal'd Comedies, I cannot but wonder why any Poet should speak of former Times, but rather acknowledg that the want of Abilities in this Age are largely supply'd with the Mercys of it. I deny not but there are some who resolve to like nothing; and such perhaps are not unwise, since by that general resolution they may be certainly in the right sometimes, which perhaps they would seldom be, if they should venture their Understandings in different Censures; and being forc'd to a general liking or disliking, lest they should discover too much their own weakness, 'tis to be expected they would rather chuse to pretend to Judgment than good Nature, though I wish they could find better ways to shew either.

But I forget my self, not considering, That while I entertain the Reader in the Entrance with what a good Play should be, when he is come beyond the Entrance he must be treated with what ill Plays are: But in this I resemble the greatest part of the World, that better know how to talk of things than to perform them, and live short of their own Discourses.

And now I seem like an eager Hunter, that has long pursu'd a Chase after an inconsiderable Quarry, and gives over weary, as I do.

John Dryden,

Of Dramatick Poesie, An Essay

(1668)

— *Fungar vice cotis, acutum*
Reddere quæ ferrum valet, exors ipsa secandi.
Horat. De Arte Poet.[1]

To the Right Honourable
CHARLES Lord BUCKHURST.[2]

My Lord,

AS I was lately reviewing my loose Papers, amongst the rest I found this Essay, the writing of which in this rude and indigested manner wherein your Lordship now sees it, serv'd as an amusement to me in the Country, when the violence of the last Plague had driven me from the Town.[3] Seeing then our Theaters shut up, I was engag'd in these kind of thoughts with the same delight with which men think upon their absent Mistresses: I confess I find many things in this discourse which I do not now approve; my judgment being a little alter'd[4] since the writing of it but whether for the better or the worse I know not: Neither indeed is it much material in an Essay, where all I have said is problematical. For the way of writing Playes in verse, which I have seem'd to favour, I have since that time laid the Practice of it aside, till I have more leisure, because I find it troublesome and slow. But I am no way alter'd from my opinion of it, at least with any reasons which have oppos'd it. For your Lordship may easily observe that none are very violent against it, but those who either have not attempted it, or who have succeeded ill in their attempt. 'Tis enough for me to have your Lordships example for my excuse in that little which I have done in it; and I am sure my Adversaries can bring no such Arguments against Verse, as the fourth Act of *Pompey* will furnish me with, in its defence.[5] Yet, my Lord, you must suffer me a little to complain of you, that you too soon withdraw from us a contentment, of which we expected the continuance, because you gave it us so early. 'Tis a revolt without occasion from your Party, where your merits had already rais'd you to the highest commands, and where you have not the excuse of other men that you have been ill us'd, and therefore laid down Armes. I know no other quarrel you can have to Verse, then that which *Spurina* had to his beauty, when he tore and mangled the features of his Face, onely because they pleas'd too well the lookers on.[6] It was an honour which seem'd to wait for you, to lead out a new Colony of Writers from the Mother Nation: and upon the first spreading of your Ensignes there had been many in a readiness to have follow'd so fortunate a Leader; if not all, yet the better part of Writers.[7]

> *Pars, indocili melior grege; mollis & expes*
> *Inominata perprimat cubilia.*[8]

I am almost of opinion, that we should force you to accept of the command, as sometimes the *Prætorian* Bands have compell'd their Captains to receive the Empire. The Court, which is the best and surest judge of writing, has generally allow'd of Verse; and in the Town it has found favourers of Wit and Quality. As for your own particular, My Lord, you have yet youth, and time enough to give part of it to the divertisement of the Publick, before you enter into the serious and more unpleasant business of the world. That which the French Poet[9] said of the Temple of Love, may be as well apply'd to the Temple of the Muses. The words, as near as I can remember them, were these:

> *La jeunesse a mauvaise grace.*
> *N'ayant pas adoré dans le temple d'Amour:*
> *Il faut qu'il entre, & pour le sage*
> *Si ce nest pas son vray sejour*
> *Ce'st une giste sur son passage.*

I leave the words to work their effect upon your Lordship in their

own Language, because no other can so well express the nobleness of
the thought; And wish you may be soon call'd to bear a part in the
affairs of the Nation, where I know the world expects you, and wonders
why you have been so long forgotten; there being no person amongst
our young Nobility, on whom the eyes of all men are so much bent.
But in the mean time your Lordship may imitate the course of Nature,
who gives us the flower before the fruit: that I may speak to you in
the language of the Muses, which I have taken from an excellent Poem
to the King.

> As Nature, when she fruit designes, thinks fit
> By beauteous blossoms to proceed to it;
> And while she does accomplish all the Spring,
> Birds to her secret operations sing.[10]

I confess I have no greater reason, in addressing this Essay to your
Lordship, then that it might awaken in you the desire of writing
something, in whatever kind it be, which might be an honour to our
Age and Country. And me thinks it might have the same effect upon
you, which *Homer* tells us the fight of the Greeks and Trojans before
the Fleet, had on the spirit of *Achilles*, who though he had resolved not
to ingage, yet found a martial warmth to steal upon him, at the sight
of Blows, the sound of Trumpets, and the cries of fighting Men.[11] For
my own part, if in treating of this subject I sometimes dissent from
the opinion of better Wits, I declare it is not so much to combat their
opinions, as to defend my own, which were first made publick.[12]
Sometimes, like a Schollar in a Fencing-School I put forth my self,
and show my own ill play, on purpose to be better taught. Sometimes
I stand desperately to my Armes, like the Foot when deserted by their
Horse, not in hope to overcome, but onely to yield on more honourable
termes. And yet, my Lord, this war of opinions, you well know, has
fallen out among the Writers of all Ages, and sometimes betwixt
Friends. Onely it has been prosecuted by some, like Pedants, with
violence of words, and manag'd by others like Gentlemen, with candour and ciuility. Even *Tully* had a Controversie with his dear *Atticus*;
and in one of his Dialogues makes him sustain the part of an Enemy
in Philosophy, who in his Letters is his confident of State, and made

privy to the most weighty affairs of the Roman Senate.[13] And the same respect which was paid by *Tully* to *Atticus*, we find return'd to him afterwards by *Cæsar* on a like occasion, who answering his Book in praise of *Cato*, made it not so much his business to condemn *Cato*, as to praise *Cicero*.[14] But that I may decline some part of the encounter with my Adversaries, whom I am neither willing to combate, nor well able to resist; I will give your Lordship the Relation of a Dispute betwixt some of our Wits upon this subject, in which they did not onely speak of Playes in Verse, but mingled, in the freedom of Discourse, some things of the Ancient, many of the Modern wayes of writing, comparing those with these, and the Wits of our Nation with those of others: 'tis true they differ'd in their opinions, as 'tis probable they would: neither do I take upon me to reconcile, but to relate them: and that as *Tacitus* professes of himself, *Sine studio partium aut ira*:[15] without Passion or Interest; leaving your Lordship to decide it in favour of which part you shall judge most reasonable, and withall, to pardon the many errours of,

> Your Lordships most obedient humble Servant,
> JOHN DRYDEN.

TO THE READER.

THE drift of the ensuing Discourse was chiefly to vindicate the honour of our English Writers, from the censure of those who unjustly prefer the French before them. This I intimate, least any should think me so exceeding vain, as to teach others an Art which they understand much better then my self. But if this incorrect Essay, written in the Country without the help of Books, or advice of Friends, shall find any accept-ance in the world, I promise to my self a better success of the second part, wherein the Vertues and Faults of the English Poets, who have written either in this, the Epique, or the Lyrique way, will be more fully treated of, and their several styles impartially imitated.[16]

AN ESSAY OF DRAMATICK POESIE.

IT was that memorable day, in the first Summer of the late War, when our Navy ingag'd the Dutch:[17] a day wherein the two most mighty and best appointed Fleets which any age had ever seen, disputed the command of the greater half of the Globe, the commerce of Nations, and the riches of the Universe. While these vast floating bodies, on either side, mov'd against each other in parallel lines, and our Country men, under the happy conduct of his Royal Highness,[18] went breaking, by little and little, into the line of the Enemies; the noise of the Cannon from both Navies reach'd our ears about the City: so that al men, being alarm'd with it, and in a dreadful suspence of the event, which we knew was then deciding,[19] every one went following the sound as his fancy led him; and leaving the Town almost empty, some took towards the Park,[20] some cross the River, others down it; all seeking the noise in the depth of silence.

Amongst the rest, it was the fortune of *Eugenius*, *Crites*, *Lisideius* and *Neander*,[21] to be in company together: three of them persons whom their witt and Quality have made known to all the Town: and whom I have chose to hide under these borrowed names, that they may not suffer by so ill a relation as I am going to make of their discourse.

Taking then a Barge which a servant of *Lisideius* had provided for them, they made haste to shoot the Bridge, and left behind them that great fall of waters which hindred them from hearing what they desired: after which, having disingag'd themselves from many Vessels which rode at Anchor in the *Thames*, and almost blockt up the passage towards *Greenwich*, they order'd the Watermen to let fall their Oares more gently; and then every one favouring his own curiosity with a strict silence, it was not long ere they perceiv'd the Air break about them like the noise of distant Thunder, or of Swallows in a Chimney: those little undulations of sound, though almost vanishing before they reach'd them, yet still seeming to retain somewhat of their first horrour which they had betwixt the Fleets: after they had attentively listned till such time as the sound by little and little went from them; *Eugenius* lifting up his head, and taking notice of it, was the first who congratulated to the rest that happy Omen of our Nations Victory: adding, we had but this to desire in confirmation of it, that we might hear no more of that noise which was now leaving the English Coast. When the rest had concur'd in the same opinion, *Crites*, a person of a sharp judgment, and somewhat too delicate a taste in wit, which the world have mistaken in him for ill nature, said, smiling to us, that if the concernment of this battel had not been so exceeding great, he could scarce have wish'd the Victory at the price he knew he must pay for it, in being subject to the reading and hearing of so many ill verses as he was sure would be made upon it; adding, that no Argument could scape some of those eternal Rhimers, who watch a Battel with more diligence then the Ravens and birds of Prey; and the worst of them surest to be first in upon the quarry, while the better able, either out of modesty writ not at all, or set that due value upon their Poems, as to let them be often call'd for and long expected! There are some of those impertinent people you speak of, answer'd *Lisideius*, who to my knowledg, are already so provided, either way, that they can produce not onely a Panegirick upon the Victory, but, if need be, a funeral elegy upon the Duke: and after they have crown'd his valour with many Lawrels, at last deplore the odds under which he fell, concluding that his courage deserv'd a better destiny. All the company smil'd at the conceipt of *Lisideius*; but *Crites*, more eager then before, began to make particular exceptions against some Writers, and said the publick Magistrate ought to send betimes to forbid them; and that it concern'd the peace and quiet of all honest people, that ill Poets should be as well silenc'd as seditious Preachers. In my opinion, replyed *Eugenius*, you pursue your point too far; for as to my own particular, I am so great a lover of Poesie, that I could wish them all rewarded who attempt but to do well; at least I would not have them worse us'd then *Sylla* the Dictator did one of their brethren heretofore: *Quem in concione vidimus* (says *Tully* speaking of him) *cum ei libellum malus poeta de populo subjecisset, quod epigramma in eum fecisset tantummodo alternis versibus longiusculis, statim ex iis rebus quas tunc vendebat jubere ei præmium tribui, sub ea conditione ne quid postea scriberet.*[22] I could wish with all my heart, replied *Crites*, that many whom we know were as bountifully thank'd upon the same condition, that they would never trouble us again. For

amongst others, I have a mortal apprehension of two Poets, whom
this victory with the help of both her wings will never be able to escape;
'tis easie to guess whom you intend,[23] said *Lisideius*; and without naming
them, I ask you if one of them does not perpetually pay us with
clenches upon words and a certain clownish kind of raillery? if now
and then he does not offer at a Catecresis or Clevelandism,[24] wresting
and torturing a word into another meaning: In fine, if he be not one
of those whom the French would call *un mauvais buffon*; one that is so
much a well-willer to the Satire, that he spares[25] no man; and though
he cannot strike a blow to hurt any, yet ought to be punish'd for the
malice of the action; as our Witches are justly hang'd because they
think themselves so; and suffer deservedly for believing they did
mischief, because they meant it. You have described him, said *Crites*,
so exactly, that I am affraid to come after you with my other extremity
of Poetry: He is one of those who having had some advantage of
education and converse, knows better then the other what a Poet
should be, but puts it into practice more unluckily then any man; his
stile and matter are every where alike; he is the most calm, peaceable
Writer you ever read: he never disquiets your passions with the least
concernment, but still leaves you in as even a temper as he found you;
he is a very Leveller in Poetry, he creeps along with ten little words
in every line, and helps out his Numbers with *For to*, and *Unto*, and all
the pretty Expletives he can find, till he draggs them to the end of
another line; while the Sense is left tir'd half way behind it:[26] he doubly
starves all his Verses, first for want of thought, and then of expression;
his Poetry neither has wit in it, nor seems to have it; like him in *Martiall*:

Pauper videri Cinna vult, & est pauper.[27]

He affects plainness, to cover his want of imagination: when he
writes the serious way, the highest flight of his fancy is some miserable
Antithesis, or seeming contradiction; and in the Comick he is still
reaching at some thin conceit, the ghost of a Jest, and that too flies
before him, never to be caught; these Swallows which we see before
us on the *Thames*, are the just resemblance of his wit: you may observe
how near the water they stoop, how many proffers they make to dip,
and yet how seldome they touch it: and when they do, 'tis but the

surface: they skim over it but to catch a gnat, and then mount into the ayr and leave it. Well Gentlemen, said *Eugenius*, you may speak your pleasure of these Authors; but though I and some few more about the Town may give you a peaceable hearing, yet, assure your selves, there are multitudes who would think you malicious and them injur'd: especially him whom you first described; he is the very *Withers* of the City:[28] they have bought more Editions of his Works then would serve to lay under all their Pies at the Lord Mayor's *Christmass*. When his famous Poem first came out in the year 1660,[29] I have seen them reading it in the midst of Change-time; nay so vehement they were at it, that they lost their bargain by the Candles ends: but what will you say, if he has been received amongst the great Ones? I can assure you he is, this day, the envy of a great person, who is Lord in the Art of Quibbling; and who does not take it well, that any man should intrude so far into his Province. All I would wish, replied *Crites*, is, that they who love his Writings, may still admire him, and his fellow Poet: *qui Bavium non odit, &c.*[30] is curse sufficient. And farther, added *Lisideius*, I believe there is no man who writes well, but would think himself very hardly dealt with, if their Admirers should praise any thing of his: *Nam quos contemnimus eorum quoque laudes contemnimus.*[31] There are so few who write well in this Age, said *Crites*, that me-thinks any praises should be wellcome; they neither rise to the dignity of the last Age, nor to any of the Ancients; and we may cry out of the Writers of this time, with more reason than *Petronius* of his, *Pace vestra liceat dixisse, primi omnium eloquentiam perdidistis:*[32] you have debauched the true old Poetry so far, that Nature, which is the soul of it, is not in any of your Writings.

If your quarrel (said *Eugenius*) to those who now write, be grounded onely upon your reverence to Antiquity, there is no man more ready to adore those great Greeks and Romans than I am: but on the other side, I cannot think so contemptibly of the Age I live in, or so dishonourably of my own Countrey, as not to judge we equal the Ancients in most kinds of Poesie, and in some surpass them; neither know I any reason why I may not be as zealous for the Reputation of our Age, as we find the Ancients themselves in reference to those who lived before them. For you hear your *Horace* saying,

Indignor quidquam reprehendi, non quia crassé
Compositum, illepidève putetur, sed quia nuper.

And after,

Si meliora dies, ut vina, poemata reddit,
Scire velim pretium chartis quotus arroget annus?[33]

But I see I am ingaging in a wide dispute, where the arguments are not like to reach close on either side;[34] for Poesie is of so large extent, and so many both of the Ancients and Moderns have done well in all kinds of it, that, in citing one against the other, we shall take up more time this Evening, than each mans occasions will allow him: therefore I would ask *Crites* to what part of Poesie he would confine his Arguments, and whether he would defend the general cause of the Ancients against the Moderns, or oppose any Age of the Moderns against this of ours?

Crites a little while considering upon this Demand, told *Eugenius* he approv'd his Propositions, and, if he pleased, he would limit their Dispute to *Dramatique Poesie*; in which he thought it not difficult to prove, either that the Antients were superiour to the Moderns, or the last Age to this of ours.

Eugenius was somewhat surpriz'd, when he heard *Crites* make choice of that Subject; For ought I see, said he, I have undertaken a harder Province than I imagin'd; for though I never judg'd the Plays of the Greek or Roman Poets comparable to ours; yet on the other side those we now see acted, come short of many which were written in the last Age: but my comfort is if we are orecome, it will be onely by our own Countreymen: and if we yield to them in this one part of Poesie, we more surpass them in all the other; for in the Epique or Lyrique way it will be hard for them to show us one such amongst them, as we have many now living, or who lately were so. They can produce nothing so courtly writ, or which expresses so much the Conversation of a Gentleman, as Sir *John Suckling*; nothing so even, sweet, and flowing as Mr. *Waller*; nothing so Majestique, so correct as Sir *John Denham*; nothing so elevated, so copious, and full of spirit, as Mr. *Cowley*; as for the Italian, French and Spanish Plays, I can make it evident that those who now write, surpass them; and that the *Drama* is wholly ours.

All of them were thus far of *Eugenius* his opinion, that the sweetness of English Verse was never understood or practis'd by our Fathers; even *Crites* himself did not much oppose it: and every one was willing to acknowledge how much our Poesie is improv'd, by the happiness of some Writers yet living; who first taught us to mould our thoughts into easie and significant words; to retrench the superfluities of expression, and to make our Rime so properly a part of the Verse, that it should never mis-lead the sence, but it self be led and govern'd by it.

Eugenius was going to continue this Discourse, when *Lisideius* told him it was necessary, before they proceeded further, to take a standing measure of their Controversie; for how was it possible to be decided who writ the best Plays, before we know what a Play should be? but, this once agreed on by both Parties, each might have recourse to it, either to prove his own advantages, or discover the failings of his Adversary.

He had no sooner said this, but all desir'd the favour of him to give the definition of a Play; and they were the more importunate, because neither *Aristotle*, nor *Horace*, nor any other, who writ of that Subject, had ever done it.

Lisideius, after some modest denials, at last confess'd he had a rude Notion of it; indeed rather a Description then a Definition: but which serv'd to guide him in his private thoughts, when he was to make a judgment of what others writ: that he conceiv'd a Play ought to be, *A just and lively Image of Humane Nature, representing its Passions and Humours, and the Changes of Fortune to which it is subject; for the Delight and Instruction of Mankind.*

This Definition, though *Crites* rais'd a Logical Objection against it; that it was onely *a genere & fine*, and so not altogether perfect;[35] was yet well received by the rest: and after they had given order to the Water-men to turn their Barge, and row softly, that they might take the cool of the Evening in their return; *Crites*, being desired by the Company to begin, spoke on behalf of the Ancients, in this manner:

If Confidence presage a Victory, *Eugenius*, in his own opinion, has already triumphed over the Ancients; nothing seems more easie to him, than to overcome those whom it is our greatest praise to have

24

imitated well: for we do not onely build upon their foundation; but by their modells. *Dramatique Poesie* had time enough, reckoning from *Thespis* (who first invented it) to *Aristophanes*, to be born, to grow up, and to flourish in Maturity. It has been observed of Arts and Sciences, that in one and the same Century they have arriv'd to a great perfection; and no wonder, since every Age has a kind of Universal Genius, which inclines those that live in it to some particular Studies: the Work then being push'd on by many hands, must of necessity go forward.

Is it not evident, in these last hundred years (when the Study of Philosophy has been the business of all the *Virtuosi* in *Christendome*) that almost a new Nature has been revealed to us? that more errours of the School have been detected, more useful Experiments in Philosophy have been made, more Noble Secrets in Opticks, Medicine, Anatomy, Astronomy, discover'd, than in all those credulous and doting Ages from *Aristotle* to us? so true it is that nothing spreads more fast than Science, when rightly and generally cultivated.

Add to this the more than common emulation that was in those times of writing well; which though it be found in all Ages and all Persons that pretend to the same Reputation; yet Poesie being then in more esteem than now it is, had greater Honours decreed to the Professors of it; and consequently the Rivalship was more high between them; they had Judges ordain'd to decide their Merit, and Prizes to reward it: and Historians have been diligent to record of *Eschylus, Euripides, Sophocles, Lycophron,* and the rest of them, both who they were that vanquish'd in these Wars of the Theater, and how often they were crown'd: while the Asian Kings, and Grecian Common-wealths scarce afforded them a Nobler Subject then the unmanly Luxuries of a Debauch'd Court, or giddy Intrigues of a Factious City. *Alit æmulatio ingenia* (says *Paterculus*) *& nunc invidia, nunc admiratio incitationem accendit*:[36] Emulation is the Spur of Wit, and sometimes Envy, sometimes Admiration quickens our Endeavours.

But now since the Rewards of Honour are taken away, that Vertuous Emulation is turn'd into direct Malice; yet so slothful, that it contents it self to condemn and cry down others, without attempting to do better: 'Tis a Reputation too unprofitable, to take the necessary pains for it; yet wishing they had it, is incitement enough to hinder others from it. And this, in short, *Eugenius*, is the reason, why you have now so few good Poets; and so many severe Judges: Certainly, to imitate the Antients well, much labour and long study is required: which pains, I have already shown, our Poets would want incouragement to take, if yet they had ability to go through with it. Those Ancients have been faithful Imitators and wise Observers of that Nature which is so torn and ill represented in our Plays, they have handed down to us a perfect resemblance of her; which we, like ill Copyers, neglecting to look on, have rendred monstrous and disfigur'd.[37] But, that you may know how much you are indebted to those your Masters, and be ashamed to have so ill requited them: I must remember you that all the Rules by which we practise the *Drama* at this day, either such as relate to the justness and symmetry of the Plot; or the Episodical Ornaments, such as Descriptions, Narrations, and other Beauties, which are not essential to the Play; were delivered to us from the Observations that *Aristotle* made, of those Poets, which either liv'd before him, or were his Contemporaries: we have added nothing of our own, except we have the confidence to say our wit is better; which none boast of in our Age, but such as understand not theirs. Of that Book which *Aristotle* has left us περί τῆς Ποιητικῆς, *Horace* his Art of Poetry is an excellent Comment, and, I believe, restores to us that Second Book of his concerning Comedy, which is wanting in him.[38]

Out of these two has been extracted the Famous Rules which the French call, *Des Trois Unitez*, or, The Three Unities, which ought to be observ'd in every Regular Play; namely, of Time, Place, and Action.[39]

The unity of Time they comprehend in 24 hours, the compass of a Natural Day; or as near it as can be contriv'd: and the reason of it is obvious to every one, that the time of the feigned action, or fable of the Play, should be proportion'd as near as can be to the duration of that time in which it is represented; since therefore all Playes are acted on the Theater in a space of time much within the compass of 24 hours, that Play is to be thought the nearest imitation of Nature, whose Plot or Action is confin'd within that time; and, by the same Rule which concludes this general proportion of time, it follows, that all the parts of it are to[40] be equally subdivided; as namely, that one act take not up the suppos'd time of half a day; which is out of proportion to the rest: since the other four are then to be straightned within the compass of the remaining half; for it is unnatural that one Act, which being spoke or written, is not longer than the rest, should be suppos'd longer by the Audience; 'tis therefore the Poets duty, to take care that no Act should be imagin'd to exceed the time in which it is represented on the Stage; and that the intervalls and inequalities of time be suppos'd to fall out between the Acts.

This Rule of Time how well it has been observ'd by the Antients, most of their Playes will witness; you see them in their Tragedies (wherein to follow this Rule, is certainly most difficult) from the very beginning of their Playes, falling close into that part of the Story which they intend for the action or principal object of it; leaving the former part to be delivered by Narration: so that they set the Audience, as it were, at the Post where the Race is to be concluded: and, saving them the tedious expectation of seeing the Poet set out and ride the beginning of the Course, you behold him not, till he is in sight of the Goal, and just upon you.

For the Second Unity, which is that of place, the Antients meant by it, That the Scene ought to be continu'd through the Play, in the same place where it was laid in the beginning: for the Stage, on which it is represented, being but one and the same place, it is unnatural to conceive it many; and those far distant from one another. I will not deny but by the variation of painted Scenes, the fancy (which in these cases will contribute to its own deceit) may sometimes imagine it several places, with some appearance of probability; yet it still carries the greater likelihood of truth, if those places be suppos'd so near each other, as in the same Town or City; which may all be comprehended under the larger Denomination of one place: for a greater distance will bear no proportion to the shortness of time, which is allotted in the acting, to pass from one of them to another; for the Observation of this, next to the Antients, the French are to be most commended. They tie themselves so strictly to the unity of place, that you never see in any of their Plays, a Scene chang'd in the middle of an Act: if the Act begins in a Garden, a Street, or Chamber, 'tis ended in the same place; and that you may know it to be the same, the Stage is so supplied with persons that it is never empty all the time: he that enters the second has business with him who was on before; and before the second quits the Stage, a third appears who has business with him.

This *Corneil* calls *La Liaison des Scenes*, the continuity or joyning of the Scenes; and 'tis a good mark of a well contriv'd Play when all the Persons are known to each other, and every one of them has some affairs with all the rest.

As for the third Unity which is that of Action, the Ancients meant no other by it then what the Logicians do by their *Finis*, the end or scope of any action: that which is the first in Intention, and last in Execution: now the Poet is to aim at one great and compleat action, to the carrying on of which all things in his Play, even the very obstacles, are to be subservient; and the reason of this is as evident as any of the former.

For two Actions equally labour'd and driven on by the Writer, would destroy the unity of the Poem; it would be no longer one Play, but two: not but that there may be many actions in a Play, as *Ben. Johnson* has observ'd in his *Discoveries*;[41] but they must be all subservient to the great one, which our language happily expresses in the name of under-plots: such as in *Terences Eunuch* is the difference and reconcilement of *Thais* and *Phædria*, which is not the chief business of the Play, but promotes the marriage of *Chærea* and *Chremes's* Sister, principally intended by the Poet. There ought to be but one action, sayes *Corneile*,[42] that is one compleat action which leaves the mind of the Audience in a full repose: But this cannot be brought to pass but by many other imperfect ones which conduce to it, and hold the Audience in a delightful suspence of what will be.

If by these Rules (to omit many other drawn from the Precepts and Practice of the Ancients) we should judge our modern Playes; 'tis probable, that few of them would endure the tryal: that which should be the business of a day, takes up in some of them an age; instead of one action they are the Epitomes of a mans life; and for one spot of ground (which the Stage should represent) we are sometimes in more Countries then the Map can show us.

But if we allow the Ancients to have contriv'd well, we must acknowledge them to have writ better; questionless we are depriv'd of a great stock of wit in the loss of *Menander* among the Greek Poets, and of *Cæcilius*, *Affranius* and *Varius*, among the Romans: we may guess of *Menanders* Excellency by the Plays of *Terence*, who translated some of his, and yet wanted so much of him that he was call'd by *C. Cæsar* the Half-*Menander*, and of *Varius*, by the Testimonies of *Horace*, *Martial*, and *Velleius Paterculus*:[43] 'Tis probable that these, could they be recover'd, would decide the controversie; but so long as *Aristophanes* in the old Comedy, and *Plautus* in the new are extant; while the Tragedies of *Eurypides*, *Sophocles*, and *Seneca* are to be had, I can never see one of those Plays which are now written, but it encreases my admiration of the Ancients; and yet I must acknowledge further, that to admire them as we ought, we should understand them better then we do. Doubtless many things appear flat to us, whose wit depended upon some custome or story which never came to our knowledge, or perhaps upon some Criticism in their language, which being so long dead, and onely remaining in their Books, 'tis not possible they should make us know it perfectly. To read *Macrobius*, explaining the propriety and elegancy of many words in *Virgil*,[44] which I had before pass'd over without consideration, as common things, is enough to assure me that I ought to think the same of *Terence*; and that in the purity of his style (which *Tully* so much valued that he ever carried his works about him) there is yet left in him great room for admiration, if I knew but where to place it. In the mean time I must desire you to take notice, that the greatest man of the last age (*Ben. Johnson*) was willing to give place to them in all things: He was not onely a professed Imitator of *Horace*, but a learned Plagiary of all the others; you track him every where in their Snow: If *Horace*, *Lucan*, *Petronius Arbiter*, *Seneca*, and *Juvenal*, had their own from him, there are few serious thoughts which are new in him; you will pardon me therefore if I presume he lov'd their fashion when he wore their cloaths. But since I have otherwise a great venera-tion for him, and you, *Eugenius*, prefer him above all other Poets, I will use no farther argument to you then his example: I will produce Father *Ben.* to you, dress'd in all the ornaments and colours of the Ancients, you will need no other guide to our Party if you follow him; and whether you consider the bad Plays of our Age, or regard the good ones of the last, both the best and worst of the Modern Poets will equally instruct you to esteem the Ancients.

Crites had no sooner left speaking, but *Eugenius* who waited with some impatience for it, thus began:

I have observ'd in your Speech that the former part of it is convincing as to what the Moderns have profitted by the rules of the Ancients, but in the latter you are careful to conceal how much they have excell'd them: we own all the helps we have from them, and want neither veneration nor gratitude while we acknowledge that to overcome them we must make use of the advantages we have receiv'd from them; but to these assistances we have joyned our own industry; for (had we sate down with a dull imitation of them) we might then have lost somewhat of the old perfection, but never acquir'd any that was new. We draw not therefore after their lines, but those of Nature; and having the life before us, besides the experience of all they knew, it is no wonder if we hit some airs and features which they have miss'd: I deny not what you urge of Arts and Sciences, that they have flourish'd in some ages more then others; but your instance in Philosophy makes for me: for if Natural Causes be more known now then in the time of *Aristotle*, because more studied, it follows that Poesie and other Arts may with the same pains arrive still neerer to perfection, and, that granted, it will rest for you to prove that they wrought more perfect images of humane life then we; which, seeing in your Discourse you have avoided to make good, it shall now be my task to show you some part of their defects, and some few Excellencies of the Moderns; and I think there is none among us can imagine I do it enviously, or with purpose to detract from them; for what interest of Fame or Profit can the living lose by the reputation of the dead? on the other side, it is a great truth which *Velleius Paterculus* affirms, *Audita visis libentius laudamus; & præsentia invidia, præterita admiratione prosequimur; & his nos obrui, illis instrui credimus:*[45] That praise or censure is certainly the most sincere which unbrib'd posterity shall give us.

Be pleased then in the first place to take notice, that the Greek Poesie, which *Crites* has affirm'd to have arriv'd to perfection in the Reign of the old Comedy, was so far from it, that the distinction of it into Acts was not known to them; or if it were, it is yet so darkly deliver'd to us that we cannot make it out.

All we know of it is from the singing of their Chorus, and that too is so uncertain that in some of their Playes we have reason to conjecture they sung more then five times: *Aristotle* indeed divides the integral parts of a Play into four:[46] First, The *Protasis* or entrance, which gives light onely to the Characters of the persons, and proceeds very little into any part of the action: 2ly, The *Epitasis*, or working up of the Plot where the Play grows warmer: the design or action of it is drawing on, and you see something promising that it will come to pass: Thirdly, the *Catastasis*, or Counterturn,[47] which destroys that expectation, imbroyles the action in new difficulties, and leaves you far distant from that hope in which it found you, as you may have observ'd in a violent stream resisted by a narrow passage; it runs round to an eddy, and carries back the waters with more swiftness then it brought them on: Lastly, the *Catastrophe*, which the Grecians call'd λύσις, the French *le denouement*, and we the discovery or unravelling of the Plot: there you see all things setling again upon their first foundations, and the obstacles which hindred the design or action of the Play once remov'd, it ends with that resemblance of truth and nature, that the audience are satisfied with the conduct of it. Thus this great man deliver'd to us the image of a Play, and I must confess it is so lively that from thence much light has been deriv'd to the forming it more perfectly into Acts and Scenes; but what Poet first limited to five the number of the Acts I know not; onely we see it so firmly establish'd in the time of *Horace*, that he gives it for a rule in Comedy; *Neu brevior quinto, neu sit productior actu*:[48] So that you see the Grecians cannot be said to have consummated this Art; writing rather by Entrances then by Acts, and having rather a general indigested notion of a Play, then knowing how and where to bestow the particular graces of it.

But since the Spaniards at this day allow but three Acts,[49] which they call *Jornadas*, to a Play; and the Italians in many of theirs follow them, when I condemn the Antients, I declare it is not altogether because they have not five Acts to every Play, but because they have not confin'd themselves to one certain number; 'tis building an House without a Modell: and when they succeeded in such undertakings, they ought to have sacrific'd to Fortune, not to the Muses.

Next, for the Plot, which *Aristotle* call'd τό μυθος and often τῶν πραγμάτων σύνθεσις, and from him the Romans *Fabula*, it has already been judiciously observ'd by a late Writer,[50] that in their Tragedies it was onely some Tale deriv'd from *Thebes* or *Troy*, or at least some thing that happen'd in those two Ages; which was worn so thred-bare by the Pens of all the Epique Poets, and even by Tradition it self of the Talkative Greeklings (as *Ben Johnson* calls them) that before it came upon the Stage, it was already known to all the Audience: and the people so soon as ever they heard the Name of *Oedipus*, knew as well as the Poet, that he had kill'd his Father by a mistake, and committed Incest with his Mother, before the Play; that they were now to hear of a great Plague, an Oracle, and the Ghost of *Laius*: so that they sate with a yawning kind of expectation, till he was to come with his eyes pull'd out, and speak a hundred or two of Verses in a Tragick tone, in complaint of his misfortunes. But one *Oedipus*, *Hercules*, or *Medea*, had been tollerable; poor people they scap'd not so good cheap: they had still the *Chapon Bouillé*[51] set before them, till their appetites were cloy'd with the same dish, and the Novelty being gone, the pleasure vanish'd: so that one main end of *Dramatique Poesie* in its Definition, which was to cause Delight, was of consequence destroy'd.

In their Comedies, the Romans generally borrow'd their Plots from the Greek Poets; and theirs was commonly a little Girle stollen or wandred from her Parents, brought back unknown to the same City, there got with child by some lewd young fellow; who, by the help of his servant, cheats his father, and when her time comes, to cry *Juno Lucina fer opem*;[52] one or other sees a little Box or Cabinet which was carried away with her, and so discovers her to her friends, if some God do not prevent it, by coming down in a Machine, and take the thanks of it to himself.

By the Plot you may guess much of the Characters of the Persons. An Old Father that would willingly before he dies, see his Son well married; his Debauch'd Son, kind in his Nature to his Wench, but miserably in want of Money; a Servant or Slave, who has so much wit to strike in with him, and help to dupe his Father, a Braggadochio Captain, a Parasite, and a Lady of Pleasure.

As for the poor honest Maid, whom all the Story is built upon, and who ought to be one of the principal Actors in the Play, she is commonly a Mute in it: She has the breeding of the Old *Elizabeth* way, for Maids to be seen and not to be heard; and it is enough you know she is willing to be married, when the Fifth Act requires it.

These are Plots built after the Italian Mode of Houses, you see thorow them all at once; the Characters are indeed the Imitations of Nature, but so narrow as if they had imitated onely an Eye or an Hand, and did not dare to venture on the lines of a Face, or the Proportion of a Body.

But in how straight a compass soever they have bounded their Plots and Characters, we will pass it by, if they have regularly pursued them, and perfectly observ'd those three Unities of Time, Place, and Action: the knowledge of which you say is deriv'd to us from them. But in the first place give me leave to tell you, that the Unity of Place, how ever it might be practised by them, was never any of their Rules: We neither find it in *Aristotle*, *Horace*, or any who have written of it, till in our age the French Poets first made it a Precept of the Stage. The unity of time, even *Terence* himself (who was the best and most regular of them) has neglected: His *Heautontimoroumenos* or Self-Punisher takes up visibly two days; therefore, sayes *Scaliger*, the two first Acts concluding the first day, were acted over-night; the three last on the ensuing day: and *Eurypides*, in tying himself to one day, has committed an absurdity never to be forgiven him: for in one of his Tragedies he has made *Theseus* go from *Athens* to *Thebes*, which was about 40 English miles, under the walls of it to give battel, and appear victorious in the next Act; and yet from the time of his departure to the return of the *Nuntius*, who gives the relation of his Victory, *Æthra* and the Chorus have but 36 Verses; that is not for every Mile a Verse.

The like errour is as evident in *Terence* his Eunuch, when *Laches*, the old man, enters in a mistake the house of *Thais*, where betwixt his Exit and the entrance of *Pythias*, who comes to give an ample relation of the Garboyles he has rais'd within, *Parmeno* who was left upon the Stage, has not above five lines to speak: *C'est bien employer un temps si court*, sayes the French Poet,[53] who furnish'd me with one of the observations; And almost all their Tragedies will afford us examples of the like nature.

'Tis true, they have kept the continuity, or as you call'd it, *Liaison des Scenes* somewhat better: two do not perpetually come in together, talk, and go out together; and other two succeed them, and do the same throughout the Act, which the English call by the name of single Scenes; but the reason is, because they have seldom above two or three Scenes, properly so call'd, in every act; for it is to be accounted a new Scene, not every time the Stage is empty, but every person who enters, though to others, makes it so; because he introduces a new business: Now the Plots of their Plays being narrow, and the persons few, one of their Acts was written in a less compass then one of our well wrought Scenes, and yet they are often deficient even in this: To go no further then *Terence*, you find in the Eunuch *Antipho* entring single in the midst of the third Act, after *Chremes* and *Pythias* were gone off: In the same Play you have likewise *Dorias* beginning the fourth Act alone; and after she has made a relation of what was done at the Souldiers entertainment (which by the way was very inartificial to do, because she was presum'd to speak directly to the Audience, and to acquaint them with what was necessary to be known, but yet should have been so contriv'd by the Poet as to have been told by persons of the *Drama* to one another, and so by them to have come to the knowledge of the people) she quits the Stage, and *Phædria* enters next, alone likewise: He also gives you an account of himself, and of his returning from the Country in *Monologue*, to which unnatural way of narration *Terence* is subject in all his playes: In his *Adelphi* or Brothers, *Syrus* and *Demea* enter; after the Scene was broken by the departure of *Sostrata*, *Geta* and *Canthara*; and indeed you can scarce look into any of his Comedies, where you will not presently discover the same interruption.

But as they have fail'd both in laying of their Plots, and managing of them, swerving from the Rules of their own Art, by mis-representing Nature to us, in which they have ill satisfied one intention of a Play, which was delight, so in the instructive part they have err'd worse: instead of punishing Vice and rewarding Virtue, they have often shown a Prosperous Wickedness, and an Unhappy Piety: They have set before us a bloudy image of revenge in *Medea*, and given her Dragons to convey her safe from punishment. A *Priam* and *Astyanax* murder'd, and *Cassandra* ravish'd, and the lust and murder ending in the victory of him that acted them: In short, there is no indecorum in any of our modern Playes, which if I would excuse, I could not shaddow with some Authority from the Ancients.

And one farther note of them let me leave you: Tragedies and Comedies were not writ then as they are now, promiscuously, by the same person, but he who found his genius bending to the one, never attempted the other way. This is so plain, that I need not instance to you, that *Aristophanes*, *Plautus*, *Terence*, never any of them writ a Tragedy; *Æschylus*, *Eurypides*, *Sophocles* and *Seneca*, never medled with Comedy; the Sock and Buskin[54] were not worn by the same Poet: having then so much care to excel in one kind, very little is to be pardon'd them if they miscarried in it; and this would lead me to the consideration of their wit, had not *Crites* given me sufficient warning not to be too bold in my judgment of it; because the languages being dead, and many of the Customes and little accidents on which it depended, lost to us, we are not competent judges of it. But though I grant that here and there we may miss the application of a Proverb or a Custom, yet a thing well said will be wit in all Languages; and though it may lose something in the Translation, yet, to him who reads it in the Original, 'tis still the same; He has an Idea of its excellency, though it cannot pass from his mind into any other expression or words then those in which he finds it. When *Phædria* – in the Eunuch had a command from his Mistress to be absent two dayes; and encouraging himself to go through with it, said; *Tandem ego non illa caream, si opus sit, vel totum triduum?* *Parmeno* to mock the softness of his Master, lifting up his hands and eyes, cryes out as it were in admiration; *Hui! universum triduum!*[55] the elegancy of which *universum*, though it cannot be rendred in our language, yet leaves an impression of the wit upon our souls: but this happens seldom in him, in *Plautus* oftner; who is infinitely too bold in his Metaphors and coyning words; out of which many times his wit is nothing, which questionless was one reason why *Horace* falls upon him so severely in those Verses:

Sed Proavi nostri Plautinos & numeros, &
Laudavere sales, nimium patienter utrumque
Ne dicam stolidè.

For *Horace* himself was cautious to obtrude a new word upon his Readers, and makes custom and common use the best measure of receiving it into our writings.

Multa renascentur quæ nunc cecidere, cadentq;
Quæ nunc sunt in honore vocabula, si volet usus,
Quem penes, arbitrium est, & jus, & norma loquendi.[56]

The not observing this Rule is that which the world has blam'd in our Satyrist *Cleveland*; to express a thing hard and unnaturally, is his new way of Elocution: 'Tis true, no Poet but may sometimes use a *Catachresis*; *Virgil* does it;

Mistaque ridenti Colocasia fundet Acantho.

In his Eclogue of *Pollio*, and in his 7th *Æneid*.

—Mirantur & undæ,
Miratur nemus, insuetum fulgentia longe,
Scuta virum fluvio, pictasq; innare carinas.[57]

And *Ovid* once so modestly, that he askes leave to do it;

Si verbo audacia detur
Haud metuam summi dixisse Palatia cæli.

Calling the Court of *Jupiter* by the name of *Augustus* his Pallace, though in another place he is more bold, where he sayes, *Et longas visent Capitolia pompas*.[58] But to do this alwayes, and never be able to write a line without it, though it may be admir'd by some few Pedants, will not pass upon those who know that wit is best convey'd to us in the most easie language; and is most to be admir'd when a great thought comes drest in words so commonly receiv'd that it is understood by the meanest apprehensions, as the best meat is the most easily digested:[59] but we cannot read a verse of *Cleveland's* without making a face at it, as if every word were a Pill to swallow: he gives us many times a hard Nut to break our Teeth, without a Kernel for our pains. So that there is this difference betwixt his *Satyres* and Doctor *Donns*, That the one gives us deep thoughts in common language, though rough cadence; the other gives us common thoughts in abstruse words: 'tis true, in some places his wit is independent of his words, as in that of the Rebel *Scot*:

> Had Cain been Scot God would have chang'd his doom;
> Not forc'd him wander, but confin'd him home.[60]

Si sic, omnia dixisset![61] This is wit in all languages: 'tis like Mercury, never to be lost or kill'd; and so that other;

> For Beauty like White-powder makes no noise,
> And yet the silent Hypocrite destroyes.[62]

You see the last line is highly Metaphorical, but it is so soft and gentle, that it does not shock us as we read it.

But, to return from whence I have digress'd, to the consideration of the Ancients Writing and their Wit, (of which by this time you will grant us in some measure to be fit judges,) Though I see many excellent thoughts in *Seneca*, yet he, of them who had a Genius most proper for the Stage, was *Ovid*; he had a way of writing so fit to stir up a pleasing admiration and concernment, which are the objects of a Tragedy, and to show the various movements of a Soul combating betwixt two different Passions, that, had he liv'd in our age, or in his own could have writ with our advantages, no man but must have yielded to him; and therefore I am confident the *Medea* is none of his: for, though I esteem it for the gravity and sententiousness of it, which he himself concludes to be suitable to a Tragedy, *Omne genus scripti gravitate Tragædia vincit*,[63] yet it moves not my soul enough to judge that he, who in the Epique way wrote things so near the *Drama*, as the Story of *Myrrha*, of *Caunus* and *Biblis*, and the rest, should stir up no more concernment where he most endeavour'd it. The Master piece of *Seneca* I hold to be that Scene in the *Troades*, where *Ulysses* is seeking for *Astyanax* to kill him;[64] There you see the tenderness of a Mother, so represented in Andromache, that it raises compassion to a high degree in the Reader, and bears the nearest resemblance of any thing in their

Tragedies to the excellent Scenes of Passion in *Shakespeare*, or in *Fletcher*: for Love-Scenes you will find few among them, their Tragique Poets dealt not with that soft passion, but with Lust, Cruelty, Revenge, Ambition, and those bloody actions they produc'd; which were more capable of raising horrour then compassion in an audience: leaving Love untoucht, whose gentleness would have temper'd them, which is the most frequent of all the passions, and which being the private concernment of every person, is sooth'd by viewing its own image in a publick entertainment.

Among their Comedies, we find a Scene or two of tenderness, and that where you would least expect it, in *Plautus*; but to speak generally, their Lovers say little, when they see each other, but *anima mea, vita mea*; ζωη και Ψυχη,[65] as the women in *Juvenal*'s time us'd to cry out in the fury of their kindness: then indeed to speak sense were an offence. Any sudden gust of passion (as an extasie of love in an unexpected meeting) cannot better be express'd than in a word and a sigh, breaking one another. Nature is dumb on such occasions, and to make her speak, would be to represent her unlike her self. But there are a thousand other concernments of Lovers, as jealousies, complaints, contrivances and the like, where not to open their minds at large to each other, were to be wanting to their own love, and to the expectation of the Audience; who watch the movements of their minds, as much as the changes of their fortunes. For the imaging of the first is properly the work of a Poet, the latter he borrows of the Historian.

Eugenius was proceeding in that part of his Discourse, when *Crites* interrupted him. I see, said he, *Eugenius* and I are never like to have this Question decided betwixt us; for he maintains the Moderns have acquir'd a new perfection in writing, I can onely grant they have alter'd the mode of it. *Homer* describ'd his Heroes men of great appetites, lovers of beef broild upon the coals, and good fellows; contrary to the practice of the French Romances, whose Heroes neither eat, nor drink, nor sleep, for love. *Virgil* makes *Æneas* a bold Avower of his own virtues,

Sum pius Æneas fama super æthera notus;[66]

which in the civility of our Poets is the Character of a Fanfaron or Hector: for with us the Knight takes occasion to walk out, or sleep, to avoid the vanity of telling his own Story, which the trusty Squire is ever to perform for him. So in their Love Scenes, of which *Eugenius* spoke last, the Ancients were more hearty, we more talkative: they writ love as it was then the mode to make it, and I will grant thus much to *Eugenius*, that perhaps one of their Poets, had he liv'd in our Age,

Si foret hoc nostrum fato delapsus in ævum (as *Horace* says of *Lucilius*)[67]

he had alter'd many things; not that they were not as natural before, but that he might accommodate himself to the Age he liv'd in: yet in the mean time we are not to conclude any thing rashly against those great men; but preserve to them the dignity of Masters, and give that honour to their memories, (*Quos libitina sacravit*;)[68] part of which we expect may be paid to us in future times.

This moderation of *Crites*, as it was pleasing to all the company, so it put an end to that dispute; which, *Eugenius*, who seem'd to have the better of the Argument, would urge no farther: but *Lisideius* after he had acknowledged himself of *Eugenius* his opinion concerning the Ancients; yet told him he had forborn, till his Discourse were ended, to ask him why he prefer'd the English Plays above those of other Nations? and whether we ought not to submit our Stage to the exactness of our next Neighbours?

Though, said *Eugenius*, I am at all times ready to defend the honour of my Countrey against the French, and to maintain, we are as well able to vanquish them with our Pens as our Ancestors have been with their swords; yet, if you please, added he, looking upon *Neander*, I will commit this cause to my friend's management; his opinion of our Plays is the same with mine: and besides, there is no reason, that *Crites* and I, who have now left the Stage, should re-enter so suddenly upon it; which is against the Laws of Comedie.

If the Question had been stated, replied *Lysideius*, who had writ best, the French or English forty years ago, I should have been of your opinion, and adjudg'd the honour to our own Nation; but since that time, said he, (turning towards *Neander*) we have been so long together bad Englishmen, that we had not leisure to be good Poets; *Beaumont*, *Fletcher*, and *Johnson* (who were onely capable of bringing us to that degree of perfection which we have) were just then leaving the world; as if in an Age of so much horror, wit and those milder studies of humanity, had no farther business among us. But the Muses, who ever follow Peace, went to plant in another Countrey; it was then that the great Cardinal of *Richlieu* began to take them into his protection; and that, by his encouragement, *Corneil* and some other Frenchmen reform'd their Theatre,[69] (which before was as much below ours as it now surpasses it and the rest of *Europe*;) but because *Crites*, in his Discourse for the Ancients, has prevented me, by touching upon many Rules of the Stage, which the Moderns have borrow'd from them; I shall onely, in short, demand of you, whether you are not convinc'd that of all Nations the French have best observ'd them? In the unity of time you find them so scrupulous, that it yet remains a dispute among their Poets, whether the artificial day of twelve hours more or less, be not meant by *Aristotle*, rather than the natural one of twenty four; and consequently whether all Plays ought not to be reduc'd into that compass? This I can testifie, that in all their *Drama*'s writ within these last 20 years and upwards, I have not observ'd any that have extended the time to thirty hours: in the unity of place they are full as scrupulous, for many of their Criticks limit it to that very spot of ground where the Play is suppos'd to begin; none of them exceed the compass of the same Town or City.

The unity of Action in all their Plays is yet more conspicuous, for they do not burden them with under-plots, as the English do; which is the reason why many Scenes of our Tragi-comedies carry on a design that is nothing of kinne to the main Plot; and that we see two distinct webbs in a Play; like those in ill wrought stuffs; and two actions, that is, two Plays carried on together, to the confounding of the Audience;[70] who, before they are warm in their concernments for one part, are diverted to another; and by that means espouse the interest of neither. From hence likewise it arises that the one half of our Actors are not known to the other. They keep their distances as if they were *Mountagues* and *Capulets*, and seldom begin an acquaintance till the last Scene of the Fifth Act, when they are all to meet upon the Stage.

There is no Theatre in the world has any thing so absurd as the English Tragi-comedie, 'tis a *Drama* of our own invention, and the fashion of it is enough to proclaim it so; here a course of mirth, there another of sadness and passion; a third of honour, and fourth a Duel: Thus in two hours and a half we run through all the fits of *Bedlam*. The French affords you as much variety on the same day, but they do it not so unseasonably, or *mal a propos* as we: Our Poets present you the Play and the farce together; and our Stages still retain somewhat of the Original civility of the Red-Bull;

Atque ursum & pugiles media inter carmina poscunt.[71]

The end of Tragedies or serious Playes, sayes *Aristotle*, is to beget admiration, compassion, or concernment; but are not mirth and compassion things incompatible? and is it not evident that the Poet must of necessity destroy the former by intermingling of the latter? that is, he must ruine the sole end and object of his Tragedy to introduce somewhat that is forced in, and is not of the body of it: Would you not think that Physician mad, who having prescribed a Purge, should immediately order you to take restringents upon it?

But to leave our Playes, and return to theirs, I have noted one great advantage they have had in the Plotting of their Tragedies; that is, they are always grounded upon some known History: according to that of *Horace, Ex noto fictum carmen sequar*,[72] and in that they have so imitated the Ancients that they have surpass'd them. For the Ancients, as was observ'd before, took for the foundation of their Playes some Poetical Fiction, such as under that consideration could move but little concernment in the Audience, because they already knew the event of it. But the French goes farther;

Atque ita mentitur; sic veris falsa remiscet,
Primo ne medium, medio ne discrepet imum:[73]

He so interweaves Truth with probable Fiction, that he puts a pleasing Fallacy upon us; mends the intrigues of Fate, and dispenses with the severity of History, to reward that vertue which has been rendred to us there unfortunate. Sometimes the story has left the success so doubtful, that the Writer is free, by the priviledge of a Poet, to take that which of two or more relations will best sute with his design: As for example, the death of *Cyrus*, whom *Justin* and some others report to have perish'd in the *Scythian* war, but *Xenophon* affirms to have died in his bed of extream old age.[74] Nay more, when the event is past dispute, even then we are willing to be deceiv'd, and the Poet, if he contrives it with appearance of truth; has all the audience of his Party; at least during the time his Play is acting: so naturally we are kind to vertue, when our own interest is not in question, that we take it up as the general concernment of Mankind. On the other side, if you consider the Historical Playes of *Shakespeare*, they are rather so many Chronicles of Kings, or the business many times of thirty or forty years, crampt into a representation of two hours and a half, which is not to imitate or paint Nature, but rather to draw her in miniature, to take her in little; to look upon her through the wrong end of a Perspective, and receive her Images not onely much less, but infinitely more imperfect then the life: this, instead of making a Play delightful, renders it ridiculous.

Quodcunque ostendis mihi sic, incredulus odi.[75]

For the Spirit of man cannot be satisfied but with truth, or at least verisimility; and a Poem is to contain, if not τὰ ετυμα, yet ἐτύμοισιν ὁμοῖα, as one of the Greek Poets have express'd it.[76]

Another thing in which the French differ from us and from the Spaniards, is, that they do not embarass, or cumber themselves with too much Plot: they onely represent so much of a Story as will constitute one whole and great action sufficient for a Play; we, who undertake more, do but multiply adventures; which, not being produc'd from one another, as effects from causes, but barely following, constitute many actions in the Drama, and consequently make it many Playes.

But by pursuing close one argument, which is not cloy'd with many turns, the French have gain'd more liberty for verse, in which they write: they have leisure to dwell upon a subject which deserves it; and to represent the passions (which we have acknowledg'd to be the Poets work) without being hurried from one thing to another, as we are in the Playes of *Calderon*, which we have seen lately upon our Theaters, under the name of Spanish Plotts. I have taken notice but of one

Tragedy of ours, whose Plot has that uniformity and unity of design in it which I have commended in the French; and that is *Rollo*, or rather, under the name of *Rollo*, The Story of *Bassianus* and *Geta* in *Herodian*,[77] there indeed the Plot is neither large nor intricate, but just enough to fill the minds of the Audience, not to cloy them. Besides, you see it founded upon the truth of History, onely the time of the action is not reduceable to the strictness of the Rules; and you see in some places a little farce mingled, which is below the dignity of the other parts; and in this all our Poets are extreamly peccant, even *Ben Johnson* himself in *Sejanus* and *Catiline* has given us this Oleo of a Play; this unnatural mixture of Comedy and Tragedy, which to me sounds just as ridiculously as the History of *David* with the merry humours of *Golias*.[78] In *Sejanus* you may take notice of the Scene betwixt *Livia* and the Physician, which is a pleasant Satyre upon the artificial helps of beauty: In *Catiline* you may see the Parliament of Women; the little envies of them to one another; and all that passes betwixt *Curio* and *Fulvia*: Scenes admirable in their kind, but of an ill mingle with the rest.[79]

But I return again to the French Writers; who, as I have said, do not burden themselves too much with Plot, which has been reproach'd to them by an *ingenious person*[80] of our Nation as a fault, for he says they commonly make but one person considerable in a Play; they dwell upon him, and his concernments, while the rest of the persons are onely subservient to set him off. If he intends this by it, that there is one person in the Play who is of greater dignity then the rest, he must tax, not onely theirs, but those of the Ancients, and which he would be loth to do, the best of ours; for 'tis impossible but that one person must be more conspicuous in it then any other, and consequently the greatest share in the action must devolve on him. We see it so in the management of all affairs; even in the most equal Aristocracy, the ballance cannot be so justly poys'd, but some one will be superiour to the rest; either in parts, fortune, interest, or the consideration of some glorious exploit; which will reduce the greatest part of business into his hands.

But, if he would have us to imagine that in exalting of one character the rest of them are neglected, and that all of them have not some share or other in the action of the Play, I desire him to produce any of *Corneilles* Tragedies, wherein every person (like so many servants in a well govern'd Family) has not some employment, and who is not necessary to the carrying on of the Plot, or at least to your understanding it.

There are indeed some protatick persons[81] in the Ancients, whom they make use of in their Playes, either to hear, or give the Relation: but the French avoid this with great address, making their narrations onely to, or by such who are some way interessed in the main design. And now I am speaking of Relations, I cannot take a fitter opportunity to add this in favour of the French, that they often use them with better judgment and more *a propos* then the English do. Not that I commend narrations in general, but there are two sorts of them; one of those things which are antecedent to the Play, and are related to make the conduct of it more clear to us, but, 'tis a fault to choose such subjects for the Stage which will inforce us upon that Rock; because we see they are seldome listned to by the Audience, and that is many times the ruin of the Play: for, being once let pass without attention, the Audience can never recover themselves to understand the Plot; and indeed it is somewhat unreasonable that they should be put to so much trouble, as, that to comprehend what passes in their sight, they must have recourse to what was done, perhaps, ten or twenty years ago.

But there is another sort of Relations, that is, of things hapning in the Action of the Play, and suppos'd to be done behind the Scenes: and this is many times both convenient and beautiful: for, by it, the French avoid the tumult, which we are subject to in *England*, by representing Duells, Battells, and the like; which renders our Stage too like the Theaters, where they fight Prizes. For what is more ridiculous then to represent an Army with a Drum and five men behind it; all which, the Heroe of the other side is to drive in before him, or to see a Duel fought, and one slain with two or three thrusts of the foyles, which we know are so blunted, that we might give a man an hour to kill another in good earnest with them.

I have observ'd that in all our Tragedies, the Audience cannot forbear laughing when the Actors are to die; 'tis the most Comick part of the whole Play. All *passions* may be lively represented on the Stage, if to the well-writing of them the Actor supplies a good commanded voice, and limbs that move easily, and without stifness; but there are many *actions* which can never be imitated to a just height: dying especially is a thing which none but a Roman Gladiator could naturally perform upon the Stage when he did not imitate or represent, but naturally do it; and therefore it is better to omit the representation of it.

The words of a good Writer which describe it lively, will make a deeper impression of belief in us then all the Actor can perswade us to,[82] when he seems to fall dead before us; as a Poet in the description of a beautiful Garden, or a Meadow, will please our imagination more then the place it self can please our sight. When we see death represented we are convinc'd it is but Fiction; but when we hear it related, our eyes (the strongest witnesses) are wanting, which might have undeceiv'd us; and we are all willing to favour the sleight when the Poet does not too grosly impose upon us. They therefore who imagine these relations would make no concernment in the Audience, are deceiv'd, by confounding them with the other, which are of things antecedent to the Play; those are made often in cold blood (as I may say) to the audience, but these are warm'd with our concernments, which are before awaken'd in the Play. What the Philosophers say of motion, that when it is once begun it continues of it self, and will do so to Eternity without some stop put to it,[83] is clearly true on this occasion; the soul being already mov'd with the Characters and Fortunes of those imaginary persons, continues going of its own accord, and we are no more weary to hear what becomes of them when they are not on the Stage, then we are to listen to the news of an absent Mistress. But it is objected, That if one part the Play may be related, then why not all? I answer, Some parts of the action are more fit to be represented, some to be related. *Corneille* sayes judiciously, that the Poet is not oblig'd to expose to view all particular actions which conduce to the principal: he ought to select such of them to be seen which will appear with the greatest beauty, either by the magnificence of the show, or the vehemence of passions which they produce, or some other charm which they have in them, and let the rest arrive to the audience by narration.[84] 'Tis a great mistake in us to believe the French present no part of the action upon the Stage: every alteration or crossing of a design, every new sprung passion, and turn of it, is a part of the action, and much the noblest, except we conceive nothing to be action till they come to blows; as if the painting of the Heroes mind were not more properly the Poets work then the strength of his body. Nor does this any thing contradict the opinion of *Horace*, where he tells us,

> *Segnius irritant animos demissa per aurem*
> *Quam quæ sunt oculis subjecta fidelibus.* —

For he says immediately after,

> — *Non tamen intus*
> *Digna geri promes in scenam, Multaq; tolles*
> *Ex oculis, quæ mox narret facundia præsens.*

Among which many he recounts some.

> *Nec pueros coram populo Medea trucidet,*
> *Aut in avem Progne mutetur, Cadmus in anguem, &c.*[85]

That is, those actions which by reason of their cruelty will cause aversion in us, or by reason of their impossibility unbelief, ought either wholly to be avoided by a Poet, or onely deliver'd by narration. To which, we may have leave to add such as to avoid tumult, (as was before hinted) or to reduce the Plot into a more seasonable compass of time, or for defect of Beauty in them, are rather to be related then presented to the eye. Examples of all these kinds are frequent, not onely among all the Ancients, but in the best receiv'd of our English Poets. We find *Ben. Johnson* using them in his Magnetick Lady, where one comes out from Dinner, and relates the quarrels and disorders of it to save the undecent appearing of them on the Stage, and to abreviate the Story: and this in express imitation of *Terence*, who had done the same before him in his Eunuch, where *Pythias* makes the like relation of what had happen'd within at the Souldiers entertainment.[86] The relations likewise of *Sejanus's* death, and the prodigies before it are remarkable; the one of which was hid from sight to avoid the horrour and tumult of the representation; the other to shun the introducing of things impossible to be believ'd.[87] In that excellent Play the King and no King, *Fletcher* goes yet farther; for the whole unravelling of the Plot is done by narration in the fifth Act, after the manner of the Ancients; and it moves great concernment in the Audience, though it be onely a relation of what was done many years before the Play. I could multiply other instances, but these are sufficient to prove that there is no errour in choosing a subject which requires this sort of narrations; in the ill managing of them, there may.

But I find I have been too long in this discourse since the French have many other excellencies not common to us, as that you never see any of their Playes end with a conversion, or simple change of will, which is the ordinary way our Poets use to end theirs. It shows little art in the conclusion of a Dramatick Poem, when they who have hinder'd the felicity during the four Acts, desist from it in the fifth without some powerful cause to take them off; and though I deny not but such reasons may be found, yet it is a path that is cautiously to be trod, and the Poet is to be sure he convinces the Audience that the motive is strong enough. As for example, the conversion of the Usurer in the Scornful Lady,[88] seems to me a little forc'd; for being an Usurer, which implies a lover of Money to the highest degree of covetousness, (and such the Poet has represented him) the account he gives for the sudden change is, that he has been dup'd by the wilde young fellow, which in reason might render him more wary another time, and make him punish himself with harder fare and courser cloaths to get it up again: but that he should look upon it as a judgment, and so repent, we may expect to hear of in a Sermon, but I should never indure it in a Play.

I pass by this; neither will I insist upon the care they take, that no person after his first entrance shall ever appear, but the business which brings him upon the Stage shall be evident: which, if observ'd, must needs render all the events in the Play more natural; for there you see the probability of every accident, in the cause that produc'd it; and that which appears chance in the Play, will seem so reasonable to you, that you will there find it almost necessary; so that in the exits of their Actors you have a clear account of their purpose and design in the next entrance: (though, if the Scene be well wrought, the event will commonly deceive you) for there is nothing so absurd, sayes *Corneille*,[89] as for an Actor to leave the Stage, onely because he has no more to say.

I should now speak of the beauty of their Rhime, and the just reason I have to prefer that way of writing in Tragedies before ours in Blanck-verse; but because it is partly receiv'd by us, and therefore not altogether peculiar to them, I will say no more of it in relation to their Playes. For our own I doubt not but it will exceedingly beautifie them, and I can see but one reason why it should not generally obtain, that is, because our Poets write so ill in it. This indeed may prove a more prevailing argument then all others which are us'd to destroy it, and therefore I am onely troubled when great and judicious Poets, and those who are acknowledg'd such, have writ or spoke against it;[90] as for others they are to be answer'd by that one sentence of an ancient Authour.

Sed ut primo ad consequendos eos quos priores ducimus accendimur, ita ubi aut præteriri, aut æquari eos posse desperavimus, studium cum spe senescit: quod, scilicet, assequi non potest, sequi desinit; præteritoq; eo in quo eminere non possumus, aliquid in quo nitamur conquirimus.[91]

Lisideius concluded in this manner; and *Neander* after a little pause thus answer'd him.

I shall grant *Lisideius*, without much dispute, a great part of what he has urg'd against us, for I acknowledg the French contrive their Plots more regularly, observe the Laws of Comedy, and decorum of the Stage (to speak generally) with more exactness then the English. Farther I deny not but he has tax'd us justly in some irregularities of ours which he has mention'd; yet, after all, I am of opinion that neither our faults nor their virtues are considerable enough to place them above us.

For the lively imitation of Nature being in the definition of a Play, those which best fulfil that law ought to be esteem'd superiour to the others. 'Tis true, those beauties of the French-poesie are such as will raise perfection higher where it is, but are not sufficient to give it where it is not: they are indeed the Beauties of a Statue, but not of a Man, because not animated with the Soul of Poesie, which is imitation of humour and passions: and this *Lisideius* himself, or any other, however byassed to their Party, cannot but acknowledg, if he will either compare the humours of our Comedies, or the Characters of our serious Playes with theirs. He that will look upon theirs which have been written till these last ten years or thereabouts, will find it an hard matter to pick out two or three passable humours amongst them. *Corneille* himself, their Arch-Poet, what has he produc'd except *the Lier*,[92] and you know how it was cry'd up in *France*; but when it came upon the English Stage, though well translated, and that part of *Dorant* acted to so much advantage by Mr. *Hart*, as I am confident it never received in its own Country, the most favourable to it would not put in competition with many of *Fletchers* or *Ben. Johnsons*. In the rest of *Corneilles* Comedies you have little humour; he tells you himself his way is first to show two Lovers in good intelligence with each other; in the working up of the Play to embroyle them by some mistake, and in the latter end to clear it up.[93]

But of late years *de Moliere*, the younger *Corneille*, *Quinault*,[94] and some others, have been imitating of afar off the quick turns and graces of the English Stage. They have mix'd their serious Playes with mirth, like our Tragicomedies since the death of Cardinal *Richlieu*, which *Lisideius* and many others not observing, have commended that in them for a virtue which they themselves no longer practice. Most of their new Playes are like some of ours, deriv'd from the Spanish Novells. There is scarce one of them without a vail, and a trusty *Diego*, who drolls much after the rate of the *Adventures*.[95] But their humours, if I may grace them with that name, are so thin sown that never above one of them comes up in any Play: I dare take upon me to find more variety of them in some one Play of *Ben. Johnsons* then in all theirs together: as he who has seen the Alchymist, the silent Woman, or *Bartholmew*-Fair, cannot but acknowledge with me.

I grant the French have performed what was possible on the ground-work of the Spanish Playes; what was pleasant before they have made regular; but there is not above one good Play to be writ upon all those Plots; they are too much alike to please often, which we need not the experience of our own Stage to justifie. As for their new way of mingling mirth with serious Plot I do not with *Lysideius* condemn the thing, though I cannot approve their manner of doing it: He tells us we cannot so speedily recollect our selves after a Scene of great passion and concernment as to pass to another of mirth and humour, and to enjoy it with any relish: but why should he imagine the soul of man more heavy then his Sences? Does not the eye pass from an unpleasant object to a pleasant in a much shorter time then is requir'd to this? and does not the unpleasantness of the first commend the beauty of the latter? The old Rule of Logick might have convinc'd him, that contraries when plac'd near, set off each other.[96] A continued gravity keeps the spirit too much bent; we must refresh it sometimes, as we bait upon a journey, that we may go on with greater ease. A Scene of mirth mix'd with Tragedy has the same effect upon us which our musick has betwixt the Acts, and that we find a relief to us from the best Plots and language of the Stage, if the discourses have been long. I must therefore have stronger arguments ere I am convinc'd, that compassion and mirth in the same subject destroy each other; and in the mean time cannot but conclude, to the honour of our Nation, that we have invented, increas'd and perfected a more pleasant way of writing for the Stage then was ever known to the Ancients or Moderns of any Nation, which is Tragicomedie.

And this leads me to wonder why *Lisideius* and many others should cry up the barrenness of the French Plots above the variety and copiousness of the English. Their Plots are single, they carry on one design which is push'd forward by all the Actors, every Scene in the Play contributing and moving towards it: Ours, besides the main design, have under plots or by-concernments, of less considerable Persons, and Intrigues, which are carried on with the motion of the main Plot: just as they say the Orb of the fix'd Stars, and those of the Planets, though they have motions of their own, are whirl'd about by the motion of the *primum mobile*, in which they are contain'd: that similitude expresses much of the English Stage: for if contrary motions may be found in Nature to agree; if a Planet can go East and West at the same time; one way by virtue of his own motion, the other by the force of the first mover; it will not be difficult to imagine how the under Plot, which is onely different, not contrary to the great design, may naturally be conducted along with it.

Eugenius[97] has already shown us, from the confession of the French Poets, that the Unity of Action is sufficiently preserv'd if all the imperfect actions of the Play are conducing to the main design: but when those petty intrigues of a Play are so ill order'd that they have no coherence with the other, I must grant *Lisideius* has reason to tax that want of due connexion; for Co-ordination[98] in a Play is as dangerous and unnatural as in a State. In the mean time he must acknowledge our variety, if well order'd, will afford a greater pleasure to the audience.

As for his other argument, that by pursuing one single Theme they gain an advantage to express and work up the passions, I wish any example he could bring from them would make it good: for I confess their verses are to me the coldest I have ever read: Neither indeed is it possible for them, in the way they take, so to express passion, as that the effects of it should appear in the concernment of an Audience: their Speeches being so many declamations, which tire us with the length; so that instead of perswading us to grieve for their imaginary Heroes, we are concern'd for our own trouble, as we are in the tedious visits of bad company; we are in pain till they are gone. When the French Stage came to be reform'd by Cardinal *Richelieu*, those long Harangues were introduc'd, to comply with the gravity of a Churchman. Look upon the *Cinna* and the *Pompey*, they are not so properly to be called Playes, as long discourses of reason of State: and *Polieucte*[99] in matters of Religion is as solemn as the long stops upon our Organs. Since that time it is grown into a custome, and their Actors speak by the Hour-glass, as our Parsons do; nay, they account it the grace of their parts: and think themselves disparag'd by the Poet, if they may not twice or thrice in a Play entertain the Audience with a Speech of an hundred or two hundred lines.[100] I deny not but this may sute well enough with the French; for as we, who are a more sullen people, come to be diverted at our Playes; they who are of an ayery and gay temper come thither to make themselves more serious: And this I conceive to be one reason why Comedy is more pleasing to us, and Tragedies to them. But to speak generally, it cannot be deny'd that short Speeches and Replies are more apt to move the passions, and beget concernment in us then the other: for it is unnatural for any one in a gust of passion to speak long together, or for another in the same condition, to suffer him, without interruption. Grief and Passion are like floods rais'd in little Brooks by a sudden rain; they are quickly up, and if the concernment be powr'd unexpectedly in upon us, it overflows us: But a long sober shower gives them leisure to run out as they came in, without troubling the ordinary current. As for Comedy, Repartee is one of its chiefest graces; the greatest pleasure of the Audience is a chase of wit kept up on both sides, and swiftly manag'd. And this our forefathers, if not we, have had in *Fletchers* Playes, to a much higher degree of perfection then the French Poets can arrive at.[101]

There is another part of *Lisideius* his Discourse, in which he has rather excus'd our neighbours then commended them; that is, for aiming onely to make one person considerable in their Playes. 'Tis very true what he has urged, that one character in all Playes, even without the Poets care, will have advantage of all the others; and that the design of the whole *Drama* will chiefly depend on it. But this hinders not that there may be more shining characters in the Play: many persons of a second magnitude, nay, some so very near, so almost equal to the first, that greatness may be oppos'd to greatness, and all the persons be made considerable, not onely by their quality, but their action. 'Tis evident that the more the persons are, the greater will be the variety of the Plot. If then the parts are manag'd so regularly that the beauty of the whole be kept intire, and that the variety become not a perplex'd and confus'd mass of accidents, you will find it infinitely pleasing to be led in a labyrinth of design, where you see some of your way before you, yet discern not the end till you arrive at it. And that all this is practicable, I can produce for examples many of our English Playes: as the Maids Tragedy,[102] the Alchymist, the Silent Woman; I was going to have named the Fox,[103] but that the unity of design seems not exactly observ'd in it; for there appears two actions in the Play; the first naturally ending with the fourth Act; the second forc'd from it in the fifth: which yet is the less to be condemn'd in him, because the disguise of *Volpone*, though it suited not with his character as a crafty or covetous person, agreed well enough with that of a voluptuary: and by it the Poet gain'd the end he aym'd at, the punishment of Vice, and the reward of Virtue, which that disguise produc'd. So that to judge equally of it, it was an excellent fifth Act, but not so naturally proceeding from the former.

But to leave this, and pass to the latter part of *Lisideius* his discourse, which concerns relations, I must acknowledge with him, that the French have reason when they hide that part of the action which would occasion too much tumult upon the Stage, and choose rather to have it made known by narration to the Audience. Farther I think it very convenient, for the reasons he has given, that all incredible actions were remov'd; but, whither custome has so insinuated it self into our Country-men, or nature has so form'd them to fierceness, I know not; but they will scarcely suffer combats & other objects of horrour to be taken from them. And indeed, the indecency of tumults is all which can be objected against fighting: For why may not our imagination as well suffer it self to be deluded with the probability of it, as with any other thing in the Play? For my part, I can with as great ease perswade my self that the blowes which are struck are given in good earnest, as I can, that they who strike them are Kings or Princes, or those persons which they represent. For objects of incredibility I would be satisfied from *Lisideius*, whether we have any so remov'd from all appearance of truth as are those of *Corneilles Andromede*?[104] A Play which has been frequented the most of any he has writ? If the *Perseus*, or the Son of an Heathen God, the *Pegasus* and the Monster were not capable to choak a strong belief, let him blame any representation of ours hereafter. Those indeed were objects of delight; yet the reason is the same as to the probability: for he makes it not a Ballette or Masque, but a Play, which is to resemble truth. But for death, that it ought not to be represented, I have besides the Arguments alledg'd by *Lisideius*, the authority of *Ben. Johnson*, who has forborn it in his Tragedies; for both the death of *Sejanus* and *Catiline* are related: though in the latter I cannot but observe one irregularity of that great Poet: he has remov'd the Scene in the same Act, from *Rome* to *Catiline*'s Army, and from thence again to *Rome*; and besides, has allow'd a very inconsiderable time, after *Catilines* Speech, for the striking of the battle, and the return of *Petreius*, who is to relate the event of it to the Senate: which I should not animadvert upon him, who was otherwise a painful observer of τὸ πρέπον, or the decorum of the Stage, if he had not us'd extream severity in his judgment upon the incomparable *Shakespeare* for the same fault. To conclude on this subject of Relations, if we are to be blam'd for showing too much of the action, the French are as faulty for discovering too little of it: a mean betwixt both should be observed by every judicious Writer, so as the audience may neither be left unsatisfied by not seeing what is beautiful, or shock'd by beholding what is either incredible or undecent. I hope I have already prov'd in this discourse, that though we are not altogether so punctual as the French, in observing the lawes of Comedy; yet our errours are so few, and little, and those things wherein we excel them so considerable, that we ought of right to be prefer'd before them. But what will *Lisideius* say if they themselves acknowledge they are too strictly ti'd up by those lawes, for breaking which he has blam'd the English? I will alledge *Corneille's* words, as I find them in the end of his Discourse of the three Unities; *Il est facile aux speculatifs d'estre severes, &c.* " 'Tis easie for speculative persons to judge severely; but if they would produce to publick view ten or twelve pieces of this nature, they would perhaps give more latitude to the Rules then I have done, when by experience they had known how much we are bound up and constrain'd by them, and how many beauties of the Stage they banish'd from it." To illustrate a little what he has said, by their servile observations of the unities of time and place, and integrity of Scenes, they have brought upon themselves that dearth of Plot, and narrowness of Imagination, which may be observ'd in all their Playes. How many beautifull accidents might naturally happen in two or three dayes, which cannot arrive with any probability in the compass of 24 hours? There is time to be allowed also for maturity of design, which amongst great and prudent persons, such as are often represented in Tragedy, cannot, with any likelihood of truth, be brought to pass at so short a warning. Farther, by tying themselves strictly to the unity of place, and unbroken Scenes, they are forc'd many times to omit some beauties which cannot be shown where the Act began; but might, if the Scene were interrupted, and the Stage clear'd for the persons to enter in another place; and therefore the French Poets are often forc'd upon absurdities: for if the Act begins in a chamber all the persons in the Play must have some business or other to come thither, or else they are not to be shown that Act, and sometimes their characters are very unfitting to appear there; As, suppose it were the Kings Bed-chamber, yet the meanest man in the Tragedy must come and dispatch his business there rather then in the Lobby or Court-yard (which is fitter for him) for fear the Stage should be clear'd, and the Scenes broken. Many times they fall by it into a greater inconvenience; for they keep their Scenes unbroken, and yet change the place; as in one of their newest Playes,[105] where the Act begins in the Street. There a Gentleman is to meet his Friend; he sees him with his man, coming out from his Fathers house; they talk together, and the first goes out: the second, who is a Lover, has made an appointment with his Mistress; she appears at the window, and then we are to imagine the Scene lies under it. This Gentleman is call'd away, and leaves his servant with his Mistress: presently her Father is heard from within; the young Lady is affraid the Servingman should be discover'd, and thrusts him in through a door which is suppos'd to be her Closet. After this, the Father enters to the Daughter, and now the Scene is in a House: for he is seeking from one room to another for this poor *Philipin*, or French *Diego*, who is heard from within, drolling and breaking many a miserable conceit upon his sad condition. In this ridiculous manner the Play goes on, the Stage being never empty all the while: so that the Street, the Window, the two Houses, and the Closet, are made to walk about, and the Persons to stand still. Now what I beseech you is more easie than to write a regular French Play, or more difficult then to write an irregular English one, like those of *Fletcher*, or of *Shakespeare*.

If they content themselves as *Corneille* did, with some flat design, which, like an ill Riddle, is found out e're it be half propos'd; such Plots we can make every way regular as easily as they: but when e're they endeavour to rise up to any quick turns and counterturns of Plot, as some of them have attempted, since *Corneilles* Playes have been less in vogue, you see they write as irregularly as we, though they cover it more speciously. Hence the reason is perspicuous, why no French Playes, when translated, have, or ever can succeed upon the English Stage. For, if you consider the Plots, our own are fuller of variety, if the writing ours are more quick and fuller of spirit: and therefore 'tis a strange mistake in those who decry the way of writing Playes in Verse, as if the English therein imitated the French. We have borrow'd nothing from them; our Plots are weav'd in English Loomes: we endeavour therein to follow the variety and greatness of characters which are deriv'd to us from *Shakespeare* and *Fletcher*: the copiousness and well-knitting of the intrigues we have from *Johnson*, and for the Verse it self we have English Presidents of elder date than any of *Corneilles*'s Playes: (not to name our old Comedies before *Shakespeare*, which were all writ in verse of six feet, or *Alexandrin's*, such as the French now use) I can show in *Shakespeare*, many Scenes of rhyme together, and the like in *Ben. Johnsons* Tragedies: In *Catiline* and *Sejanus* sometimes thirty or forty lines; I mean besides the Chorus, or the Monologues, which by the way, show'd *Ben.* no enemy to this way of writing, especially if you look upon his *Sad Shepherd*[106] which goes sometimes upon rhyme, sometimes upon blanck Verse, like an Horse who eases himself upon Trot and Amble. You find him likewise commending *Fletcher's* Pastoral of the Faithful Shepherdess;[107] which is for the most part Rhyme, though not refin'd to that purity to which it hath since been brought: And these examples are enough to clear us from a servile imitation of the French.

But to return from whence I have digress'd, I dare boldly affirm these two things of the English *Drama*: First, That we have many Playes of ours as regular as any of theirs; and which, besides, have more variety of Plot and Characters: And secondly, that in most of the irregular Playes of *Shakespeare* or *Fletcher* (for *Ben. Johnson's* are for the most part regular) there is a more masculine fancy and greater spirit in all the writing, then there is in any of the French. I could produce even in *Shakespeare's* and *Fletcher's* Works, some Playes which are almost exactly form'd, as the Merry Wives of *Windsor*, and the Scornful Lady:[108] but because (generally speaking) *Shakespeare*, who writ first, did not perfectly observe the Laws of Comedy, and *Fletcher*, who came nearer to perfection, yet through carelessness made many faults; I will take the pattern of a perfect Play from *Ben. Johnson*, who was a careful and learned observer of the Dramatique Lawes, and from all his Comedies I shall select *The Silent Woman*;[109] of which I will make a short Examen, according to those Rules which the French observe.

As *Neander* was beginning to examine the Silent Woman, *Eugenius*, looking earnestly upon him; I beseech you *Neander*, said he, gratifie the company and me in particular so far, as before you speak of the Play, to give us a Character of the Authour; and tell us franckly your opinion, whether you do not think all Writers, both French and English, ought to give place to him?

I fear, replied *Neander*, That in obeying your commands I shall draw a little envy upon my self. Besides, in performing them, it will be first necessary to speak somewhat of *Shakespeare* and *Fletcher*, his Rivalls in Poesie; and one of them, in my opinion, at least his equal, perhaps his superiour.

To begin then with *Shakespeare*; he was the man who of all Modern, and perhaps Ancient Poets, had the largest and most comprehensive soul. All the Images of Nature were still present to him, and he drew them not laboriously, but luckily: when he describes any thing, you more than see it, you feel it too. Those who accuse him to have wanted learning, give him the greater commendation: he was naturally learn'd; he needed not the spectacles of Books to read Nature; he look'd inwards, and found her there.[110] I cannot say he is every where alike; were he so, I should do him injury to compare him with the greatest of Mankind. He is many times flat, insipid; his Comick wit degenerating into clenches, his serious swelling into Bombast. But he is alwayes great, when some great occasion is presented to him: no man can say he ever had a fit subject for his wit, and did not then raise himself as high above the rest of Poets,

Quantum lenta solent, inter viberna cupressi.[111]

The consideration of this made Mr. *Hales* of *Eaton* say, That there was no subject of which any Poet ever writ, but he would produce it much better treated of in *Shakespeare*; and however others are now generally prefer'd before him, yet the Age wherein he liv'd, which had contemporaries with him, *Fletcher* and *Johnson* never equall'd them to him in their esteem: And in the last Kings Court, when *Ben*'s reputation was at highest, Sir *John Suckling*, and with him the greater part of the Courtiers, set our *Shakespeare* far above him.

Beaumont and *Fletcher* of whom I am next to speak, had with the advantage of *Shakespeare*'s wit, which was their precedent, great natural gifts, improv'd by study. *Beaumont* especially being so accurate a judge of Playes, that *Ben. Johnson* while he liv'd, submitted all his Writings to his Censure, and 'tis thought, us'd his judgement in correcting, if not contriving all his Plots. What value he had for him, appears by the Verses he writ to him;[112] and therefore I need speak no farther of it. The first Play which brought *Fletcher* and him in esteem was their *Philaster*: for before that, they had written two or three very unsuccessfully: as the like is reported of *Ben. Johnson*, before he writ *Every Man in his Humour*.[113] Their Plots were generally more regular then *Shakespeare's*, especially those which were made before *Beaumont's* death; and they understood and imitated the conversation of Gentlemen much better; whose wilde debaucheries, and quickness of wit in reparties, no Poet can ever paint as they have done.[114] This Humour of which *Ben. Johnson* deriv'd from particular persons, they made it not their business to describe: they represented all the passions very lively, but above all, Love. I am apt to believe the English Language in them arriv'd to its highest perfection; what words have since been taken in, are rather superfluous then necessary. Their Playes are now the most pleasant and frequent entertainments of the Stage; two of theirs being acted through the year for one of *Shakespeare's* or *Johnsons*: the reason is, because there is a certain gayety in their Comedies, and Pathos in their more serious Playes, which suits generally with all mens humours. *Shakespeares* language is likewise a little obsolete, and *Ben. Johnson's* wit comes short of theirs.

As for *Johnson*, to whose Character I am now arriv'd, if we look upon him while he was himself, (for his last Playes were but his dotages) I think him the most learned and judicious Writer which any Theater ever had. He was a most severe Judge of himself as well as others. One cannot say he wanted wit, but rather that he was frugal of it. In his works you find little to retrench or alter. Wit and Language, and Humour also in some measure we had before him; but something of Art was wanting to the *Drama* till he came. He manag'd his strength to more advantage then any who preceded him. You seldome find him making Love in any of his Scenes, or endeavouring to move the Passions; his genius was too sullen and saturnine to do it gracefully, especially when he knew he came after those who had performed both to such an height. Humour was his proper Sphere, and in that he delighted most to represent Mechanick people. He was deeply conversant in the Ancients, both Greek and Latine, and he borrow'd boldly from them: there is scarce a Poet or Historian among the Roman Authours of those times whom he has not translated in *Sejanus* and *Catiline*. But he has done his Robberies so openly, that one may see he fears not to be taxed by any Law. He invades Authours like a Monarch, and what would be theft in other Poets, is onely victory in him. With the spoils of these Writers he so represents old *Rome* to us, in its Rites, Ceremonies and Customs, that if one of their Poets had written either of his Tragedies, we had seen less of it then in him. If there was any fault in his Language, 'twas that he weav'd it too closely and laboriously in his serious Playes;[115] perhaps too, he did a little too much Romanize our Tongue, leaving the words which he translated almost as much Latine as he found them: wherein though he learnedly followed the Idiom of their language, he did not enough comply with ours. If I would compare him with *Shakespeare*, I must acknowledge him the more correct Poet, but *Shakespeare* the greater wit. *Shakespeare* was the *Homer*, or Father of our Dramatick Poets; *Johnson* was the *Virgil*, the pattern of elaborate writing; I admire him, but I love *Shakespeare*. To conclude of him, as he has given us the most correct Playes, so in the precepts which he has laid down in his *Discoveries*, we have as many and profitable Rules for perfecting the Stage as any wherewith the French can furnish us.

Having thus spoken of the Authour, I proceed to the examination of his Comedy, *The Silent Woman*.

EXAMEN OF THE SILENT WOMAN.

To begin first with the length of the Action, it is so far from exceeding the compass of a Natural day, that it takes not up an Artificial one. 'Tis all included in the limits of three hours and an half, which is no more than is requir'd for the presentment on the Stage. A beauty perhaps not much observ'd; if it had, we should not have look'd upon the Spanish Translation of five hours with so much wonder.[116] The scene of it is laid in *London*; the latitude of place is almost as little as you can imagine: for it lies all within the compass of two Houses, and after the first Act, in one.[117] The continuity of Scenes is observ'd more than in any of our Playes, excepting his own Fox and Alchymist. They are not broken above twice or thrice at most in the whole Comedy, and in the two best of *Corneille's* Playes, the *Cid* and *Cinna*, they are interrupted once apiece. The action of the Play is intirely one; the end or aim of which is the setling *Morose*'s Estate on *Dauphine*. The Intrigue of it is the greatest and most noble of any pure unmix'd Comedy in any Language: you see in it many persons of various characters and humours, and all delightful: As first, *Morose*, or an old Man, to whom all noise but his own talking is offensive. Some who would be thought Criticks, say this humour of his is forc'd: but to remove that objection, we may consider him first to be naturally of a delicate hearing, as many are to whom all sharp sounds are unpleasant; and secondly, we may attribute much of it to the peevishness of his Age, or the wayward authority of an old man in his own house, where he may make himself obeyed; and this the Poet seems to allude to in his name *Morose*. Besides this, I am assur'd from diverse persons, that *Ben. Johnson* was actually acquainted with such a man, one altogether as ridiculous as he is here represented. Others say it is not enough to find one man of such an humour; it must be common to more, and the more common the more natural. To prove this, they instance in the best of Comical Characters, *Falstaff*: There are many men resembling him; Old, Fat, Merry, Cowardly, Drunken, Amorous, Vain, and Lying: But to convince these people, I need but tell them, that humour is the ridiculous extravagance of conversation, wherein one man differs from all others. If then it be common, or communicated to many, how differs it from other mens? or what indeed causes it to be ridiculous so much as the singularity of it? As for *Falstaffe*, he is not properly one humour, but a Miscellany of Humours or Images, drawn from so many several men; that wherein he is singular in his wit, or those things he says, *præter expectatum*, unexpected by the Audience; his quick evasions when you imagine him surpriz'd, which as they are extreamly diverting of themselves, so receive a great addition from his person; for the very sight of such an unwieldy old debauch'd fellow is a Comedy alone. And here having a place so proper for it I cannot but enlarge somewhat upon this subject of humour into which I am fallen. The Ancients had little of it in their Comedies; for the τὸ γελοῖον,[118] of the old Comedy, of which *Aristophanes* was chief, was not so much to imitate a man, as to make the people laugh at some odd conceit, which had commonly somewhat of unnatural or obscene in it. Thus when you see *Socrates* brought upon the Stage, you are not to imagine him made ridiculous by the imitation of his actions, but rather by making him perform something very unlike himself: something so childish and absurd, as by comparing it with the gravity of the true *Socrates*, makes a ridiculous object for the Spectators.[119] In their new Comedy which succeeded, the Poets sought indeed to express the ἦθος, as in their Tragedies the πάθος of Mankind.[120] But this ἦθος contain'd onely the general Characters of men and manners; as old men, Lovers, Servingmen, Courtizans, Parasites, and such other persons as we see in their Comedies; all which they made alike: that is, one old man or Father; one Lover, one Courtizan so like another, as if the first of them had begot the rest of every sort: *Ex homine hunc natum dicas.*[121] The same custome they observ'd likewise in their Tragedies. As for the *French*, though they have the word *humeur* among them, yet they have small use of it in their Comedies, or Farces; they being but ill imitations of the *ridiculum*, or that which stirr'd up laughter in the old Comedy. But among the *English* 'tis otherwise: where by humour is meant some extravagant habit, passion, or affection; particular (as I said before) to some one person: by the oddness of which, he is immediately distinguish'd from the rest of men; which being lively and naturally represented, most frequently begets that malicious pleasure in the Audience which is testified by laughter: as all things which are deviations from common customes are ever the aptest to produce it: though by the way this laughter is onely accidental, as the person represented is Fantastick or Bizarre, but pleasure is essential to it, as the imitation of what is natural. The description of these humours, drawn from the knowledge and observation of particular persons, was the peculiar genius and talent of *Ben. Johnson*; To whose Play I now return.

Besides *Morose*, there are at least 9 or 10 different Characters and humours in the *Silent Woman*, all which persons have several concernments of their own, yet are all us'd by the Poet, to the conducting of the main design to perfection. I shall not waste time in commending the writing of this Play, but I will give you my opinion, that there is more wit and acuteness of Fancy in it then in any of *Ben. Johnson's*. Besides, that he has here describ'd the conversation of Gentlemen in the persons of *True-Wit*, and his Friends, with more gayety, ayre and freedom, then in the rest of his Comedies. For the contrivance or the Plot 'tis extream elaborate, and yet withal easie; for the λύσις, or untying of it, 'tis so admirable, that when it is done, no one of the Audience would think the Poet could have miss'd it; and yet it was conceald so much before the last Scene, that any other way would sooner have enter'd into your thoughts. But I dare not take upon me to commend the Fabrick of it, because it is altogether so full of Art, that I must unravel every Scene in it to commend it as I ought. And this excellent contrivance is still the more to be admir'd, because 'tis Comedy where the persons are onely of common rank, and their business private, not elevated by passions or high concernments as in serious Playes. Here every one is a proper Judge of all he sees; nothing is represented but that with which he daily converses: so that by consequence all faults lie open to discovery, and few are pardonable. 'Tis this which *Horace* has judiciously observ'd:

> *Creditur ex medio quia res arcessit habere*
> *Sudoris minimum, sed habet Comedia tanto*
> *Plus oneris, quanto veniæ minus.* —[122]

But our Poet, who was not ignorant of these difficulties, had prevail'd himself of all advantages; as he who designes a large leap takes his rise from the highest ground. One of these advantages is that which *Corneille* has laid down as the greatest which can arrive to any Poem, and which he himself could never compass above thrice in all his Playes, *viz.* the making choice of some signal and long expected day, whereon the action of the Play is to depend.[123] This day was that design'd by *Dauphine* for the setling of his Uncles Estate upon him; which to compass he contrives to marry him: that the marriage had been plotted by him long beforehand is made evident by what he tells

Truwit in the second Act, that in one moment he had destroy'd what he had been raising many months.

There is another artifice of the Poet, which I cannot here omit, because by the frequent practice of it in his Comedies, he has left it to us almost as a Rule, that is, when he has any Character or humour wherein he would show a *Coup de Maistre*, or his highest skill; he recommends it to your observation by a pleasant description of it before the person first appears. Thus, in *Bartholomew Fair* he gives you the Pictures of *Numps* and *Cokes*, and in this those of *Daw*, *Lafoole*, *Morose*, and the *Collegiate Ladies*; all which you hear describ'd before you see them. So that before they come upon the Stage you have a longing expectation of them, which prepares you to receive them favourably; and when they are there, even from their first appearance you are so far acquainted with them, that nothing of their humour is lost to you.

I will observe yet one thing further of this admirable Plot; the business of it rises in every Act. The second is greater then the first; the third then the second, and so forward to the fifth. There too you see, till the very last Scene, new difficulties arising to obstruct the action of the Play; and when the Audience is brought into despair that the business can naturally be effected, then, and not before, the discovery is made. But that the Poet might entertain you with more variety all this while, he reserves some new Characters to show you, which he opens not till the second and third Act. In the second, *Morose*, *Daw*, the *Barber* and *Otter*; in the third the *Collegiat Ladies*: All which he moves afterwards in by-walks, or under-Plots, as diversions to the main design, least it should grow tedious, though they are still naturally joyn'd with it, and somewhere or other subservient to it. Thus, like a skilful Chess-player, by little and little he draws out his men, and makes his pawns of use to his greater persons.

If this Comedy, and some others of his, were translated into French Prose (which would now be no wonder to them, since *Moliere* has lately given them Playes out of Verse which have not displeas'd them) I believe the controversie would soon be decided betwixt the two Nations, even making them the Judges. But we need not call our Hero's to our ayde; Be it spoken to the honour of the English, our Nation can never want in any Age such who are able to dispute the Empire of Wit with any people in the Universe. And though the fury of a Civil War, and Power, for twenty years together, abandon'd to a barbarous race of men, Enemies of all good Learning, had buried the Muses under the ruines of Monarchy; yet with the restoration of our happiness, we see reviv'd Poesie lifting up its head, & already shaking off the rubbish which lay so heavy on it. We have seen since His Majesties return, many Dramatick Poems which yield not to those of any forreign Nation, and which deserve all Lawrels but the English. I will set aside Flattery and Envy: it cannot be deny'd but we have had some little blemish either in the Plot or writing of all those Playes which have been made within these seven years: (and perhaps there is no Nation in the world so quick to discern them, or so difficult to pardon them, as ours:) yet if we can perswade our selves to use the candour of that Poet, who (though the most severe of Criticks) has left us this caution by which to moderate our censures;

— *Ubi plura nitent in carmine non ego paucis offendar maculis.*[124]

If in consideration of their many and great beauties, we can wink at some slight, and little imperfections; if we, I say, can be thus equal to our selves, I ask no favour from the French. And if I do not venture upon any particular judgment of our late Playes, 'tis out of the consideration which an Ancient Writer gives me; *Vivorum, ut magna admiratio ita censura difficilis*: betwixt the extreams of admiration and malice, 'tis hard to judge uprightly of the living.[125] Onely I think it may be permitted me to say, that as it is no less'ning to us to yield to some Playes, and those not many of our own Nation in the last Age, so can it be no addition to pronounce of our present Poets that they have far surpass'd all the Ancients, and the Modern Writers of other Countreys.

This, my Lord, was the substance of what was then spoke on that occasion; and *Lisideius*, I think was going to reply, when he was prevented thus by *Crites*: I am confident, said he, the most material things that can be said, have been already urg'd on either side; if they have not, I must beg of *Lisideius* that he will defer his answer till another time, for I confess I have a joynt quarrel to you both, because you have concluded, without any reason given for it, that Rhyme is proper for the Stage. I will not dispute how ancient it hath been among us to write this way; perhaps our Ancestours knew no better till *Shakespeare's* time. I will grant it was not altogether left by him, and that *Fletcher* and *Ben. Johnson* us'd it frequently in their Pastorals, and sometimes in other Playes. Farther, I will not argue whether we receiv'd it originally from our own Countrymen, or from the French; for that is an inquiry of as little benefit, as theirs who in the midst of the great Plague were not so sollicitous to provide against it, as to know whether we had it from the malignity of our own air, or by transportation from *Holland*. I have therefore onely to affirm, that it is not allowable in serious Playes; for Comedies I find you already concluding with me. To prove this, I might satisfie my self to tell you, how much in vain it is for you to strive against the stream of the peoples inclination; the greatest part of which are prepossess'd so much with those excellent Playes of *Shakespeare, Fletcher,* and *Ben. Johnson,* (which have been written out of Rhyme) that except you could bring them such as were written better in it, and those too by persons of equal reputation with them, it will be impossible for you to gain your cause with them, who will still be judges. This it is to which in fine all your reasons must submit. The unanimous consent of an Audience is so powerful, That even *Julius Cæsar* (as *Macrobius* reports of him) when he was perpetual Dictator, was not able to ballance it on the other side. But when *Laberius,* a *Roman* Knight, at his request contended in the *Mime* with another Poet, he was forc'd to cry out, *Etiam favente me victus es Laberi.*[126] But I will not on this occasion, take the advantage of the greater number, but onely urge such reasons against Rhyme, as I find in the Writings of those who have argu'd for the other way.[127] First then I am of opinion, that Rhyme is unnatural in a Play, because Dialogue there is presented as the effect of sudden thought. For a Play is the imitation of Nature; and since no man, without premeditation speaks in Rhyme, neither ought he to do it on the Stage; this hinders not but the Fancy may be there elevated to an higher pitch of thought then it is in ordinary discourse: for there is a probability that men of excellent and quick parts may speak noble things *ex tempore*: but those thoughts are never fetter'd with the numbers or sound of Verse without study, and therefore it cannot be but unnatural to present the most free way of speaking, in that which is the most constrain'd. For this Reason, sayes *Aristotle*, 'Tis best to write Tragedy in that kind of Verse which is the least such, or which is nearest Prose:[128] and this amongst the Ancients was the Iambique, and with us is blank verse, or the measure of verse, kept exactly without rhyme. These numbers therefore are fittest for a Play; the others for a paper of Verses, or a Poem, Blank verse being as much below them as rhyme is improper for the *Drama*. And if it be objected that neither are blank verses made *ex tempore*, yet as nearest Nature, they are still to be preferr'd. But there are two particular exceptions which many besides my self have had to verse; by which it will appear yet more plainly, how improper it is in Playes. And the first of them is grounded upon that very reason for which some have commended Rhyme: they say the quickness of repartees in argumentative Scenes receives an ornament from verse. Now what is more unreasonable then to imagine that a man should not onely light upon the Wit, but the Rhyme too upon the sudden? This nicking of him who spoke before both in sound and measure, is so great an happiness, that you must at least suppose the persons of your Play to be born Poets, *Arcades omnes & cantare pares & respondere parati*: they must have arriv'd to the degree of *quicquid conabar dicere*:[129] to make Verses almost whether they will or no: if they are any thing below this, it will look rather like the design of two then the answer of one: it will appear that your Actors hold intelligence together, that they perform their tricks like Fortune-tellers, by confederacy. The hand of Art will be too visible in it against that maxime of all Professions; *Ars est celare artem*,[130] That it is the greatest perfection of art to keep it self undiscover'd. Nor will it serve you to object, that however you manage it, 'tis full known to be a Play; and consequently the Dialogue of two persons understood to be the labour of one Poet. For a Play is still an imitation of Nature; we know we are to be deceiv'd, and we desire to be so; but no man ever was deceiv'd but with a probability of truth, for who will suffer a gross lie to be fasten'd on him? Thus we sufficiently understand that the Scenes which represent Cities and Countries to us, are not really such, but onely painted on boards and Canvas: But shall that excuse the ill Painture or designment of them; Nay rather ought they not to be labour'd with so much the more diligence and exactness to help the imagination? since the mind of man does naturally tend to, and seek after Truth; and therefore the nearer any thing comes to the imitation of it, the more it pleases.

Thus, you see, your Rhyme is uncapable of expressing the greatest thoughts naturally, and the lowest it cannot with any grace: for what is more unbefitting the Majesty of Verse, then to call a Servant, or bid a door be shut in Rhime? And yet this miserable necessity you are forc'd upon. But Verse, you say, circumscribes a quick and luxuriant fancy, which would extend it self too far on every subject, did not the labour which is requir'd to well turn'd and polish'd Rhyme, set bounds to it. Yet this Argument, if granted, would onely prove that we may write better in Verse, but not more naturally. Neither is it able to evince that; for he who wants judgment to confine his fancy in blank Verse, may want it as much in Rhyme; and he who has it will avoid errours in both kinds. Latine verse was as great a confinement to the imagination of those Poets, as Rhime to ours: and yet you find *Ovid* saying too much on every subject. *Nescivit* (sayes *Seneca*) *quod bene cessit relinquere*: of which he gives you one famous instance in his Discription of the Deluge.

Omnia pontus erat, deerant quoque Litora Ponto.[131]

Now all was Sea, Nor had that Sea a shore. Thus *Ovid's* fancy was not limited by verse, and *Virgil* needed not verse to have bounded his.

In our own language we see *Ben. Johnson* confining himself to what ought to be said, even in the liberty of blank Verse; and yet *Corneille*, the most judicious of the *French* Poets, is still varying the same sence an hundred wayes, and dwelling eternally upon the same subject, though confin'd by Rhyme. Some other exceptions I have to Verse, but being these I have nam'd are for the most part already publick; I conceive it reasonable they should first be answer'd.

It concerns me less then any, said *Neander*, (seeing he had ended) to reply to this Discourse; because when I should have prov'd that Verse may be natural in Playes, yet I should alwayes be ready to confess, that those which I have written in this kind come short of that perfection which is requir'd. Yet since you are pleas'd I should undertake this Province, I will do it, though with all imaginable respect and deference both to that person from whom you have borrow'd your strongest Arguments, and to whose judgment when I have said all, I finally submit. But before I proceed to answer your objections, I must first remember you, that I exclude all Comedy from my defence; and next that I deny not but blank verse may be also us'd, and content my self onely to assert, that in serious Playes where the subject and characters are great, and the Plot unmix'd with mirth, which might allay or divert these concernments which are produc'd, Rhyme is there as natural, and more effectual then blank Verse.

And now having laid down this as a foundation, to begin with *Crites*, I must crave leave to tell him, that some of his Arguments against rhyme reach no farther then from the faults or defects of ill rhime, to conclude against the use of it in general. May not I conclude against blank verse by the same reason? If the words of some Poets who write in it, are either ill chosen, or ill placed (which makes not onely rhyme, but all kind of verse in any language unnatural;) Shall I, for their vitious affectation condemn those excellent lines of *Fletcher*, which are written in that kind? Is there any thing in rhyme more constrain'd than this line in blank verse? *I Heav'n invoke, and strong resistance make*,[132] where you see both the clauses are plac'd unnaturally; that is, contrary to the common way of speaking, and that without the excuse of a rhyme to cause it: yet you would think me very ridiculous, if I should accuse the stubbornness of blank Verse for this, and not rather the stifness of the Poet. Therefore, *Crites*, you must either prove that words, though well chosen, and duly plac'd, yet render not Rhyme natural in it self; or, that however natural and easie the rhyme may be, yet it is not proper for a Play. If you insist upon the former part, I would ask you what other conditions are requir'd to make Rhyme natural in it self, besides an election of apt words, and a right disposing of them? For the due choice of your words expresses your sence naturally, and the due placing them adapts the rhyme to it. If you object that one verse may be made for the sake of another, though both the words and rhyme be apt; I answer it cannot possibly so fall out; for either there is a dependance of sence betwixt the first line and the second, or there is none: if there be that connection, then in the natural position of the words, the latter line must of necessity flow from the former: if there be no dependance, yet still the due ordering of words makes the last line as natural in it self as the other: so that the necessity of a rhime never forces any but bad or lazy Writers to say what they would not otherwise. 'Tis true, there is both care and Art requir'd to write in Verse; A good Poet never concludes upon the first line, till he has sought out such a rhime as may fit the sense, already prepar'd to heighten the second: many times the close of the sense falls into the middle of the next verse, or farther off, and he may often prevail himself of the same advantages in English which *Virgil* had in Latine, he may break off in the *Hemystich*, and begin another line: indeed, the not observing these two last things, makes Playes which are writ in verse so tedious: for though, most commonly, the sence is to be confin'd to the Couplet, yet nothing that does *perpetuo tenore fluere*,[133] run in the same channel, can please alwayes. 'Tis like the murmuring of a stream, which not varying in the fall, causes at first attention, at last drowsiness. Variety of cadences is the best rule, the greatest help to the Actors, and refreshment to the Audience.

If then Verse may be made natural in it self, how becomes it improper to a Play? You say the Stage is the representation of Nature, and no man in ordinary conversation speaks in rhime. But you foresaw when you said this, that it might be answer'd; neither does any man speak in blank verse, or in measure without rhime. Therefore you concluded, that which is nearest Nature is still to be preferr'd. But you took no notice that rhime might be made as natural as blank verse, by the well placing of the words, &c. all the difference between them when they are both correct, is the sound in one, which the other wants; and if so, the sweetness of it, and all the advantage resulting from it, which are handled in the Preface to the *Rival Ladies*, will yet stand good. As for that place of *Aristotle*, where he sayes Playes should be writ in that kind of Verse which is nearest Prose; it makes little for you, blank verse being properly but measur'd Prose. Now measure alone in any modern Language, does not constitute verse; those of the Ancients in Greek and Latine, consisted in quantity of words, and a determinate number of feet. But when, by the inundation of the *Goths* and *Vandals* into *Italy* new Languages were brought in, and barbarously mingled with the Latine (of which the *Italian*, *Spanish*, *French*, and ours, (made out of them and the *Teutonick*) are Dialects:) a new way of Poesie was practis'd; new, I say in those Countries, for in all probability it was that of the Conquerours in their own Nations.[134] This new way consisted in measure or number of feet and rhyme. The sweetness of Rhyme, and observation of Accent, supplying the place of quantity in words, which could neither exactly be observ'd by those *Barbarians* who knew not the Rules of it, neither was it suitable to their tongues as it had been to the Greek and Latine. No man is tied in modern Poesie to observe any farther rule in the feet of his verse, but that they be dissylables; whether *Spondee*, *Trochee*, or *Iambique*, it matters not; onely he is obliged to rhyme: Neither do the *Spanish*, *French*, *Italian* or *Germans* acknowledge at all, or very rarely any such kind of Poesie as blank verse amongst them. Therefore at most 'tis but a Poetick Prose, *a Sermo pedestris*, and as such most fit for Comedies, where I acknowledge Rhyme to be improper. Farther, as to that quotation of *Aristotle*, our Couplet Verses may be rendred as near Prose as blank verse it self, by using those advantages I lately nam'd, as breaks in a Hemistick, or running the sence into another line, thereby making Art and Order appear as loose and free as Nature: or not tying our selves to Couplets strictly, we may use the benefit of the Pindarique way, practis'd in the Siege of *Rhodes*;[135] where the numbers vary and the rhyme is dispos'd carelesly, and far from often chymeing. Neither is that other advantage of the Ancients to be despis'd, of changing the kind of verse when they please with the change of the Scene, or some new entrance: for they confine not themselves alwayes to Iambiques, but extend their liberty to all Lyrique numbers, and sometimes, even to Hexameter. But I need not go so far to prove that Rhyme, as it succeeds to all other offices of Greek and Latine Verse, so especially to this of Playes, since the custome of all Nations at this day confirms it: All the *French*, *Italian* and *Spanish* Tragedies are generally writ in it, and sure the Universal consent of the most civiliz'd parts of the world, ought in this, as it doth in other customs, include the rest.

But perhaps you may tell me I have propos'd such a way to make rhyme natural, and consequently proper to Playes, as is unpracticable, and that I shall scarce find six or eight lines together in any Play, where the words are so plac'd and chosen as is requir'd to make it natural. I answer, no Poet need constrain himself at all times to it. It is enough he makes it his general Rule; for I deny not but sometimes there may be a greatness in placing the words otherwise; and sometimes they may sound better, sometimes also the variety it self is excuse enough. But if, for the most part, the words be plac'd as they are in the negligence of Prose, it is sufficient to denominate the way practicable; for we esteem that to be such, which in the Tryal oftner succeeds then misses. And thus far you may find the practice made good in many Playes; where you do not, remember still, that if you cannot find six natural Rhymes together, it will be as hard for you to produce as many lines in blank Verse, even among the greatest of our Poets, against which I cannot make some reasonable exception.

And this, Sir, calls to my remembrance the beginning of your discourse, where you told us we should never find the Audience favourable to this kind of writing, till we could produce as good Playes in Rhyme, as *Ben. Johnson, Fletcher,* and *Shakespeare,* had writ out of it. But it is to raise envy to the living, to compare them with the dead. They are honour'd, and almost ador'd by us, as they deserve; neither do I know any so presumptuous of themselves as to contend with them. Yet give me leave to say thus much without injury to their Ashes, that not onely we shall never equal them, but they could never equal themselves, were they to rise and write again. We acknowledge them our Fathers in wit, but they have ruin'd their Estates themselves before they came to their childrens hands. There is scarce an Humour, a Character, or any kind of Plot, which they have not blown upon: all comes sullied or wasted to us: and were they to entertain this Age, they could not make so plenteous treatments out of such decay'd Fortunes. This therefore will be a good Argument to us either not to write at all, or to attempt some other way. There is no bayes to be expected in their Walks; *Tentanda via est quà me quoque possum tollere humo.*[136]

This way of writing in Verse, they have onely left free to us; our age is arriv'd to a perfection in it, which they never knew; and which (if we may guess by what of theirs we have seen in Verse as the *Faithful*

Shepherdess, and *Sad Shepherd*:)[137] 'tis probable they never could have reach'd. For the Genius of every Age is different; and though ours excel in this, I deny not but that to imitate Nature in that perfection which they did in Prose, is a greater commendation then to write in verse exactly. As for what you have added, that the people are not generally inclin'd to like this way; if it were true, it would be no wonder, that betwixt the shaking off an old habit, and the introducing of a new, there should be difficulty. Do we not see them stick to *Hopkins* and *Sternholds* Psalmes, and forsake those of *David*, I mean *Sandys* his Translation of them? If by the people you understand the multitude, the οἱ πολλοί. 'Tis no matter what they think; they are sometimes in the right, sometimes in the wrong; their judgment is a meer Lottery. *Est ubi plebs rectè putat, est ubi peccat.*[138] *Horace* sayes it of the vulgar, judging Poesie. But if you mean the mix'd audience of the populace, and the Noblesse, I dare confidently affirm that a great part of the latter sort are already favourable to verse; and that no serious Playes written since the Kings return have been more kindly receiv'd by them, then the Seige of *Rhodes*, the *Mustapha*, the *Indian* Queen, and *Indian* Emperour.[139]

But I come now to the inference of your first Argument. You said the Dialogue of Playes is presented as the effect of sudden thought, but no man speaks suddenly, or *ex tempore* in Rhyme: And you inferr'd from thence, that Rhyme, which you acknowledge to be proper to Epique Poesie cannot equally be proper to Dramatick, unless we could suppose all men born so much more then Poets, that verses should be made in them, not by them.

It has been formerly urg'd by you, and confess'd by me, that since no man spoke any kind of verse *ex tempore*, that which was nearest Nature was to be preferr'd. I answer you therefore, by distinguishing betwixt what is nearest to the nature of Comedy, which is the imitation of common persons and ordinary speaking, and what is nearest the nature of a serious Play: this last is indeed the representation of Nature, but 'tis Nature wrought up to an higher pitch. The Plot, the Characters, the Wit, the Passions, the Descriptions, are all exalted above the level of common converse, as high as the imagination of the Poet can carry them, with proportion to verisimility. Tragedy we know is wont to image to us the minds and fortunes of noble persons, and to portray these exactly; Heroick Rhime is nearest Nature, as being the noblest kind of modern verse.

> *Indignatur enim privatis, & prope socco.*
> *Dignis carminibus narrari cæna Thyestæ.* (Sayes *Horace.*)

And in another place,

> *Effutire leves indigna tragædia versus.*[140]

Blank Verse is acknowledg'd to be too low for a Poem, nay more, for a paper of verses; but if too low for an ordinary Sonnet, how much more for Tragedy, which is by *Aristotle* in the dispute betwixt the Epique Poesie and the Dramatick; for many reasons he there alledges ranck'd above it.[141]

But setting this defence aside, your Argument is almost as strong against the use of Rhyme in Poems as in Playes; for the Epique way is every where interlac'd with Dialogue, or discoursive Scenes; and therefore you must either grant Rhyme to be improper there, which is contrary to your assertion, or admit it into Playes by the same title which you have given it to Poems. For though Tragedy be justly preferr'd above the other, yet there is a great affinity between them as may easily be discover'd in that definition of a Play which *Lisideius* gave us. The Genus of them is the same, a just and lively Image of humane nature, in its Actions, Passions, and traverses of Fortune: so is the end, namely for the delight and benefit of Mankind. The Characters and Persons are still the same, *viz.* the greatest of both sorts, onely the manner of acquainting us with those Actions, Passions and Fortunes is different. Tragedy performs it *viva voce*, or by action, in Dialogue, wherein it excels the Epique Poem which does it chiefly by narration, and therefore is not so lively an Image of Humane Nature. However, the agreement betwixt them is such, that if Rhyme be proper for one, it must be for the other. Verse 'tis true is not the effect of sudden thought; but this hinders not that sudden thought may be represented in verse, since those thoughts are such as must be higher then Nature can raise them without premeditation, especially to a continuance of them even out of verse, and consequently you cannot imagine them to have been sudden either in the Poet, or the Actors. A Play, as I have said to be like Nature, is to be set above it; as Statues which are plac'd on high are made greater then the life, that they may descend to the sight in their just proportion.

Perhaps I have insisted too long upon this objection; but the clearing of it will make my stay shorter on the rest. You tell us *Crites*, that rhyme appears most unnatural in repartees, or short replyes: when he who answers, (it being presum'd he knew not what the other would say, yet) makes up that part of the verse which was left incompleat, and supplies both the sound and measure of it. This you say looks rather like the confederacy of two, then the answer of one.

This, I confess, is an objection which is in every ones mouth who loves not rhyme: but suppose, I beseech you, the repartee were made onely in blank verse, might not part of the same argument be turn'd against you? for the measure is as often supply'd there as it is in Rhyme. The latter half of the Hemystich as commonly made up, or a second line subjoyn'd as a reply to the former; which any one leaf in *Johnson's* Playes will sufficiently clear to you. You will often find in the Greek Tragedians, and in *Seneca*, that when a Scene grows up into the warmth of repartees (which is the close fighting of it) the latter part of the Trimeter is supply'd by him who answers; and yet it was never observ'd as a fault in them by any of the Ancient or Modern Criticks. The case is the same in our verse as it was in theirs; Rhyme to us being in lieu of quantity to them. But if no latitude is to be allow'd a Poet, you take from him not onely his license of *quidlibet audendi*,[142] but you tie him up in a straighter compass then you would a Philosopher. This is indeed *Musas colere severiores*:[143] You would have him follow Nature, but he must follow her on foot: you have dismounted him from his *Pegasus*. But you tell us this supplying the last half of a verse, or adjoyning a whole second to the former, looks more like the design of two then the answer of one. Suppose we acknowledge it: how comes this confederacy to be more displeasing to you then in a Dance which is well contriv'd? You see there the united design of many persons to make up one Figure: after they have separated themselves in many petty divisions, they rejoyn one by one into a gross: the confederacy is plain amongst them; for chance could never produce any thing so beautiful, and yet there is nothing in it that shocks your sight. I acknowledg the hand of Art appears in repartee, as of necessity it must in all kind of verse. But there is also the quick and poynant brevity of it (which is an high imitation of Nature in those sudden gusts of passion) to mingle with it: and this joyn'd with the cadency and sweetness of the Rhyme, leaves nothing in the soul of the hearer to desire. 'Tis an Art which appears; but it appears onely like the shadowings of Painture, which being to cause the rounding of it, cannot be absent; but while that is consider'd they are lost: so while we attend to the other beauties of the matter, the care and labour of the Rhyme is carry'd from us, or at least drown'd in its own sweetness, as Bees are sometimes bury'd in their Honey. When a Poet has found the repartee, the last perfection he can add to it, is to put it into verse. However good the thought may be; however apt the words in which 'tis couch'd, yet he finds himself at a little unrest while Rhyme is wanting: he cannot leave it till that comes naturally, and then is at ease, and sits down contented.

From Replies, which are the most elevated thoughts of Verse, you pass to the most mean ones: those which are common with the lowest of houshold conversation. In these, you say, the Majesty of Verse suffers. You instance in the calling of a servant, or commanding a door to be shut in rhyme. This, *Crites*, is a good observation of yours, but no argument: for it proves no more but that such thoughts should be wav'd, as often as may be, by the address of the Poet. But suppose they are necessary in the places where he uses them, yet there is no need to put them into rhime. He may place them in the beginning of a Verse, and break it off, as unfit, when so debas'd for any other use: or granting the worst, that they require more room then the Hemystich will allow; yet still there is a choice to be made of the best words, and least vulgar (provided they be apt) to express such thoughts. Many have blam'd Rhyme in general, for this fault, when the Poet, with a little care, might have redress'd it. But they do it with no more justice, then if English Poesie should be made ridiculous for the sake of the Water Poet's Rhymes.[144] Our language is noble, full and significant; and I know not why he who is Master of it may not cloath ordinary things in it as decently as the Latine; if he use the same diligence in his choice of words.

Delectus verborum Origo est Eloquentiæ.[145]

It was the saying of *Julius Cæsar*, one so curious in his, that none of them can be chang'd but for a worse. One would think unlock the door was a thing as vulgar as could be spoken; and yet *Seneca* could make it sound high and lofty in his Latine. –

Reserate clusos Regii postes Laris.[146]

But I turn from this exception, both because it happens not above twice or thrice in any Play that those vulgar thoughts are us'd; and then too (were there no other Apology to be made, yet) the necessity of them (which is alike in all kind of writing) may excuse them.[147] Besides that the great eagerness and præcipitation with which they are spoken makes us rather mind the substance then the dress; that for which they are spoken, rather then what is spoke. For they are alwayes the effect of some hasty concernment, and something of consequence depends upon them.

Thus, *Crites*, I have endeavour'd to answer your objections; it remains onely that I should vindicate an Argument for Verse, which you have gone about to overthrow. It had formerly been said, that the easiness of blank verse, renders the Poet too luxuriant; but that the labour of Rhyme bounds and circumscribes an over-fruitful fancy, The sence there being commonly confin'd to the couplet, and the words so order'd that the Rhyme naturally follows them, not they the Rhyme. To this you answer'd, that it was no Argument to the question in hand, for the dispute was not which way a man may write best: but which is most proper for the subject on which he writes.

First, give me leave, Sir, to remember you that the Argument against which you rais'd this objection, was onely secondary: it was built upon this *Hypothesis*, that to write in verse was proper for serious Playes. Which supposition being granted (as it was briefly made out in that discourse, by showing how verse might be made natural) it asserted, that this way of writing was an help to the Poets judgment, by putting bounds to a wilde overflowing Fancy. I think therefore it will not be hard for me to make good what it was to prove: But you add, that were this let pass, yet he who wants judgment in the liberty of his fancy, may as well show the defect of it when he is confin'd to verse: for he who has judgment will avoid errours, and he who has it not, will commit them in all kinds of writing.

This Argument, as you have taken it from a most acute person,[148] so I confess it carries much weight in it. But by using the word Judgment here indefinitely, you seem to have put a fallacy upon us: I grant he who has Judgment, that is, so profound, so strong, so infallible a judgment, that he needs no helps to keep it alwayes pois'd and upright, will commit no faults either in rhyme or out of it. And on the other extream, he who has a judgment so weak and craz'd that no helps can correct or amend it, shall write scurvily out of Rhyme, and worse in it. But the first of these judgments is no where to be found, and the latter is not fit to write at all. To speak therefore of judgment as it is in the best Poets; they who have the greatest proportion of it, want other helps than from it within. As for example, you would be loth to say, that he who was indued with a sound judgment had no need of History, Geography, or Moral Philosophy, to write correctly. Judgment is indeed the Master-workman in a Play: but he requires many subordinate hands, many tools to his assistance. And Verse I affirm to be one of these: 'Tis a Rule and line by which he keeps his building compact and even, which otherwise lawless imagination would raise either irregularly or loosly. At least if the Poet commits errours with this help, he would make greater and more without it: 'tis (in short) a slow and painfull, but the surest kind of working. *Ovid* whom you accuse for luxuriancy in Verse, had perhaps been farther guilty of it had he writ in Prose. And for your instance of *Ben. Johnson*, who you say, writ exactly without the help of Rhyme; you are to remember 'tis onely an aid to a luxuriant Fancy, which his was not: As he did not want imagination, so none ever said he had much to spare. Neither was verse then refin'd so much to be an help to that Age as it is to ours. Thus then the second thoughts being usually the best, as receiving the maturest digestion from judgment, and the last and most mature product of those thoughts being artful and labour'd verse, it may well be inferr'd, that verse is a great help to a luxuriant Fancy, and this is what that Argument which you oppos'd was to evince.

Neander was pursuing this Discourse so eagerly, that *Eugenius* had call'd to him twice or thrice ere he took notice that the Barge stood still, and that they were at the foot of *Somerset*-Stairs, where they had appointed it to land. The company were all sorry to separate so soon, though a great part of the evening was already spent; and stood a while looking back upon the water, which the Moon-beams play'd upon, and made it appear like floating quick-silver: at last they went up through a crowd of French people who were merrily dancing in the open air, and nothing concern'd for the noise of Guns which had allarm'd the Town that afternoon. Walking thence together to the *Piazze*[149] they parted there; *Eugenius* and *Lysideius* to some pleasant appointment they had made, and *Crites* and *Neander* to their several Lodgings.

FINIS.

Sir Robert Howard,
'Preface' to *The Great Favourite*
(1668)

I CANNOT plead the usual excuse for publishing this trifle, which is commonly the Subject of most Prefaces; by charging it upon the importunity of friends; for, I confess, I was my selfe willing, at the first desire of Mr. *Herringman* to print it; not for any great opinion that I had entertain'd; but for the opinion that others were pleas'd to express: which being told me by some friends, I was concern'd to let the World judge what subject matter of offence was contain'd in it: some were pleas'd to believe, little of it mine: but they are both obliging to me; though perhaps not intentionally; the last, by thinking there was any thing in it that was worth so ill design'd an Envy, as to place it to another Author; the others (perhaps the best bred Informers) by continuing their displeasure towards me, since I most gratefully acknowledge to have received some advantage in the opinion of the sober part of the World, by the loss of theirs.

For the Subject, I came accidentally to write upon it; for a Gentleman brought a Play to the Kings Company, call'd, *The Duke of* Lerma;[1] and by them I was desir'd to peruse it, and return my opinion whether I thought it fit for the Stage; after I had read it, I acquainted them, that in my judgement it would not be of much use for such a design, since the contrivance, scarce would merit the name of a plot; and some of that, assisted by a disguise; and it ended abruptly: and on the Person of *Philip* the 3. there was fixt such a mean Character, and on the Daughter of the Duke of *Lerma*, such a vitious one, that I cou'd not but judge it unfit to be presented by any that had a respect, not only to Princes, but indeed to either Man or Woman; and about that time, being to go into the Countrey, I was perswaded by Mr. *Hart* to make it my diversion there that so great a hint might not be lost, as the Duke of *Lerma* saving himself in his last extremity, by his unexpected disguise, which is as well in the true story as the old Play; and besides that and the Names, my altering the most part of the Characters, and the whole design, made me uncapable to use much more; though perhaps written with higher Stile and Thoughts, than I cou'd attain to.

I intend not to trouble myself nor the World any more in such Subjects, but take my leave of these my too long acquaintances; since that little fancy and liberty I once enjoy'd, is now fetter'd in business of more unpleasant Natures; yet were I free to apply my thoughts as my own choice directed them; I should hardly again venter into the Civil Wars of Censures.

Ubi – Nullos habitura Triumphos.[2]

In the next place, I must ingeniously confess, that the manner of Plays which now are in most esteem, is beyond my pow'r to perform; nor do I condemn in the least any thing of what Nature soever that pleases; since nothing cou'd appear to me a ruder folly, than to censure the satisfaction of others; I rather blame the unnecessary understanding of some that have labour'd to give strict rules to things that are not Mathematical, and with such eagerness, persuing their own seeming reasons, that at last we are to apprehend such Argumentative Poets will grow as strict as *Sancho Pancos* Doctor[3] was to our very Appetites; for in the difference of *Tragedy* and *Comedy*, and of *Fars* it self, there can be no determination but by the Taste; nor in the manner of their Composure; and who ever wou'd endeavour to like or dislike by the Rules of others, he will be as unsuccessful, as if he should try to be perswaded into a power of believing; not what he must, but what others direct him to believe.

But I confess, 'tis not necessary for Poets to study strict reason, since they are so us'd to a greater Latitude then is allow'd by that severe Inquisition; that they must infringe their own Jurisdiction, to profess themselves oblig'd to argue well: I will not therefore pretend to say, why I writ this Play, some Scenes in blank Verse, others in Rhime, since I have no better a reason to give then Chance, which waited upon my present Fancy; and I expect no better a reason from any ingenious person, then his Fancy for which he best relishes.

I cannot therefore but beg leave of the Reader, to take a little notice of the great pains the Author of an Essay of Drammatick Poesie has taken, to prove Rhime as natural in a serious Play, and more effectual than blank Verse: thus he states the question, but persues that which he calls Natural in a wrong Application; for 'tis not the question, whether Rhime or not Rhime, be best, or most Natural for a grave and serious Subject; but what is neerest the nature of that which it presents. Now after all the endeavours of that ingenious Person, a Play will still be supposed to be a Composition of several Persons speaking, *ex tempore*; and 'tis as certain, that good Verses are the hardest things that can be imagin'd to be so spoken; so that if any will be pleas'd to impose the rule of measuring things to be the best, by being nearest Nature; it is granted by consequence, that which is most remote from the thing supposed, must needs be most improper; and therefore I may justly say, that both I and the question were equally mistaken, for I do own, I had rather read good Uerses, then either blank Verse or Prose, and therefore the Author did himself injury, if he like Verse so well in Plays, to lay down rules to raise Arguments, only unanswerable against himself.

But the same Author being fill'd with the presidents of the Antients writing their Plays in Verse, commends the thing, and assures us, that our Language is Noble, Full, and Significant; charging all defects upon the ill placing of words, and proves it by quoting *Seneca*, loftily expressing such an ordinary thing as shutting a door.

Reserate Clusos Regii postes Laris.[4]

I suppose he was himself highly affected with the sound of these words; but to have Compleated his Dictates together with his Arguments, he should have oblig'd us, by charming our Eares with such an Art of placing words, as in an English Verse to express so loftily the shutting of a Door, that we might have been as much affected with the sound of his words; this, in stead of being an argument upon the question rightly stated, is an attempt, to prove that nothing may seeme something, by the help of a Verse, which I easily grant to be the ill-fortune of it; and therefore the question being so much mistaken, I wonder to see that Author trouble himself twice about it, with such an absolute triumph declared by his own imagination: But I have heard that a Gentleman in Parliament going to speak twice, and being interrupted by another Member, as against the Orders of the House, he was excused by a third, assuring the House he had not yet spoken to the Question.

But if we examine the general rules laid down for Playes by strict Reason, we shall find the errors equally gross; for the great foundation that is laid to build upon is nothing, as it is generally stated; which will appear upon the examination of the particulars.

First, We are told the Plot should not be so rediculously contriv'd, as to crowd two several Countries into one stage; secondly, to cramp the Accidents of many years or dayes into the representation of two houres and a halfe: And Lastly, a Conclusion drawn, that the only remaining dispute is concerning time, whether it should be contain'd in twelve, or four and twenty hours, and the place to be limited to the spot of ground, either in Town or City, where the Play is suppos'd to begin; And this is call'd neerest to Nature: For that is concluded most natural, which is most probable, and neerest to that which it presents.

I am so well pleas'd with any ingenuous offers, as all these are, that I should not examine this strictly, did not the confidence of others force me to it; there being not any thing more unreasonable to my Judgment, then the attempt to infringe the Liberty of Opinion by Rules so little demonstrative.

To shew therefore upon what ill grounds they dictate Lawes for *Dramatick Poesie*, I shall endeavour to make it evident, that there's no such thing as what they all pretend; for, if strictly and duely weigh'd, 'tis as impossible for one stage to present two Houses, or two Roomes truely, as two Countreys or Kingdomes; and as impossible that five houres, or four and twenty houres should be two houres and a halfe, as that a thousand houres or yeares should be less then what they are; or the greatest part of time to be comprehended in the less; for all being impossible, they are none of them nearest the truth, or nature, of what they present, for Impossibilities are all equal, and admit no degrees: and then if all those Poets that have so fervently labour'd to give Rules as Maximes, would but be pleased to abreviate, or endure to hear their Reasons reduc't into one strict definition, it must be, that there are degrees in impossibilities, and that many things which are not possible, may yet be more or less impossible; and from this pro- ceed to give rules to observe the least absurdity in things which are not at all.[5]

I suppose I need not trouble the Reader with so impertinent a delay to attempt a farther Confutation of such ill-grounded reasons, then thus by opening the true state of the Case, nor do I design to make any farther use of it, then from hence to draw this modest Conclusion, That I would have all attempts of this nature be submitted to the fancy of others, and bear the name of Propositions, not of Confident Lawes, or Rules made by Demonstration; and then I shall not discom- mend any Poet that dresses his Play in such a fashion as his fancy best approves; and fairly leave it for others to follow, if it appears to them most convenient, and fullest of ornament.

But writing this Epistle in so much haste, I had almost forgot one Argument, or Observation, which that Author has most good fortune in; It is in his *Epistle Dedicatory*, before his *Essay* of *Dramaticke Poesie*; where, speaking of Rhyme in Playes, he desires it may be observ'd, That none are violent against it, but such as have not attempted it, or who have succeeded ill in the attempt; which as to my self and him I easily acknowledge; for I confess none has written in that way better then himself, nor few worse than I: Yet, I hope, he is so ingenuous, that he would not wish this Argument should extend further then to him and me; for if it should be received as a good one, all *Divines* and *Philosophers*, would find a readier way of Confutation then they yet have done, of any that should oppose the least Thesis or Definition, by saying, they were denied by none but such as never attempted to write, or succeeded ill in the attempt.

Thus as I am one that am extreamly well pleas'd with most of the *Propositions*, which are ingeniously laid down in that Essay for regulating the Stage; so I am also alwayes Concern'd for the true honour of reason, and would have no spurious issue Father'd upon her. Fancy may be allow'd her wantonness; but reason is alwayes pure and chast: and as it resembles the Sun, in making all things clear, it also resembles it in its several positions, when it shines in full height and directly ascendant over any Subject, it leaves but little shaddow; But when descended and grown low, its oblique shining renders the shaddow larger then the substance, and gives the deceiv'd person a wrong measure of his own proportion.

Thus begging the *Readers* Excuse for this seeming Impertinency, I submit what I have written to the liberty of his unconfin'd Opinion, which is all the favour I ask of others to afford to me.[6]

Thomas Shadwell,
'Preface' to *The Humorists*
(1671)

This Play (besides the Errors in the writing of it) came upon the Stage with all the disadvantages imaginable: First, I was forced, after I had finish'd it, to blot out the main design of it; finding that, contrary to my intention, it had given offence. The second disadvantage was, that notwithstanding I had (to the great prejudice of the Play) given satisfaction to all the exceptions made against it, it met with the clamorous opposition of a numerous party, bandied against it, and resolved, as much as they could to damn it, right or wrong, before they had heard or seen a word on't. The last, and not the least, was, that the *Actors* (though since they have done me some right) at first were extreamly imperfect in the Action of it. The least of these had been enough to have spoil'd a very good Comedy, much more such a one as mine. The last (*viz.*) imperfect Action, had like to have destroyd *She would if she could*,[1] which I think (and I have the Authority of some of the best Judges in *England* for't) is the best Comedy that has been written since the Restauration of the Stage: And even that, for the imperfect representation of it at first, received such prejudice, that, had it not been for the favour of the *Court*, in all probability it had never got up again; and it suffers for it, in a great measure, to this very day. This of mine, after all these blows, had fallen beyond redemption, had it not been revived, after the second day, by her kindness (which I can never enough acknowledge) who, for four days together, beautified it with the most excellent *Dancings* that ever has been seen upon the Stage. This drew my enemies, as well as friends, till it was something better acted, understood, and liked, than at first. By this means the poor Play's life was prolonged, and, I hope, will live in spight of Malice; if not upon the Stage, at least in Print.

Yet do not think I will defend all the faults of it: Before it was alter'd, I could better have answer'd for it: yet, as it is, I hope it will not wholly displease you in the reading. I should not say so much for it, if I did not find so much undeserved malice against it.

My design was in it, to reprehend some of the Vices and Follies of the Age, which I take to be the most proper, and most useful way of writing Comedy. If I do not perform this well enough, let not my endeavors be blam'd.

Here I must take leave to Dissent from those, who seem to insinuate that the ultimate end of a Poet is to delight, without correction or instruction:[2] Methinks a Poet should never acknowledge this, for it makes him of as little use to Mankind as a Fidler, or Dancing Master, who delights the fancy onely, without improving the Judgement.

Horace, the best judge of Poetry, found other business for a Poet

> *Pectus præceptis format amicis,*
> *Asperitatis & Invidiæ, corrector, & Iræ,*
> *Recte facta refert, orientia tempora notis*
> *Instruit Exemplis:*[3]

I confess a Poet ought to do all that he can, decently to please, that so he may instruct. To adorn his Images of *Vertue* so delightfully to affect people with a secret veneration of it in others, and an emulation to practice it in themselves: And to render their Figures of *Vice* and *Folly* so ugly and detestable, to make people hate and despise them, not onely in others, but (if it be possible) in their dear selves. And in this latter I think Comedy more useful than Tragedy; because the Vices and Follies in *Courts* (as they are too tender to be touch'd) so they concern but a few; whereas the Cheats, Villanies, and troublesome Follies, in the common conversation of the World, are of concernment to all the Body of Mankind.

And a Poet can no more justly be censured for ill nature, in detesting such *Knaveries*, and troublesome impertinencies as are an imposition on all good men, and a disturbance of Societies in general, than the most vigilant of our Judges can be thought so, for detesting Robbers and High-way-men; who are hanged, not for the sake of the money they take (for of what value can that be to the life of a man) but for interrupting common communication, and disturbing Society in general. For the sake of good men ill should be punished; and 'tis ill nature to the first, not to punish the last. A man cannot truly love a good man, that does not hate a bad one; nor a Wiseman, that does not hate a Fool; this love and hatred are correlatives, and the one necessarily implies the other. I must confess it were ill nature, and below a man, to fall upon the natural imperfections of men, as of Lunaticks, Ideots, or men born monstrous. But these can never be made the proper subject of a Satyr, but the affected vanities, and artificial fopperies of men, which (sometimes even contrary to their natures) they take pains to acquire, are the proper subject of a Satyr.

As for the reformation of Fopps and Knaves, I think Comedy most useful, because to render Vices and Fopperies very ridiculous, is much a greater punishment than Tragedy can inflict upon 'em. There we do but subject 'em to hatred, or at worst to death; here we make them live to be despised and laugh'd at, which certainly makes more impression upon men, than even death can do.

Again, I confess a Poet ought to endeavour to please, and by this way of writing may please, as well as by any way whatsoever, (if he writes it well) when he does

Simul & Jucunda & idonea dicere vitæ.[4]

Men of Wit and Honour, and the best Judges (and such as cannot be touch'd by Satyr) are extreamly delighted with it; and for the rest

Odi profanum vulgus & Arceo.[5]

The rabble of little people, are more pleas'd with *Jack Puddings* being soundly kick'd, or having a Custard handsomely thrown in his face, than with all the wit in Plays: and the higher sort of Rabble (as there may be a rabble of very fine people in this illiterate age) are more pleased with the extravagant and unnatural actions, the trifles, and fripperies of a Play, or the trappings and ornaments of Nonsense, than with all the wit in the world.

This is one reason why we put our Fopps into extravagant, and unnatural habits; it being a cheap way of conforming to the understanding of those brisk, gay Sparks, that judge of Wit or Folly by the Habit; that being indeed the onely measure they can take in judging of Mankind, who are Criticks in nothing but a Dress.

Extraordinary pleasure was taken of old, in the Habits of the Actors, without reference to sense, which *Horace* observes, and reprehends in his Epistle to *Augustus*

> *Garganum mugire putes nemus, aut Mare Tuscum,*
> *Tanto cum strepitu ludi spectantur, & Artes,*
> *Divitiæque peregrinæ, quibus oblitus actor,*
> *Cum stetit in scena, concurrit dextera Lævæ,*
> *Dixit adhuc aliquid! nil sane, quid placet ergo?*[26]

But for a Poet to think (without wit or good humor, under such a Habit) to please men of sense, is a presumption inexcusable. If I be guilty of this, it is an error of my understanding, not of my will. But I challenge the most clamorous and violent of my Enemies (who would have the Town believe that every thing I write, is too nearly reflecting upon persons) to accuse me, with truth, of representing the real actions, or using the peculiar, affected phrases, or manner of speech of any particular Man, or Woman living.

I cannot indeed create a new Language, but the Phantastick Phrases, used in any Play of mine, are not appropriate to any one *Fop*, but applicable to many.

Good men, and men of sence, can never be represented but to their advantage, nor can the Characters of Fools, Knaves, Whores, or Cowards (who are the people I deal most with in Comedies) concern any that are not eminently so: Nor will any apply to themselves what I write in this kind, that have but the wit, or honesty, to think tolerably well of themselves.

But it has been objected, that good men, and men of sence enough, may have blind-sides, that are liable to reprehension, and that such men should be represented upon a Stage, is intollerable.

'Tis true, excellent men may have errors, but they are not known by them, but by their excellencies: their prudence overcomes all gross follies, or conceals the less vanities, that are unavoidable Concomitants of humane nature; or if some little errors do escape 'em, and are known, they are the least part of those men, and they are not distinguished in the world by them, but by their perfections; so that (if such blind-sides or errors be represented) they do not reflect upon them, but upon such on whom these are predominant; and that receive such a Bias from 'em, that it turns 'em wholly from the wayes of wisdom or Morality.

And, even this representation, does not reflect upon any particular man, but upon very many of the same kind: For if a man should bring such a humor upon the Stage (if there be such a humor in the world) as onely belongs to one, or two persons, it would not be understood by the Audience, but would be thought (for the singularity of it) wholly unnatural, and would be no jest to them neither.

But I have had the fortune to have had a general humor (in a Play of mine) applied to three, or four men (whose persons I never saw, or humors ever heard of till the Play was acted).

As long as men wrest the Writings of Poets to their own corrupted sense, and with their Clamors prevail too, you must never look for a good Comedy of Humor, for a humor (being the representation of some extravagance of Mankind) cannot but in some thing resemble some man, or other, or it is monstrous, and unnatural.

After this restraint upon Poets, there is little scope left, unless we retrieve the exploded Barbarismes of Fool, Devil, Giant, or Monster, or translate French Farces, which, with all the wit of the English, added to them, can scarce be made tollerable.

Mr. *Johnson*, I believe, was very unjustly taxed for personating particular men,[7] but it will ever be the fate of them, that write the humors of the *Town*, especially in a foolish, and vicious Age. Pardon me (*Reader*) that I name him in the same page with my self; who pretend to nothing more, than to joyn with all men of sense and learning in admiration of him; which, I think, I do not out of a true understanding of him; and for this I cannot but value my self. Yet, by extolling his way of writing, I would not insinuate to you that I can practise it; though I would if I could, a thousand times sooner than any mans.

And here I must make a little digression, and take liberty to dissent from my particular friend,[8] for whom I have a very great respect, and whose Writings I extreamly admire; and though I will not say his is the best way of writing, yet, I am sure, his manner of writing it is much the best that ever was. And I may say of him, as was said of a Celebrated Poet, *Cui unquam Poetarum magis proprium fuit subito æstro incalescere? Quis, ubi incaluit, fortius, & fælicius debacchatur.*[9] His Verse is smoother and deeper, his thoughts more quick and surprising, his raptures more mettled and higher; and he has more of that in his writing, which *Plato* calls σώφρονα μανίαν,[10] than any other Heroick Poet. And those who shall go about to imitate him, will be found to flutter, and make a noise, but never rise. Yet (after all this) I cannot think it impudence in him, or any man to endeavour to imitate Mr. *Johnson*, whom he confesses to have fewer failings than all the English Poets, which implies he was the most perfect, and best Poet; and why should not we endeavour to imitate him? because we cannot arrive to his excellence? 'Tis true we cannot, but this is no more an argument, than for a Soldier (who considers with himself he cannot be so great a one as *Julius Cæsar*) to run from his Colours, and be none; or to speak of a less thing, why should any man study *Mathematicks* after *Archimedes*, *&c*. This Principle would be an obstruction to the progress of all learning and knowledge in the world. Men of all Professions ought certainly to follow the best in theirs, and let not their endeavours be blamed, if they go as far as they can in the right way, though they be unsuccessful and attain not their ends. If Mr. *Johnson* be the most faultless Poet, I am so far from thinking it impudence to endeavour to imitate him, that it would rather (in my opinion) seem impudence in me not to do it.

I cannot be of their opinion who think he wanted wit, I am sure, if he did, he was so far from being the most faultless, that he was the most faulty Poet of his time, but it may be answered, that his Writings were correct, though he wanted fire; but I think flat and dull things are as incorrect, and shew as little Judgment in the Author, nay less, than sprightly and mettled Nonsense does. But I think he had more true wit than any of his Contemporaries; that other men had sometimes things that seemed more fiery than his, was because they were placed with so many sordid and mean things about them, that they made a greater show.

> *Inter quæ verbum emicuit, si fortè, decorum,*
> *Si versus paulo concinnior, unus, & alter,*
> *Injuste totum ducit, venditque Poema.*[11]

Nor can I think, to the writing of his humors (which were not onely the follies, but vices and subtleties of men) that wit was not required, but judgment; where, by the way, they speak as if judgment were a less thing than wit. But certainly it was meant otherwise by nature, who subjected wit to the government of judgment, which is the noblest faculty of the mind. Fancy rough-draws, but judgement smooths and finishes; nay, judgment does in deed comprehend wit, for no man can have that who has not wit. In fancy mad men equal, if not excel all others, and one may as well say that one of those mad men is as good a man as a temperate wiseman, as that one of the very fancyful Plays (admired most by Women) can be so good a Play as one of *Johnson's* correct, and well-govern'd Comedies.

The reason given by some, why *Johnson* needed not wit in writing humor, is, because humor is the effect of observation, and observation the effect of judgment; but observation is as much necessary in all other Plays, as in Comedies of humor: For first, even in the highest Tragedies, where the Scene lies in Courts, the Poet must have observed the Customs of Courts, and the manner of conversing there, or he will commit many indecencies, and make his Persons too rough and ill-bred for a Court.

Besides Characters in Plays being representations of the Vertues or Vices, Passions or Affections of Mankind, since there are no more new Vertues, or Vices; Passions or Affections, the Idea's of these can no other way be received into the imagination of a Poet, but either from the Conversation or Writings of Men. After a Poet has formed a Character (as suppose of an Ambitious Man) his design is certainly to write it naturally, and he has no other rule to guid him in this, but to compare him with other men of that kind, that either he has heard of, or conversed with in the world, or read of in Books (and even this reading of Books is conversing with men) nay, more; (besides judging of his Character) the Poet can fancy nothing of it, but what must spring from the Observation he has made of Men, or Books.

If this argument (that the enemies of humor use) be meant in this sense, that a Poet, in the writing of a Fools Character, needs but have a man sit to him, and have his words and actions taken; in this case there is no need of wit. But 'tis most certain, that if we should do so, no one fool (though the best about the Town) could appear pleasantly upon the Stage, he would be there too dull a Fool, and must be helped out with a great deal of wit in the Author. I scruple not to call it so, first, because 'tis not your down-right Fool that is a fit Character for a Play, but like Sir *John Dawe* and Sir *Amorous la Foole*[12] your witty, brisk, aiery *Fopps*, that are *Entreprennants*. Besides, wit in the Writer (I think, without any Authority for it) may be said to be the invention of remote and pleasant thoughts of what kind soever; and there is as much occasion for such imaginations in the writing of a Curious Coxcomb's part, as in writing the greatest Hero's; and that which may be folly in the Speaker, may be so remote and pleasant, to require a great deal of wit in the Writer. The most Excellent *Johnson* put wit into the mouths of the meanest of his people, and which, is infinitely difficult, made it proper for 'em. And I once heard a Person, of the greatest Wit and Judgement of the Age, say, that *Bartholomew Fair* (which consists most of low persons) is one of the Wittiest Plays in the World. If there be no wit required in the rendering Folly ridiculous, or Vice odious, we must accuse *Juvenal* the best Satyrist, and wittiest Man of all the Latine Writers, for want of it.

I should not say so much of Mr. *Johnson* (whose Merit sufficiently justifies him to all Men of Sense) but that I think my self a little obliged to vindicate the Opinion I publickly declared, in my *Epilogue* to this Play; which I did upon mature consideration, and with a full satisfaction in my Judgement, and not out of a bare affected vanity in being thought his Admirer.

I have onely one word more, to trouble you with, concerning this Trifle of my own, which is, that, as it is at present, it is wholly my own, without borrowing a tittle from any man; which I confess is too bold an attempt for so young a Writer; for (let it seem what it will) a Comedy of humor (that is not borrowed) is the hardest thing to write well; and a way of writing, of which a man can never be certain.

> *Creditur, ex medio quia res accessit, habere*
> *Sudoris minimum, sed habet comœdia tanto*
> *Plus oneris, quanto veniæ minus.*[13]

That which (besides judging truly of Mankind) makes Comedy more difficult, is that the faults are naked and bare to most people, but the wit of it understood, or valued, but by few. Wonder not then if a man of ten times my parts, miscarries in the Attempt.

I shall say no more of this of mine, but that the Humors are new (how well chosen I leave to you to judge) and all the words and actions of the Persons in the Play, are alwayes sutable to the Characters I have given of them; and, in all the Play, I have gone according to that definition of humor, which I have given you in my *Epilogue*, in these words:

> *A Humor is the Biasse of the Mind,*
> *By which, with violence, 'tis one way inclin'd.*
> *It makes our actions lean on one side still,*
> *And, in all Changes, that way bends the Will.*

Vale.

II
Poetical Correctness,
1682–1701

Buckingham,
An Essay Upon Poetry
(1682)

OF Things in which Mankind does most excell,
Nature's chief Master-piece is writing well;
And of all sorts of Writing none there are
That can the least with *Poetry* compare;
No kind of work requires so nice a touch,
And if well done, there's nothing shines so much;
But Heav'n forbid we should be so prophane,
To grace the vulgar with that sacred name;
'Tis not a Flash of Fancy which sometimes
10   Dasling our Minds, sets off the slightest Rimes,
Bright as a blaze, but in a moment done;
True Wit is everlasting, like the Sun;
Which though sometimes beneath a cloud retir'd,
Breaks out again, and is by all admir'd.
Number, and Rime, and that harmonious sound,
Which never does the Ear with harshness wound,
Are necessary, yet but vulgar Arts,
For all in vain these superficial parts
Contribute to the structure of the whole
20   Without a Genius too, for that's the Soul;
A Spirit which inspires the work throughout,
As that of Nature moves this World about;
A heat that glows in every word that's writ,
That's something of Divine, and more than Wit;
It self unseen, yet all things by it shown
Describing all men, but describ'd by none;

Where dost thou dwell? what caverns of the Brain
Can such a vast and mighty thing contain?
When I at idle hours in vain thy absence mourn,
30   O where dost thou retire? and why dost thou return,
Sometimes with powerful charms to hurry me away
From pleasures of the night, and business of the day?
Ev'n now too far transported I am fain
To check thy course, and use the needfull rein;
As all is dullness, when the Fancy's bad,
So without Judgment, Fancy is but mad;
And Judgment has a boundless influence;
Not upon words alone, or only sence,
But on the world, of manners, and of men,
40   Fancy is but the Feather of the Pen;
Reason is that substantial useful part,
Which gains the Head, while t'other wins the Heart.

Here I should all the differing kinds reherse
Of *Poetry* with various sorts of Verse;
But who that task can after *Horace* do?
That mighty Master and Example too?
Ecchoes at best; all we can say is vain,
Dull the design, and fruitless were the pain;
'Tis true, the Ancients we may rob with ease,
50   But who with that sad shift himself can please,
Without an Actor's pride? a Players Art
Is more than his who writes the borrow'd part.
Yet modern Laws are made for later Faults,
And new Absurdities inspire new thoughts;
What need has *Satyr* then to live on theft,
When so much fresh occasion still is left?
Folly abounds, nay flourishes at Court,
Where on its sphere it finds a kind support;
But hold, *White-Hall* has nothing now to fear,
60   'Tis Wit and Sence that is the Subject here.

98

Defects of witty Men deserve a Cure,
And those who are so, will the worst endure.

    First then of *Songs*, that now so much abound,
Without his Song no Fop is to be found,
A most offensive Weapon which he draws,
On all he meets, against *Apollo's* Laws:
Though nothing seems more easy, yet no part
Of Poetry requires a nicer Art;
For as in rows of richest Pearl there lyes
70   Many a blemish that escapes our Eyes,
The least of which Defects is plainly shewn
In some small Ring, and brings the value down;
So Songs should be to just perfection wrought,
Yet where can we see one without a fault;
Exact propriety of words and thought?
Th' expression easy, and the fancy high,
Yet that not seem to creep, nor this to fly;
No words transpos'd, but in such just cadance,
As, though hard wrought, may seem the effect of chance;
80   Here, as in all things else, is most unfit
Bawdry barefac'd, that poor pretence to Wit;
Such nauseous Songs as the late Convert[1] made,
Which justly call this censure on his Shade;
Not that warm thoughts of the transporting joy,
Can shock the Chastest, or the Nicest cloy;
But obscene words, too gross to move desire,
Like heaps of Fuel do but choak the Fire.
That Author's Name has undeserved praise,
Who pall'd the appetite he meant to raise.

90   Next, *Elegie*, of sweet but solemn voice,
And of a Subject grave, exacts the choice,
The Praise of Beauty, Valour, Wit contains,
And there too oft despairing Love complains.

In vain alas, for who by Wit is moved?
That Phoenix-she deserves to be beloved.
But Noisy Nonsence, and such Fops as vex
Mankind, take most with that fantastick Sex.
This to the praise of those who better know,
The many raise the value of the few.
100 But here, as I too oft alas have tryed,
Women have drawn my wandring thoughts aside.
Their greatest fault, who in this kind have writ,
Is neither want of words, nor dearth of wit;
But though this Muse harmonious numbers yield,
And every Couplet be with fancy fill'd;
If yet a just coherence be not made
Between each thought, and the whole model layed
So right, that every step may higher rise,
As in a Ladder, till it reach the Skies;
110 Trifles like these perhaps of late have past,
And may be lik'd awhile, but never last;
'Tis Epigram, 'tis Point, 'tis what you will,
But not an Elegie, nor writ with skill,
No *Panegyrick**, nor a *Coopers-Hill*.²   *Wallers.

A higher flight and of a happier force,
Are *Odes*, the Muses most unruly Horse;
That bounds so fierce, the Rider has no rest,
But foams at mouth, and speaks like one possest.
The Poet here must be indeed Inspired,
120 And not with fancy, but with fury fired.
Cowley might boast to have perform'd this part,
Had he with Nature joyn'd the rules of Art:
But ill expression gives too great Allay
To that rich Fancy, which can ne're decay.
Though all appears in heat and fury done,
The Language still must soft and easy run.
These Laws may seem a little too severe,
But Judgment yields, and Fancy governs there;

Which, though extravagant, this Muse allows,
130 And makes the work much easier than it shews.

Of all the ways that Wisest Men could find
To mend the Age, and mortify Mankind,
Satyr well writ has most successful prov'd,
And cures, because the remedy is lov'd.
'Tis hard to write on such a Subject more,
Without repeating things said oft before.
Some vulgar Errors only Lets remove,
That stain this Beauty, which we chiefly love.
Of well-chose words some take not care enough,
140 And think they may be as the Subject rough.
This great work must be more exactly made,
And sharpest thoughts in smoothest words convey'd:
Some think if sharp enough, they cannot fail,
As if their only business was to rail;
But 'tis mens *Foibles* nicely to unfold,
Which makes a Satyr different from a Scold.
Rage you must hide, and prejudice lay down,
A Satyr's Smile is sharper than his Frown.
So while you seem to scorn some Rival Youth,
150 Malice it self may pass sometimes for Truth.
The Laureat here may justly claim our praise,
Crown'd by *Mac-Fleckno* with immortal Bays;
Though prais'd and punish'd for another's Rimes,[3]
His own deserve that glorious fate sometimes;
Were he not forc'd to carry now dead weight,
Rid by some Lumpish Minister of State.

Here rest my Muse, suspend thy cares awhile,
A greater Enterprize attends thy toil;
And as some Eagle that intends to fly
160 A long and tedious Journy through the Sky,
Considers first the perils of her case,
Over what Lands and Seas she is to pass;

Doubts her own strength so far, and justly fears
That lofty Road of Airy Travellers;
But yet incited by some great design,
That does her hopes beyond her fears incline,
Prunes every feather, views her self with care,
Then on a sudden flounces in the Air.
Away she flies so strong, so high, so fast,
170   She lessens to us, and is lost at last.
So greater things my Muse prepares to sing,
Things that will Malice, and may Envy bring;
Yet why should Truth offend, when only told
T' inform the Ignorant, and warn the Bold?
On then, my Muse, adventrously engage
To give Instructions that concern the Stage.
The *Unites* of Action, Time, and Place,
Which, if observed, give Plays so great a grace,
Are, though but little practis'd, too well known
180   To be taught here, where we pretend alone
From nicer faults to purge the present Age,
Less obvious Errors of the *English* Stage.

   First then, *Soliloquies* had need be few,
Extreamly short, and spoke in passion too.
Our Lovers talking to themselves, for want
Of others, make the Pit their Confidant;
Nor is the matter mended much, if thus
They trust a friend only to tell it us.
Th' occasion should as naturally fall,
190   As when *Bellario*[4] confesses all.

   Figures of *Speech*, which Poets think so fine,
Art's needless Varnish to make Nature shine,
Are all but Paint upon a beauteous Face,
And in Descriptions only claim a place.
But to make Rage declame, and Grief discourse,
From Lovers in despair fine things to force,

Must needs succeed, for who can chuse but pity
To see poor Hero's miserably witty?
But O the Dialogues, where jest and mock
200   Is held up like a rest at Shittle-cock!
Or else like Bells eternally they Chime,
Men dye in Simile, and live in Rime.
What things are these, who would be Poets thought,
By Nature not inspir'd, nor Learning taught?
Some Wit they have, and therefore may deserve
A better way than this by which they starve:
But to write Plays? why, 'tis a bold pretence,
To Language, Breeding, Fancy and good Sense;
Nay more, for they must look within to find
210   Those secret turns of Nature in the mind.
Without this part in vain would be the whole,
And but a Body all without a Soul:
All this together yet is but a part
Of Dialogue, that great and powerful Art,
Now almost lost, which the old *Grecians* knew,
From whence the *Romans* fainter Copies drew,
Scarce comprehended since but by a few.
Plato and *Lucian* are the best Remains
Of all the wonders which this art contains;
220   Yet to our selves we Justice must allow,
Shakespear and *Fletcher* are the wonders now:
Consider them, and read them o're and o're,
Go see them play'd, then read them as before.
For though in many things they grosly fail,
Over our Passions still they so prevail,
That our own grief by theirs is rockt asleep,
The dull are forc'd to feel, the wise to weep.
Their Beauties Imitate, avoid their faults;
First on a Plot employ thy carefull thoughts,
230   Turn it with time a thousand several waies,
This oft alone has given success to Plays;

Reject that vulgar error which appears
So fair, of making perfect characters,
There's no such thing in Nature, and you'l draw
A faultless Monster which the world ne're saw.
Some faults must be, that his misfortunes drew,
But such as may deserve compassion too.
Besides the main Design composed with Art,
Each moving Scene must be a Plot a part,
240　Contrive each little turn, mark every place,
As Painters first chalk out the future face,
Yet be not fondly your own slave for this,
But change hereafter what appears amiss.
Think not so much where shining thoughts to place,
As what a man would say in such a case.
Neither in Comedy will this suffice,
The Actor too must be before your eyes,
And though 'tis Drudgery to stoop so low,
To him you must your utmost meaning show.
250　Expose no single Fop, but lay the load
More equally, and spread the Folly broad;
The other way 's too common, oft we see
A fool derided by as bad as he;
Hawks fly at nobler game, but in his way,
A very *Owl* may prove a Bird of prey;
Some *Poets* so will one poor Fop devour;
But to Collect, like Bees from every flower,
Ingredients to compose that precious juice,
Which serves the world for pleasure and for use,
260　In spite of faction this will favour get,
But *Falstaff* seems unimitable yet.

Another fault which often does befall,
Is when the wit of some great *Poet* shall
So overflow, that is, be none at all,
That all his Fools speak sence, as if possest,
And each by Inspiration breaks his jest;

If once the Justness of each part be lost,
Well may we laugh, but at the *Poets* cost.
That silly thing men call sheer Wit avoid,
270 With which our Age so nauseously is cloy'd,
Humour is all, and 'tis the top of wit
T' express agreeably a thing that's fit.
But since the *Poets* we of late have known,
Shine in no dress so well as in their own,
The better by example to convince,
Lets cast a view on this wrong side of sence.

   First a Soliloquie is calmly made,
Where every reason is most nicely weigh'd,
At the end of which most opportunely comes
280 Some Hero frighted at the noise of Drums,
For her dear sake whom at first sight he loves,
And all in Metaphor his passion proves;
But some sad accident, that's yet unknown,
Parting this pair, to leave the man alone,
He's Jealous presently, we know not why,
Then, to oblige his Rival needs must dy;
But first he makes a Speech, wherein he tells
The absent Nymph how much his flame excells,
And yet bequeaths her generously now
290 To that dear Rival whom he does not know,
Who, coming in, sent sure by Fate's command,
Too late alas withholds his hasty hand,
Which now has given that most lamented stroke,
At which this very Stranger's heart is broke;
Who more to his new friend than Mistress kind,
Mourns the sad Fate of being left behind,
Most naturally prefers those dying Charms
To Love, and living in his Ladyes Arms.
How shamefull, and what monstrous things are these?
300 And then they rail at th' Age they cannot please,

Conclude us only partial for the dead,
And grudge the Sign of old *Ben. Johnson's* head.
When the Intrinsick value of the Stage
Can scarce be judg'd, but by the following Age;
For Dances, Flutes, *Italian* Songs, and rime
May keep up sinking Nonsence for a time,
But that will fail, which now so much o're rules,
And sence no longer will submit to fools.

    By painfull steps we are at last got up
310 *Pernassus* hill, upon whose Airy top
The *Epick* Poets so divinely show,
And with just pride behold the rest below.
Heroick Poems have a just pretence
To be the chief effort of humane sence,[5]
A work of such inestimable worth,
There are but two the world has yet brought forth,
Homer and *Virgil*: with what awfull sound
Each of those names the trembling Air does wound?
Just as a Changeling seems below the rest
320 Of men, or rather is a two legg'd beast,
So those Gigantick souls amaz'd we find
As much above the rest of humane kind.
Nature's whole strength united; endless fame,
And universal shouts attend their name.
Read Homer once, and you can read no more,
For all things else will seem so dull and poor,
You'l wish 't unread; but oft upon him look,
And you will hardly need another book;
Had *Bossu* never writ, the world had still
330 Like *Indians* view'd this wondrous piece of Skill;
As something of Divine the work admired,
Hoped not to be Instructed, but Inspired;
Till he disclosing sacred Mysteries,
Has shewn where all the mighty Magick lyes,

Describ'd the Seeds, and in what order sown,
That have to such a vast proportion grown.
Sure from some Angel he the secret knew,
Who through this Labyrinth has given the clue.
But what alas avails it poor Mankind
340   To see this promised Land, yet stay behind?
The way is shewn, but who has strength to go?
Who can all Sciences exactly know?
Whose fancy flyes beyond weak reason's sight,
And yet has Judgment to direct it right?
Whose nice distinction, *Virgil*-like, is such,
Never to say too little nor too much?
Let such a man begin without delay,
But he must do much more than I can say,
Must above *Cowley*, nay and *Milton* too prevail,
350   Succeed where great *Torquato*,[6] and our greater *Spencer* fail.

FINIS.

Roscommon,
An Essay On Translated Verse
(1685)

HAPPY that Author, whose correct Essay[1]
Repairs so well our Old *Horatian* way
And happy you, who (by propitious fate)
On great *Apollo's* sacred Standard wait,
And with strict discipline instructed right,
Have learn'd to *use* your arms before you *fight*.[2]
But since the *Press*, the *Pulpit*, and the *Stage*,
Conspire to censure and expose our Age.
Provok'd, Too far, we resolutely must[3]

10 To the few Vertues that we have, be just.
For who have long'd, or who have labour'd more
To search the Treasures of the *Roman* store;
Or dig in *Grecian Mines* for *purer Oar*;
The noblest Fruits Transplanted in our Isle
With early Hope, and fragrant Blossoms smile.
Familiar *Ovid* tender thoughts inspires,
And *Nature* seconds all his soft *Desires*:
Theocritus do's now to *Vs* belong;
And *Albion's Rocks* repeat his *Rural Song*.

20 Who has not heard how *Italy* was blest,
Above the *Medes*, above the wealthy *East*?
Or *Gallus* Song, so tender, and so true,
As evn *Lycoris* might with pity view!
When *Mourning Nymphs* attend their *Daphni's Herse*
Who do's not *Weep*, that *Reads* the *moving Verse*!

But hear, oh hear, in what exalted streins
Sicilian Muses through these happy Plains,
Proclaim *Saturnian* Times, our own *Apollo* Reigns.

When *France* had breath'd, after intestine *B*roils,
30   And Peace, and Conquest crown'd her forreign Toils,
There (cultivated by a Royal Hand)
Learning grew fast, and spread, and blest the Land;
The choicest *B*ooks, that *Rome*, or *Greece* have known,
Her excellent *Translators* made her own:
And *Europe* still considerably gains,[4]
*B*oth by their good *Example* and their *Pains*.
From hence our gen'rous Emulation came,
We undertook, and we perform'd the same.
But now, *We* shew the world a nobler way,
40   And in *Translated Verse*, do more than *They*.
Serene, and clear, Harmonious *Horace* flows,
With sweetness not to be exprest in *Prose*.[5]
Degrading *Prose* explains his meaning ill,
And shews the *Stuff*, but not the Workman's skill.
I (who have serv'd him more than twenty years)
Scarce know my Master as he there appears.
Vain are our *Neighbours Hopes*, and *Vain* their *Cares*,
The *Fault* is more their *Languages*, than theirs.
'Tis Courtly, florid, and abounds in words;
50   Of softer sound than our perhaps affords.[6]
But who did ever in *French Authors* see
The Comprehensive, *English Energy*?
The weighty *Bullion* of *One Sterling Line*,
Drawn to *French Wire*, would thro' whole *Pages* shine.
I speak my *private*, but *impartial sense*,
With *Freedom*, and (I hope) without *offence*:
For I'le Recant, when *France* can shew me *Wit*,
As strong as *Ours*, and as *succinctly Writ*.

'Tis true, *Composing* is the *Nobler* Part,
60 But good *Translation* is no *easie* Art:
For tho *Materials* have long since been found,
Yet both your *fancy*, and your *Hands* are *bound*;
And by *Improving* what was writ *Before*;
Invention Labours *Less*, but *Judgment*, *more*.

The *Soil* intended for *Pierian*[7] *seeds*;
Must be well *purg'd* from *rank Pedantick Weeds*.
Apollo starts, and all *Parnassus* shakes,
At the rude Rumbling *Baralipton*[8] makes.
For none have been with *Admiration*, read,
70 But who (beside their *Learning*) were *Well-bred*.

THE first great work, (a Task perform'd by few)
Is, that *your self* may to *your self* be *True*:
No *Masque*, no *Tricks*, no *Favour*, no *Reserve*;
Dissect your Mind, examine ev'ry *Nerve*.
Whoever *Vainly* on his *strength* depends,
Begins like *Virgil*, but like *Mævius*, *Ends*:
That wretch (in spight of his forgotten Rhymes)
Condemn'd to Live to all succeeding Times,
With *pompous Nonsense* and a *bellowing sound*
80 Sung *lofty Ilium*, *Tumbling* to the *Ground*.
And (if my Muse can through past Ages see)
That *Noisy*, *Nauseous*, *Gaping Fool* was *He*;
Exploded, when with universal scorn,
The *Mountains Labour'd* and a *Mouse* was *Born*.

Learn, learn, *Crotona*'s brawny Wrestler cryes
Audacious Mortals, and be *Timely* Wise!
'Tis I that call, remember *Milo's End*,
Wedgd in that Timber which, he strove to *Rend*.

Each Poet, with a *different Talent* writes,
90 One *Praises*, One *Instructs*, Another *Bites*.

Horace did ne're aspire to *Epick Bays*,
Nor lofty *Maro* stoop to *Lyrick Lays*.
Examine how your *Humour* is inclin'd,
And which the *Ruling Passion* of your Mind;[9]
Then, seek a *Poet* who *your* way do's bend,
And chuse an *Author* as you chuse a *Friend*.
United by this *Sympathetick Bond*,
You grow *Familiar*, *Intimate* and *Fond*;
Your *thoughts*, your *Words*, your *Stiles*, your *Souls* agree,
100   No Longer his *Interpreter*, but *He*.

    With how much ease is a *young Muse Betray'd*,
How *nice* the *Reputation* of the *Maid*!
Your *early*, *kind*, *paternal* care appears,
By *chast Instruction* of her *Tender Years*.
The *first Impression* in her *Infant* Breast
Will be the *deepest*, and should be the best
Let no Austerity breed servile *Fear*,[10]
No *wanton* Sound offend her *Virgin-Ear*.
Secure from *foolish Pride's affected state*,
110   And *specious Flattery's more pernicious Bait*,
Habitual Innocence adorns her *Thoughts*
But your neglect must answer for her *Faults*[11]

Immodest words admit of no defence;
For want of *Decency*, is want of *Sense*.[12]
What mod'rate *Fop* would rake the *Park*, or *Stews*,
Who among Troops of *faultless Nymphs* may chuse?
Variety of *such* is to be found;
Take then a Subject, *proper* to expound:
But *Moral*, *Great*, and worth a *Poet's Voice*,
120   For Men of *sense despise a trivial Choice*:
And such *Applause* it must expect to meet,
As wou'd some Painter, busie in a Street,
To copy *Bulls* and *Bears*, and ev'ry *Sign*
That calls the *staring Sots* to *nasty Wine*

    Yet 'tis not all to have a Subject *Good*,
It must *Delight* us when 'tis *understood*.
He that brings *fulsome Objects* to my view,
(As many *Old* have done, and many *New*)
With *nauseous Images* my Fancy fills,

130   And all, goes down like *Oxymel* of *Squils*.[13]
Instruct the list'ning world how *Maro* sings
Of *useful subjects*, and of *lofty Things*.
These will such true, such bright *Idea's* raise,
As merit *Gratitude*, as well as *Praise*,
But *foul Descriptions* are *offensive* still,
Either for being *Like*, or being *Ill*.
For who, without a *Qualm*, hath ever lookt,
On *Holy Garbage*, tho by *Homer Cookt*?
Whose *Rayling Hero's*, and whose *wounded Gods*,

140   Make some suspect, He *Snores*, as well as *Nods*.[14]
But I offend – *Virgil* begins to *frown*,
And *Horace* looks with *Indignation* down;
My blushing Muse with *Conscious fear* retires,
And whom *They like*, *Implicitely Admires*.

    On *sure Foundations* let your *Fabrick Rise*,
And with attractive *Majesty* surprise,[15]
Not by affected, *meritricious Arts*,
But strict *harmonious Symetry* of *Parts*.
Which through the *Whole*, insensibly must pass,

150   With vital Heat to animate the Mass.
A *pure*, an *Active*, an *Auspicious flame*,
And *bright* as *Heav'n*, from whence the *Blessing* came;
But few, oh few, Souls, præordain'd by *Fate*,
The Race of *Gods*, have reach'd that *envy'd Height*.
No *Rebel-Titan's sacrilegious Crime*,
By heaping Hills on Hills can *thither climb*.
The grizly *Ferry-man of Hell*[16] deny'd
Æneas entrance, till he knew his *Guid*;

How justly then will impious Mortals fall,
160   Whose *Pride* would soar to *Heav'n* without a *Call?*

Pride (of all others the most *dangerous* Fau't)
Proceeds from want of *Sense* or want of *Thought,*[17]
The Men, who *labour* and *digest* things *most,*
Will be much apter to *despond,* than *boast.*
For if your Author be *profoundly good,*
'Twill cost you *dear* before he's *understood.*
How many Ages since has *Virgil* writ?
How few are they who understand him *yet?*
Approach his Altars with *religious Fear,*[18]
170   No *vulgar Deity* inhabits *there:*[19]
Heav'n shakes not more at *Jove's imperial Nod,*
Then *Poets* shou'd before their *Mantuan God.*[20]
Hail, mighty *MARO!* may that Sacred Name,
Kindle *my Breast* with *thy cælestial Flame;*
Sublime Ideas, and *apt Words* infuse.
The *Muse* instruct *my Voice,* and *Thou* inspire the *Muse!*

What I have instanced only in the *best,*
Is, in proportion true of All the *rest.*
Take pains the *genuine* Meaning to explore,
180   There *Sweat,* there *Strain,* tug the laborious *Oar.*
Search *ev'ry Comment,* that your Care can find,
Some here, some there, may hit the Poets *Mind;*
Yet be not blindly guided by the *Throng;*
The Multitude is always in the *Wrong.*[21]
When Things appear *unnatural* or *hard,*
Consult your *Author,* with *Himself* compar'd;
Who knows what blessing *Phæbus* may bestow,
And future Ages to your Labour owe?
Such Secrets are not easily found out,
190   But once Discover'd, leave no Room for Doubt.
Truth Stamps *Conviction* in your Ravisht Breast,
And *Peace,* and *Joy* attend the glorious Guest.[22]

Truth still is *One*; *Truth* is Divinely *bright*,
No cloudy *Doubts* obscure her *Native light*,
While in your *Thoughts* you find the *least* debate,
You may *Confound*, but *never* can *Translate*.
Your *Stile* will this through all Disguises show,
For none, *explain*, more clearly than they *Know*.
He only proves he *Understands* a Text,
200   Whose *Exposition* leaves it *unperplex'd*.
They, who too faithfully on *Names* insist,[23]
Rather Create than *Dissipate* the *Mist*.
And grow *Unjust* by being *over nice*,
(For *Superstitious Virtue* turns to *Vice*.)
Let *Crassus's* Ghost, and *Labienus* tell   *Hor. l. 3. Od. 6.*
How twice in *Parthian* plains their *Legions* fell.
Since *Rome* hath been so Jealous of her Fame,
That few know *Pacorus* or *Monæses* Name.[24]

Words in One Language Elegantly us'd,
210   Will hardly in another be excus'd.
And some that *Rome* admir'd in *Cæsars* Time,
May neither suit *Our Genius* nor our *Clime*.[25]
The *Genuine Sence*, *intelligibly* Told,
Shews a *Translator* both *Discreet*, and *Bold*.

Excursions are *inexpiably Bad*.
And 'tis much safer to leave out than *Add*,
Abstruse and Mystick thoughts you must express,
With painful Care but seeming easiness,
For truth shines brightest through the plainest dress.
220   Th' *Ænæean Muse* when she appears in *state*,
Makes all *Joves Thunder* on her *Verses* wait,
Yet writes sometimes as soft and moving things
As *Venus* speaks or *Philomela* sings.
Your Author alwayes will the best advise,[26]
Fall when *He falls*, and when *He Rises*, *Rise*.
Affected *Noise* is the most *wretched* Thing,

That to *Contempt* can *Empty Scriblers* bring.
Vowels and *Accents*, *Regularly plac'd*
On *even Syllables* (and still the *Last*)
230 Tho gross innumerable *Faults* abound,
In spight of non sense never *fail* of *Sound*.[27]
But this is meant of *even Verse* alone
As being most harmonious and most known,
For if you will unequal numbers try,
There accents on odd *Syllables* must lie.[28]
Whatever Sister of the learned Nine
Do's to your suit a willing Ear incline,
Urge your success, deserve a lasting Name,
She'l crown a *Grateful* and a *Constant Flame*.
240 But if a wild *Uncertainty* prevail,
And turn your *Veering heart* with *ev'ry Gale*,
You lose the *Fruit* of all your *former care*
For the sad *Prospect* of a *Just Despair*.

A *Quack* (too scandalously mean to Name)
Had, by *Man-Midwifry*, got *Wealth*, and *Fame*;
As if *Lucina* had forgot her *Trade*,
The *Lab'ring Wife* invok's *his surer Aid*.
Well-season'd Bowls the Gossips Spirits raise,
Who while she Guzzles, Chats the *Doctor's* Praise.
250 And largely, what she wants in *Words*, supplies
With *Maudlin-Eloquence* of *trickling Eyes*.
But what a thoughtless *Animal* is *Man*,
(How very *Active* in his own *Trepan*!)
For greedy of *Physicians* frequent *Fees*,
From *Female Mellow Praise* He takes Degrees?
Struts in a new *Unlicens'd Gown*, and then,
From *saving Women* falls to *Killing Men*.
Another Such had left the *Nation Thin*,
In spight of all the *Children* he brought in.
260 His *Pills*, as thick as *Hand Granadoes* flew,
And where they *Fell*, as Certainly, they *slew*.

His *Name* struck ev'ry where as great a *Damp*
As *Archimedes* through the *Roman Camp.*[29]
With this, the *Doctors Pride* began to *Cool,*
For *Smarting soundly* may *convince* a Fool.
But now *Repentance* came too late, for *Grace*;
And meager *Famine* star'd him in the Face.
Fain would he to the *Wives* be reconcil'd,
But found no *Husband* left *to own a Child.*
270 The *Friends,* that *got* the Brats, were poyson'd too;
In this sad case what could our *Vermin* do?[30]
Worry'd with *Debts* and past all *Hope* of *Bail,*
Th' unpity'd wretch lies *Roting* in a *Jail.*
And There with *Basket-Alms,* scarce kept *Alive,*
Shews how *Mistaken Talents* ought to *Thrive.*[31]

I pity, from my Soul, Unhappy men,
Compell'd by *want* to *Prostitute* their *Pen*;
*W*ho must, like *Lawyers,* either *Starve* or *Plead,*
And *follow,* right or wrong, where *Guynny's Lead*;
280 But you, *Pompilian,*[32] *wealthy, pamper'd Heirs,*
*W*ho to your *Country* owe your *Swords* and *Cares.*
Let no vain hope your easie mind seduce,
For *Rich Ill Poets* are without *Excuse.*
'Tis very Dangerous, *Tampring* with a *Muse.*
The *Profit's small,* and you have *much* to *lose*;
For, tho *true Wit adorns* your *Birth,* or *Place,*
Degenerate lines *degrade* th' *attainted Race,*
No Poet any *Passion* can Excite;
But what they feel transport them when they write.[33]
290 Have you been led through the *Cumæan Cave.*
And heard th' Impatient Maid *Divinely Rave?*[34]
I hear her now; I see her Rowling Eyes;
And panting; *Lo!* the *God,* the *God* she cries;
With words, not *Hers,* and more then *humane sound,*
She makes th' obedient *Ghosts* peep trembling thro the
    ground,

But tho we *must obey* when *heaven Commands*,
And man in vain the *Sacred Call withstands*,
Beware *what Spirit* rages in your breast.
For ten inspir'd ten thousand are Possest.
300   Thus make the *proper use* of each *Extream*,
And *write* with *fury* but *correct* with *Phleam.*
And when the Chearful hours too freely Pass,
And sparkling wine smiles in the tempting Glass,
Your *Pulse* advises, and Begins to beat
Through Every swelling Vein a *loud retreat.*
So when a *Muse Propitiously invites*
Improve her favours, and *Indulge* her flights,
But when you find that vigorous heat *abate*,
Leave off, and for *another summons* wait.
310   Before the *Radiant Sun*, a *Glimmering Lamp*;
Adult'rate Metals to the *Sterling Stamp*,
Appear not *meaner*, than *mere humane Lines*,
Compar'd with those whose *Inspiration shines*;
These, Nervous, bold; those Languid, and *remiss*;
There, cold salutes, But *here*, a *Lovers kiss.*
Thus have I seen a Rapid, headlong Tide,
With foaming Waves the Passive *Soan* Divide
Whose Lazy Waters without Motion lay,
While he, with eager force, urg'd his Impetuous way.

320   The *Priviledge* that Ancient Poets claim
Now turn'd to *License* by too *just* a Name,
Belongs to none but an *Establisht Fame*,
Which *scorns* to *Take* it –
Absur'd Expressions, crude, Abortive Thoughts,
All the lewd *Legion* of *Exploded fau'ts*,
Base Fugitives to that *Asylum* fly,
And sacred *Laws* with *Insolence* Defy.
Not thus our *Heroes* of the *former* Days,
Deserv'd and *Gain'd* their never fading *Bayes*;

330   For I mistake, or far the greatest Part,
Of what some call *Neglect* was *study'd Art*.
When *Virgil* seems to *Trifle* in a Line,
'Tis like a *Warning-piece*, which gives the *Sign*
To *Wake* your *Fancy*, and *prepare* your *Sight*,
To reach the noble Height of some *unusual Flight*.
I lose my Patience, when, with *Sawcy Pride*,
By *untun'd Ears* I hear *His Numbers* try'd.
Reverse of *Nature*! shall *such Copies*, then
Arraign th' *Originals* of *Maro's* Pen!
340   And the *rude Notions* of *Pedantick Schools*
Blaspheme the sacred *Founder* of *Our Rules*!

    The Delicacy of the nicest Ear
Finds nothing *harsh*, or out of *Order* There.
Sublime or *Low*, *unbended* or *Intense*,
The *sound* is still a *Comment* to the *Sense*.[35]

    A skilful *Ear*, in *Numbers* shou'd preside,
And all *Disputes* without *Appeal* decide.
This ancient Rome, and *Elder Athens* found,
Before *mistaken stops debauch'd* the *sound*.

350   When, by Impulse from Heaven, *Tyrtæus* Sung,
In drooping Souldiers a new Courage sprung
Reviving Sparta now the fight mantain'd,
And what *Two Gen'rals Lost*, a *Poet Gain'd*.
By secret influence of Indulgent Skyes,
Empire, and *Poesy Together* rise.
True Poets are the *Guardians* of a *State*,
And when *They Fail*, portend approaching *Fate*,
For that which *Rome* to *Conquest* did Inspire,
Was not the *Vestal*, but the *Muses fire*;
360   *Heaven joyns* the *Blessings* no *declining* Age
E're felt the *Raptures* of *Poetick Rage*.

118

Of many faults, *Rhyme* is (perhaps) the *Cause*,
Too *strict* to *Rhyme* We slight more *useful* Laws.
For *That*, in *Greece* or *Rome*, was never *known*,
Till by *Barbarian* Deluges *o'reflown*,
Subdu'd, Undone, They did at Last, *Obey*,
And change their *Own* for their *Invaders* way.

I grant that from some *Mossie, Idol Oak*,
In *Double Rhymes* our *Thor* and *Woden* spoke;
370　And by Succession of unlearned Times,
As *Bards began*, so *Monks Rung on* the *Chimes*.

But now that *Phœbus* and the *sacred Nine*,
With all their Beams on our blest Island shine,
Why should not *We* their *ancient Rites restore*
And *be*, what *Rome* or *Athens* were *Before*?[36]

Have we forgot how Raphaels *Num'rous Prose*   An Essay on
Led our exalted Souls through heavenly Camps,   blanc Verse out
And mark'd the ground where proud Apostate Thrones,   of the *6th* Book
Defy'd Jehovah! *Here, 'twixt Host and Host,*   of *Paradise* lost.
380　*(A narrow but a dreadful Interval)*
Portentous sight! before the Cloudy van,
Satan with vast and haughty Strides advanc'd,
Came tow'ring arm'd in Adamant and Gold.
There Bellowing Engines, with their fiery Tubes,
Dispers'd Æthereal forms, and down they fell
By thousands, Angels on Arch-Angels rowl'd;
Recover'd, to the hills they ran, they flew,
Which, (with their pond'rous load, Rocks, Waters, Woods)
From their firm Seats torn by the shaggy Tops,
390　*They bore like shields before them through the Air,*
Till more incens'd they hurl'd them at their Foes,
All was Confusion; Heavens Foundations shook,
Threatning no less than Universal Wrack,
For Michael's *arm main Promontories flung,*

And over prest whole Legions weak with Sin;
Yet they Blasphem'd and struggled as they lay
Till the great Ensign of Messiah *blaz'd,*
And (arm'd with vengeance) Gods Victorious Son
(Effulgence of Paternal Deity)
400   *Grasping ten thousand Thunders in his hand*
Drove th' old Original Rebels headlong down
And sent them flameing to the vast Abysse.

O may I live to hail the Glorious day,[37]
And sing loud *Pæans* through the crowded way,
When in Triumphant State the *British* Muse,
True to her self, shall barb'rous aid Refuse,
And in the *Roman* Majesty appear,
Which none know better, and none come so near.[38]

FINIS.

Francis Atterbury,
'Preface' to the Second Part
of Waller's *Poems*
(1690)

The Reader need be told no more in commendation of these Poems, than that they are Mr. *Waller*'s; A Name that carries every thing in it, that's either Great or Graceful in Poetry. He was indeed the Parent of *English* Verse, and the first that shew'd us our Tongue had Beauty and Numbers in it. Our Language owes more to him than the *French* does to *Cardinal Richlieu*, and the whole Academy. A Poet cannot think of him, without being in the same rapture *Lucretius* is in, when *Epicurus* comes in his way.

> *Tu pater & rerum inventor, Tu patria nobis*
> *Suppeditas præcepta: Tuesque ex Inclyte, chartis,*
> *Floriferis ut Apes in sallibus omnia libant,*
> *Omnia Nos itidem depascimur aurea dicta:*
> *Aurea, perpetua semper dignissima vita.*[1]

The Tongue came into his hands, like a rough Diamond; he polish'd it first, and to that degree that all Artists since him have admired the Workmanship, without pretending to mend it. *Sucklyn* and *Carew*, I must confess, wrote some few things smoothly enough, but as all they did in this kind was not very considerable, so 'twas a little later than the earliest pieces of Mr. *Waller*. He undoubtedly stands first in the List of Refiners, and for ought I know, last too; for I question whether in *Charles* the Second's Reign, *English* did not come to its full perfection; and whether it has not had its *Augustan Age*,[2] as well as the *Latin*. It seems to be already mix'd with Foreign Languages, as far as its purity will bear; and, as Chymists say of their *Menstruums*,[3] to be quite sated with the Infusion. But Posterity will best judge of this – In the mean time, 'tis a surprizing Reflection, that between what *Spencer* wrote last, and *Waller* first, there should not be much above twenty years distance: and yet the one's Language, like the Money of that time, is as currant now as ever; whilst the other's words are like old Coyns, one must go to an Antiquary to understand their true meaning and value. Such advances may a great Genius make, when it undertakes any thing in earnest!

Some Painters will hit the chief Lines, and master strokes of a Face so truly, that through all the differences of Age, the Picture shall still bear a Resemblance. This Art was Mr. *Waller*'s; he sought out, in this flowing Tongue of ours, what parts would last, and be of standing use and ornament; and this he did so successfully, that his Language is now as fresh as it was at first setting out. Were we to judge barely by the wording, we could not know what was wrote at twenty, and what at fourscore. He complains indeed of a Tyde of words that comes in upon the *English* Poet, o'reflows whate'er he builds: but this was less his case than any man's, that ever wrote; and the mischief on't is, this very complaint will last long enough to confute it self. For though *English* be mouldring Stone, as he tells us there, yet he has certainly pick'd the best out of a bad Quarry.

We are no less beholding to him for the new turn of Verse, which he brought in, and the improvement he made in our Numbers. Before his time, men Rhym'd indeed, and that was all: as for the harmony of measure, and that dance of words, which good ears are so much pleas'd with, they knew nothing of it. Their *Poetry* then was made up almost entirely of monosyllables; which, when they come together in any cluster, are certainly the most harsh untunable things in the World.[4] If any man doubts of this, let him read ten lines in *Donne*, and he'll be quickly convinc'd. Besides, their Verses ran all into one another, and hung together, throughout a whole Copy, like the *hook't Attoms*, that compose a Body in *Des Cartes*.[5] There was no distinction of parts, no regular stops, nothing for the Ear to rest upon – But as soon as the Copy began, down it went, like a Larum, incessantly; and the Reader was sure to be out of Breath, before he got to the end of it. So that really Verse in those days was but down-right Prose, tagg'd with Rhymes. Mr. *Waller* remov'd all these faults, brought in more Polysyllables, and smoother measures; bound up his thoughts better, and in a cadence more agreeable to the nature of the Verse he wrote in: So that where-ever the natural stops of that were, he contriv'd the little breakings of his sense so as to fall in with 'em. And for that reason, since the stress of our Verse lyes commonly upon the last Syllable, you'll hardly ever find him using a word of no force there. I would say if I were not afraid the Reader would think me too nice, that he commonly closes with Verbs, in which we know the Life of Language consists.

Among other improvements, we may reckon that of *his Rhymes*: Which are always good, and very often the better for being *new*. He had a fine Ear, and knew how quickly that Sense was cloy'd by the same round of chiming Words still returning upon it.[6] 'Tis a decided Case by the great Master of Writing. *Quæ sunt ampla & Pulchra, diu placere possunt; quæ lepida & concinna*, (amongst which Rhyme must, whether it will or no, take its place) *cito satietate afficiunt aurium sensum fastidiosissimum.*[7] This he understood very well, and therefore, to take off the danger of a Surfeit that way, strove to please by Variety, and new sounds. Had he carried this Observation (among others) as far as it would go, it must, methinks, have shown him the incurable fault of this jingling kind of Poetry, and have led his later judgment to blank Verse. But he continu'd an obstinate Lover of Rhyme to the very last: 'Twas a Mistress, that never appear'd unhandsome in his Eyes, and was courted by him long after *Sacharissa* was forsaken. He had rais'd it, and brought it to that perfection we now enjoy it in: And the Poet's temper (which has always a little vanity in it) would not suffer him ever to slight a thing, he had taken so much pains to adorn. My Lord *Roscommon* was more impartial: No man ever Rhym'd truer and evener than he; yet he is so just as to confess, that 'tis but a Trifle, and to wish the Tyrant dethron'd, and blank Verse set up in its room. There is a third person, the living Glory of our English Poetry,[8] who has disclaim'd the use of it upon the Stage, tho no man ever employ'd it there so happily as He. 'Twas the strength of his Genius that first brought it into credit in Plays; and 'tis the force of his Example that has thrown it out agen. In other kinds of writing it continues still; and will do so, till some excellent Spirit arises, that has leisure enough, and resolution to break the charm, and free us from the *troublesome bondage of Rhyming*,[9] as Mr. Milton very well calls it, and has prov'd it as well, by what he has wrote in another way. But this is a thought for times at some distance; the present Age is a little too Warlike: It may perhaps furnish out matter for a good Poem in the next, but 'twill hardly encourage one now: Without Prophesying, a Man may easily know, what sort of Lawrels are like to be in request?

Whilst I am talking of Verse, I find my self, I don't know how, betray'd into a great deal of Prose. I intended no more than to put the Reader in mind, of what respect was due to any thing that fell from the Pen of Mr. *Waller.* I have heard his last Printed Copies, which are added in the several Editions of his Poems, very slightly spoken of; but certainly they don't deserve it. They do indeed discover themselves to be his last, and that's the worst we can say of 'em. He is there *Jam Senior; Sed cruda Deo viridisque Senectus*.[10] The same censure perhaps will be past on the pieces of this second part. I shall not so far engage for 'em, as to pretend they are all equal to whatever he wrote in the vigour of his Youth. Yet they are so much of a piece with the rest, that any Man will at first sight know 'em to be Mr. *Waller*'s. Some of 'em were wrote very early, but not put in former Collections, for reasons obvious enough, but which are now ceas'd. The Play was alter'd, to please the Court: 'Tis not to be doubted who sat for the two Brothers Characters. 'Twas agreeable to the sweetness of Mr. *Waller*'s Temper, to soften the rigour of the Tragedy, as he expresses it; but whether it be so agreeable to the Nature of Tragedy it self, to make every thing come off easily, I leave to the Criticks. In the Prologue, and Epilogue, there are a few Verses that he has made use of upon another occasion. But the Reader may be pleased to allow that in him, that has been allowed so long in *Homer* and *Lucretius*. Exact Writers dress up their thoughts so very well always, that when they have need of the same sense, they can't put it into other words, but it must be to its prejudice. Care has been taken in this Book to get together everything of Mr. *Waller*'s, that's not put into the former Collection; so that between both, the Reader may make the set compleat.

It will perhaps be contended after all, that some of these ought not to have been Publish'd: And Mr. *Cowly*'s decision will be urg'd, that a neat Tomb of Marble is a better Monument, than a great Pile of Rubbish, *&c.*[11] It might be answer'd to this, that the Pictures and Poems of great Masters have been always valu'd, tho the last hand weren't put to 'em. And I believe none of those Gentlemen that will make the objection would refuse a Sketch of *Raphael*'s, or one of *Titian*'s draughts of the first sitting.

I might tell 'em too, what care has been taken by the Learned, to preserve the Fragments of the Ancient Greek and Latin Poets: There has been thought to be a Divinity in what they said, and therefore the least pieces of it have been kept up and reverenc'd, like Religious reliques. And I am sure, take away the *mille anni*,[12] and Impartial reasoning will tell us, there is as much due to the Memory of Mr. *Waller*, as to the most celebrated names of Antiquity.

But to wave the dispute now of what *ought* to have been done; I can assure the Reader, what *would* have been had this Edition been delay'd. The following Poems were got abroad, and in a great many hands: It were vain to expect that amongst so many admirers of Mr. *Waller*, they should not meet with one fond enough to Publish 'em. They might have staid indeed, till by frequent transcriptions they had been corrupted extreamly, and jumbled together with things of another kind: But then they would have found their way into the World. So 'twas thought a greater piece of kindness to the Author, to put 'em out; whilst they continue genuine and unmix'd; and such, as he himself, were he alive might own.

Lansdowne,
Concerning Unnatural Flights in Poetry
(1701)

By the Honorable *George Granvil* Esq;

AS when some Image, of a charming face,
In living Paint, An Artist tries to trace
He carefully consults, each beauteous line,
Adjusting to his Object, his design;
We Praise the Peice, And give the Painter Fame,
But as the bright resemblance,[1] speaks the Dame.
Poets, are Limners of another kind,
To copy out, Idæas in the Mind,
Words are the paint, by which their thoughts are shown,
10   And Nature is their Object[2] to be drawn;
The written Picture, we applaud, or blame,
But as the just proportions,[3] are the same.

  Who, driven with ungovernable fire,
Or void of Art, beyond these bounds aspire,
Gygantick forms, and monstrous Births alone
Produce, which Nature shockt, disdains to own
By true reflection, I would see my face;
Why brings the Fool, a magnifying Glass?
  But Poetry in Fiction takes delight,   Obj. (1.)
20   And mounting up, in Figures out of Sight,
Leaves Truth behind, in her audacious flight:

Fables, and Metaphors, that always lie,   (2.)
And bold Hyperboles,[4] that soar so high,   (3.)
And every Ornament of Verse must die.

Mistake me not – No Figures I exclude,   *Ans.*
And but forbid Intemperance, not Food.
Who would with care, some happy Fiction frame,
So mimicks Truth, it looks the very same,
Not rais'd to force, or feign'd in nature's scorn,
30   But meant to grace, illustrate and adorn:
Important Truths, still let your Fables hold,
And moral misteries, with art unfold:
Ladies and Beaux, to Please, is all the task,
But the sharp Critick, will Instruction ask.

As Veils transparent cover, but not hide,
Such metaphors appear, when right apply'd;
When thro' the phrase, we plainly see the sense,
Truth, when the meaning's obvious, will dispense;
The Reader, what in Reason's due, believes,
40   Nor can we call that false, which not deceives.

Hyperboles, so daring and so bold,
Disdaining bounds, Are yet by Rules controul'd:
Above the Clouds, but yet within our sight,
They mount with truth, and make a tow'ring flight,
Presenting things impossible to view,
They wander, thro' incredible to True;
Falshoods thus mixt, Like metalls are refind.
And Truth, like Silver, leaves the dross behind.

Thus Poetry has ample space to soar,
50   Nor needs forbidden Regions to explore.
Such Vaunts as his who can with patience bear,
Who thus describes his Hero, in the War.[5]

In heat of Action, combats being slain,   (4.)
And after death, still do's the fight maintain.[*][6]

The noisy Culvering, O're charg'd lets fly,
And bursts unaiming, in the rended sky,
Such frantick flights, are like a Mad-mans dream,
And nature suffers, in the wild extream.[7]

    The Roman Wit, who impiously divides   (5.)
60 His Heroe and his Gods, to different sides,[8]
I would condemn, but that in spight of sense,
Th' admiring World, still stands in his defence.
How o'ft Alas! the best of men in vain
Contend for blessings, that the worst obtain!
The Gods permitting Traitors to succeed:
Become not Parties, in an impious deed,
And by the Tyrants Murder, we may find
That *Cato* and the Gods, were of a mind.

    Thus forcing truth, with such prepostrous praise,
70 Our Characters we lessen, when we'd raise,
Like Castles built, by magick Art, in air,
That vanish at approach, such thoughts appear,
But rais'd on Truth, by some judicious hand,
As on a Rock, they shall for Ages stand.

    Our King return'd, and banisht Peace restor'd,
The Muse ran Mad, to see her exil'd Lord;
On the crackt Stage, the Bedlam Heroes roar'd,
And scarce cou'd speak one reasonable word:
Dryden himself, to please a frantick Age,   (6.)
80 Was forc'd to let his judgment, stoop to Rage;
To a wild Audience, he conform'd his voice,
Comply'd to Custom, but not err'd thro' Choice;

* *Taken from* Ariosto.

Deem then the Peoples, not the Writer's Sin,
Almanzor's Rage, and Rants of *Maximin*:[9]
That fury spent, in each elaborate Peice
He vies for Fame, with ancient *Rome*, and *Greece*.

    Roscommon first, Then *Mulgrave* rose, Like light
To clear our Darkness, and to guide our flight,
With steady Judgment, and in lofty Sounds,
90   They gave us patterns, and they set us bounds,
The *Stagyrite*,[10] and *Horace*, laid aside,
Inform'd by Them, we need no foreign Guide.

    Who seek from Poetry, a lasting Name,
May in their Lessons, learn the road to Fame;
But let the bold Adventurer be sure
That every line, the test of Truth endure,
On this Foundation, may the Fabrick rise
Firm and unshaken, till it touch the Skies.

    From Pulpits banisht, from the Court, from Love,
100 Abandon'd Truth, seeks shelter in the Grove,
Cherish ye Muses, the forsaken Fair,
And take into Your Train, this Wanderer.

EXPLANATORY ANNOTATIONS ON
THE FOREGOING POEM[11]

(1.) The Poetic World is nothing but Fiction; Pernassus, Pegasus, and the Muses, pure imagination and Chimæra: But being however a system universally agreed on, all that shall be contriv'd or invented upon this Foundation according to Nature, shall be reputed, as truth: But what so ever shall diminish from, or exceed the just proportions of Nature, shall be rejected, as False, and pass for extravagance, as Dwarfs and Gyants, for Monsters.

(2.) When *Homer* mentioning *Achilles*, terms him a Lyon, this is a metaphor, And the Meaning is obvious and true, tho' the litteral sense be false: The Poet intending thereby to give his Reader some Idæa of the strength and fortitude of his Heroe – Had he said – That Wolf, or that Bear, this had bin false by, presenting an Image not conformable to the Nature, Or Character of a Heroe. &c.

(3.) Hyperboles are of diverse sorts, And the manner of introducing them, is different. Some are, as it were, Naturaliz'd and established by a Customary way of expression, as when we say, such a one's as swift as the wind; whiter then snow, or the like: *Homer* speaking of *Nireus* calls him Beauty it self:[12] *Martial* of *Zoilus*, Lewdness it self.[13] such Hiperboles lie indeed, but deceive us not, And therefore *Seneca* terms 'em Lyes, that readily conduct our imagination to Truths, and have an intelligible signification, tho' the expression be strain'd beyond credibility.[14] Custom has likewise familiaris'd another way for Hyperboles, for example, by Irony, as when we say of some very infamous Woman, she's a Civil person, where the meaning's to be taken in a sense quite opposite to the letter. These few Figures are mention'd only for examples sake: it will be understood that all others are to be us'd with the like care and discretion.

(4.) These lines are taken from *Ariosto*. The Authour need not have travel'd so far from home, to fetch nonsense. But he chose rather to correct in the gentlest manner, by a foreign Example, hoping that such, as are conscious of the like extravagances, will take the hint, and secretly reprove themselves. *Quodcunq; ostendis mihi sic, incredulus Odi.*[15] It may be possible for some tempers to maintain Rage and indignation to the last gasp. But the Soul and Body once parted, there must necessarily be a determination of Action &c.[16]

(5.) *Victrix Causa deis placuit, sed Victa Catoni*:[17] The consent of so many Ages having establish'd the reputation of this Line, the Author perhaps may be judg'd too presuming in this attack. But he cou'd not suppose that *Cato*, who is describ'd to have been a Man of strict devotion, and more resembling the Gods, than men, would choose any party in opposition to the Gods. The Poet would give us to understand, that his Heroe was too generous to accompany the Gods themselves in an unjust Cause. But to represent a Man to be either wiser, or juster, than God, may show the impiety of the Writer, but can add nothing to the lustre of the Heroe, since neither Reason, nor Religion will allow it, and it is impossible in nature for a corrupt being to be more excellent, than a divine. Besides, success implies permission, and not approbation: to place the Gods always on the thriving side, is to make 'em partakers in all successfull wickedness: They judge before the conclusion of the Action: The Catastrophe will best determine on which side is Providence: And the Violent death of *Cæsar* acquits the Gods, from being Companions of his *Usurpation*.

(6.) Mr. *Dryden* in some Prologue has these two Lines,

> *He's bound to please, not to write well, And knows*
> *There is a mode in Plays, as well as Cloaths.*[18]

Let the Censurers of Mr. *Dryden* therefore be satisfied that where he has expos'd himself to be criticiz'd, it has been only when he has endeavour'd to follow the fashion: To humour others, and not to please himself. It may likewise be observ'd that at the time when those Characters were form'd, Bullying was altogether the Mode, off the Stage, as well as upon it: And tho' that humour is since much abated in the Conversation of the World, yet there remains so far a relish for it, that to this day, an Audience is never so well pleas'd, as when an Actor foams with some extravagant rant. neither can we ever expect a thorow reformation of this Sacrifice to the People, till the writer has some more certain encouragement, than the bare profits of a third day:[19] For those who write to live, will be always under a necessity to comply in some measure; with the Generality, by whose approbation they subsist.

Mr. *Dryden* for further Satisfaction in his Epistle Dedicatory to the *Spanish-Fryar*, thus censures himself. "I remember some Verses of my own *Maximin* and *Almansor*, which cry vengeance upon me for their extravagance *&c.* All I can say for these passages which are I hope not many, is that I knew they were bad enough to please, Even when I writ them: But I repent of them among my sins: And if any of their fellows intrude by chance into my present writing, I draw a Stroke over all those *Dalilahs* of the Theatre: and am resolv'd I will Settle my self no reputation by the applause of Fools: 'Tis not that I am mortify'd to all Ambition, but I scorn as much to take it from half-witted Judges, as I should to raise an Estate, by cheating of Bubbles. Neither doe I discommend the lofty stile in Tragedy, which is naturally pompous and Magnificent: But nothing is truly sublime that is not Just and proper."[20] *Ep. Dedic.* to the *Spanish-Fryar.*

This may serve for a standing Apology for Mr. *Dryden* against all his Criticks; and likewise for an unquestionable, Authority to confirm those principles which the Authour of the foregoing Poem has pretended to lay down. *&c.*

III
Criticism and the War of the
Spanish Succession,
1704-1711

John Dennis,
Selections from *The Grounds of Criticism in Poetry*
(1704)

THE PREFACE

THE following Treatise is but a small part of a Volume of Criticism intended to be publish'd in Folio, in which in Treating of the works of the most Celebrated English Poets Deceas'd, I design'd to shew both by Reason and Examples, that the use of Religion in Poetry was absolutely necessary to raise it to the greatest exaltation, of which so Noble an Art is capable, and on the other side, that Poetry was requisite to Religion in order to its making more forcible Impressions upon the Minds of Men.

And this I thought would be an effectual way of Reconciling People to a Regulated Stage, in spight of the Grimaces of some Spiritual Comedians; who have themselves a mind to be the only Actors in Vogue; and who in order to a total suppression of the Stage, have endeavour'd to set up private Authorities against the common Sense of Mankind, and the Errors of two or three Churchmen against Divine Inspiration.[1] For I appeal to any impartial Reader, whether the constant practice in all Ages of the best and the bravest Nations in their most flourishing States, may not pass for the common Sense of Men: And we know very well that St. *Paul*, whom we believe to be divinely inspir'd, has made use of Heathen Poets nay ev'n Heathen Dramatick Poets, for the Reformation of Mankind. Witness that famous passage, *Evil Communications corrupt good manners*; which St. *Paul* makes use of in his Second Epistle to the *Corinthians*, and which *Grotius* informs us that he borrow'd from the *Thais* of the famous *Menander*.[2] Now how that which was the Language of the Holy Ghost, in the

Mouth of St. *Paul*, comes to be the Language of the Devil in ours, I believe our Bigots will find it a Difficult matter to shew.

It is plain then that these Persons by designing totally to suppress the Stage, which is the only encouragement that we have in these Islands of Poetry, manifestly intended to drive out so noble and useful an Art from among us, and by that means endeavour'd with all their might to weaken the power of Religion, which has need of Poetry to make its utmost Impression upon the Minds of Men.

In short, almost all but the Ceremonial and Historical part of the old Testament, was deliver'd in Poetry and that is almost Half of it. And a considerable part of the Doctrine of the Gospel was deliver'd in Parables, which, as my Lord *Bacon* has justly observ'd in his Advancement of Learning *Lib. 2 Chap. 1.* are a kind of Divine Poesy. I might here very truly observe, that not only *Job* and *Solomon*'s Song and part of the Prophets, but several too of our Saviours Parables, are tho' not Dramatick Poems, yet Poesy that is Dramatical, that is Poesy in which Persons are introduc'd who are talking in Dialogue.

From what has been said, this Consequence must undeniably follow, that either they who deliver'd our Religion were mistaken in the manner of doing it, which will by no means consist with our Belief of the Divinity of one of them, or the Divine Inspiration of the Rest, or that our Religion must be most powerfully propagated by the same means, by which it was at first deliver'd.

I believe that it would be an easie matter to prove, that it was the use of exalted Poesy, such as the lofty Hymn of St. *Ambrose*, that blew up the Flame of Christian zeal to such a transporting height, in the Primitive and Apostolical times, and that the neglect of so Divine an art, has not only in these latter Days considerably lessen'd the force of Religion, but has with some People among us gone a very great way towards the making the Publick Worship contemptible. But I leave it to our Prelates and Pastors to consider, whether, since they are satisfy'd that there is a necessity, for an Harmonious and a Numerous Style, in some parts of our Publick Worship, they ought so long to have remain'd contented with the vile Meetre of *Hopkins*, and by that proceeding to suffer the most Lofty and most Pathetick Divine Poetry to be Burlesqu'd and Ridicul'd in our Churches, which is all one, as if each Sunday they should dress up a Bishop in some Antick Habit, and expose him in that merry Garb in Order to raise the Veneration of the People.

That Poetry is necessary for the inforcing Religion upon the Minds of Men, may I think appear very plainly from what has been said, and from what will be said upon that Subject in the following Treatise. But since our Clergy by their constant practise appear to be already satisfyed of it, I leave it to them to consider, whether they ought not rather to make it part of their business, to set Poetry and consequently the Stage upon a good Foot, than to endeavour with all their might to drive out both from among us.

Since I mention'd my Lord *Bacon* above, I desire the Readers leave to lay before him a most Beautiful Passage of that great genius concerning the worth and the use of Poetry, which he esteems to be the Second principal Branch of Learning.

As for Narrative Poesy (*says he in the 13* Ch. *of the 2* Lib. *of his Advancement of Learning*) or, if you please, Heroical, so you understand it of the Matter, not of the Verse, it seems to be rais'd altogether from a noble Foundation, which makes much for the Dignity of Man's Nature. For seeing the sensible World is in Dignity inferior to the Soul of Man, Poesy seems to endow human Nature, with that which History denies, and to give satisfaction to the Mind, with at least the Shadow of things, where the Substance cannot be had. For if the matter be throughly consider'd a strong Argument may be drawn from Poetry, that a more stately Greatness of things, a more perfect Order, and a more beautiful Variety, delights the Soul of Man, than can be any way found in Nature, since the fall. Wherefore seeing the Acts and events, which are the Subject of True History, are not of that amplitude as to content the Mind of Man, Poesy is ready at Hand to fain Acts more Heroical. Because true History reports the Successes of Business not proportionable to the merit of Virtues and Vices, Poesy corrects it, and presents Events and Fortunes according to Desert; and according to the Law of Providence. Because true History, through the frequent Satiety and Similitude of things, works a Distast and Misprision in the Mind of Men, Poetry Cheereth and Refreshes the Soul; Chanting things rare and various, and full of Vicissitudes, so as Poetry serveth and conferreth to Delectation, Magnanimity, and Morality; and therefore it may seem deservedly to have some Participation of Divineness; because it doth raise the Mind, and exalt the Spirit with high Raptures, by proportioning the Shews of things to the Desires of the Mind, and not submitting the Mind to things, as Reason and History do. And by these Allurements and Congruities, whereby it cherisheth the Soul of Men, joyned also with Consort of Musick, whereby it may more sweetly insinuate it self, it hath won such Access, that it hath been in Estimation, even in Rude Times, and barbarous Nations, when other Learning stood excluded.

But because that Poetry which we call Heroick, has been but barely neglected among us, and the great Cry has been against the Dramatick, let us see what the same extraordinary Person says in Defence of that.

Dramatick or Representative Poesy, *says he*, which brings the World upon the Stage, is of excellent use if it were not abus'd. For the Instructions and Corruptions of the Stage may be great; but the Corruptions in this kind abound; the Discipline is altogether neglected in our times. For altho' in Modern Commonwealths, Stage-Plays be but esteemed a Sport or Pastime, unless they draw from the Satyr and be mordant; yet the Care of the Antients was, that the Stage should instruct the Minds of Men unto Virtue. Nay, wise Men and great Philosophers, have accounted it as the Archet or Musical Bow of the Mind. And certainly it is most true, and as it were a Secret of Nature, that the Minds of Men are more patent to Affections, and Impressions Congregate than Solitary.[3]

In this last Observation which is perfectly Beautiful, my Lord *Bacon* has given a very solid Reason, why the Drama must be more useful than History, and more prevalent than Philosophy. And a little lower he has given two more, though he has applied them to a sort of Poetry which is somewhat different, and those are, that Dramatick Fables are more sensible than Arguments; and more fit than Examples.

At the same time, that extraordinary Man declares like a most just and discerning Judge, that the Modern Stage was but a Shadow of the Antient, and an imperfect Shadow; that it had something of its Shew, but nothing of its Reality; that is, that it was not only a vain and an empty, but a dangerous Amusement. And he plainly taxes the Modern Policy with the Neglect of its Discipline. Indeed in this as well as other things, there is as great a difference between Antient and Modern Policy, as there is between Antient and Modern Extent of Empire.

But the Wisdom of the Queen can never be too much extolled, who has vouchsafed to take care of that which all Her Predecessors neglected.

That Discerning Princess is resolved to support the Stage, that it may be instrumental to the Reforming Her People; and She is resolved to Regulate it, that it may no longer be justly accus'd of corrupting their Manners.[4]

The following Treatise, as has been said above, is but a small Portion of a much larger which was design'd for the Improvement of Modern Poetry, and of the Drama particularly. And here I desire the Reader's Leave to do two things. First to lay down the Design and Method of the larger Treatise, and then to give an Account to the World why no more is Published.

The Design then, and the Method of the whole Treatise, as they were deliver'd in the Second Proposal, are as follows.

THE PROPOSAL

First, The Design is To restore Poetry to all its Greatness, and to all its Innocence.

That Poetry is miserably fall'n, is, I suppose, granted: And, as there never was more occasion for a just and impartial *Criticism* on account of the generality of the Writers; so, there never was more necessity for one on account of the Readers and the Spectators. For the taste of both the Readers and the Spectators was never so debauch'd as it is at present; of which we have given the Reasons in another place.[5] Some of them would be thought to approve of every thing that they either Read or See, and value themselves upon that; that is, upon their want of Discernment to distinguish right from wrong: Others are so squeamish, that they like nothing, and value themselves even upon that too; that is, upon the sickliness and the unsoundness of their Minds; because he who likes nothing tastes nothing, and want of Taste is want of Sense. But this is not all: even they who pretend to like nothing, will at the Play-houses be pleas'd with ev'ry thing; and they who would be thought to approve of every thing, like nothing long; For nothing but Truth can be long esteem'd, and Truth it self, to be long esteem'd, must be distinguish'd from Falshood. From these random ways of Judging it comes to pass, that this Town, in the compass of ten Years, happens to have one and the same Author in the greatest Admiration and in the utmost Contempt; which is infinitely a greater Satyr upon the Town, than it can be on the Author; for the Town is certainly in the wrong in one of the Extreams at least, and perhaps in both; whereas the Authors, for the most part, give no occasion for either of them. This random or this partial way of Judging, has been the cause that Poetry is banish'd from the rest of *Europe*, and is upon its last Legs in *England*.

The Design of the foresaid Treatise is, not only to retrieve so noble an Art, and to fix the Rules both of Writing and of Judging, that both Readers and Writers may be at some certainty; but, to raise it to a height which it has never known before among us, and to restore it, as we said above, to all its Greatness, and to all its Innocence.

But whereas several may imagine that the Design is chimerical, of restoring Poetry either to its Greatness or to its Innocence, we think it proper to satisfie the Reader, in as few words as we can, that both may be easily effected.

1. Poetry may easily be restored to its former Greatness, because the discovering the Cause of a Disease is more than half the Cure of it: but the true and almost only Cause of the Declention of Poetry, that Cause which has lain hid for so many Ages, has been already discovered in a little Tract that was published two Years ago*, for which I have the Opinion of several of the best Judges in *England*, and that matter will be set in so clear a Light in the beginning of the foresaid Treatise, without repeating any thing that was said before, or at least as little as may be, as may satisfie the most incredulous. But,

2. Poetry may easily be restored to its Innocence by taking a proper

---

* *Advancement and Reformation of Modern Poetry.*

Method, a Method that may be more prevalent with the Writers than either Law or Philosophy, which have been us'd in vain. For let us but consider the Character that *Horace* has giv'n of a Poet,

> *Vatis avarus*
> *Non temere est animus, versus amet, hoc studet unum,*
> *Detrimenta, fugas servorum, incendia ridet.*[6]

In short, a Poet will contemn every thing but the acquiring the Reputation of a good Poet. This is what he makes his only Business, and the sole design of his Life; and there is no Reprimand that you can give him, and no Remonstrance that you can make him, that he will not laugh at, until you convince him that he is an ill Poet. And indeed he is partly in the right; for an ill Poet is ten times more ridiculous than a Blockhead of any other Profession: for an ill Physician, or an ill Lawyer, know their own Ignorance, and make it their business to be esteem'd by the People: but, on the contrary, an ill Poet is found out by every body, and admires himself, than which nothing can be more a Jest. So that there is nothing he will refuse to do to avoid the Infamy of that Reputation. From whence it follows that in the foresaid *Criticism* there is a Motive that will work more strongly upon them than the Censures of our Reformers: for there we clearly shew them, that Poetry, by losing its Innocence, loses its very Nature; for if Poetry be more philosophical, and more instructive, than History, as *Aristotle* is pleas'd to affirm of it,[7] and no Man ever knew the Nature either of Poetry, or of History, or of Philosophy, better than he did; why then that Art, or rather that Artifice, with which a great many Writers of Verses and Plays debauch and corrupt the People, is a thing to which Poetry is as directly contrary, as a Virgin is to a Whore. And these People are no more Poets, than those Empricks are Physicians who make their *Jack-Puddings* swallow Potions to recommend them to the People.

In the foresaid Treatise we clearly shew them, that Piety and Virtue was not only the first Original, but that it has been, is and will be the only solid Basis, nay and the very Life and Soul of the Greater Poetry. That the farther Poetry declines from that, the farther it recedes from its very Nature and Essence; and that the true Poetry is as inconsistent and as incompatible with Vice, as the Harmony, and Light, and Raptures of Heaven with the gloomy Horrors of Hell; and the proving this in so clear a manner as we pretend to do, will oblige those Poets who are never so profligate in their Inclinations, to be virtuous at least in their Writings.

Both they and their Readers will then be satisfied, that the true Poetical Genius is a great and a sacred thing; and, to quote an Admirable passage from *Milton*, "Is, wherever it is found, the inspir'd Gift of God, rarely bestow'd, but yet to some (says he) in ev'ry Nation, tho' most abuse it: and is of power, beside the Office of a Pulpit, to imbreed and cherish in a great People the Seeds of Virtue and publick Civility, to allay the Perturbations of the Mind, and set the Affections in a right Tune, to celebrate in glorious and lofty Hymns the Throne and Equipage of God's Almightiness, and what he works, and what he suffers to be wrought with high providence in his Church; to sing victorious Agonies of Martyrs and Saints, the Deeds and Triumphs of just and pious Nations, doing valiantly, thro' Faith, against the Enemies of Christ; to deplore the general Relapses of Kingdoms and States from Justice and God's true Worship. Lastly, Whatever in Religion is holy and sublime, in Virtue amiable or grave, whatever hath Passion or Admiration in all the changes of that which is call'd Fortune from without, or the wily Subtleties and Refluxes of Man's Thoughts from within; all these things with a solid and treatable Smoothness to point out and describe; teaching over the whole Book of Sanctity and Virtue, thro' all the instances of example, with such delight, to those especially of soft and delicious temper, who will not so much as look upon Truth her self, unless they see her elegantly drest; that whereas the paths of Honesty and Good-life appear now rugged and difficult, tho' they be indeed easie and pleasant, they would then appear to all Men both easie and pleasant, tho' they were rugged and difficult indeed. And what a Benefit this would be to our Youth and Gentry (continues he) may be soon guest by what we know of the Corruption and Bane which they suck in daily from the Writings and Interludes of libidinous and ignorant Poetasters, who having scarce ever heard of that which is the main Consistence of a true Poem, the Choice of such persons as they ought to introduce, and what is moral and decent to each one, do for the most part lap up vicious Principles in sweet Pills to be swallow'd down, and make the taste of virtuous Documents harsh and sour."[8] Thus far goes *Milton*: And the Reader may see that it was his Opinion, That tho Poetry was in the main miserably sunk among us; yet, that it might be restor'd to its Innocence, and its Greatness. In order then to the doing this we come to display,

Secondly, The Method that we follow in the foremention'd *Criticism*

We begin then with a *Criticism* upon Poetry in general; in which we endeavour to shew its Nature, and its End, and the means which it ought to use for the attaining that End. And then we come to divide Poetry into its two great Branches, the Greater and the Less.

1. We treat of the Greater Poetry, shew what its Nature and its End are; and that the only certain Method for the attaining its End, is, the keeping strictly up to its Nature, which seems to have been hitherto not very clearly understood. And here we shall lay down some general Rules, which are both few and short, but eternal and unalterable; and for the want of observing which, it will appear throughout this whole Treatise, that the very best among the Ancients, and among the Moderns, have not only made gross Mistakes, but have deviated sometimes, in a great degree, from the Art.

And here too we endeavour to shew the mutual Dependance that the Greater Poetry has on Religion, and Religion on the Greater Poetry; and to make it appear, that all those parts of the Old Testament which were writ in Verse, ought to be translated in Verse, by Reasons which may have force enough to convince us, that Verse translated into Prose is but half translated.

When we have done this, we come to Heroick Poetry; which being a Branch of the Greater Poetry, must have the same End, and must participate of the same Nature; and must besides, have something particular in its Nature to distinguish it from the other two Branches, which are Tragedy, and the Greater Ode. But because too much bare Speculation may prove tedious to several Readers, we shew what every Poet who writes an Epick Poem is oblig'd to do, to make that

Poem keep to the Nature of Epick Poetry in general, and to its own: This, I say, we endeavour to shew, not by laying down the Rules after the common Method, but by shewing what *Virgil* has done; because that great Poet is so exact, that he may be said to have written a *Criticism* upon Epick Poetry by Examples, and because he is now, by Mr. *Dryden*'s Translation, to be reckon'd among our own Poets; and so comes within the compass of my Design.

When by doing this we have laid down the Rules, we come briefly to examine, Whether those Rules are always to be kept inviolable; and if they are not, in what parts, and by whom, they may be alter'd. Then we shew how *Spencer*, by not following those Rules, fell so very far short of the Ancients: And afterwards we endeavour to make it appear, how *Milton*, by daring to break a little loose from them in some particulars, kept up in several others to the Nature of the Greater Poetry in general, and of Epick Poetry in particular, better than the best of the Ancients. After this we treat of the other *English* Poets, who have written any thing that comes near to Heroick Poetry; and shew of them all, as we go along, how they differ from one another, how from the best of the Ancient Poets, and the best of the Moderns of other Countries.

The Branch of the Greater Poetry which we consider next is Tragedy, which we treat of after the same manner with Heroick Poetry, and shew what ev'ry one who writes a Tragedy is oblig'd to do, to make that Poem come up to the Nature of the Greater Poetry in general, and of Tragedy in particular, by shewing what *Sophocles* has done in his *Œdipus* (which will be there translated) and for what Reasons; where we endeavour to display the Beauties of his admirable Conduct, and to clear the Moral by a very different Method from what *Monsieur Dacier* has taken.[9] And after that by doing this we have laid down the Rules, the first of any length that were ever extant in *English*, we by those examine the Plays of our most celebrated Tragick Poets, in their Fables, Characters, Sentiments, Expressions, Harmony; shew what distinguishes them, from one another, from the best of the Ancients, and the most famous Moderns of other Countries. And here we make it our business to shew how much the present *English* Stage is degenerated from the Virtue and Greatness of the Ancient Tragedy, and what is to be done to restore Modern Tragedy first to the Innocence, and secondly to the Greatness of the *Grecian* Stage. And here we examine whether it is not possible to advance *English* Tragedy to a greater Height than ever the *Grecian* Poets arriv'd.

In the next place we descend to the third and last Branch of the Greater Poetry, which is the Greater Ode, which we treat of after the same manner with the two preceding, and shew what the composer of such an Ode is oblig'd to do, to make it keep up to the Nature of the Greater Poetry in general, and to its own. And here we have occasion to take notice, that of these three Branches of Poetry, the Ode is the most degenerated: For since the Nature of Poetry consists in Passion; and that of the Greater Poetry in great Passion, as we make it appear in the foremention'd *Criticism*; and since that which we commonly call Passion is very rarely to be found in the Greater Ode, it follows that the excellence of the Greater Ode must consist in extraordinary Passion, which can be nothing but strong *Enthusiasm*; but Religion is the greatest, noblest, strongest source of *Enthusiasm* as we very clearly shew; so that the Modern Ode, by forsaking Religion, and becoming for the most part prophane, has parted with that from which it deriv'd its greatest excellence.

And that the excellence of the Greater Ode is deriv'd from Religion, we make appear not only by the Examples of those very few which are admirable among our own, but by those of *Pindar* and *Horace*; and we shew that the first of those great Masters was so throughly convinc'd of this at the same time, that he was oblig'd, by the desire of Gain, to celebrate the Triumphs of worthless Coachmen and Jockeys, that his numerous extravagant Digressions are to be attributed, in a great measure, to that Conviction join'd with that Obligation.[10] When we have done this,

2. We descend to the other division of Poetry, which is the Less; and shall treat of those Branches of it in which our *English* Poets are most concern'd, after the same Method that we treated of those of the Greater. Where first we shall speak of the Little Ode, and shew for what Reasons our *English* Poets have, for the most part miscarried in it. Then we shall give the Reader a large *Criticism* upon Comedy, the first of any Moment that will be extant upon it in any Language.

And here we shall endeavour to make it appear, that as the Moderns have apparently the advantage of the Ancients in Comedy, the *English* have it of the rest of the Moderns.

We shall end with a *Criticism* upon Satyr, where we shall shew the true difference between that and a Libel or Lampoon; and the usefulness of the one, and destructiveness of the other.

Thus we laid before the Reader the Design and Method of the Work. But because the discerning Reader cannot but see, that it is impossible for any Bookseller to make it worth the Undertaker's Trouble in employing so much Time and Thought as so great and important a Design requires, the lovers of *Criticism* are therefore desir'd, at least those who have Spirit enough to promote so generous an Undertaking, to encourage it by their Subscriptions at the Rate of a Guinea a Book, paying half a Guinea down at the time of subscribing, and half at the delivery of the Book in Quires; the Undertaker at the same time promising, that not a Book shall be printed more than the number subscribed.

For the greater variety, the Lives of the several *English* Poets will be added in their proper places.

SPECIMEN.

*Being the Substance of what will be said in the
Beginning of the* Criticism *upon* Milton.

THE next Poet of whom we shall treat is *Milton*, one of the greatest and most daring Genius's that has appear'd in the World, and who has made his Country a glorious present of the most lofty, but most irregular Poem, that has been produc'd by the Mind of Man. That great Man had a desire to give the World something like an Epick Poem; but he resolv'd at the same time to break thro' the Rules of *Aristotle*. Not that he was ignorant of them, or contemn'd them. On the contrary, no Man knew them better, or esteemed them more, because no Man had an Understanding that was more able to comprehend the necessity of them; and therefore when he mention'd them in the little Treatise which he wrote to Mr. *Hartlib*, he calls the Art which treats of them, a sublime Art.[11] But at the same time he had discernment enough to see, that if he wrote a Poem which was within the compass of them, he should be subjected to the same Fate which has attended all who have wrote Epick Poems ever since the time of *Homer*, and that is to be a Copyist instead of an Original. Tis true, the Epick Poets who have liv'd since *Homer*, have most of them been Originals in their Fables, which are the very Souls of their Poems; but in their manner of treating those Fables, they have too frequently been Copyists, They have Copyed the Spirit and the Images of *Homer*, even the great *Virgil* himself is not to be excepted. *Milton* was the first, who in the space of almost 4000 Years, resolved, for his Country's Honour and his own, to present the World with an Original Poem; that is to say, a Poem that should have his own Thoughts, his own Images, and his own Spirit. In order to this he was resolved to write a Poem, that, by vertue of its extraordinary Subject, cannot so properly be said to be against the Rules, as it may be affirmed to be above them all. He had observ'd, that *Aristotle* had drawn his Rules which he has given us for Epick Poetry from the Reflections which he had made upon *Homer*. Now he knew very well, that in *Homer* the Action lay chiefly between Man and Man: For *Achilles* and *Hector* are properly the Principals, and the Gods are but Seconds. He was resolved therefore, that his Principals should be the Devil on one side and Man on the other: and the Devil is properly his Hero, because he gets the better. All the persons in his Poem, excepting two, are either Divine or Infernal. So that most of the Persons and particularly one of the Principals, being so very different from what *Homer* or *Aristotle* ever thought of, could not possibly be subjected to their Rules, either for the Characters or the Incidents. We shall now shew for what Reasons the choice of *Milton*'s Subject, as it set him free from the Obligation which he lay under to the Poetical Laws, so it necessarily threw him upon new Thoughts, new Images, and an Original Spirit. In the next place we shall shew, that his Thoughts, his Images, and by consequence too his Spirit, are actually new, and different from those of *Homer* and *Virgil*. Thirdly, We shall shew, that besides their Newness, they have vastly the Advantage of those of *Homer* and *Virgil*. And we shall make this appear from several things, but principally from the Description of Hell, which has been describ'd by those three great Poets with all their Force and with all their Art. After that, we shall proceed to say something of *Milton*'s Expression and his Harmony; and then we shall come to mark his Defects with so much the more exactness, because some of them ought to be avoided with the utmost Caution, as being so great, that they would be Insupportable in any one who had not his extraordinary Distinguishing Qualities.

CHAP. I.

The Design of the following Treatise, is the Re-establishment of Poetry.

THE Design of the ensuing Treatise, whether we consider the Importance or the Extent of it, is perhaps the greatest in this kind of Writing, that has been conceiv'd by the Moderns; for 'tis no less than an Attempt to restore and re-establish the noblest Art in every Branch of it: an Art, that by the Barbarity of the Times, is fallen and sunk in them all, and has been driven and banish'd from every Country excepting *England* alone; and is even here so miserably fallen for the most part by the Extravagance of its Professors, and by the Unskilfulness of its Admirers, that we have reason to apprehend it to be departing from hence too.

That Poetry is the noblest of all Arts, and by consequence the most instructive and most beneficial to Mankind, may be prov'd by the concording Testimony of the greatest Men, who have liv'd in every Age; the greatest Philosophers, the greatest Heroes, and the greatest Statesmen, who have, as it were, unanimously cherish'd, esteem'd, admir'd it: and never has it been disesteem'd or neglected by any but some Pretenders to Wisdom, and by some contemptible Politicasters, Persons who have got into the Management of Affairs only by the Weakness of those who have employ'd them, and who have utterly wanted Capacity to know what a glorious Use may be made of it, for the Benefit of Civil Society. But in the Sequel of this Discourse, by discovering the Nature of Poetry in general (which seems to me to have been hitherto but little understood) I shall clearly shew its Excellence, and the Importance of this Undertaking. And by laying down either the general Rules of it, or by tracing out that sublime Art, which to make use of *Milton*'s Expression, teaches what the Laws are of a true Epick Poem, what of a Dramatick, what of a Lyrick, what Decorum is, what is the grand Masterpiece to observe; I shall not only lay a good Foundation for the judging of the Performance of the several Poets, whose Works I have undertaken to examine, but shall, as *Milton* says in his Treatise of Education to Mr. *Hartlip*,[12] soon make the World perceive what despicable Creatures our common Rhymers and Play-wrights are, and shew them what religious, what glorious, and magnificent Use may be made of Poetry, both in Divine and in Human Things.

CHAP. II.

That Poetry is to be establish'd, by laying down the Rules.

THAT an Art, so Divine in its Institution, is sunk and profan'd, and miserably debas'd, is a thing that is confess'd by all. But since Poetry is fallen from the Excellence which it once attain'd to, it must be fallen either by the want of Parts, or want of Industry, or by the Errors of its Professors. But that it cannot be for want of Parts, we have shewn clearly in the Advancement of modern Poetry; nor can it be suppos'd to be for want of Industry, since so many of its Professors have no other Dependance. It remains then that it must have fallen by their Errors, and for want of being guided right. Since therefore 'tis for want of knowing by what Rules they ought to proceed, that Poetry is fallen so low, it follows then that it is the laying down of those Rules alone, that can re-establish it. In short, Poetry is either an Art, or whimsy and Fanaticism. If it is an Art, it follows that it must propose an End to it self, and afterwards lay down proper Means for the attaining that End: For this is undeniable, that there are proper Means for the attaining of every End, and those proper Means in Poetry we call the Rules. Again, if the End of Poetry be to instruct and reform the World, that is, to bring Mankind from Irregularity, Extravagance, and Confusion, to Rule and Order, how this should be done by a thing that is in it self irregular and extravagant, is difficult to be conceiv'd. Besides, the Work of every reasonable Creature must derive its Beauty from Regularity; for Reason is Rule and Order, and nothing can be irregular either in our Conceptions or our Actions, any further than it swerves from Rule, that is, from Reason. As Man is the more perfect, the more he resembles his Creator; the Works of Man must needs be more perfect, the more they resemble his Maker's. Now the Works of God, tho infinitely various, are extremely regular.

The Universe is regular in all its Parts, and it is to that exact Regularity that it owes its admirable Beauty. The Microcosm owes the Beauty and Health both of its Body and Soul to Order, and the Deformity and Distempers of both to nothing but the want of Order. Man was created, like the rest of the Creatures, regular, and as long as he remain'd so, he continu'd happy; but as soon as he fell from his Primitive State, by transgressing Order, Weakness and Misery was the immediate Consequence of that universal Disorder that immediately follow'd in his Conceptions, in his Passions and Actions.

The great Design of Arts is to restore the Decays that happen'd to human Nature by the Fall, by restoring Order: The Design of Logick is to bring back Order, and Rule, and Method to our Conceptions, the want of which causes most of our Ignorance, and all our Errors. The Design of moral Philosophy is to cure the Disorder that is found in our Passions, from which proceeds all our Unhappiness, and all our Vice; as from the due Order that is seen in them, comes all our Virtue and all our Pleasure. But how should these Arts re-establish Order, unless they themselves were regular? Those Arts that make the Senses instrumental to the Pleasure of the Mind, as Painting and Musick, do it by a great deal of Rule and Order: Since therefore Poetry comprehends the Force of all these Arts of Logick, of Ethicks, of Eloquence, of Painting, of Musick; can any thing be more ridiculous than to imagine, that Poetry it self should be without Rule and Order?

CHAP. III.

What Poetry is, and that it attains its End by exciting of Passion.

WE have said above, that as Poetry is an Art, it must have a certain End, and that there must be Means that are proper for the attaining that End, which Means are otherwise call'd the Rules: But that we may make this appear the more plainly, let us declare what Poetry is. Poetry then is an Art, by which a Poet excites Passion (and for that very Cause entertains Sense) in order to satisfy and improve, to delight and reform the Mind, and so to make Mankind happier and better: from which it appears that Poetry has two Ends, a subordinate, and a final one; the subordinate one is Pleasure, and the final one is Instruction.

First, The subordinate End of Poetry is to please, for that Pleasure is the Business and Design of Poetry is evident; because Poetry, unless it pleases, nay and pleases to a height, is the most contemptible thing in the World. Other things may be borne with if they are indifferent, but Poetry, unless it is transporting, is abominable: nay, it has only the name of Poetry, so inseparable is Pleasure from the very nature of the Thing.

But, *Secondly,* The final End of Poetry is to reform the Manners: As Poetry is an Art, Instruction must be its final End; but either that Instruction must consist in reforming the Manners, or it cannot instruct at all, and consequently be an Art; for Poetry pretends to no other Instruction as its final End. But since the final End of Poetry is to reform the Manners, nothing can be according to the true Art of it, which is against Religion, or which runs counter to moral Virtue, or to the true Politicks, and to the Liberty of Mankind: and every thing which is against the last, tends to the Corruption and Destruction of Mankind; and consequently every thing against the last, must be utterly inconsistent with the true Art of Poetry.

Now the proper Means for Poetry, to attain both its subordinate and final End, is by exciting Passion.

1*st,* The subordinate End of Poetry, which is to please, is attain'd by exciting Passion, because every one who is pleas'd is mov'd, and either desires, or rejoices, or admires, or hopes, or the like. As we are mov'd by Pleasure which is Happiness, to do every thing we do, we may find upon a little Reflection, that every Man is incited by some Passion or other, either to Action, or to Contemplation; and Passion is the result either of Action or of Contemplation, as long as either of them please; and the more either of them pleases, the more they are attended with Passion. The Satisfaction that we receive from Geometry it self, comes from the Joy of having found out Truth, and the Desire of finding more. And the Satiety that seizes us upon too long a Lecture, proceeds from nothing but from the Weariness of our Spirits, and consequently from the Cessation or the Decay of those two pleasing Passions. But,

2dly, Poetry attains its final End, which is the reforming the Minds of Men, by exciting of Passion. And here I dare be bold to affirm, that all Instruction whatever depends upon Passion. The moral Philosophers themselves, even the dryest of them, can never instruct and reform, unless they move; for either they make Vice odious and Virtue lovely, or they deter you from one by the Apprehension of Misery, or they incite you to the other by the Happiness they make you expect from it; or they work upon your Shame, or upon your Pride, or upon your Indignation. And therefore Poetry instructs and reforms more powerfully than Philosophy can do, because it moves more powerfully: And therefore it instructs more easily too. For whereas all Men have Passions, and great Passions of one sort or another; and whereas those Passions will be employ'd, and whatever way they move, they that way draw the Man; it follows, that Philosophy can instruct but hardly, because it moves but gently: for the violent Passions not finding their account in those faint Emotions, begin to rebel and fly to their old Objects; whereas Poetry, at the same time that it instructs us powerfully, must reform us easily; because it makes the very Violence of the Passions contribute to our Reformation. For the Generality of Mankind are apparently sway'd by their Passions, nay, and perhaps the very best and wisest of them. The greatest Philosophers and the greatest princes are influenc'd by their Favourites, and so are the wisest Magistrates. And 'tis for this reason that not only the Devil, who must be suppos'd to understand human Nature, corrupts Mankind by their Passions; (for Temptation is nothing but the inclining Men to such and such Actions, by the raising such and such Passions in them) but God himself, who made the Soul, and best understands its Nature, converts it by its Passions. For whereas Philosophy pretends to correct human Passions by human Reason, that is, things that are strong and ungovernable, by something that is feeble and weak; Poetry by the force of the Passion, instructs and reforms the Reason: which is the Design of the true Religion, as we have shewn in another place.[13] So that we have here already laid down one great Rule, necessary for the succeeding in Poetry: for since it can attain neither its subordinate nor its final End, without exciting of Passion, it follows, That where there is nothing which directly tends to the moving of that, there can be no Poetry; and that consequently a Poet ought to contrive every thing in order to the moving of Passion, that not only the Fable, the Incidents and Characters, but the very Sentiments and the Expressions, ought all to be design'd for that. For since Poetry pleases and instructs us more even than Philosophy it self, only because it moves us more, it follows, That the more Poetry moves, the more it pleases and instructs: and it is for this reason that Tragedy, to those who have a Taste of it, is both more pleasing and more instructing than Comedy. And this naturally brings us to the dividing Poetry into the greater and the less.

1. The greater Poetry is an Art by which a Poet justly and reasonably excites great Passion, that he may please and instruct; and comprehends Epick, Tragick, and the greater Lyrick Poetry.

2. The less Poetry is an Art by which a Poet excites less Passion for the foremention'd Ends; and includes in it Comedy and Satire, and the little Ode, and Elegiack and Pastoral Poems. But first we shall treat of the former.

CHAP. IV.

What the greater Poetry is, what Enthusiasm is.

THE greater Poetry then, is an Art by which a Poet justly and reasonably excites great Passion, in order to please and instruct, and make Mankind better and happier; so that the first and grand Rule in the greater Poetry is, that a Poet must every where excite great Passion: but in some Branches of the greater Poetry, it is impossible for a Poet every where to excite in a very great degree, that which we vulgarly call Passion: as in the Ode, for example, and in the Narration of the Epick Poem. It follows then, that there must be two sorts of Passion: *First*, That which we call Vulgar Passion; and *Secondly*, Enthusiasm.

First, Vulgar Passion, or that which we commonly call Passion, is that which is moved by the Objects themselves, or by the Ideas in the ordinary Course of Life; I mean, that common Society which we find in the World. As for example, Anger is moved by an Affront that is offer'd us in our presence, or by the Relation of one; Pity by the Sight of a mournful Object, or the Relation of one; Admiration or Wonder, (the common Passion, I mean; for there is an Enthusiastick Admiration, as we shall find anon) by the Sight of a strange Object, or the Relation of one. But,

Secondly, Enthusiastick Passion or Enthusiasm, is a Passion which is moved by the Ideas in Contemplation, or the Meditation of things that belong not to common Life. Most of our Thoughts in Meditation are naturally attended with some sort and some degree of Passion; and this Passion, if it is strong, I call Enthusiasm. Now the Enthusiastick Passions are chiefly six, Admiration, Terror, Horror, Joy, Sadness, Desire, caus'd by Ideas occurring to us in Meditation, and producing the same Passions that the Objects of those Ideas would raise in us, if they were set before us in the same light that those Ideas give us of them. And here I desire the Reader to observe, that Ideas in Meditation are often very different from what Ideas of the same Objects are, in the course of common Conversation. As for example, the Sun mention'd in ordinary Conversation, gives the Idea of a round flat shining Body, of about two foot diameter. But the Sun occurring to us in Meditation, gives the Idea of a vast and glorious Body, and the top of all the visible Creation, and the brightest material Image of the Divinity. I leave the Reader therefore to judge, if this Idea must not necessarily be attended with Admiration; and that Admiration I call Enthusiasm. So Thunder mention'd in common Conversation, gives an Idea of a black Cloud, and a great Noise, which makes no great Impression upon us. But the Idea of it occurring in Meditation, sets before us the most forcible, most resistless, and consequently the most dreadful Phænomenon in Nature: So that this Idea must move a great deal of Terror in us, and 'tis this sort of Terror that I call Enthusiasm. And 'tis this sort of Terror, or Admiration, or Horror, and so of the rest, which express'd in Poetry make that Spirit, that Passion, and that Fire, which so wonderfully please.

Thus there are two sorts of Passions to be rais'd in Poetry, the Vulgar and the Enthusiastick; to which last, the Vulgar is preferable, because all Men are capable of being moved by the Vulgar, and a Poet writes to all: But the Enthusiastick are more subtle, and thousands have no feeling and no notion of them. But where the Vulgar cannot be moved in a great degree, there the Enthusiastick are to be rais'd. Therefore in those parts of Epick Poetry, where the Poet speaks himself, or the eldest of the Muses for him, the Enthusiastick Passions are to prevail, as likewise in the greater Ode. And the Vulgar Passions are to prevail in those parts of an Epick and Dramatick Poem, where the Poet introduces Persons holding Conversation together. And perhaps this might be one Reason, for which *Aristotle* might prefer Tragedy to Epick Poetry,[14] because the Vulgar Passions prevail more in it, and are more violently moved in it; and therefore Tragedy must necessarily both please and instruct, more generally than Epick Poetry. We shall then treat of the Vulgar Passions when we come to speak of Tragedy, in which Poem they ought most to prevail: we shall then more particularly shew the surest and most powerful ways of raising Compassion and Terror, which are the true Tragical Passions.

We shall at present treat of the Enthusiastick Passions, and how they are to be rais'd. We have taken notice above, that they are to be mov'd by Ideas occurring in Contemplation; that they are to be mov'd in a great degree, and yet justly and reasonably. We shall now shew, that the strongest Enthusiastick Passions, that are justly and reasonably rais'd, must be rais'd by religious Ideas; that is, by Ideas which either shew the Attributes of the Divinity, or relate to his Worship. And this we shall endeavour to prove, 1st, By Reason: 2dly, By Authority: 3dly, By Examples.

1st, We shall endeavour to prove it by Reason. Since the foresaid Passions are to be mov'd in a great degree, and are to be mov'd by their Ideas, it follows, that to be justly and reasonably mov'd, they must be mov'd by great Ideas. And therefore the stronger the Enthusiasm is, the greater must the Ideas be. Now those Ideas are certainly the greatest, which are worthiest to move the greatest and the wisest Men: for there the Enthusiastick Passions in Poetry are truly admirable, when the greater and more violent they are, the more they show the Largeness of Soul, and Greatness of Capacity of the Writer. For Men are mov'd for two Reasons, either because they have weak Minds and Souls, that are capable of being mov'd by little Objects, and consequently by little and ordinary Ideas; or because they have Greatness of Soul and Capacity, to discern and feel the great ones: for the Enthusiastick Passions being caus'd by the Ideas, it follows, that the more the Soul is capable of receiving Ideas whose Objects are truly great and wonderful, the greater will the Enthusiasm be that is caus'd by those Ideas. From whence it follows, that the greater the Soul is, and the larger the Capacity, the more will it be mov'd by religious Ideas; which are not only great and wonderful, but which almost alone are great and wonderful to a great and wise Man; and which never fail to move very strongly, unless it is for want of due Reflection, or want of Capacity in the Subject.

Since therefore the Enthusiasm in the greater Poetry, is to hold proportion with the Ideas; and those Ideas are certainly the greatest, which are worthiest to move the greatest and the wisest Men: and Divine Ideas, or Ideas which shew the Attributes of God, or relate to his Worship, are worthiest to move the greatest and the wisest Men; because such Ideas belong to Objects which are only truly above them, and consequently truly Admirable, Desirable, Joyful, Terrible, &c. it follows, That the greatest and strongest Enthusiasm that can be employ'd in Poetry, is only justly and reasonably to be deriv'd from Religious Ideas.

But here we desire the Reader's leave to make this Observation, That since Religious and Divine Ideas, or Ideas which shew the Attributes or relate to the Worship of the Divinity, are the worthiest to move the greatest and the wisest Men; and the greater and wiser the Men are, the more they must move and raise them; as for example, the greater and more comprehensive the Soul is, which reflects upon the Idea of God, the more that Idea must fill that Soul with Admiration: it follows, That as great Passion only is the adequate Language of the greater Poetry, so the greater Poetry is only the adequate Language of Religion; and that therefore the greatest Passion is the Language of that sort of Poetry, because that sort of Poetry is the worthiest Language of Religion.

But, 2*dly*, We shall proceed to prove by Authority, That the strongest Enthusiastick Passions in Poetry are only justly and reasonably to be rais'd by religious Ideas: And this we shall show by the Authority of the greatest Criticks among the Antients, *Aristotle*, *Hermogenes*, and *Longinus*.

(1.) *Aristotle* says, in the third Book of his Rhetorick, *cap.* 2, & 3. That the frequent Use of Methaphors, Dialects, Epithets, is a great deal fitter for Poetry than it is for Prose, because they are the Language of Passion; and Poetry is more Passionate or more Enthusiastick than Prose, for this Reason, because the Persons and the Things of which Poetry treats, are many degrees above those which are the Subjects of Prose. Now all the World knows, that the *Grecians* treated of the greatest human Persons and Things in their Prose, but that Poetry was a Language which they reserv'd for their Gods, and for the Things which related to them. And I am apt to believe, that Poetry from hence was call'd the Language of the Gods, because whenever the *Grecians* in the Poetical Times introduced their Gods speaking, they were sure to speak in Verse. But,

(2.) *Hermogenes*, in the sixth Chapter of the first Book of his Treatise, concerning the Forms of Speech, tells us, that there are four kinds of Thoughts or Ideas, or Conceptions, which were proper to give that

Elevation and Gravity to a Discourse, which by their Union compose that Quality in Writing which we call Majesty.

1. The first and principal of them are all such Thoughts or Ideas of God, as are worthy of the Divinity; not like some of the *Homerical* Conceptions of *Jupiter*, which, says *Hermogenes*, being more Human than Divine, and unworthy of the Divinity, are contrary to true Majesty.

2. Next to these the Conceptions which give Elevation and Gravity, and consequently Majesty to a Discourse, are such Thoughts or Ideas concerning the Works of God, as are worthy the Divine Workmanship.

3. The third sort of Conceptions are, of such Things as are indeed themselves Divine, but they are such Emanations of Divinity, as are to be seen in Men; as Justice, Temperance, Fortitude, Nature, Law, and the like; to which may be added, Number, Power and Might.

4. The fourth sort are, of Things that indeed are Human, but are reputed Great and Illustrious, as Conquest, Riches, Nobility, &c. But here I desire the Reader to observe, that *Hermogenes* is here speaking concerning Pieces of Eloquence, and such Discourses as are writ in Prose; for it is certain, that these last Ideas, as they are of Things that are merely Human, can never afford the greatest Spirit that can be employ'd in Poetry. For as the Objects themselves are not truly great, because, as *Longinus* says, a Man who has it in his power to possess them, shows himself great by contemning them; it is impossible that a Spirit that is very great, can flow from these Ideas, because the Spirit that is very great, must hold proportion with its Ideas, as the Ideas must with their Objects: and therefore these Ideas cannot be great, because their Objects are not great.[15]

We ought now, in the third place, to proceed to the Authority of *Longinus*. But that we may diversify this Treatise the more, and make it the more entertaining, we shall first shew Examples of the several Kinds of the foremention'd Thoughts, producing that sort of Spirit in Poetry which we call Enthusiastick Admiration: and that we may show the Reader more plainly how that Spirit is produc'd, we shall set before him as near as we can, such kind of Thoughts as inspire the

Soul with Admiration alone, uncomplicated with Terror, or any other Passion. . . .[16]

I now come to the Precepts of *Longinus*, and pretend to shew from them, that the greatest Sublimity is to be deriv'd from Religious Ideas. But why then, says the Reader, has not *Longinus* plainly told us so? He was not ignorant that he ought to make his Subject as plain as he could. For he has told us in the beginning of his Treatise, that every one who gives Instruction concerning an Art, ought to endeavour two things: The first is to make his Reader clearly understand what that is which he pretends to teach: The second is to shew him how it may be attain'd.[17] And he blames *Cecilius* very severely for neglecting the last; how then, says the Objector, comes he himself to have taken no care of the first? Is it because *Cecilius* had done it before him? If so, it was a very great Fault in *Longinus* to publish a Book which could not be understood but by another Man's Writings; especially when he saw that those Writings were so very defective, that they would not probably last. But what, continues the Objector, if *Cecilius* had not done it before him? For *Longinus* tells us, that *Cecilius* makes use of a multitude of Words to shew what it is; now he who knows any thing clearly, may in a few Words explain it clearly to others; and he who does not, will make it obscure by many.

To this I answer, that tho *Longinus* did by long Study and Habitude know the Sublime when he saw it, as well as any Man, yet he had not so clear a Knowledge of the nature of it, as to explain it clearly to others. For if he had done that, as the Objector says, he would have defin'd it; but he has been so far from defining it, that in one place he has given an account of it that is contrary to the true nature of it. For he tells us in that Chapter which treats of the Fountains of Sublimity, that Loftiness is often without any Passion at all; which is contrary to the true nature of it.[18] The Sublime is indeed often without common Passion, as ordinary Passion is often without that. But then it is never without Enthusiastick Passion: For the Sublime is nothing else but a great Thought, or great Thoughts moving the Soul from its ordinary Situation by the Enthusiasm which naturally attends them. Now *Longinus* had a notion of Enthusiastick Passion, for he establishes it in that very Chapter for the second Source of Sublimity. Now

Longinus, by affirming that the Sublime may be without not only that, but ordinary Passion, says a thing that is not only contrary to the true nature of it, but contradictory to himself. For he tells us in the beginning of the Treatise, that the Sublime does not so properly persuade us, as it ravishes and transports us, and produces in us a certain Admiration, mingled with Astonishment and with Surprize, which is quite another thing than the barely pleasing, or the barely persuading;[19] that it gives a noble Vigour to a Discourse, an invincible Force, which commits a pleasing Rape upon the very Soul of the Reader; that whenever it breaks out where it ought to do, like the Artillery of *Jove*, it thunders, blazes, and strikes at once, and shews all the united Force of a Writer. Now I leave the Reader to judge, whether *Longinus* has not been saying here all along that Sublimity is never without Passion.

That the foremention'd Definition is just and good, I have reason to believe, because it takes in all the Sources of Sublimity which *Longinus* has establish'd. For, first, Greatness of Thought supposes Elevation, they being synonymous Terms: And, secondly, the Enthusiasm or the Pathetique, as *Longinus* calls it, follows of course; for if a Man is not strongly mov'd by great Thoughts, he does not sufficiently and effectually conceive them. And, thirdly, the figurative Language is but a Consequence of the Enthusiasm, that being the natural Language of the Passions. And so is, fourthly, the Nobleness of the Expression, supposing a Man to be Master of the Language in which he writes. For as the Thoughts produce the Spirit or the Passion, the Spirit produces and makes the Expression, which is known by Experience to all who are Poets; for never any one, while he was wrapt with Enthusiasm or ordinary Passion, wanted either Words or Harmony, as is self-evident to all who consider that the Expression conveys and shows the Spirit, and consequently must be produc'd by it.

Thus the Definition which we have laid down being, according to *Longinus*'s own Doctrine, the true Definition of the Sublime, and shewing clearly the thing which he has not done, nor given any Definition at all of it; it seems plain to me, that he had no clear and distinct Idea of it; and consequently Religion might be the thing from which 'tis chiefly to be deriv'd, and he but obscurely know it: but that

Religion is that thing from which the Sublime is chiefly to be deriv'd, let us shew by the Marks which he has given of the latter; which will further strengthen our Definition.[20] 1. Says he, that which is truly Sublime has this peculiar to it, that it exalts the Soul, and makes it conceive a greater Idea of it self, filling it with Joy, and with a certain noble Pride, as if it self had produc'd what it but barely reads.

Now here it is plain, that the highest Ideas must most exalt the Soul, but Religious Ideas are the highest.

The more the Soul is moved by the greatest Ideas, the more it conceives them; but the more it conceives of the greatest Ideas, the greater Opinion it must have of its own Capacity. By consequence the more it is moved by the Wonders of Religion, the more it values it self upon its own Excellences. Again, the more the Soul sees its Excellence, the more it rejoices. Besides, Religious Ideas are the most admirable; and what is most admirable, according to the Doctrine of *Aristotle*, is most delightful.[21] Besides, Religious Ideas create Passion in such a manner, as to turn and incline the Soul to its primitive Object. So that Reason and Passion are of the same side, and this Peace between the Faculties causes the Soul to rejoice; of which we shall have occasion to say more anon.

2. The second Mark that *Longinus* gives of the Sublime, is, when a Discourse leaves a great deal for us to think. But now this is certain, that the Wonders of Religion are never to be exhausted; for they are always new, and the more you enter into them, the more they are sure to surprize.

3. The third Mark is, when it leaves in the Reader an Idea above its Expression. Now no Expressions can come up to the Ideas which we draw from the Attributes of God, or from his wondrous Works, which only the Author of them can comprehend.

4. The fourth Mark is, when it makes an Impression upon us, which it is impossible to resist.

God, who made Man for himself, and for his own Glory, and who requires chiefly his Heart, must by consequence have form'd him of such a nature, as to be most strongly moved with Religious Ideas, if once he enters into them. So that the Impressions which they make, are impossible to be resisted.

5. The fifth Mark is, when the Impression lasts, and is difficult to be defaced. Now that the Impressions which religion makes upon us are difficult to be defaced, is plain from this, that they who think it their Interest to deface them, can never bring it about.

6. The sixth Mark is, when it pleases universally, People of different Humours, Inclinations, Sexes, Ages, Times, Climates. Now there is nothing so agreeable to the Soul, or that makes so universal an Impression, as the Wonders of Religion. Some Persons are moved by Love, and are not touch'd by Ambition; others are animated by Ambition, and only laugh at Love. Some are pleas'd with a brave Revenge, others with a generous Contempt of Injuries; but the Eternal Power, and the Infinite Knowledge of God, the Wonders of the Creation, and the beautiful Brightness of Virtue, make a powerful Impression on all.

I must confess I have wonder'd very much, upon Reflection, how it could happen that so great a Man as *Longinus*, who whenever he met a Passage in any Discourse that was lofty enough to please him, had Discernment enough to see that it had some of the preceding Marks, should miss of finding so easy a thing as this, that never any Passage had all these Marks, or so much as the Majority of them, unless it were Religious.

But to return to Terror, we may plainly see by the foregoing Precepts and Examples of *Longinus*, that this Enthusiastick Terror contributes extremely to the Sublime; and, secondly, that it is most produced by Religious Ideas.

First, Ideas producing Terror, contribute extremely to the Sublime. All the Examples that *Longinus* brings of the Loftiness of the Thought, consist of terrible Ideas. And they are principally such Ideas that work the Effects, which he takes notice of in the beginning of his Treatise, *viz.* that ravish and transport the Reader, and produce a certain Admiration, mingled with Astonishment and with Surprize. For the Ideas which produce Terror, are necessarily accompany'd with Admiration, because ev'ry thing that is terrible, is great to him to whom it is terrible; and with Surprize, without which Terror cannot subsist; and with Astonishment, because everything which is very terrible, is wonderful and astonishing: and as Terror is perhaps the violentest of all the Passions, it consequently makes an Impression which we cannot resist, and which is hardly to be defaced: and no Passion is attended with greater Joy than Enthusiastick Terror, which proceeds from our reflecting that we are out of danger at the very time that we see it before us. And as Terror is one of the violentest of all Passions, if it is very great, and the hardest to be resisted, nothing gives more Force, nor more Vehemence to a Discourse.

But, secondly, it is plain from the same *Longinus*, that this Enthusiastick Terror is chiefly to be deriv'd from Religious Ideas. For all the Examples which he has brought of the Sublime, in his Chapter of the Sublimity of the Thoughts, consists of most terrible and most religious Ideas; and at the same time every Man's Reason will inform him, that every thing that is terrible in Religion, is the most terrible thing in the World.

But that we may set this in a clearer Light, let us lay before the Reader the several Ideas which are capable of producing this enthusiastick Terror; which seem to me to be those which follow, *viz.* Gods, Dæmons, Hell, Spirits and Souls of Men, Miracles, Prodigies, Enchantments, Witchcrafts, Thunder, Tempests, raging Seas, Inundations, Torrents, Earthquakes, Volcanos, Monsters, Serpents, Lions, Tygers, Fire, War, Pestilence, Famine, *&c.*

Now of all these Ideas none are so terrible as those which shew the Wrath and Vengeance of an angry God; for nothing is so wonderful in its Effects: and consequently the Images or Ideas of those Effects must carry a great deal of Terror with them, which we may see was *Longinus*'s Opinion, by the Examples which he brings in his Chapter of the Sublimity of the Thoughts. Now of things which are terrible, those are the most terrible which are the most wonderful; because that seeing them both threatning and powerful, and not being able to fathom the Greatness and Extent of their Power, we know not how far and how soon they may hurt us.

But further, nothing is so terrible as the Wrath of infinite Power, because nothing is so unavoidable as the Vengeance design'd by it. There is no flying nor lying hid from the great universal Monarch. He may deliver us from all other Terrors, but nothing can save and defend us from him. And therefore Reason, which serves to dissipate our Terrors in some other Dangers, serves but to augment them when we are threatened by infinite Power; and that Fortitude, which may be heroick at other times, is downright Madness then.

For the other Ideas, which we mention'd above, they will be found to be more terrible as they have more of Religion in them. But we shall have so many necessary Occasions of giving Examples of them, in the Sequel of this Treatise, that it will be altogether needless to do it now. But here it will be convenient to answer an Objection: For how come some of the foremention'd Ideas, which seem to have but little to do with Religion, to be terrible to great and to wise Men? as it is plain that such, when they read the Descriptions of them in *Homer* and *Virgil*, are terrify'd.

To which we answer, That the Care, which Nature has inrooted in all, of their own Preservation, is the Cause that Men are unavoidably terrify'd with any thing that threatens approaching Evil. 'Tis now our Business to shew how the Ideas of Serpents, Lions, Tygers, &c. were made by the Art of those great Poets, to be terrible to their Readers, at the same time that we are secure from their Objects.

'Tis very plain that it is the Apprehension of Danger which causes that Emotion in us which we call Terror, and it signifies nothing at all to the purpose whether the Danger is real or imaginary; and 'tis as plain too, that the Soul never takes the Alarm from any thing so soon as it does from the Senses, especially those two noble ones of the Eye and the Ear, by reason of the strict Affinity which they have with the Imagination; and the Evil always seems to be very near, when those two Senses give notice of it; and the nearer the Evil is, the greater still is the Terror. But now let us see how those two Poets did, by virtue of their Ideas, bring even absent terrible Objects within the reach of those two noble Senses. First then, to bring an absent terrible Object before our Sight, they drew an Image or Picture of it; but to draw an Image or Picture of a terrible Object, so as to surprize and astonish the Soul by the Eye, they never fail'd to draw it in violent Action or Motion; and in order to that, they made choice of Words and Numbers, which might best express the Violence of that Action or Motion. For an absent Object can never be set before the Eye in a true Light, unless it be shewn in violent Action or Motion; because unless it is shewn so, the Soul has leisure to reflect upon the Deceit. But violent Motion can never be conceiv'd without a violent Agitation of Spirit, and that sudden Agitation surprizes the Soul, and gives it less time to reflect; and at the same time causes the Impressions that the Objects make to be so deep, and their Traces to be so profound, that it makes them in a manner as present to us, as if they were really before us. For the Spirits being set in a violent Emotion, and the Imagination being fir'd by that Agitation; and the Brain being deeply penetrated by those Impressions, the very Objects themselves are set as it were before us, and consequently we are sensible of the same Passion that we should feel from the things themselves. For the warmer the Imagination is, the less able we are to reflect, and consequently the things are the more present to us of which we draw the Images; and therefore when the Imagination is so inflam'd, as to render the Soul utterly incapable of reflecting, there is no difference between the Images and the Things themselves; as we may see, for example, by Men in raging Fevers. But those two great Poets were not satisfy'd with setting absent Objects before our Eyes, by shewing them in violent Motion; but if their Motion occasion'd any extraordinary Sounds that were terrifying, they so contriv'd their Numbers and Expressions, as that they might be sure to ring those Sounds in the very Ears of their Readers.

We ought now to treat of the other Enthusiastick Passions, as Horror, Grief, Joy, and Desire: But to the end that we may diversify this Treatise as much as we can, and not tire out the Reader with too much Speculation at a time, we shall omit speaking of them till we come to the Epick Poets.

CHAP. V.

*Recapitulation; and that Religion is the Basis and
Foundation of the greater Poetry.*

BUT now let us recapitulate: We have shewn in the foregoing part
of this Discourse, that Passion is the Characteristical Mark of Poetry,
and that all Poetry is pathetick; and then we divided it into two
kinds, the greater and the less; and shew'd that the greater Poetry
comprehends Epick, Tragick, and the greater Lyrick, and that our
Design was in the first place to treat of it. Then we proceeded to shew,
that as Passion is the Characteristical Mark of Poetry, great Passion
must be the Characteristical Mark of the greater Poetry, and consequently that this last must have every where great Passion; but that
since what we commonly call Passion cannot be every where, there
must be something distinct from ordinary Passion, and that must be
Enthusiasm. Then we endeavour'd to discover what Enthusiasm is,
and how many several sorts there are of it; and that Admiration and
Terror make the principal Greatness of Poetry, and are the chief of
the Enthusiastick Passions; that those two Passions are to bear proportion with the Ideas from which they are deriv'd, and that consequently the greatest must flow from religious Ideas. We shall shew
too in the Sequel of this Discourse, that not only the remaining
Enthusiastick Passions, Horror, Sadness, Joy, and Desire; but that
even the ordinary Passions, which contribute most to the Greatness
of Poetry, as Admiration, Terror, and Pity, are chiefly to be deriv'd
from Religion; but that the Passions of both sorts must, for the most
part, flow greater from Revelation than from Natural Religion; because
all Reveal'd Religion, whether true or pretended, speaks to the Senses,
brings the Wonders of another World more home to us, and so makes
the Passions which it raises the greater.

The fundamental Rule then that we pretend to lay down, for the
succeeding or excelling in the greater Poetry, is, That the Constitution
of the Poem be religious, that it may be throughout pathetick.

And we pretend to prove undeniably, that not only the Gentlemen, whose Works we design to examine, have succeeded and excell'd no further than their Poems have been so constituted; but that never any Poets of any Nation, or any Age, ever did or can excel without it. I have already prov'd in the Advancement of modern Poetry, beyond all manner of doubt, to those who have Capacity enough to comprehend the Arguments, that the antient Poets excell'd the Moderns in the Greatness of Poetry, for no other reason, but because their Subjects were religious in their Constitution: And therefore all that I shall say of it here, is, That Poetry is the natural Language of Religion, and that Religion at first produc'd it, as a Cause produces its Effect. In the first Ages of writing among the *Grecians*, there was nothing writ but Verse, because they wrote of nothing but Religion, which was necessary for the cementing the Societies which in those times were but just united; and Nature had taught them, that Poetry was the only Language in which they could worthily treat of the most important Parts of Religion, or worthily perform its most important Duties. But as soon as Religion was sufficiently imprinted in the Minds of Men, and they had leisure to treat of human things in their Writings, they invented Prose, and invented it in imitation of Verse, as *Strabo* tells us in the first Book of his Geography;[22] but after that Prose was invented by them, never any of them treated of their Gods or their religious Matters in Prose, before the Age of *Socrates*, because they found that that way of Writing was by no means proper for it. For the Wonders of Religion naturally threw them upon great Passions, and great Passions naturally threw them upon Harmony and figurative Language, as they must of necessity do any Poet, as long as he continues Master of them. Which is known by Experience to all who are Poets; for never any one, while he was wrapt with Enthusiasm, or with ordinary Passion, wanted either Words or Harmony; and therefore Poetry is more harmonious than Prose, because it is more pathetick: Even in Prose your Orators, and all who pretend to move the Passions, have more harmonious Periods than they who barely speak to the Reason. And in Poetry, they who write with a great deal of Passion, are generally very harmonious; whereas those who write with but little, are not so musical. *Horace* is an illustrious Example of this: No Man, who has read his Odes, can doubt of the Fineness and the delicacy of his Ear; and therefore his Satires are often harsh and rugged, because the Spirit in them is mean and little. No Man can believe that *Juvenal* had a finer Ear than *Horace*, but yet his Satires are more musical, because they have a greater Spirit in them. At the same time 'tis a little odd to consider, that Passion, which disturbs the Soul, should occasion it to produce Harmony, which seems to imply the Order and Composure of it. Whether this proceeds from the secret Effort that the Soul makes to compose it self, or whatever the Cause is, the Effect is certain. But as Passion, which is the Disorder of the Soul, produces Harmony, which is Agreement; so Harmony, which is Concord, augments and propagates Passion, which is Discord. All who are acquainted with Poetry or Musick; must be as sensible of this, as Mr. *Waller* was fully convinc'd of it.

> Well sounding Verses are the Charm we use,
> Heroick Thoughts and Virtue to infuse;
> Things of deep Sense we may in Prose unfold,
> But they move more in lofty Numbers told;
> By the loud Trumpet which our Courage aids,
> We learn that Sound as well as Sense persuades.[23]

Thus we may see by Mr. *Waller*, that Numbers are proper to move Passion, and for that reason are inseparable from Poetry, which has no other Design. But we shall have occasion to treat of Harmony more at large, when we come to the particular sorts of Poems; in the mean time let us return to the Business from which we may seem to have digress'd.

As we have formerly undeniably prov'd, in the Advancement of modern Poetry, that the antient Poets deriv'd that Advantage which they have over the Moderns, to the constituting their Subjects after a religious manner; so I shall make it appear, in the Sequel of this Discourse, that it was owing to the same thing that the antient Poets very often excell'd themselves.

And I have reason to believe, that one of the principal Reasons that has made the modern Poetry so contemptible, is, That by divesting it self of Religion, it is fallen from its Dignity, and its original Nature and Excellence; and from the greatest Production of the Mind of Man, is dwindled to an extravagant and a vain Amusement. For the modern Poetry being for the most part profane, has either very little Spirit; or if it has a great one, that Spirit is out of Nature, because it bears no manner of Proportion to the Ideas from which it is forcibly deriv'd, nor the Ideas very often to the Objects from which they are taken: for as Mr. *Waller* says,

> In boundless Verse the Fancy soars too high
> For any Object but the Deity:
> What Mortal can with Heav'n pretend to share
> In the Superlatives of Wise and Fair?
> A meaner Object when with these we grace,
> A Giant Habit on a Dwarf we place.[24]

But that the modern Poetry, as miserably as it is fallen from the Dignity of its original Nature, might gloriously arise and lift up its Head, surpassing even that of the Antients, if the Poets would but constitute their Subjects religious, I have formerly clearly shewn, in the second Part of the *Advancement of modern Poetry*; by shewing that the Design of the Christian Religion is the very same with that of Poetry, which can be said of no other Religion; that the Business of both is to delight and reform Mankind, by exciting the Passions in such a manner, as to reconcile them to Reason, and restore the Harmony of the human Faculties. And therefore that I may repeat nothing at present that I have formerly said there, I shall only add, that if 'tis Religion that gives the Warmth and the Passion to Poetry, it follows that the less mixture that Religion has of any thing profane and human in it, the greater Warmth and Passion it must give to Poetry; for that which moves us in effect in a false Religion, must be the Imagination of that which is true. As for example, in the above-mention'd Passage of the Wrath of *Neptune*, the Anger of *Neptune* is Fiction, and so is the Stroke of his Trident; but that which moves us at the bottom of this Fiction is true, which is, that the Anger of a Deity, and the Effects of it are very terrible. The Reason why Religion moves the Soul so extremely, is because the Soul was created by God, to find its Happiness in him; and all Happiness consists in Pleasure, and all Pleasure in Passion. Now the less mixture Religion has of any thing of human

Invention in it, the more divine it is, and the nearer it brings us to God. . . .[25]

But here it will be necessary to answer an Objection: for it may be urg'd perhaps that common Experience will destroy these new Speculations. For several of the Moderns have attempted Divine Poetry, and yet some of them have been contemptible to the last degree, and not one of them has excell'd the Antients.

To which we answer, That *Milton* has clearly the advantage of the Antients in several points, as shall be shewn in its proper place: and if the rest of the Moderns, who have attempted Sacred Poetry, have faln so very much short of them, it has been either for want of Genius, or for want of Art to know how to make use of Religion. For Sacred Poetry apparently requires a greater Capacity than the Profane does; because the greater the Ideas are, the greater must the Capacity be that receives them. But Sacred Ideas are greater than the Profane, as hath been shewn above. And therefore if the Rule of *Horace* be true, that a Poet ought to proportion his Subject to his Strength,[26] it follows, that a Man may succeed pretty well in Human Poetry, and yet be despicable in the Divine. Besides, as Religion supplies us with greater Ideas than any thing Human can do; so it requires greater Enthusiasm, and a greater Spirit to attend them, as has been shewn above too. So that Sacred Poetry requires not only a very great Capacity, but a very warm and strong Imagination; which is a happy Mixture that is to be met with in a very few, and even of those few not one in a thousand perhaps applies himself to Sacred Poetry. And even of those rare ones who have apply'd themselves, hardly one of the Moderns has known the true use that ought to be made of Religion in Poetry. *Milton* indeed happen'd upon it, in his *Paradise Lost*; I say, happen'd upon it, because he has err'd very widely from it in his *Paradise Regain'd*, as shall be shewn in its proper place. The Rules for employing Religion in Poetry, are principally these which follow.

1. The first is, That the Religion ought to be one, that the Poet may be mov'd by it, and that he may appear to be in earnest. And the not observing of this Rule, was one Reason why *Spencer* miscarry'd, as we shall shew anon.

2. The second Rule, That the Religion which the Poet employs,

ought to be the reigning one, that both the Poet and the Readers may be mov'd the more by a Religion in which they were bred. And this Rule may acquaint us with one of the Reasons why all who have translated *Homer* and *Virgil*, have succeeded so very indifferently.

3. The third is, That it may run through and be incorporated with the Action of the Poem, and consequently that it may always be a part of Action, and productive of Action; for from the Neglect of this third Rule, strange Inequalities would follow in a Poem, as shall be shewn more at large, when we treat of *Spencer* and *Cowley*.

4. The fourth Rule is, That the Religion may be managed so as to promote the Violence of the Enthusiastick Passions, and their Change and Variety; and the constituting his Subject contrary to this Rule, was one great Reason why *Milton* did not succeed in his *Paradise Regain'd*.

5. That it may not hinder the Violence of the ordinary Passions, nor the Change and Variety of them; and the not constituting his Subject according to this Rule, is the chief Reason why *Homer* in his *Odysses* fell so far short of his *Iliads*; and *Milton* of his *Paradise Lost*, in his *Paradise Regain'd*.

6. That the Religion be managed so as not to obstruct the Violence of Action, which is always attended by the Violence of ordinary Passion; and the not observing of this, was one great Reason of the Miscarriage of *Homer* and *Milton*, in the fore-mention'd Poems.

7. That the divine and human Persons, if there be any, may have Inclinations and Affections; which *Tasso*'s celestial Persons have not, nor as I remember, *Cowley*'s.

8. That they be fairly distinguish'd from one another by those Inclinations and Affections. And this is the great advantage that the *Grecian* Machines have, for the most part, over those in our Religion. Yet *Milton* has pretty well distinguish'd his celestial Persons from one another, and his infernal ones admirably.

9. That they be fairly distinguish'd from the human Persons by the same Inclinations and Affections. And here *Milton*, in his infernal Persons, has undeniably the advantage both of Antients and Moderns. The Passions and Inclinations of the *Grecian* Gods are downright human Inclinations and Affections. The Passions of *Milton*'s Devils

have enough of Humanity in them to make them delightful, but then they have a great deal more to make them admirable, and may be said to be the true Passions of Devils: but the time to speak more largely of this, will be when we come to the Epick Poets.

But now, as we have shewn that the Religion reveal'd in the Old and New Testament is proper, nay necessary, to give the last Force and Elevation to Poetry; we shall now endeavour to convince the Reader, that Poetry is proper, if not necessary, to give Force to that Religion. For indeed there are Duties in this Religion, which cannot be worthily perform'd without the assistance of Poetry: as the offering up Praise and Thanksgiving, and several sorts of Prayer to God, and the celebrating the Wonders of his Might. Because if the Ideas which these Subjects afford, are express'd with Passion equal to their Greatness, that which expresses them is Poetry: for that which makes Poetry to be what it is, is only because it has more Passion than any other way of writing.

It is ridiculous to imagine that there can be a more proper way to express some Parts and Duties of a Religion which we believe to be divinely inspired, than the very way in which they were at first deliver'd. Now the most important Part of the Old Testament was deliver'd not only in a Poetical Style, but in Poetical Numbers. The most important Parts of the Old Testament to us, are the Prophecies; because without them we could never be satisfy'd that *Jesus* is the Messiah. For the Prophets were Poets by the Institution of their Order, and Poetry was one of the Prophetick Functions, which were chiefly three: 1. Predicting or foretelling things to come. 2. Declaring the Will of God to the People. And, 3. Praising God with Songs of the Prophets composing, accompany'd with the Harp and other Instrumental Musick. From whence it came to pass, that praising God upon such kind of Instruments, is often in the Scriptures call'd Prophesying, as Mr. *Mede* has observ'd in his *Diatribæ*; and has prov'd it from several Passages of the Old Testament, and more particularly from the three first Verses of the 25th Chapter of the *Chronicles*, which are as follow.[27]

Ver. 1. *Moreover* David *and the Captains of the Host separated to the Service of the Sons of* Asaph, *and of* Heman, *and of* Jeduthun, *such as should prophesy with Harps,*

with Psalteries, and with Cymbals; and the Number of the Workmen according to their
Service was,

Ver. 2. *Of the Sons of* Asaph; Zaccar, *and* Joseph, *and* Nethaniah *and* Asarelah,
the Sons of Asaph; *under the hands of* Asaph, *which prophesy'd according to the Order*
of the King.

Ver. 3. *Of* Jeduthun, *the Sons of* Jeduthun, Gedaliah, *and* Zeri, *and* Jeshaiah,
Hashabiah, *and* Metithiah *six, under the hands of their Father* Jeduthun, *who*
prophesied with a Harp, to give thanks and to praise the Lord.

Nor was the Poetical Talent confin'd to their Praise and Thanksgiving, but is to be seen in their Predictions too, as we said before,
and in their declaring the Will of God to the People.

As the Prophets were Poets by their Institution, so when the Son
of God himself came down from Heaven in order to reform the Earth,
he who was a Prophet as well as a Priest and a King, did by consequence
discharge the three Prophetical Functions, of which the Poetical has
been shewn to be one. And consequently tho our Saviour did not
make use of a Style that was Figurative and Enthusiastick, because he
instructed the World as God, and as God he could not feel either
Admiration or Terror, or the rest of the Enthusiastick Passions; yet
we find that he not only prais'd God with spiritual Songs, but that the
Method of his Instruction was intirely Poetical: that is, by Fables or
Parables, contriv'd, and plac'd, and adapted to work very strongly
upon human Passions.

Thus the Prophets among the *Jews* were Poets; and the Divine
Institutor of the Christian Religion being a Prophet, by a Poetical
Method instructed and reform'd the World: And even the *Grecian*
Poets pretending to discharge the three Prophetical Functions, were
not only vulgarly reputed Prophets, but were stil'd so by St. *Paul*
himself, who quoting a Verse out of *Epimenides*, in the Epistle which
he wrote to *Titus*, calls that *Cretensian* Poet a Prophet: *As one of their own*
Prophets has said.[28]

Thus we have made it very plain, that not only the Predictions, but
the Praise and Thanksgiving in the inspir'd Writers, were written in
Verse; as were likewise several of the Prayers, and the Instructions,
and in short the noblest and most important part of the Old Testament.

Now if they were written in Poetry, it could be for no other reason, but because they who wrote them, believ'd that the figurative passionate Style, and the Poetical Numbers, did by Right of Nature belong to them, and consequently were requisite to inforce them upon the Minds of Men. And here we cannot as it were help observing, that for the Scriptures to make all the Impression that they are capable of making upon Men of very good Parts, and perhaps too upon others, all those Parts of them that were written in Verse, ought to be translated in Verse, and by Persons who are the most qualify'd to do it with Force and Harmony. For if the Passion and Harmony were thought requisite by the Original Writers, who were divinely inspir'd, to give Force to the *Hebrew*; why should not Spirit and Passion, and Numbers in a Translation, give a proportionable Force to that? For if Harmony of it self is of force to lift up our Thoughts to Heaven, as our Clergy seem to imply by the use of it in our Churches; and may be gather'd from what happen'd to *Elisha* in the second of *Kings*, when they would have had him prophesy at a time when the Spirit of Prophesy was not upon him, *Ch.* 3. *ver.* 15. where the Prophet says, *Now bring me a Minstrel, and it came to pass as the Minstrel plaid, that the Hand of the Lord came upon him:* If Harmony, I say, is of it self so efficacious, what must it not be, when incorporated with a Religious Sense, and a Poetical Style? There can certainly be no better way to reform the World, than the reading of those Writings which we believe to be divinely inspir'd: But this is as certain, that the greater the Pleasure is with which we read them, we shall the more frequently discharge that Duty; but to make us read them with more Pleasure than we do, they must have more of the Agreeableness of their Originals, that is, more Perspicuity, more Force, and more Harmony. This would more particularly attract the Gentry, and particularly those of the most extraordinary Parts among them, whose Examples would influence the rest, as the rest would influence the People. For they of extraordinary Parts for the most part being extremely delighted with Poetry, and finding the greatest and most exalted Poetry upon Religious Subjects, would by degrees become more us'd to be mov'd by Sacred Ideas, than they would by Profane; that is, would by degrees become reform'd. That this is by no means a Chimera, Experience may serve to convince us: For I know several

Gentlemen of very good Sense, who are extremely mov'd by *Milton*'s Hymn, in the fifth Book of *Paradise Lost*, and hardly at all stir'd with the Translation of the 148th Psalm, from whence that Hymn is taken. But if Men of very good Parts are more mov'd by the Hymn, it follows that they ought to be more mov'd by it; because Men of very good Sense are only mov'd to that degree by things by which they ought to be mov'd. So that we may conclude, that the Passion or Enthusiasm in that Hymn is exactly in Nature; that is, that the Enthusiasm, or Passion, or Spirit, call it what you will, flows from the Ideas, and bears a just Proportion to them.

But from hence at the same time it follows, that since those Persons, who are so much mov'd by the Hymn, are not equally stir'd by the translated Psalm, the Passion or Spirit is less in the latter, and does not come up to the Ideas; and therefore we may conclude, that *Milton*, by his Genius and Harmony, has restor'd that Spirit in composing the Hymn, which had been lost by the Weakness of the Translation, and the Want of Poetical Numbers: which last, as we have said before, contribute very much to the raising of Passion.

What *Milton* has done in relation to the 148th Psalm, others may do in a less proportion to other parts of the Old Testament, till the Favour of the Prince and publick Encouragement causes another *Milton* to arise, and apply himself to so necessary and so noble a Work. For this is certain, that there are not wanting great Genius's to every Age: But they do not equally appear in every Age, sometimes for want of knowing themselves, and sometimes for want of Encouragement and Leisure to exert themselves. The Business of the Treatise intended is to shew them how they may try, and know, and form themselves, which is all that I am capable of attempting towards the restoring so useful and so noble an Art. If I were in a Condition to give them Encouragement too, they should not be long without it. If they who so much exceed me in Power, did but equal me in Will, we should soon see Poetry raise up its dejected Head, and our own might come to emulate the happiest of *Grecian* and *Roman Ages*.

And thus much may suffice to shew the Nature of Poetry, but chiefly of the greater Poetry, and the Importance of this Design. For since Poetry has been thought not only by Heathens, but by the Writers of the Old Testament, and consequently by God himself who inspir'd them, to be the fittest Method for the enforcing Religion upon the Minds of Men; and since Religion is the only solid Foundation of all Civil Society, it follows, that whoever endeavours to re-establish Poetry, makes a generous Attempt to restore an Art, that may be highly advantageous to the Publick, and beneficial to Mankind.

Sir Richard Blackmore,

Advice to the Poets:
A Poem[1]
(1706)

OH! let the Conqueror stop his swift Career,
A while the Foe, a while the Poet spare.
What Muse can follow with an equal Pace,
Thro' the bright Stages of his rapid Race?
He, like the Orbs of Light, that roll above,
Does in his glorious Course so swiftly move;
His Conquests are so sudden, so compleat,
He does so oft his Miracles repeat,
The Muse exhausted pants, and hangs the Wing,
10   Has no more Strength to rise, and no more Breath to sing.
He Danger seeks, he asks unequal Fight,
He Conquers faster, than our Bards can Write.
So thick Illustrious Victories on them throng,
That half his Triumphs must be left unsung.

To sink the Proud, the Innocent to save,
To scourge the Tyrant, and release the Slave,
Two Winters past, at *Anna*'s high Command,
The Chief prepar'd to leave *Britannia*'s Land.
He shone in Arms, and to the Great Campaign,
20   The radiant Tempest flew across the Main.
He lands, and at their Great Asserter's Sight,
Fair Liberty rejoyc'd, and publick Right.
The Hero march'd, and on the *Danube*'s Tyde
He chang'd the Balance to *Germania*'s side,
And terribly chastis'd the *Gaul*'s aspiring Pride.

With vital Purple he the Stream distains,
Or from *Bavarian*, or from *Gallic* Veins.
By *Marlbro*'s Sword upheld, the wond'ring Flood
Was like *Egyptian* Rivers, turn'd to Blood.
30 *Danaw* oppress'd with *Gallia*'s ruin'd Pride,
With Spoil and Trophies rolling in, his Tyde
Flow'd on, *Britannia*'s Triumphs to convey
To Eastern Empires, and the *Caspian* Sea.
The *Hellespont*, and proud *Byzantia*'s Tow'rs
Shook with the Thunder of the *British* Pow'rs.
The numerous Nations of the spacious East
Were with Amazement struck, when from the West
They saw so bright a Luminary rise,
And with his Rival Beams adorn their Skies.

40 The Muse forsaking fair *Britannia*'s *Thames*,
Attends the Chief to *Danaw*'s noble Streams.
She pass'd the *German* Sea, and *Belgia*'s Soil,
To sing Immortal Deeds, and *Blenheim*'s glorious Toil.²
Now high *Augusta*, now *Britannia* rung
With Lyric Numbers, and Heroic Song.
Adulter Bards rehears'd their noble Thoughts,
And Infant Poets lisp'd their tender Notes.
Harmonious Striplings, by an early Bloom,
Promis'd ripe Numbers, and Great Men to come:
50 They all their Stores of Wit and Language drain'd;
They rais'd their Voices, and their Sinews strain'd.
Lavish of Force, and at a vast Expence
Of noble Fire, and tuneful Eloquence,
The *British* Poets labour'd to display
The Martial Toil of *Blenheim*'s wond'rous Day.
A Day, which fatal *Albion*'s Isle regards
To *Gallic* Warriors, and to *British* Bards:
Those by contending *Marlbro*' to repel,
And these by singing his Atchievements, fell.

60 For *Blenheim* was a Theme too bright, too strong
    For any Rapture, any master Song.
    In this Attempt, they did their Stock exhaust,
    They spent their Genius, and their Vigor lost.
    Say, ye uncautious Sons of Eloquence,
    Wastful of Wit, and prodigal of Sense,
    Could you believe the *British* Hero's Sword
    Would no more Triumphs, no more Themes afford?
    That here the Chief's victorious Course would cease?
    That you and *Gallia* might indulge your Ease?
70 This Judgment had been right, had *Marlbro'* fought
    For Martial Fame, and only Laurels sought.
    For one brave Toil, like that of *Blenheim*'s Field,
    To which the twelve *Herculean* Labours yield,
    Consummate Vertue to the World displays,
    We own the Hero, and we sing his Praise.
    Had therefore low Designs, had Wealth and Fame,
    Had mean Ambition kindled *Marlbro*'s Flame,
    Had he, as vulgar Warriors do, with Care
    And Caution, play'd the doubtful Game of War;
80 After the wond'rous Deeds at *Blenheim* done,
    Where all, that Thirst of Glory seeks, was won,
    The Hero had resign'd his high Command,
    And rose from Combate with a winning Hand.
    He had retir'd with noble Laurels crown'd,
    Had a delightful Seat on *Isis* found;[3]
    There liv'd from publick Labour free, and far
    From Fields of Slaughter, and rude Shocks of War.
    But 'tis his Country's, 'tis *Europa*'s Cause,
    That to the Field the mighty *Briton* draws.
90 Divine Compassion to oppress'd Mankind,
    Like that which dwells in *Anna*'s gen'rous Mind,
    To lead her Armies forth, the Hero's Heart inclin'd.
    Fair Liberty, and Right, and ancient Laws,
    And *Anna*'s, which is Human Nature's Cause,

Invite the Chief, his Labours to repeat,
Europa, thy Redemption to compleat.

He yields; he undertakes the Pious Toil;
Laden with Trophies, and with *Gallic* Spoil,
With Laurels sprung from *Danaw*'s Banks adorn'd,
His rapid Course of Glory back he turn'd.
Bless'd by the numerous States to Peace restor'd,
And Princes rescu'd by his conquering Sword,
The Great Deliv'rer marches to the *Rhine*,
To break his Chains, and drive encroaching *Sein*.
'Tis done. The *Sein*'s ambitious Waves subside,
Reluctant roar, and backward roll their Tyde.
Oh! had not Envy, had not Discord reign'd,
And the swift Progress of his Arms restrain'd,
The next Campaign had equal Wonders shown,
And Laurels giv'n, like those at *Blenheim* won.
But then the next did on the Chief confer
Vict'ries post-pon'd, and Glory's full Arrear.

The Solar Orb did from the South retreat,
And thro' the Air diffuse reviving Heat;
Solace the Soil, exhilerate the Swain,
And Nature loose from Winter's Crystal Chain.
When the Great Chief, at *Anna*'s high Command,
Return'd to cheer *Batavia*'s joyful Land.
Dreadful in Arms he march'd to *Brabant*'s Coast,
And Terror struck thro' *Gallia*'s shudd'ring Host;
Whose Numbers o'er the Ground, like Locusts, spread,
Each Herb devour'd, and crop'd each verdant Head.
The Veteran Troops, innur'd to Blood, advance,
The Plague of *Europe*, and the Pride of *France*.
The Squadrons reach'd thy frighted Fords, *Mehaigne*,
And cover'd all *Ramillia*'s spacious Plain.
Here their Brigades, in Battel rang'd, appear,
Determin'd to sustain th'advancing War.

The *Briton* saw: Transported with the Sight,
130 And bravely eager of decisive Fight,
     March'd swiftly on, but march'd in Pain and Fear,
     Lest *Gallia* should decline the proffer'd War.[4]
     Should, to elude his threat'ning Arms, retreat,
     The only way the Hero to defeat.
     He drew, he brandish'd his victorious Sword,
     Blenheim, remember *Blenheim*, was the Word.
     That magic Sound the Cohorts did inspire,
     Their Courage rous'd, and set their Veins on Fire.
     With *Blenheim*, ring the Hills and Vales around,
140 *Louvania*'s[5] trembling Tow'rs reverberate the Sound.

     Unguided Muse, say, whither dost thou stray,
     In *Marlbro*'s rapid Vortex caught away,
     In the bright Eddy lost, and blind with too much Day?
     Stop thy ambitious Flight, with Rev'rence yield
     Thy Strength unequal to *Ramillia*'s Field.
     For thee the Theme is too sublime and bright,
     Thou art not wing'd to rise to such a Height,
     Nor Eagle-Ey'd, to bear this Blaze, this Stress of Light.
     Can'st thou to Heav'n, secure from sinking, rise,
150 And soar with Strength amidst superior Skies?
     Can'st thou, supported with thy vig'rous Wing,
     To list'ning Orbs around *Ramillia* sing,
     And make the ecchoing Spheres with *Marlbro*'s Actions ring?
     Hast thou of noble Words a Stock immense,
     Vast Stores of rich inestimable Sense,
     To furnish all the Pow'r and Pomp of Eloquence?
     Can'st thou warm Fancy, and cool Judgment show?
     Make Numbers charm, and Words like Colours glow?
     Then take the Lyre, and in a lofty Strain
150 Sing *Marlbro*'s Triumph, sing *Ramillia*'s Plain.
     But wanting this, attempt not, Muse, to sing;
     Weak is thy Voice, and weary is thy Wing.

Thou art too poor to bear the vast Expence,
The rich Profusion and Magnificence
Fit to adorn a Subject so sublime;
Prevent inglorious Fall, and do not climb.
Proportion'd Strength, Invention, Numbers, Skill,
All things to thee are wanting, but a Will.
Be then advis'd, and prudently forbear,
170   For this Attempt more unprovided far,
Than *German* Circles, when engag'd in War.

    But since the Bards, whose Laurels spring and thrive
By *Marlbro*'s, should to *Marlbro*' Tribute give:
Should to remotest Realms, their Envoy Fame
Dispatch, their Hero's Triumphs to proclaim.
Since *Cam* and *Ouze*, which, from the *Gaul*'s Alarms,
And thine, O *Rome*, preserv'd by *Marlbro*'s Arms,
Do Peace enjoy, and gently murmuring flow,
Should tell the World, what they to *Marlbro*' owe.
180   And since superior in the Field, 'tis fit
We should assert the Empire too of Wit,
And make the haughty *Gaul* in both submit.
To sing *Ramillia*'s Field, ye Bards, awake,
The tuneful Lyre let none but Masters take.

    Ye mercenary Wits, who Rime for Bread,
Ye unfledg'd Muses, this high Subject dread.
Let not th'inferior Race, who can indite
A pretty Prologue, or a Sonnet write;
Tho' none so forward are, so bold as they,
190   Make on this Theme an Impotent Essay.
All who can raise a Shed, must not presume
To frame a Palace, or erect a Dome.
No more let *Milton*'s Imitator dare
Torture our Language, to torment our Ear
With Numbers harsher than the Din of War.

Let him no more his horrid Muse employ
In uncouth Strains, pure *English* to destroy,
And from its Ruins, yell his hideous Joy.
Away, ye Triflers, who all Rule disdain.
200 Who in *Pindaric* sing *Philander*'s Pain,
And Camps, and Arms, in *Paster-Fido*'s Strain.[6]
Hence, vain Pretenders to the Song sublime,
Turners of Verse, and Finishers of Rime,
Who think with Fame Immortal you are Crown'd,
By flowing Numbers, and harmonious Sound:
Who without Fire, and mindless of Design,
Ply hard the Pump, and labour every Line,
To make, like empty Clouds, your Diction shine.
So many Masters of this tuneful Skill,
210 With their melodious songs the Kingdom fill,
That to compleat Poetic Eloquence,
Nothing is wanting, but Design, and Sense.
Yet of the Few, who can with Judgment praise,
And sing Great Actions in becoming Lays,
Let none, betray'd by generous Thirst of Fame,
Adventure singly on this Mighty Theme:
Lest crush'd beneath th'unsufferable Weight,
He curse th'ambitious Flame, that caus'd his Fate,
And learn his Error in his Fall too late.
220 Let many Master Bards their Force unite,
And with Confederate Fire a Song Heroic write.
The Muses richest Treasures let 'em drain,
Lavish their Genius, and exhaust their Vein.
Let 'em this generous Resolution own,
That they are pleas'd, and proud to be undone,
While they adorn, with all the Muses Charms,
Bright *Anna*'s Empire, and brave *Marlbro*'s Arms.
Tho' any one unvulgar Bard might raise
The *Briton*'s Triumphs, in superior Lays,
230 To my unfinish'd Songs, and crude Essays;

Yet a distinguish'd, and consummate Piece,
Excelling that of *Mantua*,[7] that of *Greece*,
A wond'rous, unexampled *Epick* Song,
Where all is just, and beautiful, and strong,
Worthy of *Anna*'s Arms, of *Marlbro*'s Fire,
Does our best Bards united Strength require.

The Poets, who assume this noble Theme,
Must have their Hero's Fire, their Hero's Flegm.
They must have Judgment to direct their Flight,
240   Be never low, and never out of Sight.
Calm they must be, and yet, with equal Grace,
Enthusiastick in a proper Place.
Then *Prior*, for distinguish'd Lays renown'd,
And *Congreve* with repeated Laurels crown'd,
Harmonious *Granville* of superior Name,
Stepny and *Walsh*, both of establish'd Fame,
And in a tuneful Genius happy *Hughes*,
Strike your concordant Lyre, and join your noble Muse.
For this great Task, let all these Sons of Art,
250   Their utmost Skill and Energy exert;
Let each his Genius know, each take his proper Part.
Let *Summers*,[8] and let *Montague* preside,
Correct their Labours, and their Progress guide.
One is with all politer Science grac'd,
Of Thought refin'd, and delicate of Taste.
All to his Judgment, as decisive fly,
By that just Standard all their Notions try;
Like the fam'd *Grecian*'s chief Intelligence,
He sits sublime, in the first Sphere of Sense:[9]
260   He rules the rest by his superior Force,
Puts them in Motion, and directs their Course.
And one, like *Rome*'s Immortal *Angelo*,[10]
Does rich and universal Genius show.
This Master, this Poetic Architect,
Can stately Domes and Palaces erect:

The Painter too, and Sculptor in his Turn,
He can the Building, which he rears, adorn.
Let these sustain the chief Surveyors Care;
By these directed, can the Poets err?
270   The Age in Taste, grown curious to a Vice;
(O, that it were as delicate, as nice!)
And all contending Parties will submit
To such a Sovereign Court of Sense and Wit.
Let those employ'd the Building to erect,
Some Hero worthy of the Song elect,
Whose conquering Arms in *Albion*'s Annals shine,
And let the Action suit the Great Design.

Ye Bards, let all the noble Scheme be wrought
With Art, and Care, and deep deliberate Thought.
280   Before the Basis of the Frame you lay,
The famous Plans of *Greece* and *Rome* survey.
The *Iliad*, and the *Æneid*, well inspect,
All that is Just, and Bright, and Great select:
You know their Errors, those you will correct.
With due Connexion let the Parts cohere,
Lean on each other, and each other bear.
Let Order, Rule, and Symetry proclaim
The Artful Wonders of the happy Frame.
Believe no Cost too great, but every where
290   Let Plenty, Wealth, Magnificence appear.
A Plan so firm, so beautiful contrive,
As may the Critick mock, and Time survive.
A nobler Subject will your Care employ,
Than *Latian* Conquests, or the Wars of *Troy*.
Let the stupendous, everlasting Pile,
Worthy of *Albion*'s Arms, of *Marlbro*'s Toil;
The Glory of *Ramillia*'s Field sustain,
Longer than *Woodstock*'s Tow'rs can that of *Blenheim*'s Plain.

Let those appointed to adorn the Song,
300   Be bold with Care, with Delicacy strong.
Let *Mantuan* Judgment, and *Horatian* Words,
And all the noble Fire which *Greece* affords,
With all the Beauties which in *Spencer* shine,
To form their Diction's Dignity, combine:
Let all the Charms of Sound, and Strength of Sense,
Let all the Pride and Force of Eloquence,
Let all the bold, and beauteous Images,
Which by their Master-Strokes amaze, and Please,
The fairest Forms of all the airy Train,
310   With which the brightest Fancy fills the Brain.
Let Gilding, and Poetic Painting, grace
The Roofs and Rooms of all the stately Case.
Let *Episodes*, contriv'd with Art, suprize,
Which from the Subject unconstrain'd arise:
Like Walks and Gardens, charming to the Sight,
And Pleasure-Houses, let 'em give Delight.
In your Machines you will no Gods employ,
Who by the Poet listed fought at *Troy*.
The *Pagan* Gods might grace a *Pagan* Scheme,
320   But will they too adorn a *Christian* Theme?
Can you Concern, or Admiration move,
By introducing *Pallas*, *Mars*, or *Jove*?
No more than *Indian* Pa-Gods, *Jove* we fear,
And *Mars* no more than *Mahomet* revere.
Yet should you these employ to grace your Plan,
You may the *Indian* please, or *Musselman*,
The *Christian*, who reflects, you never can.

When you the *Briton*'s Character pursue,
Design *Æneas*, and *Achilles* too,
330   Else you but half the Hero set in View.
Let him in Steel bright, as *Achilles*, shine;
Give him his God-like Port, and Arms Divine.

186

So let his Mien, and Martial Charms surprize,
Let such a Flame irradiate his Eyes.
Make him to fight, *Achilles* like, advance,
So let him wave his Sword, so grasp his trembling Lance.
With such an Ardor, and intrepid Air,
To Danger fly, and plunge himself in War.
Make him augment the *Dyle* with hostile Blood,
340   As the *Greek* Hero did *Scamander*'s Flood.[11]
Then *Marlbro'* draw, for Poets too can paint,
They never Lights, or Shades, or Colours want:
Give us his Picture, when engag'd in Fight,
Let him with glorious Slaughter smear'd, affright
And please us too, with terrible Delight.

But by this famous *Greek*'s, ye Poets know,
The *Briton*'s Courage you imperfect show.
Fierce is the *Greek*, and rugged as the Age,
And too near Brutal is his Martial Rage.
350   The *Briton* is courageous and serene,
To the Angelic Warriors more akin.
If you would Justice to the Hero do,
In a true Light would you his Valour shew,
Delineate Fury mixt with God-like Grace,
And Indignation in a Seraph's Face.
Describe the Leader of the Guards above,
Tell how he charg'd, how he in Battle strove,
How o'er the Plains of Heav'n he raging *Satan* drove.
Then let the Hero's noble Mind be crown'd
360   With all the Vertues in *Æneas* found.
Give him his pious Soul, his gen'rous Heart,
Leave out his boastful, and ungallant Part,
In *Marlbro'* none can these Defects assert.
Did the good *Trojan* bear his aged Sire,
On his strong Shoulders from the raging Fire?[12]
Marlbro' on his sustains a nobler Weight,
His Kindred's, Country's, and *Europa*'s Fate.

The Heads by me suggested to your Muse,
And those, which you with more Success shall chuse,
370   As Epic Laws demand, should be express'd
In proper Types, and in Allusion dress'd.
Thus you'll Mankind with greater Pleasure strike
By side Advances, and by Views oblique.

    Tell how the Prince, who to retrieve his Fame
From *Boian* Fields,[13] to those of *Belgia* came,
To make the *Dola* and *Ramillia* clear,
The *Danube*'s Debt, and *Blenheim*'s vast Arrear,
Eager of Conquest, to the Battel flies,
Revenge and Fury flashing in his Eyes.
380   As when a Panther has with gen'rous Pride,
His Strength in Combate with the Lyon try'd,
And quickly vanquish'd by superior Might,
All maim'd and wounded, sav'd himself by Flight,
If when grown whole, he meets the mighty Foe,
His Hair erect, his raging Eye-balls glow:
Fierce he extends his Paws, he threat'ning stands,
And with revengeful Looks new War demands.
He calls to mind, to animate his Flame,
His painful Wounds, and his more painful Shame.
390   The noble Beast once more his Fortune trys,
The former to repair, to greater Ruin flies.
The *Boian* so. – Ye Bards, forgive me, you
Will of that Prince a nobler Image shew.

    Tell how the *Gallic* Gen'ral was distrest,
What Grief, what wast Disturbance fill'd his Breast,
When first he saw his plying Cohorts yield,
And to th'advancing *Briton* quit the Field.
Tell how amidst the trembling Troops he flies,
With Tears and Fury mingled in his Eyes.
400   How to prevent their Flight, and his Defeat,
He some did menace, and did some intreat.

How he exclaim'd aloud amidst the Host,
Oh *Gallia*! have thy Sons their Courage lost?
By *Gallia*'s Safety, and your Monarch's Name,
By your past Deeds, and Military Fame,
Return. – Be for your Lives and Honour brave,
Your King, your Country, and your Altars save.
In vain. The *Gauls*, unable to sustain
Unequal War, forsake the fatal Plain.

410   Tell the Distraction, tell the dreadful Cry
Of *Gallia*'s Troops, while from the Foe they fly.
Describe their haughty Leader's Mein and Air,
Forc'd by his Troops away, and in Despair
Born with th'impetuous Tyde of refluent War.
But first, to form this Image strong and true,
In *Raphael*'s famous Piece *Maxentius* view,
Whom such another Briton did pursue.[14]
Observe him plung'd in *Tiber*'s troubled Tyde,
Remark his sullen Rage, and melancholly Pride;
420   His vast Amazement, Anguish, Horror, Care,
And Indignation finish'd by Despair.
See how he frowns like a black Tempest driv'n
By warring winds thro' the blue Chace of Heav'n.
Of *Vill'roy*[15] in his Flight, this Picture give,
In his wild Looks let all these Passions strive.
Let *Marlbro'* on his Rear conspicuous shine,
Make him advance like *Raphael's Constantine*.
Give him his Ardor, and Majestic Grace,
Give all the Martial Beauties of his Face.
430   Give him a noble, unaffected Mein,
Sedate in Triumph, as in Fight serene.
Give him the Conqueror's, and the Judge's Air,
Oblig'd to punish, tho' inclin'd to spare.
So the destroying Angels look'd, who came
To cast on *Sodom*'s Tow'rs vindictive Flame.

They with Reluctance did their Arms employ,
With Pity touch'd, and backward to destroy.
They would have spar'd, they would have Mercy shown,
Had not her Crimes to full Perfection grown,
440   Extorted Wrath, and pull'd Destruction down.

Since I the mighty *Constantine* have nam'd,
Renown'd in Arms, for Moderation fam'd,
A Christian Hero, and a *Briton* born,
Why may not he, ye Bards, the Song adorn?
Think, if he may not be your noble Theme,
A proper Hero for your Epic Scheme.
In this Illustrious Warrior, may not you
Brave *Marlbro*'s Praises with Success pursue,
And of the Hero give an allegoric View?
450   The Piety and Love to Human Kind,
Which fill'd, Great *Constantine*, thy gen'rous Mind,
Are the same Vertues we in *Marlbro'* find.
Did not thy States and subject Realms, O *Rome*,
From *Constantine*'s Success expect their Doom?
Like vast Events on *Marlbro*'s Progress wait,
Whose Sword, O *Europe*, will decide thy Fate.
In this indeed the Heros diff'rent are,
One gain'd an Empire by successful War.
One greater Glory wins, who by his Sword
460   Reduces Countries for their rightful Lord.

In some fit Place, which you know best to chuse,
Bring in a Stranger, who in *Paris* views
The Place, in which the *Gaul*'s proud Statue stands,
And Veneration from the Crowd demands.[16]
Let the disdainful Stranger point, and say,
How swift, amazing Change! is thy Decay?
The strong Foundations, which thy Pride sustain,
Break with the Thunder of *Ramillia*'s Plain.

The Tow'rs around thee tremble at th'Alarms
470   Of *Anna*'s Anger, and her Gen'ral's Arms.
The *Briton*'s blasting Flame thy Head invades,
Thy Laurels wither, and thy Glory fades.
This Place, this Scene of Pride must change its Name,
No more the Place of Vict'ry, but of Shame.
See the resistless *Briton* does advance,
Europe's Deliv'rer, and the scourge of *France*.
He'll of its Honours strip thy haughty Head,
And in the Dust thy ruin'd Glory tread.
The States and Cities, which in Fetters bound,
480   At thy triumphant Feet here lie around,
Th'Immortal Foe of Tyrants shall release,
Unchain thy Slaves, and give *Europa* Peace.
He'll from its tow'ring Heights thy Marble thrust,
Pollute thy Pride, and spurn thee in the Dust.
Thy Titles, and thy Trophies he'll deface,
Thy Arrogance, thy Blasphemy erase.

You the Narration will so well dispose,
That all the Great Campaign it may enclose.
Tell all the Wonders done on *Belgia*'s Plain,
490   The Countries conquer'd, and the Numbers slain
In the short Compass of one circling Moon;
Superior Orbs with greater Swiftness run.
In a few Days such Actions are atchiev'd,
As will with Pain hereafter be believ'd.
One Month so full of Miracles, contains
The mighty Deeds of many Great Campaigns.
The *Briton*'s Course of Glory does out-shine
Thy Progress, *Cæsar*, and *Adolphus*, thine.
So thick, so great the confluent Triumphs come,
500   Confin'd and crowded in such narrow Room,
That this bright Month redundant Fame bestows,
And with a swelling Tyde of Glory overflows.

If you in Hangings, or in Painting show,
For that an Epic Song may fitly do,
What Tow'rs, what Towns, what stately Cities yield,
To crown the Labour of *Ramillia*'s Field.
Let her high Gates *Lovania* open lay,
Receive the Conqu'ror, and Protection pray.
Then to *Brussella* let his Arms advance,
510   Driving along the frighted Herds of *France*.
Pour'd from the Gates of fair *Brabantia*'s Head,
Of rescu'd Captives let a Deluge spread:
Let them with wond'rous Joy the *Briton* meet,
Bless their Deliv'rer, and embrace his Feet;
Who has releas'd, by one amazing Stroke,
Their Feet from *Gallia*'s Chains, their Necks from *Gallia*'s
    Yoke.

Describe him ent'ring high *Brussella*'s Gate,
'Midst loud Applauses, in triumphant State.
Express his God-like unelated Air;
520   Oh! who can conquer so? who Conquest so can bear?
Th'Illustrious Vertues, which in *Marlbro*' shone,
As once the Glory that did *Moses* crown,[17]
Dazled the Crowd around, but were to him unknown.
Let all the eager *Belgians* throng to see
The Mighty Chief, who set their Nation free,
The Fence of *Europe*'s Rights, the Prop of Liberty.
Let Princes, Lords, and Counsellors of State,
Augment the Pomp, and on the Triumph wait.
Let 'em deliver to the Conqu'ror's Hand
530   Their Keys, and all their Ensigns of Command.

Shew all the Ways of fair *Brabantia*'s Soil
With Trav'llers throng'd, and smoaking with their Toil:
Great Prelates, Princes, Magistrates supream,
High Soveraign States, and Lords of greatest Fame.

Let some from high *Mechlinia*'s Tow'rs,[18] and some
Pour'd from the Gates of fam'd *Antwerpia* come.
Be these from *Bruges*, those from spacious *Ghent*,
From *Oudenard* some, and some from *Lier* sent.
From every Region let a num'rous Train
540   Fill ev'ry Road, and cover ev'ry Plain.
Panting in Clouds of Dust, and bath'd in Sweat,
Let 'em advance to fair *Brussella*'s Gate;
There to the Conqu'ror humbly to submit,
And throw themselves obedient at his Feet.
Let 'em his Favour and his Aid implore,
And to be safe, resign to him their Pow'r.
Thus *Marlbro*'s Arms excel ev'n *Cæsar*'s Fame,
Conqu'ring before he saw, before he came.
You in your Plan will leave capacious Room
550   For promis'd Triumphs, and great Deeds to come.
What a luxuriant Harvest of Renown,
What full ripe Glory will the *Autumn* crown,
Since early Seeds so thick, so bright appear,
That *Fame* a nobler Bloom did never wear,
Nor pregnant *Time* Events of more Importance bear?
   While I so near, so long the Hero view,
And Hints suggest to be improv'd by you,
My fading Flame does in my Veins renew.
I feel an inward Impulse not unknown,
560   Urging your Muse, I have provok'd my own.
Oh! did a Portion of the noble Fire,
With which the Hero fought, my Breast inspire;
I'd raise my Voice, and with a lofty Strain
Would to Etherial Fields uplift *Ramillia*'s Plain.
The Laurel I would win from *Maro*'s Brow,
My happy Lays the *Grecian*'s should out do.
The *Trojan* Chief should to the *Briton* yield,
The *Latian* Triumphs to *Ramillia*'s Field.
Scamander's Flood should own superior *Dyle*,
570   And *Grecian* Deeds submit to *Marlbro*'s Toil.

'Tis done. I've compass'd my ambitious Aim,
The Hero's Fire restores the Poet's Flame.
The Inspiration comes, my Bosom glows,
I strive with strong Enthusiastic Throws.
Oh! I am all in Rapture, all on Fire,
Give me, to ease the Muse's Pangs, the Lyre.
How can a Muse, that *Albion* loves, forbear
To sing the Wonders of the glorious War?
I rise, O whither am I caught away?
580   I mount, I must the tow'ring Muse obey.
I cut the Space immense, and reach the Realms of Day.
Where will the Flight, where will the Labour end?
Thro' the steep Gulph I to the Stars ascend.
Stars, which I now behold vast Orbs of Light,
Only by Distance little to the Sight.
All Suns of equal Bulk, and equal Flame
With that, which rules the World from whence I came.
All glorious Centers, whose attractive Sway
Revolving Moons and wand'ring Worlds obey,
590   Each is a Globe immense, each is a Source of Day.
Amazing Prospect! ravishing Delight!
How vastly great they are? How dazling bright?
In beauteous Order, how they hang around?
Good Heav'ns! – but hark, I hear an ecchoing Sound,
It does from Sphere to Sphere, from World to World
    rebound.
The Noise augments; attend, it seems to rise
From *Belgia*'s Land; hark, how it fills the Skies?
This mighty Noise is Triumph, 'tis Applause,
'Tis loud Rejoycing for some Victor Cause.
600   'Tis known. I hear, I hear these Accents plain,
Arms, Anna, Marlbro', Dyle, Ramillia's Plain.
But see, with radiant Wings, see, yonder flies
One of th'Immortal Envoys of the Skies;
From the Terrestrial World he seems to rise.

How bright, how strong, how swift he wings his Way?
How mild a Glory, what a circling Day
Does the Cœlestial Youth around display?
Important Joy does his glad Looks possess,
I follow, I attend the bright Express.
610   With him I climb the steep Empyreal Height,
Swift as an Angel's is the Muse's Flight.
We now arrive at Heav'n's Eternal Gate,
Where the Immortal Guards in Arms Immortal wait.
Thronging about Heav'n's Courier, they demand,
What happy Tydings from the *Belgian* Land.
Of *Albion*'s Captain Guardian Seraph, say,
What great Events, and what new Triumphs pay
The noble Labour of *Ramillia*'s Day?
That Chief, the shining Minister replies,
620   Who on the Justice of his Cause relies,
His prosp'rous Ensigns daily does advance,
To sink the Pride, and break the Pow'r of *France*.
The Conqu'ror all things does before him bear,
Like Torrents in the Hills, or Tempests in the Air.
The stately Cities, which *Brabantia* crown,
And *Flandria*'s fairest Towns their Sov'raign own,
And from their Necks proud *Gallia*'s Yoke have thrown.

      Hark! now I hear the Shouts of Joy around,
I hear the Triumph's multiplying Sound.
630   Th'Angelic Acclamation grows, it fills
All the blue Plains, and all the crystal Hills.
They shew by this, repeated loud Applause,
Those fight in Heav'n's, who fight in *Anna*'s Cause.
The Shouts of Joy diminish, but behold
Yon Seraph takes his Harp of Heav'nly Gold:
Hark! the bless'd Poet of the glorious Choir
Begins, he strikes his bright Cœlestial Lyre.

How the Terrestrial *Lucifer*,
The Son of Pride, the haughty *Gaul*,
640   Does from his high Imperial Sphere,
Struck with *Britannia*'s Thunder, fall?
Th'Almighty gave his high Command,
From all the Hills and Tow'rs of *Belgia*'s Land,
Hang out the Flag, and let the Banner stream,
Terror denounce, and growing War proclaim.
Call forth my Warriors from *Batavia*'s Soil,
        My Gen'rals from *Britannia*'s Isle:
        Warriors, to whom proud Tyrants yield,
        To *Gallia* known at *Blenheim*'s Field:
650 Warriors, who only God-like Fame respect,
Despite the Danger, and the Spoil neglect.
Let confluent Cohorts crown the Mountain's Head,
Let o'er the Plain a Martial Deluge spread.
Let them extend their Front, collect their Rear,
And terribly advance the congregated War.
        Lutetia,[19] tremble, see the Clouds arise,
        The Tempest darkens all the Skies.
'Tis with Destruction charg'd, and will unload
        The Terrors of an angry God.
660   On thee he'll pour his Viols forth,
Of high fermented Rage, and old digested Wrath.
        Justice no longer will delay,
        It will the Debt of Vengeance pay.
Aspiring City! which did'st raise thy Head,
Did'st tow'ring midst the Skies thy Glory spread.
        Who, mad with Pride, wer't wont to say
        Europa's Realms shall my Commands obey,
        The ruin'd Nation's woeful Cries,
        The Widow's Tears, and Orphan's Cries,
670 The Seas of Blood by thy Ambition spilt,
And all th'Effects of thy enormous Guilt,
Provoke just Heav'n on thy proud Head to pour
Fury reserv'd, and as thy Crimes, mature.

See, drunk with Wrath Divine, the Tyrant reels,
  What Anguish, what Distress he feels?
  Against the *Gaul* th'Almighty does declare,
Against th'Oppressor he denounces War.
His Arm stretch'd out, descends with ling'ring Sway,
But heavier Wrath will Recompense delay.
680 Arm'd with his glitt'ring Sword and Sun-like Shield,
  The Lord of Armies takes the Field.
  Grasping his bright Immortal Lance,
  To *Belgia*'s Plain he does advance.
The Earth's Foundations quake, the Mountains bow,
  Affrighted Rivers backward flow.
  Nature's strong Fears, and vast Distress,
  The awful Presence of her Lord confess.
Torrents of Glory his dread March proclaim,
Clouds, and thick Darkness, and Tempestuous Flame.
690 The *Gaul* before his Terrors flies,
  A hideous Yell, and lamentable Cries
  Of routed Warriors, fill the Skies.
How red with Slaughter is *Ramillia*'s Plain?
How are the Mountains cover'd with the Slain?
  How deeply dy'd with *Gallic* Blood
  Belgia's polluted Rivers roll their Flood!

Ye *Flandrian* Hills and Tow'rs around, declare,
  For you beheld the wond'rous War;
  You heard *Britannia*'s terrible Alarms,
700 You heard the Shouts of her victorious Arms:
  You saw the Foe subdu'd in Fight,
You saw the Rout, and ignominious Flight;
Tell how against the *Gaul* the Battle turn'd,
  How from the Field their Cohorts fled
Like scatt'ring Flocks upon the Mountain's Head;
How *Albion*'s Captain, dreadfully adorn'd
  With Dust and Slaughter, did pursue,
How on their Rear he hung, and how his Terrors flew.

          The *Gallic* General's Looks relate,
710   Enrag'd, and cursing their amazing Fate.
     Their Consternation, and their Woe declare,
     For you their Anguish saw, and absolute Despair.

          Let us in rapt'rous Hallelujahs sing,
          The Praises of th'Eternal King,
          Who sits above th'Empyreal Height,
          Enthron'd in uncreated Light.
          He by his Servant *Anna*'s Hand,
          On *Dola*'s Flood in *Belgia*'s Land,
          Has the proud Oppressor broke,
720   Who his just Vengeance did so long provoke.
     The wond'rous Deed does Men below suprize,
          'Tis wond'rous too in Seraph's Eyes.
          This mighty Work of Providence Divine,
          In Earth's and Heav'n's Records shall shine.
          Bless'd be *Ramillia*'s Plain, that gave
     Ease to th'Oppress'd, and Freedom to the Slave.
          That has rebuk'd th'ambitious *Gaul*,
     A glorious Promise of th'Oppressor's Fall.
          May'st thou with flow'ry Pride be crown'd,
730   With *Nature*'s richest Gifts abound.
          May Genial Show'rs and Heav'nly Dew
          Thy verdant Honours still renew.
          Let not the cruel Plough-share wound,
          Let not the Harrow tear thy Ground:
          Let thy prolific, but unlabour'd Soil,
          Enrich the Farmer, and prevent his Toil.
          Unconscious of inclement Skies,
     Be neither chill'd with Cold, or scorch'd with Heat;
          Let no destructive Meteor rise,
740   No Tempest on thy peaceful Region beat.
          Let not thy Glebe produce a Weed,
          Thy Caverns no raw Vapour feed,
     No spotted Plague, or Pestilential Seed.

Unfading Bloom and vernal Verdure wear,
    And with spontaneous Plenty blest,
    Like *Eden*'s happy Garden rest,
Thy Soil as fruitful, and as mild thy Air.
Be this its Fate, for this auspicious Plain
Has sunk th'Oppressor's Hopes and broke *Europa*'s Chain.
750 Now, *Dola*, thou, before a vulgar Stream,
Among the noblest Floods shalt have a Name.
    Danaw alone shall Rival thee,
    Thames alone superior be.

    Auspicious Chief, thy great Designs pursue,
Defend the Suff'rer, and the Proud subdue,
'Till by Defect of Foes thy Triumphs cease,
And grateful *Europe* thank thee for her Peace.
Then 'midst Applauses of the Realms restor'd,
And Nations sav'd by thy victorious Sword,
760 Return Triumphant to thy native Soil,
To honourable Ease, from glorious Toil.
Then let the Queen, with a just Umpire's Hand,
Of *Europe*'s Pow'r, the balanc'd Scales command.
Let her ambitious Monarchies restrain,
Religion guard, and publick Right maintain.
Let her be dear at Home, Abroad rever'd,
By all good Princes lov'd, and by all Tyrants fear'd.

FINIS.

Samuel Cobb,
A Discourse on Criticism and the Liberty of Writing
(1707)

In a Letter to *Richard Carter* Esq; late of the *Middle Temple*, now living in *Barbadoes*.

SIR,

THE *Muses* are said to be the Daughters of Memory:[1] A Poet therefore must lay down his Title to their Favour, who can be forgetful of a Friend, like You, whose polite Knowledge, instructive Conversation, and particular Generosity to my self, have left such strong Impressions upon my Mind, as defy the Power of Absence to remove them. I scarce believe Death it self can blot out an *Idea* so firmly imprinted. The Soul, when it leaves this earthly Habitation, and has no more Use for those Vertues, which were serviceable in the Conduct of human Life, such as *Temperance*, *Fortitude* and the like, will certainly carry *Love* and *Gratitude* along with it to Heaven. This may suffice to let the World know what Obligations you have laid upon me.

By this Letter (the room of which, for your sake I could willingly have supply'd) you will plainly see, that no Place, however remote, is able to secure you from the Zeal of a *Friend*, and the Vanity of a *Poet*.

> *For tho' retiring to the* Western Isles,
> *At the long Distance of five thousand Miles,*
> *You've chang'd* dear London *for your Native Seat,*
> *And think* Barbadoes *is a safe Retreat;*
> *You highly err: Nor is the* Wat'ry Fence
> *Sufficient Guard against Impertinence.*
> *The* Muse, *which smiles on jingling Bards, like Me,*

> *Has always Winds to waft her o'er the Sea.*
> *Blow on, ye Winds, and o'er th'*Atlantick Main,
> *Bear to my Gen'rous Friend this thankful Strain.*

You see, Sir, I have not left off that rhyming Trick of Youth; but knowing You to be a Gentleman who loves Variety in every thing, I thought it would not be ungrateful if I chequer'd my Prose with a little Verse.

After this Preamble, it is presum'd, that one who lives on the Other side of the Globe, will expect by every Pacquet-boat to know what is done on This.[2] Since Your Departure, Affairs have had a surprizing Turn every where, and particularly in *Italy*; which Success of our Armies and Allies abroad, have given a manifest Proof of our wise Counsels at home. – Parties still run between *High* and *Low*. I shall make no Remarks on either; thinking it always more prudent, as well as more safe, to live peaceably under the Government in which I was born, rather than peevishly to quarrel with it.

But You will cry, *Who expects any thing from the Politicks of a Poet? How goes the State of* Parnassus? *What has the Battle of* Ramillies *produc'd?* What Battles generally do; bad Poets, and worse Criticks. I could not perswade my self to attempt any thing above six Lines, which had not been made, were it not at the Request of a Musical Gentleman. You will look upon them with the same Countenance you us'd to do on things of a larger Size.

> *Born to surprize the World, and teach the Great*
> *The slippery Danger of exalted State,*
> *Victorious* Marlbrô *to* Ramilly *flies;*
> *Arm'd with new Lightning from bright* ANNA*'s Eyes.*
> *Wonders like These, no former Age has seen;*
> *Subjects are* Heroes, *where a Saint's the* QUEEN.

Mr. *Congreve* has given the World an ode, and prefix'd to it a Discourse on the *Pindaric Verse*,[3] of which more, when I come to speak on the same Argument: There are several others on that Subject, and some which will bear the Test; one particularly, written in the Style of *Spencer*; and goes under the Name of Mr. *Prior*;[4] I have not read it through, but *ex pede Herculem*.[5] He is a Gentleman who cannot write ill. Yet some of our *Criticks* have fell upon it, as the Viper did on the file, to the detriment of their Teeth. So that Criticism, which was formerly the Art of judging well, is now become the pure Effect of Spleen, Passion and Self-conceit. Nothing is perfect in every Part. He that expects to see any thing so, must have patience till *Dooms day*. The Worship we pay to our own Opinion, generally leads us to the Contempt of another's. This blind Idolatry of *Self* is the Mother of Errour; and this begets a secret Vanity in our *Modern Censurers*, who, when they please to think a *Meaning* for an Author, would thereby insinuate how much his Judgment is inferiour to their inlighten'd Sagacity. When, perhaps, the Failings they expose are a plain Evidence of their own Blindness.

> *For to display our Candour and our Sence,*
> *Is to discover some deep* Excellence.
> *The Critick's faulty, while the Poet's free;*
> *They raise the* Mole-hill, *who want Eyes to see.*

Excrescences are easily perceiv'd by an ordinary Eye; but it requires the Penetration of a *Lynceus*[6] to discern the Depth of a good Poem; the secret Artfulness and Contrivance of it being conceal'd from a Vulgar Apprehension.

I remember somewhere an Observation of St. *Evremont* (an Author whom you us'd to praise, and whom therefore I admire) that some Persons, who would be Poets, which they cannot be, become Criticks which they can be. The censorious Grin, and the loud Laugh, are common and easy things, according to *Juvenal*; and according to *Scripture*,[7] the Marks of a *Fool*. These Men are certainly in a deplorable Condition, who cannot be witty, but at another's Expence, and who take an unnatural kind of Pleasure in being uneasy at their Own.

> *Rules they can write, but, like the* College Tribe,
> *Take not that Physick which their Rules prescribe.*
> *I scorn to praise a plodding, formal Fool,*
> *Insipidly correct, and* dull *by Rule:*
> Homer, *with all his* Nodding, *I would chuse,*

> *Before the more exact* Sicilian *Muse.*
> *Who'd not be* Dryden*; tho' his Faults are great,*
> *Sooner than our Laborious* Laureat?
> *Not but a decent Neatness, I confess,*
> *In* Writing *is requir'd, as well as* Dress.
> *Yet still in both the* unaffected Air
> *Will always please the* Witty *and the* Fair.

I would not here be thought to be a Patron of slovenly Negligence; for there is nothing which breeds a greater Aversion in Men of a *Delicate Taste.* Yet you know, Sir, that, after all our care and Caution, the Weakness of our Nature will eternally mix it self in every thing we write; and an over curious Study of being correct, enervates the Vigour of the Mind, slackens the Spirits, and cramps the Genius of a *Free Writer.* He who creeps by the Shore, may shelter himself from a Storm, but is likely to make very few Discoveries: And the cautious Writer, who is timorous of disobliging the captious Reader, may produce you true Grammar, and unexceptionable *Prosodia*, but most stupid Poetry.

In vitium culpæ ducit fuga, si caret arte.[8]

A slavish Fear of committing an Oversight, betrays a Man to more inextricable Errours, than the Boldness of an enterprizing Author, whose artful Carelessness is more instructive and delightful than all the Pains and Sweat of the Poring and Bookish Critick.

Some Failings, like Moles in a beautiful Countenance, take nothing from the Charms of a happy Composure, but rather heighten and improve their Value. Were our modern Reflecters Masters of more Humanity than Learning, and of more Discernment than both, the Authors of the Past and Present Ages, would have no reason to complain of Injustice; nor would that Reflection be cast upon the *best-natur'd Nation* in the World, that, when rude and ignorant, we were unhospitable to Strangers, and now, being civiliz'd, we expend our Barbarity on one another. *Homer* would not be so much the Ridicule of our *Beaux Esprits*; when, with all his Sleepiness, he is propos'd as the most exquisite Pattern of Heroic Writing, by the Greatest of Philosophers, and the Best of Judges.[9] Nor is *Longinus* behind hand with *Aristotle* in his Character of the same Author, when he tells us that the greatness of *Homer*'s Soul look'd above little Trifles (which are Faults in meaner Capacities) and hurry'd on to his Subject with a Freedom of Spirit peculiar to himself.[10] A Racer at *New-market* or the *Downs*, which has been fed and drest, and with the nicest Caution prepared for the Course, will stumble perhaps at a little Hillock; while the Wings of *Pegasus* bear him o'er Hills and Mountains,

Sub pedibusq; videt nubes & sydera —[11]

Such was the Soul of *Homer*: who is more justly admir'd by those who understand him, than he is derided by the Ignorant: Whose Writings partake as much of that Spirit, as he attributes to the Actions of his *Heroes*; and whose Blindness is more truly chargeable on his *Criticks*, than on *Himself*: who, as he wrote without a Rule, was himself a Rule to succeeding Ages. Who as much deserves that Commendation which *Alcibiades* gave to *Socrates*, when he compar'd him to the statues of the *Sileni*, which to look upon, had nothing beautiful and ornamental; but open them, and there you might discover the Images of all the Gods and Goddesses.[12]

Who knows the secret Springs of the Soul, and those sudden Emotions, which excite illustrious Men, to act and speak out of the *Common Road*? They seem irregular to Us by reason of the Fondness and Bigottry we pay to *Custom*, which is no Standard to the Brave and the Wise. The Rules we receive in our first Education, are laid down with this Purpose, to restrain the *Mind*; which by reason of the Tenderness of our Age, and the ungovernable Disposition of Young Nature, is apt to start out into Excess and Extravagance. But when Time has ripen'd us, and Observation has fortify'd the Soul, we ought to lay aside those common Rules with our Leading strings; and exercise our Reason with a free, generous and manly Spirit. Thus a *Good Poet* should make use of a Discretionary Command; like a *Good General*, who may rightly wave the vulgar Precepts of the Military School (which may confine an ordinary Capacity, and curb the Rash and Daring) if by a new and surprizing Method of Conduct, he find out an uncommon Way to Glory and Success.

Bocalin, the *Italian Wit*, among his other odd Advertisements, has this remarkable one, which is parallel to the present Discourse. When *Tasso* (says he) had presented *Apollo* with his *Poem*, call'd *Giurasalemme Liberata*; the *Reformer* of the *Delphic Library*, to whose Perusal it was committed, found fault with it, because it was not written according to the Rules of *Aristotle*; which affront being complain'd of, *Apollo* was highly incens'd, and chid *Aristotle* for his Presumption in daring to prescribe Laws and Rules to the high Conceptions of the *Virtuosi*, whose Liberty of Writing and Inventing, enrich'd the Schools and Libraries with gallant Composures; and to enslave the Wits of Learned Men, was to rob the World of those alluring Charms which daily flow'd from the Productions of Poets, who follow the Dint of their own unbounded Imagination. You will find the rest in the *28*th Advertisement.[13]

The Moral is instructive; because to judge well and candidly, we must wean our selves from a slavish Bigotry to the Ancients. For, tho' *Homer* and *Virgil*, *Pindar* and *Horace* be laid before us as Examples of exquisite Writing in the Heroic and Lyric Kind, yet, either thro' the Distance of Time, or Diversity of Customs, we can no more expect to find like Capacities, than like Complexions. Let a Man follow the Talent that Nature has furnish'd him with, and his own Observation has improv'd, we may hope to see Inventions in all Arts, which may dispute Superiority with the best of the *Athenian* and *Roman* Excellencies.

> *Nec minimum meruêre decus vestigia Græca*
> *Ausi deserere.* —[14]

It is another Rule of the same Gentleman, that we should attempt nothing beyond our Strength: There are some modern *Milo*'s who have been wedg'd in that Timber which they strove to rend. Some have fail'd in the Lyric Way who have been excellent in the Dramatic. And, Sir, would you not think a Physician would gain more Profit and Reputation by *Hippocrates* and *Galen* well-studied, than by *Homer* and *Virgil* ill-copied?

Horace, who was as great a Master of Judgment, as he was an Instance of Wit, would have laid the Errours of an establish'd Writer on a pardonable Want of Care, or excus'd them by the Infirmity of Human Nature; he would have wondred at the corrupt Palates now a-days, who quarrel with their Meat, when the Fault is in their Taste. To reform which, if our Moderns would lay aside the malicious Grin and drolling Sneer, the Passions and Prejudices to Persons and Circumstances, we should have better Poems, and juster Criticisms. Nothing casts a greater Cloud on the Judgment than the Inclination (or rather Resolution) to praise or condemn, before we see the Object. The Rich and Great lay a Trap for Fame, and have always a numerous Crowd of servile Dependants, to clap their Play, or admire their Poem.

> *For noble Scriblers are with Flattery fed,
> And none dare tell their Fault who eat their bread.
>
> *Dryden's Pers.[15]

Juvenal shews his Aversion to this Prepossession, when his old disgusted Friend gives this among the rest of his Reasons why he left the Town,

> — *Mentiri nescio: librum
> Si malus est, nequeo laudare & poscere.*[16]

To conquer Prejudice is the part of a Philosopher; and to discern a Beauty is an Argument of good Sense and Sagacity; and to find a Fault with Allowances for human Frailty, is the Property of a Gentleman.

Who then is this Critick? You will find him in *Quintilius Varus*, of *Cremona*, who when any Author shew'd him his Composure, laid aside the *Fastus* common to our supercilious Readers; and when he happen'd on any Mistake, *Corrige sodes Hoc aiebat & hoc.*[17]

Such is the Critick I would find, and such would I prove my self to others. I am sorry I must go into my Enemies Country to find out another like him. Our *English* Criticks having taken away a great deal from the Value of their Judgment, by dashing it with some splenetick Reflections. Like a certain Nobleman mention'd by my Lord *Verulam*, who when he invited any Friends to Dinner, always gave a disrelish to the Entertainment by some cutting malicious Jest.

The French then seem to me to have a truer Taste of the ancient Authors than ever *Scaliger* or *Heinsius* could pretend to. *Rapin*, and above all, *Bossu*, have done more Justice to *Homer* and to *Virgil*, to *Livy* and *Thucydides*, to *Demosthenes* and to *Cicero*, &c. and have bin more beneficial to the Republick of Learning, by their nice Comparisons and Observations, than all the honest Labours of those well-meaning Men, who rummage *musty Manuscripts* for *various Lections*. They did not *Insistere in ipso cortice, verbisq; interpretandis intenti nihil ultra petere*,[18] (as *Dacier* has it) but search'd the inmost Recesses, open'd their Mysteries, and (as it were) call'd the Spirit of the Authors from the Dead. It is for this *Le Clerc* (in his *Bibliotheque Choisie*, Tom. *9*. p. *328*) commends St. *Evremont*'s Discourses on *Salust* and *Tacitus*, as also his Judgment on the Ancients, and blames the Grammarians, because they give us not a Taste of Antiquity after his Method, which would invite our Polite Gentlemen to study it with a greater Appetite. Whereas their Manner of Writing, which takes Notice only of Words, Customs, and chiefly Chronology, with a blind Admiration of all they read, is unpleasant to a fine Genius, and deters it from the pursuit of the *Belles Lettres*.

I shall say no more at present on this Head, but proceed to give you an Account of the following Sheets. What I have attempted in them is mostly of the Pindaric and Lyric Way. I have not follow'd the *Strophe* and *Antistrophe*; neither do I think it necessary; besides I had rather err with Mr. *Cowley*,[19] who shew'd us the Way, than be flat and in the right with others.

Mr. *Congreve*, an ingenious Gentleman, has affirm'd, I think too hastily, that in each particular Ode the Stanza's are alike, whereas the last Olympick has two *Monostrophicks* of different Measure, and Number of Lines.[20]

The Pacquet-boat is just going off, I am afraid of missing Tide. You may expect the rest on the *Pindaric Style*. In the mean time I beg leave to subscribe my self,

Sir, Your ever Obedient and Obliged Servant,
Samuel Cobb.

Alexander Pope,
An Essay on Criticism
(1711)

'TIS hard to say, if greater Want of Skill
Appear in *Writing* or in *Judging* ill;[1]
But, of the two, less dang'rous is th' Offence,
To tire our *Patience*, than mis-lead our *Sense*:
Some few in *that*, but Numbers err in *this*,
Ten Censure wrong for one who Writes amiss;
A *Fool* might once *himself* alone expose,
Now *One* in *Verse* makes many more in *Prose*.
　　'Tis with our *Judgments* as our *Watches*, none
10　Go just *alike*, yet each believes his own.
In *Poets* as true *Genius* is but rare,
True *Taste* as seldom is the *Critick*'s Share;
Both must alike from Heav'n derive their Light,
These *born* to Judge, as well as those to Write.
*Let such teach others who themselves excell,
And *censure freely* who have *written well*.
Authors are partial to their *Wit*, 'tis true,
But are not *Criticks* to their *Judgment* too?
　　Yet if we look more closely, we shall find
20　†Most have the *Seeds* of Judgment in their Mind;
Nature affords at least a *glimm'ring Light*;
The *Lines*, tho' touch'd but faintly, are drawn right.

---

* 　— *De Pictore, Sculptore, Fictore, nisi Artifex judicare non potest.* Pliny.[2]
† 　*Omnes tacito quodam sensu, sine ulla arte, aut ratione, quæ sint in artibus ac rationibus recta ac prava dijudicant.* Cic. de Orat. lib. 3.[3]

But as the slightest Sketch, if justly trac'd, ⎫
Is by ill *Colouring* but the more disgrac'd, ⎬
So by *false Learning* is *good Sense* defac'd; ⎭
Some are bewilder'd in the Maze of Schools,
And some made *Coxcombs* Nature meant but *Fools*.
In search of *Wit* these lose their *common Sense*,
And then turn Criticks in their own Defence.
30 Those hate as *Rivals* all that write; and others
But envy *Wits*, as *Eunuchs* envy *Lovers*.[4]
All *Fools* have still an Itching to deride,
And fain *wou'd* be upon the *Laughing Side*:
If *Mævius* Scribble in *Apollo's* spight,
There are, who *judge* still *worse* than he can *write*.
      Some have at first for *Wits*, then *Poets* past,
Turn'd *Criticks* next, and prov'd plain *Fools* at last;[5]
Some neither can for *Wits* nor *Criticks* pass,
As heavy Mules are neither *Horse* nor *Ass*.
40 Those half-learn'd Witlings, num'rous in our Isle,
As half-form'd Insects on the Banks of *Nile*;
Unfinish'd Things, one knows not what to call,
Their Generation's so *equivocal*:
To tell 'em, wou'd a *hundred Tongues* require,
Or *one vain Wit's*, that wou'd a hundred tire.
      But *you* who seek to *give* and *merit* Fame,
And justly bear a Critick's noble Name,
Be sure *your* self and your own *Reach* to know,
How far your *Genius, Taste,* and *Learning* go;
50 Launch not beyond your Depth, but be discreet,
And mark *that Point* where Sense and Dulness *meet*.
Nature to all things fix'd the Limits fit,
And wisely curb'd proud Man's pretending Wit:
As on the *Land* while *here* the *Ocean* gains,
In *other Parts* it leaves wide sandy Plains;
Thus in the *Soul* while *Memory* prevails,
The solid Pow'r of *Understanding* fails;

Where Beams of warm *Imagination* play,
The *Memory*'s soft Figures melt away.
60 One *Science* only will one *Genius* fit;[6]
So *vast* is Art, so *narrow* Human Wit:
Not only bounded to *peculiar Arts*,
But ev'n in *those*, confin'd to *single Parts*.
Like Kings we lose the Conquests gain'd before,
By vain Ambition still t'extend them more:
Each might his *sev'ral Province* well command,
Wou'd all but *stoop* to what they *understand*.

First follow NATURE,[7] and your Judgment frame
By her just Standard, which is still the same:
70 *Unerring Nature*, still divinely bright,
One *clear*, *unchang'd*, and *Universal* Light,[8]
Life, Force, and Beauty, must to all impart,
At once the *Source*, and *End*, and *Test* of *Art*.
That *Art* is best which most resembles *Her*,
Which still *presides*, yet never does *Appear*;[9]
In some fair Body thus the sprightly[10] Soul
With Spirits feeds, with Vigour fills the whole,
Each Motion guides, and ev'ry Nerve sustains;
It self unseen, but in th' *Effects*, remains.

80 There are whom Heav'n has blest with store of Wit,
Yet want as much again to manage it;[11]
For *Wit* and *Judgment* ever[12] are at strife,
Tho' meant each other's Aid, like *Man* and *Wife*.
'Tis more to *guide* than *spur* the Muse's Steed;
Restrain his Fury, than provoke his Speed;
The winged Courser, like a gen'rous Horse,
Shows most true Mettle when you *check* his Course.[13]

Those RULES of old *discover'd*, not *devis'd*,
Are *Nature* still, but *Nature Methodiz'd*;
90 *Nature*, like *Monarchy*,[14] is but restrain'd
By the same Laws which first *herself* ordain'd.

First learned *Greece* just Precepts did indite,
When to repress, and when indulge our Flight:[15]

High on *Parnassus'* Top her Sons she show'd,
And pointed out those arduous Paths they trod,
Held from afar, aloft, th' Immortal Prize,
And urg'd the rest by equal Steps to rise;
From great *Examples useful Rules* were giv'n;[16]
She drew from *them* what they deriv'd from *Heav'n*,
100 The gen'rous Critick *fann'd* the *Poet's Fire*,
And taught the World, *with Reason* to *Admire*.
Then Criticism the Muses Handmaid prov'd,
To dress her Charms, and make her more belov'd;
But following Wits from that Intention stray'd; ⎫
Who cou'd not win the Mistress, woo'd the Maid, ⎬
Set up themselves, and drove a *sep'rate* Trade:[17] ⎭
Against the Poets *their own Arms* they turn'd,
Sure to hate most the Men from whom they *learn'd*.
So modern *Pothecaries*, taught the Art
110 By *Doctor's Bills* to play the *Doctor's Part*,
Bold in the Practice of *mistaken Rules*,
Prescribe, apply, and call their *Masters Fools*.[18]
Some on the Leaves of ancient Authors prey,
Nor Time nor Moths e'er spoil'd so much as they:
Some dryly plain, without Invention's Aid,
Write dull *Receits* how Poems may be made:
These lost the Sense, their Learning to display,
And those explain'd the Meaning quite away.
  You then whose Judgment the right Course wou'd steer,
120 Know well each ANCIENT's proper *Character*,
His *Fable, Subject, Scope* in ev'ry Page,
Religion, Country, Genius of his *Age*:
Without all these at once before your Eyes,
You may *Confound*, but never *Criticize*.[19]
Be *Homer's* Works your *Study*, and *Delight*,
Read them by Day, and meditate by Night,[20]
Thence form your Judgment, thence your Notions[21] bring,
And trace the Muses *upward* to their *Spring*;

Still with *It self compar'd*, his *Text* peruse;[22]

130 And let your *Comment* be the *Mantuan Muse*.[23]

When first great[24] *Maro* in his boundless Mind

A Work, t'outlast Immortal *Rome* design'd,[25]

Perhaps he seem'd *above* the Critick's Law,

And but from *Nature's Fountains* scorn'd to draw:

But when t'examine ev'ry Part he came,

Nature and *Homer* were, he found, the *same*:

Convinc'd, amaz'd, he checkt the bold Design,

And did his Work to Rules as strict confine,[26]

As if the *Stagyrite*[27] o'erlook'd each Line.

140 Learn hence for Ancient *Rules* a just Esteem;

To copy *Nature* is to copy *Them*.

Some Beauties yet, no Precepts can declare,

For there's a *Happiness* as well as *Care*.

Musick resembles *Poetry*, in each

Are *nameless Graces* which no Methods teach,

And which a *Master-Hand* alone can reach.

*If, where the *Rules* not far enough extend,

(Since Rules were made but to promote their End)

Some Lucky LICENCE answers to the full

150 Th' Intent propos'd, *that Licence is a Rule*.

Thus *Pegasus*, a nearer way to take,

May boldly deviate from the common Track.

Great Wits sometimes may *gloriously offend*,

And *rise* to *Faults* true Criticks *dare not mend*;

From *vulgar Bounds* with *brave Disorder* part,

And *snatch* a *Grace* beyond the Reach of Art,

Which, without passing thro' the *Judgment*, gains

The *Heart*, and all its End *at once* attains.

In *Prospects*, thus, some *Objects* please our Eyes,

160 Which *out of* Nature's *common Order* rise,

The shapeless *Rock*, or hanging *Precipice*.

---

* *Neque tam sancta sunt ista Præcepta, sed hoc quicquid est, Utilitas excogitavit; Non negabo autem sic utile esse plerunque; verum si eadem illa nobis aliud suadebit utilitas, hanc, relictis magistrorum autoritatibus, sequemur.* Quintil. l. 2. cap. 13.[28]

But Care in Poetry must still be had,
It asks *Discretion* ev'n in *running Mad*;[29]
And tho' the *Ancients* thus their *Rules* invade,
(As *Kings* dispense with *Laws* Themselves have made)
Moderns, beware! Or if you must offend
Against the *Precept*, ne'er transgress its *End*,
Let it be *seldom*, and *compell'd by Need*,
And have, at least, *Their Precedent* to plead.
170 The Critick else proceeds without Remorse,
Seizes your Fame, and puts his Laws in force.
    I know there are, to whose presumptuous Thoughts
Those *Freer Beauties*, ev'n in *Them*, seem Faults:
Some Figures *monstrous* and *mis-shap'd* appear,
Consider'd *singly*, or beheld too *near*,
Which, but *proportion'd* to their *Light*, or *Place*,
Due Distance *reconciles* to Form and Grace.
A prudent Chief not always must display
His Powr's in *equal Ranks*, and *fair Array*,
180 But with th' *Occasion* and the *Place* comply,
Oft *hide*[30] his Force, nay seem sometimes to *Fly*.
Those are but[31] *Stratagems* which *Errors* seem,
Nor is it *Homer Nods*, but *We* that *Dream*.
Still green with Bays each *ancient* Altar stands,
Above the reach of *Sacrilegious* Hands,
Secure from *Flames*, from *Envy's* fiercer Rage,
Destructive *War*, and all-devouring[32] *Age*.
See, from *each Clime* the Learn'd their Incense bring;
Hear, in *all Tongues* Triumphant[33] *Pæans* ring!
190 In Praise so just, let ev'ry Voice be join'd,
And fill the *Gen'ral Chorus of Mankind*!
Hail *Bards Triumphant*! born in *happier Days*;
Immortal Heirs of *Universal* Praise!
Whose Honours with Increase of Ages *grow*,
As Streams roll down, *enlarging* as they flow!
Nations *unborn* your mighty Names shall sound,
And Worlds applaud that must not yet be *found*!

Oh may some Spark of *your* Cœlestial Fire
The last, the meanest of your Sons inspire,[34]
200   (That with weak Wings, from far, pursues your Flights;
Glows while he *reads*, but *trembles* as he *writes*)
To teach vain Wits that Science *little known*,
T'admire Superior Sense, and *doubt* their own!
    OF all the Causes which conspire to blind
Man's erring Judgment, and misguide the Mind,
What the weak Head with strongest Byass rules,
Is *Pride*, the *never-failing Vice of Fools*.
Whatever Nature has in *Worth* deny'd,
She gives in large Recruits of *needful Pride*;
210   For as in *Bodies*, thus in *Souls*, we find
What wants in *Blood* and *Spirits*, swell'd with *Wind*;
Pride, where Wit fails, steps in to our Defence,
And fills up all the *mighty Void of Sense!*[35]
If once right Reason drives *that Cloud* away,
Truth breaks upon us with *resistless Day*;
Trust not your self; but your Defects to know,
Make use of ev'ry *Friend* – and ev'ry *Foe*.
    A *little Learning* is a dang'rous Thing;
Drink deep, or taste not the *Pierian* Spring:[36]
220   There *shallow Draughts* intoxicate the Brain,
And drinking *largely* sobers us again.
Fir'd with the Charms fair *Science* does impart,
In *fearless Youth* we tempt the Heights of Art;[37]
While from the bounded *Level* of our Mind,
Short Views we take, nor see the *Lengths behind*,
But *more advanc'd*, survey[38] with strange Surprize
New, distant Scenes of *endless* Science rise:
So pleas'd at first, the towring *Alps* we try,
Mount o'er the Vales, and seem to tread the Sky;
230   Th' Eternal Snows appear already past,
And the first *Clouds* and *Mountains* seem the last:
But *those attain'd*, we tremble to survey
The growing Labours of the lengthen'd Way,

Th' *increasing* Prospect *tires* our wandring Eyes,
Hills peep o'er Hills, and *Alps* on *Alps* arise![39]
    *A perfect Judge will *read* each Work of Wit
With the same Spirit that its Author *writ*,
Survey the *Whole*, not seek slight Faults to find;
Where *Nature moves*, and *Rapture warms* the Mind;
240   Nor lose, for that malignant dull Delight,
The *gen'rous Pleasure* to be charm'd with Wit.
But in such Lays as neither *ebb*, nor *flow*,
Correctly cold, and *regularly low*,[40]
That shunning Faults, one quiet *Tenour* keep;
We cannot *blame* indeed – but we may *sleep*.
In Wit, as Nature, what affects our Hearts
Is not th' Exactness of peculiar Parts;
'Tis not a *Lip*, or *Eye*, we Beauty call,
But the joint Force and full *Result* of all.
250   Thus when we view some well-proportion'd Dome,
(The *World*'s just Wonder, and ev'n *thine* O *Rome!*)
No single Parts unequally surprize;
All comes *united* to th' admiring Eyes;
No monstrous Height, or Breadth, or Length appear;
The *Whole* at once is *Bold*, and *Regular*.
    Whoever thinks a faultless Piece to see,
Thinks what ne'er was, nor is, nor e'er shall be.[41]
In ev'ry Work regard the *Writer's End*,
Since none can compass more than they *Intend*;
260   And if the *Means* be just, the *Conduct* true,
Applause, in spite of trivial Faults, is due.
As Men of Breeding, oft the[42] Men of Wit,
T' avoid *great Errors*, must the *less* commit,
Neglect the Rules each *Verbal Critick* lays,
For *not* to know some Trifles, is a Praise.
Most Criticks fond of some subservient Art,
Still make the *Whole* depend upon a *Part*,

---

*   *Diligenter legendum est, ac pæne ad scribendi sollicitudinem: Nec per partes modo scrutanda sunt omnia, sed perlectus liber utique ex Integro resumendus.* Quintilian.[43]

They talk of *Principles*, but Parts they[44] prize,
And All to one lov'd Folly Sacrifice.

270   Once on a time, *La Mancha*'s Knight, they say,[45]
A certain *Bard* encountring on the Way,
Discours'd in Terms as just, with Looks as Sage,
As e'er cou'd *D——s*, of the Laws o' th' Stage;[46]
Concluding all were desp'rate Sots and Fools,
That durst depart from *Aristotle*'s Rules,[47]
Our Author, happy in a Judge so nice,
Produc'd his Play, and beg'd the Knight's Advice,
Made him observe the *Subject* and the *Plot*,
The *Manners*, *Passions*, *Unities*, what not?

280   All which, exact to *Rule* were brought about,
Were but a *Combate in the Lists* left out.
What! Leave the Combate out? Exclaims the Knight;
Yes, or we must renounce the *Stagyrite*.
Not so by Heav'n (he answers in a Rage)
Knights, Squires, and Steeds, must enter on the Stage.
The Stage can ne'er so vast a Throng contain.[48]
Then build a New, or act it in a Plain.

    Thus Criticks, of less *Judgment* than *Caprice*,
Curious, not *Knowing*, not *exact*, but *nice*,

290   Form *short Ideas*; and offend in *Arts*
(As most in *Manners*) by a *Love to Parts*.
Some to *Conceit* alone their Taste confine,
And glitt'ring Thoughts struck out at ev'ry Line;
Pleas'd with a Work where nothing's just or fit;
One *glaring Chaos* and *wild Heap of Wit*:
Poets like Painters, thus, unskill'd to trace
The *naked Nature* and the *living Grace*,
With *Gold* and *Jewels* cover ev'ry Part,
And hide with *Ornaments* their *Want of Art*.

300   *True Wit* is *Nature* to Advantage drest,
What oft was *Thought*, but ne'er before *Exprest*,[49]

* *Naturam intueamur, hanc sequamur; Id facillimè accipiunt animi quod agnoscunt.* Quintil. lib. 8. c. 3.[50]

Something, whose Truth convinc'd at Sight we find,
That gives us back the Image of our Mind:
As Shades more sweetly recommend the Light,
So modest Plainness sets off sprightly Wit:[51]
For *Works* may have more *Wit* than does 'em good,
As *Bodies* perish through Excess of *Blood*.
    Others for *Language* all their Care express,
And value *Books*, as Women *Men*, for *Dress*:
310   Their Praise is still – *The Stile is excellent*:
The *Sense*, they humbly take upon Content.
Words are like *Leaves*; and where they most abound,
Much *Fruit* of *Sense* beneath is rarely found.
False Eloquence, like the *Prismatic Glass*,
Its gawdy Colours spreads on *ev'ry place*;
The Face of Nature we no more Survey,
All glares *alike*, without *Distinction* gay:
But true *Expression*, like th' unchanging *Sun*,[52]
Clears, and *improves* whate'er it shines upon,
320   It *gilds* all Objects, but it *alters* none.
Expression is the *Dress* of *Thought*, and still
Appears more *decent* as more *suitable*;
A vile Conceit in pompous Style exprest,
Is like a Clown in regal Purple drest;
For diff'rent *Styles* with diff'rent *Subjects* sort,
As several Garbs with Country, Town, and Court.
*Some by *Old Words* to Fame have made Pretence;
Ancients in *Phrase*, meer Moderns in their *Sense*!
Such *labour'd Nothings*, in so *strange* a Style,
330   *Amaze* th' unlearn'd, and make the Learned *Smile*.

---

* *Abolita & abrogata retinere, insolentiæ cujusdam est, & frivolæ in parvis jactantiæ.* Quint. lib. 1. c. 6.

   Opus est ut Verba a vetustate repetita neque crebra sint, neque manifesta, quia nil est odiosius affectatione, nec utique ab ultimis repetita temporibus. Oratio, cujus summa virtus est perspicuitas, quam sit vitiosa si egeat interprete? Ergo ut novorum optima erunt maximè vetera, ita veterum maximè nova. Idem.[53]

Unlucky, as *Fungoso* in the *Play,
These Sparks with aukward Vanity display
What the Fine Gentlemen wore *Yesterday*!
And but so mimick ancient Wits at best,
As Apes our Grandsires in their *Doublets drest*.
In *Worlds*, as *Fashions*, the same Rule will hold;
Alike Fantastick, if *too New*, or *Old*;
Be not the *first* by whom the *New* are try'd,
Nor yet the *last* to lay the *Old* aside.

340 †But most by *Numbers* judge a Poet's Song,
And *smooth* or *rough*, with such, is *right* or *wrong*;
In the bright *Muse* tho' thousand *Charms* conspire,
Her *Voice* is all these tuneful Fools admire,
Who haunt *Parnassus* but to please their Ear,
Not mend their Minds; as some to *Church* repair,
Not for the *Doctrine*, but the *Musick* there.
These *Equal Syllables* alone require,[54]
‡Tho' oft the Ear the *open Vowels* tire,
While *Expletives* their feeble Aid *do* join,

350 And ten low Words oft creep in one dull Line,[55]
While they ring round the same *unvary'd Chimes*,
With sure *Returns* of still *expected Rhymes*.[56]
Where e'er you find *the cooling Western Breeze*,
In the next Line, it *whispers thro' the Trees*;
If *Chrystal Streams with pleasing Murmurs creep*,
The Reader's threaten'd (not in vain) with *Sleep*.
Then, at the *last*, and *only* Couplet fraught
With some *unmeaning* Thing they call a *Thought*,
A *needless Alexandrine* ends the Song,

360 That like a wounded Snake, drags its slow Length along.

---

* Ben. Johnson's *Every Man in his Humour*.[57]

† *Quis populi sermo est? quis enim? nisi carmine molli Nunc demum numero fluere, ut per læve severos Effugit junctura ungues: scit tendere versum, Non secus ac si oculo rubricam dirigat uno.* Persius, Sat. 1.[58]

‡ *Fugiemus crebras vocalium concursiones, quæ vastam atque hiantem orationem reddunt.* Cic. ad Herenn. lib. 4. *Vide etiam* Quintil. lib. 9. c. 4.[59]

Leave such to tune their own dull Rhimes, and know
What's *roundly smooth*, or *languishingly slow*;
And praise the *Easie Vigor* of a Line,
Where *Denham*'s Strength, and *Waller*'s Sweetness join.[60]
'Tis not enough no Harshness gives Offence,
The *Sound* must seem an *Eccho* to the *Sense*.[61]
Soft is the Strain when *Zephyr* gently blows,
And the *smooth Stream* in *smoother Numbers* flows;
But when loud Surges lash the sounding Shore,
370 The *hoarse, rough Verse* shou'd like the *Torrent* roar.
When *Ajax* strives, some Rock's vast Weight to throw,
The Line too *labours*, and the words move *slow*;
Not so, when swift *Camilla* scours the Plain,
Flies o'er th'unbending Corn, and skims along the Main.
Hear how *Timotheus' various[62] Lays surprize,
And bid Alternate Passions fall and rise!
While, at each Change, the Son of *Lybian Jove*
Now *burns* with Glory, and then *melts* with Love;
Now his *fierce Eyes* with *sparkling Fury* glow;
380 Now *Sighs* steal out, and *Tears begin to flow*:
Persians and *Greeks* like *Turns of Nature* found,
And the *World's Victor* stood subdu'd by *Sound*!
The Pow'r of Musick all our Hearts allow;
And what *Timotheus* was, is *Dryden* now.

   Avoid *Extreams*; and shun the Fault of such,
Who still are pleas'd *too little*, or *too much*.
At ev'ry Trifle scorn to take Offence,
That always shows *Great Pride*, or *Little Sense*;
Those *Heads* as *Stomachs* are not sure the best
390 Which nauseate all, and nothing can digest.
Yet let not each gay *Turn* thy Rapture move,
For Fools *Admire*, but Men of Sense *Approve*;[63]
As things seem *large* which we thro' *Mists* descry,
Dulness is ever apt to *Magnify*.[64]

---

* Alexander's *Feast, or the Power of Musick; An Ode by Mr.* Dryden.

Some the *French*[65] Writers, some our *own* despise;
The *Ancients* only, or the *Moderns* prize:
Thus *Wit*, like *Faith*, by each Man is apply'd
To *one small Sect*, and All are *damn'd beside*.
Meanly they seek the Blessing to confine,
400 And force *that Sun* but on a *Part* to Shine;
Which not alone the *Southern Wit* sublimes,
But ripens Spirits in cold *Northern Climes*;
Which from the first has shone on *Ages past*,
Enlights the *present*, and shall warm the *last*:
(Tho' *each* may feel *Increases* and *Decays*,
And see now *clearer* and now *darker Days*)
Regard not then if Wit be *Old* or *New*,
But blame the *False*, and value still the *True*.
Some ne'er advance a Judgment of their own,
410 But *catch* the *spreading Notion* of the Town;
They reason and conclude by *Precedent*,
And own *stale Nonsense* which they ne'er invent.
Some judge of Author's *Names*, not *Works*, and then
Nor praise nor damn[66] the *Writings*, but the *Men*.
Of all this *Servile Herd* the worst is He
That in *proud Dulness* joints with *Quality*,
A constant Critick at the Great-man's Board,
To *fetch and carry* Nonsense for my Lord.
What *woful stuff* this Madrigal wou'd be,
420 In some starv'd Hackny Sonneteer, or me?
But let a *Lord* once own the *happy Lines*,
How the *Wit brightens*! How the *Style refines*!
Before *his* sacred Name flies ev'ry Fault,
And each *exalted* Stanza *teems* with *Thought*![67]
The *Vulgar* thus through *Imitation* err;
As oft the *Learn'd* by being *Singular*;
So much they scorn the Crowd, that if the Throng
By *Chance* go right, they *purposely* go wrong;
So Schismatics the *dull*[68] *Believers* quit,
430 And are but damn'd for having *too much Wit*.

    Some praise at Morning what they blame at Night;
But always think the *last* Opinion *right*.
A Muse by these is like a Mistress us'd,
This hour she's *idoliz'd*, the next *abus'd*,
While their weak Heads, like Towns unfortify'd,
'Twixt Sense and Nonsense daily change their Side.
Ask them the Cause; *They're wiser still*, they say;
And still to Morrow's wiser than to Day.
We think our *Fathers* Fools, so *wise* we grow;
440   Our *wiser Sons*, no doubt, will think *us* so.
Once *School-Divines* our zealous Isle o'erspread;
Who knew most *Sentences* was *deepest read*;
Faith, Gospel, All, seem'd made to be *disputed*,
And none had *Sense enough to be Confuted.*
Scotists and *Thomists*,[69] now, in Peace remain,
Amidst their *kindred Cobwebs* in *Duck-Lane*.[70]
If *Faith* it self has *diff'rent Dresses* worn,
What wonder *Modes* in *Wit* shou'd take their Turn?
Oft, leaving what is Natural and fit,
450   The *current Folly* proves our *ready Wit*,
And Authors think their Reputation safe,
Which lives as long as *Fools* are pleas'd to *Laugh*.
    Some valuing those of their own *Side*, or *Mind*,
Still make themselves the measure of Mankind;
Fondly we think we honour Merit then,
When we but praise *Our selves* in *Other Men*.
Parties in *Wit* attend on those of *State*,
And publick Faction doubles private Hate.
Pride, Malice, Folly, against *Dryden* rose,
460   In various Shapes of *Parsons, Criticks, Beaus*;
But *Sense* surviv'd, when *merry Jests* were past;
For rising Merit will *buoy up* at last.
Might he return, and bless once more our Eyes,
New *Bl—s* and new *M—s*[71] must arise;
Nay shou'd great *Homer* lift his awful Head,
Zoilus[72] again would start up from the Dead.

Envy will *Merit* as its *Shade* pursue,
But like a Shadow, proves the *Substance* too;[73]
For envy'd Wit, like *Sol* Eclips'd, makes known
470　Th' *opposing Body's* Grossness, not its *own.*
When first that Sun too powerful Beams displays,
It draws up Vapours which obscure its Rays;
But ev'n those Clouds at last adorn its Way,
Reflect new Glories, and augment the Day.[74]
　　Be thou the *first* true Merit to befriend;
His Praise is lost, who stays till *All* commend;
Short is the Date, alas, of *Modern Rhymes*;
And 'tis but just to let 'em live *betimes.*
No longer now that Golden Age appears,
480　When *Patriarch-Wits* surviv'd a *thousand Years*;
Now Length of *Fame* (our *second* Life) is lost,
And bare Threescore is all ev'n That can boast:
Our Sons their Father's *failing Language* see,
And such as *Chaucer* is, shall *Dryden* be.
So when the faithful *Pencil* has design'd
Some *fair*[75] *Idea* of the Master's Mind,
Where a *new World* leaps out at his command,
And ready Nature waits upon his Hand;
When the ripe Colours *soften* and *unite*,
490　And sweetly *melt* into just Shade and Light,
When mellowing Time does full Perfection give,[76]
And each Bold Figure just begins to *Live*;
The *treach'rous Colours* in few Years decay,[77]
And all the bright Creation fades away!
　　Unhappy *Wit*, like most mistaken Things,
Repays not half that *Envy* which it brings:[78]
In *Youth* alone its empty Praise we boast,
But soon the Short-liv'd Vanity is lost!
Like some fair *Flow'r* that in the *Spring* does rise,[79]
500　And gaily Blooms, but ev'n in blooming *Dies.*
What is this *Wit* that does our Cares employ?
The *Owner's Wife*, that *other Men* enjoy,

The more his *Trouble* as the more *admir'd*;
Where *wanted*, scorn'd, and envy'd where *acquir'd*;
Maintain'd with *Pains*, but forfeited with *Ease*;[80]
Sure *some* to *vex*, but never *all* to *please*;
'Tis what the *Vicious fear*, the *Virtuous shun*;
By *Fools* 'tis *hated*, and by *Knaves undone*!
    Too much does *Wit* from *Ign'rance* undergo,[81]
510   Ah let not *Learning* too commence its Foe!
Of old, those found *Rewards* who cou'd *excel*,
And such were *Prais'd* who but *endeavour'd well*:
Tho' *Triumphs* were to *Gen'rals* only due,
Crowns were reserv'd to grace the *Soldiers* too.
Now those that reach *Parnassus'* lofty Crown,
Employ their Pains to spurn some others down;
And while Self-Love each jealous Writer rules,
Contending Wits become the *Sport of Fools*:
But still the *Worst* with most Regret commend,
520   And each *Ill Author* is as bad a *Friend*.
To what base Ends, and by what abject Ways,
Are Mortals urg'd by *Sacred Lust of Praise*?
Ah ne'er so *dire* a *Thirst of Glory* boast,
Not in the *Critick* let the *Man* be lost!
Good-Nature and *Good-Sense* must ever join;
To Err is *Humane*; to Forgive, *Divine*.
But if in Noble Minds some Dregs remain,
Not yet purg'd off, of Spleen and sow'r Disdain,
Discharge that Rage on more Provoking Crimes,
530   Not fear a Dearth in these Flagitious Times.
No Pardon vile *Obscenity* should find,[82]
Tho' *Wit* and *Art* conspire to move your Mind;
But *Dulness* with *Obscenity* must prove
As Shamefull sure as *Impotence* in *Love*.
In the fat Age of Pleasure, Wealth, and Ease,
Sprung the rank Weed,[83] and thriv'd with large Increase;
When *Love* was all an easie Monarch's[84] Care;
Seldom at *Council*, never in a *War*:

223

Jilts[85] rul'd the State, and Statesmen *Farces* writ;[86]
540 Nay *Wits* had *Pensions*, and *young Lords* had *Wit*:
The Fair sate panting at a *Courtier's Play*,
And not a Mask[87] went *un-improv'd* away:
The modest Fan was lifted up no more,
And Virgins *smil'd* at what they *blush'd* before –
The following Licence of a Foreign Reign[88]
Did all the Dregs of bold *Socinus*[89] drain;
Then *first* the *Belgian Morals* were extoll'd;
We their *Religion* had, and they our *Gold*:[90]
Then Unbelieving Priests reform'd the Nation,
550 And taught more *Pleasant* Methods of Salvation;[91]
Where Heav'ns Free Subjects might their *Rights* dispute,
Lest God himself shou'd seem too *Absolute*.[92]
Pulpits their *Sacred Satire* learn'd to spare,
And Vice *admir'd* to find a *Flatt'rer there*!
Encourag'd thus, Witt's *Titans* brav'd the Skies,
And the Press groan'd with Licenc'd *Blasphemies* –[93]
These Monsters, Criticks! with your Darts engage,
Here point your Thunder, and exhaust your Rage!
Yet shun their Fault, who, *Scandalously nice*,
560 Will needs *mistake* an Author *into Vice*;
All seems Infected that th'Infected spy,
As all looks yellow to the Jaundic'd Eye.

Learn then what MORALS Criticks ought to show,
For 'tis but *half* a *Judge's Task*, to *Know*.
'Tis not enough, Wit, Art, and Learning join;[94]
In all you speak, let Truth and Candor shine:
That not alone what to your *Judgment's*[95] due,
All may allow; but seek your *Friendship* too.
Be *silent* always when you *doubt* your Sense;
570 *Speak* when you're *sure*, yet speak with *Diffidence*;[96]
Some positive persisting Fops we know,
That, if *once wrong*, will needs be *always so*;

But you, with Pleasure own your Errors past,
And make each Day a *Critick* on the last.
   'Tis not enough your Counsel still be *true*,
Blunt Truths more Mischief than *nice Falshoods* do;
Men must be *taught* as if you taught them *not*;
And Things *ne'er known*[97] propos'd as Things *forgot*:
Without *Good Breeding*, *Truth* is not approv'd,[98]

580 *That* only makes *Superior* Sense *belov'd*.
   Be Niggards of Advice on no Pretence;
For the *worst Avarice* is that of *Sense*:
With mean Complacence ne'er betray your Trust,
Nor be so *Civil* as to prove *Unjust*;
Fear not the Anger of the Wise to raise;
Those best can *bear Reproof*, who *merit Praise*.
   'Twere well, might Criticks still this Freedom take;
But *Appius*[99] reddens at each Word you speak,
And *stares*, *Tremendous*! with a *threatning Eye*,

590 Like some *fierce Tyrant* in *Old Tapestry*!
Fear most to tax an *Honourable* Fool,
Whose Right it is, *uncensur'd* to be dull;
Such without *Wit* are Poets when they please,
As without *Learning* they can take *Degrees*.
Leave dang'rous *Truths* to unsuccessful *Satyrs*,
And *Flattery* to fulsome *Dedicators*,
Whom, when they *Praise*, the World believes no more,
Than when they promise to give *Scribling* o'er.
'Tis best sometimes your Censure to restrain,

600 And *charitably* let dull Fools[100] be *vain*:
Your Silence there is better than your *Spite*,
For who can *rail* so long as they can *write*?[101]
Still humming on, their old dull[102] Course they keep,
And *lash'd* so long, like *Tops*, are *lash'd asleep*.
False Steps but help them to renew the Race,
As after *Stumbling*, Jades will *mend* their Pace.
What Crouds of these, impenitently bold,
In *Sounds* and jingling *Syllables* grown old,

Still *run on* Poets in a raging Vein,
610　Ev'n to the Dregs and *Squeezings* of the *Brain*,
Strain out the last, dull droppings of their Sense,
And Rhyme with all the *Rage* of *Impotence*!
　　Such shameless *Bards* we have; and yet 'tis true,
There are as mad, abandon'd *Criticks* too.
*The Bookful Blockhead, ignorantly read,
With *Loads* of *Learned Lumber* in his Head,
With his own Tongue still edifies his Ears,
And always *List'ning to Himself* appears.
All Books he reads, and all he reads assails,
620　From *Dryden*'s *Fables* down to *D—y*'s[103] *Tales*.
With *him*, most Authors steal their Works, or buy;
Garth did not write his own *Dispensary*.[104]
Name a new *Play*, and *he's* the Poet's *Friend*,
Nay show'd his Faults – but when wou'd Poets mend?
No Place so Sacred from such Fops is barr'd,
Nor is *Paul's Church* more safe than *Paul's Church-yard*:
Nay, run to *Altars*; *there* they'll talk you dead;
For *Fools* rush in where *Angels* fear to tread.
Distrustful *Sense* with modest Caution speaks;　⎫
630　It still *looks home*, and *short Excursions* makes;　⎬
But *ratling Nonsense* in full *Vollies* breaks;　⎭
And never shock'd, and never turn'd aside,
Bursts out, resistless, with a thundring Tyde!
　　But where's the Man, who Counsel *can* bestow,
Still *pleas'd* to *teach*, and yet not *proud* to *know*?
Unbias'd, or by *Favour* or by *Spite*;
Not *dully prepossest*, or *blindly right*;
Tho' Learn'd, well-bred; and tho' well-bred, sincere;[105]
Modestly bold, and Humanly severe?
640　Who to a *Friend* his Faults can freely show,
And gladly praise the Merit of a *Foe*?

* *Nihil pejus est iis, qui paullum aliquid ultra primas litteras progressi, falsam sibi scientiæ persuasionem induerunt: Nam & cedere præcipiendi peritis indignantur, & velut jure quodam potestatis, quo ferè hoc hominum genus intumescit, imperiosi, atque interim sævientes, Stultitiam suam perdocent.* Quintil. lib. 1, ch. 1.[106]

Blest with a *Taste* exact, yet unconfin'd;
A *Knowledge* both of *Books* and *Humankind*;
Gen'rous Converse; a *Soul* exempt from *Pride*;
And *Love to Praise*, with *Reason* on his Side?
    Such once were *Criticks*, such the Happy *Few*,
Athens and *Rome* in better Ages knew.
The mighty *Stagyrite* first left the Shore,
Spread all his Sails, and durst the Deeps explore;
650 He steer'd securely, and discover'd far,
Led by the Light of the *Mæonian Star*.[107]
Not only *Nature* did his Laws obey,
But *Fancy*'s boundless Empire own'd his Sway.[108]
Poets, a *Race* long unconfin'd and free,
Still fond and proud of *Savage Liberty*,
Receiv'd his Rules, and stood convinc'd 'twas fit
Who conquer'd *Nature*, shou'd preside o'er *Wit*.
    Horace still charms with graceful Negligence,
And without Method *talks* us into Sense,
660 Does[109] like a *Friend* familiarly convey
The *truest Notions* in the *easiest way*.
He, who Supream in Judgment, as in Wit,
Might boldly censure, as he boldly writ,
Yet *judg'd* with *Coolness* tho' he sung with *Fire*;
His *Precepts* teach but what his *Works* inspire.
Our Criticks take a contrary Extream,
They *judge* with *Fury*, but they *write* with *Fle'me*:[110]
Nor suffers *Horace* more in wrong *Translations*
By *Wits*, than *Criticks* in as wrong *Quotations*.[111]
670   Fancy and Art in gay *Petronius* please,
The *Scholar's Learning*, and[112] the *Courtier's Ease*.
    In grave *Quintilian*'s copious Work we find
The justest *Rules*, and clearest *Method* join'd;
Thus *useful Arms* in Magazines we place,
All rang'd in *Order*, and dispos'd with *Grace*,
Nor thus alone the Curious Eye to please,
But to be *found*, when Need requires, with Ease.[113]

The *Muses* sure *Longinus* did inspire,[114]
And blest *their Critick* with a *Poet's Fire*.
680   An ardent *Judge*, that Zealous in his *Trust*,
With *Warmth* gives Sentence, yet is always *Just*;
Whose *own Example* strengthens all his Laws,
And *Is himself* that great *Sublime* he draws.

     Thus long succeeding Criticks justly reign'd,
Licence repress'd, and *useful Laws* ordain'd;
Learning and *Rome* alike in Empire grew,
And *Arts* still *follow'd* where her *Eagles flew*;
From the same Foes, at last, both felt their Doom,
And the same Age saw *Learning* fall, and *Rome*.
690   With *Tyranny*, then *Superstition* join'd,
As that the *Body*, this enslav'd the *Mind*;
All was *Believ'd*, but nothing *understood*,[115]
And to be *dull* was constru'd to be *good*;
A *second* Deluge Learning thus o'er-run,
And the *Monks* finish'd what the *Goths* begun.

     At length, *Erasmus*, that *great, injur'd* Name,
(The *Glory* of the Priesthood, and the *Shame*!)
Stemm'd the *wild Torrent* of a *barb'rous Age*,
And drove those *Holy Vandals* off the Stage.

700   But see! each *Muse*, in *Leo*'s Golden Days,[116]
Starts from her Trance, and trims her wither'd Bays!
Rome's ancient *Genius*, o'er its *Ruins* spread,
Shakes off the *Dust*, and rears his rev'rend Head!
Then *Sculpture* and her *Sister-Arts* revive;
Stones leap'd to *Form*, and *Rocks* began to *live*;
With *sweeter Notes* each *rising Temple* rung;
A *Raphael* painted, and a *Vida sung![117]
Immortal *Vida*! on whose honour'd Brow
The Poet's *Bays* and Critick's *Ivy* grow:
710   *Cremona* now shall ever boast thy Name,
As next in Place to *Mantua*, next in Fame!

---

*   M. Hieronymus Vida, *an excellent* Latin *Poet, who writ an Art of Poetry in Verse.*

But soon by Impious Arms from *Latium* chas'd,[118]
Their *ancient Bounds* the banish'd Muses past;
Thence Arts o'er all the *Northern World* advance;
But *Critic Learning* flourish'd most in *France*.
The *Rules*, a Nation born to serve, obeys,
And *Boileau* still in Right of *Horace* sways.
But *we*, brave *Britains*, *Foreign Laws* despis'd,
And kept *unconquer'd*, and *unciviliz'd*,
720 Fierce for the *Liberties of Wit*, and bold,
We still defy'd the *Romans*, as *of old*.

Yet *some* there were, among the *sounder Few*
Of those who *less presum'd*, and *better knew*,
Who durst assert the *juster Ancient Cause*,
And here *restor'd* Wit's *Fundamental Laws*.[119]
Such was *Roscomon* – not more *learn'd* than *good*,
With Manners gen'rous as his Noble Blood;
To him the Wit of *Greece* and *Rome* was known,
And ev'ry Author's *Merit*, but his own.

730 Such late was *Walsh*, – the Muses Judge and Friend,
Who justly knew to blame or to commend;
To Failings *mild*, but *zealous* for Desert;
The *clearest Head*, and the *sincerest Heart*.
This humble Praise, lamented *Shade*! receive,
This Praise at least a grateful Muse may give!
The Muse, whose early Voice you taught to Sing,
Prescrib'd her Heights, and prun'd her tender Wing,
(Her Guide now lost) no more attempts to *rise*,
But in low Numbers short Excursions tries:
740 Content, if hence th' Unlearn'd their Wants may view,
The Learn'd reflect on what before they knew:
Careless of *Censure*, nor too fond of *Fame*,
Still pleas'd to *praise*, yet not afraid to *blame*,
Averse alike to *Flatter*, or *Offend*,
Not *free* from Faults, nor yet too vain to *mend*.

FINIS.

John Dennis,

Reflections Critical and Satyrical, Upon a Late Rhapsody, Call'd, An Essay Upon Criticism
(1711)

THE PREFACE.

'TIS now almost seven Years, since I happen'd to say one Morning to a certain Person distinguish'd by Merit and Quality, that wherever the *Italian Opera* had come, it had driven out Poetry from that Nation, and not only Poetry, but the very Tast of Poetry, and of all the politer Arts; and that if the same Protection and Encouragement were continued to the *Opera*, by which it was then supported, the same Calamity would befal *Great Britain* which had happen'd to the Neighbouring Nations. As 'tis hard to find a Man more quick or more penetrating, than the Person to whom I spoke this; he immediately enter'd into that Sentiment, and soon after withdrew that Encouragement which he had given to the *Italians*. All that I foretold, and more than all hath happen'd.[1] For such Things, such monstrous Things have been lately writ, and such monstrous Judgments pass'd, that what has been formerly said has been sufficiently confirm'd, that 'tis impossible an Author can be so very foolish, but he will find more stupid Admirers.

A most notorious Instance of this Depravity of Genius and Tast, is the Essay upon which the following Reflections are writ, and the Approbation which it has met with. I will not deny but that there are two or three Passages in it with which I am not displeas'd; but what are two or three Passages as to the whole?

Fit Chœrilus ille
Quem bis terq; bonum cum risu miror.[2]

The approving two or Three Passages amongst a multitude of bad ones, is by no means advantageous to an Author. That little that is good in him does but set off its contrary, and make it appear more extravagant. The Thoughts, Expressions, and Numbers of this Essay are for the most part but very indifferent, and indifferent and execrable in Poetry are all one. But what is worse than all the rest, we find throughout the whole a deplorable want of that very Quality, which ought principally to appear in it, which is Judgment; and I have no Notion that where there is so great a want of Judgment, there can be any Genius.

However, I had not publish'd the following Letter, but had suffer'd his Readers to have hugg'd themselves in the Approbation of a Pamphlet so very undeserving, if I had not found things in it that have provok'd my Scorn, tho' not my Indignation. For I not only found my self attack'd without any manner of Provocation on my side, and attack'd in my Person, instead of my Writings, by one who is wholly a Stranger to me, and at a time when all the World knew that I was persecuted by Fortune;[3] I not only saw that this was attempted in a clandestine manner with the utmost Falshood and Calumny, but found that all this was done by a little affected Hypocrite, who had nothing in his mouth at the same time but *Truth*, *Candor*, *Friendship*, *good Nature*, *Humanity*, and *Magnanimity*.

'Tis for this Reason that I have publish'd the following Letter, in which if I have not treated the Author of the Essay with my usual Candor, he may thank himself and this good-natur'd Town. For having observ'd with no little Astonishment, that Persons have been censur'd for ill Nature, who have attempted to display the Errors of Authors undeservedly successful; tho' they have done this with all imaginable Candor, and with the best and noblest Designs, which are the doing Justice, the Discovery of Truth, and the Improvement of Arts; while Writers of Lampoons and infamous Libels, whose Anonymous Authors have lain lurking in the dark, sometimes in Clubs, and sometimes solitary, like so many common Rogues and Footpads, to ruin the Fortunes, and murder the Reputations of others; have been caress'd and hugg'd by their thoughtless Applauders, and treated as if they had been the most vertuous and the best natur'd Men in the

World; having observ'd all this with no little astonishment, I at last found out the reason of it, which is, because the Attempts of Libellers and Lampooners hurt only those whom they attack, and delight the rest of the Readers; whereas they who expose by a just Criticism the Absurdities of foolish fortunate Authors, attack all those who commend and admire those Authors, and disturb perhaps by opening their Eyes, no fewer than a thousand Fops in the good Opinion which they have conceiv'd of themselves. 'Tis for this Reason that I have endeavour'd to comply with this wise and good natur'd general Disposition of Minds, and to make amends for the Ill-nature of my Criticism, by the Allurements of my *Satyr*.

To Mr. — at Sunning-Hill, Berks.

SIR,

I Here send you my Answer to the two Questions which I lately received from you, which are whether the Essay upon Criticism, which I lately sent you is like to take in Town, and who is the Author of that anonymous Rhapsody.

In answer to the first Question, my Opinion is that it will take very well. For the same thing is true of great Bodies of Men, which has been observ'd of particular Persons; and that is, that when Genius thinks fit to depart from among them, good Taste never cares to be very long after it. When the *Italian* Opera drove Poetry from out this Island, Criticism thought it a very great Impertinence for her to stay long behind. Besides that the elegant Translations of the *Italian* Opera's, which Mr. *Tonson* has published by the most eminent Hands, have prepared People to like any thing that is of an equal Merit with those Translations, and with *Tom Sternhold*'s Version.

For the second *Quære*, Mr. — is of Opinion that this Essay was writ by some experienced judicious Person, who knows what Quantity of base Alloy is at this Juncture requisite to debase the Coin of *Parnassus*, and reduce it to the current Standard. But I am inclin'd to believe that it was writ by some young, or some raw Author, for the following Reasons.

First, He discovers in every Page a Sufficiency that is far beyond his little Ability; and hath rashly undertaken a Task which is infinitely above his Force; a Task that is only fit for the Author, with the just Encomium of whose Essay my Lord *Roscommon* begins his own.

> *Happy that author whose correct Essay*
> *Repairs so well our old* Horatian *way.*[4]

There is nothing more wrong, more low, or more incorrect than this Rhapsody upon Criticism. The Author all along taxes others with Faults of which he is more guilty himself. He tells us in the very two first Lines, that

> *'Tis hard to say if greater want of Skill*
> *Appear in writing, or in judging ill.*

Now whereas others have been at some Pains and Thought to shew each of these wants of Skill separately and distinctly, his comprehensive Soul hath most ingeniously contriv'd to shew them both in a supreme Degree together.

Secondly, While this little Author struts and affects the Dictatorian Air, he plainly shews that at the same time he is under the Rod; and that while he pretends to give Laws to others, he is himself a pedantick Slave to Authority and Opinion, of which I shall give some Instances.

In the beginning of his Essay he lays down this Maxim:

> *Let such teach others who themselves excel;*
> *And censure others who have written well.*

Where he would insinuate, that they alone are fit to be Criticks who have shewn themselves great Poets. And he brings in *Pliny* to confirm by his Authority the Truth of a Precept, which is denied by matter of Fact, and by the Experience of above Two thousand Years.

> *De Pictore, Sculptore, Fictore nisi Artifex judicare non potest.*[5]

It has been observed by Writers of Politicks, That they who have succeeded best in these kind of Writings, have never been either Governours of Provinces, or Ministers of State, as *Plato* and *Aristotle* in *Greece*, *Machiavel* in *Italy*, and in this Island *Harrington*. I will not say that this may be applied to Criticks. There are and have been very good ones who have been great Poets, as *Horace* in *Italy*, *Boileau* in *France*, and in *Great Britain* my Lord *Roscommon*, and a living noble Author.[6] Nay I am fully convinc'd, that there never was an admirable Poet, but he was a great Critick. For what can be more absurd than to imagine, that any Man can excel in any Art, or Business, or Profession, who does not understand that Profession, Art, or Business. Now he who understands the Art of Poetry is a Critick in Poetry. But this is undeniable at the same time, that there have been Criticks, who have been approv'd of by all the World, who never meddled with Poetry. Was *Aristotle* himself, the very Father of *Criticks*, a Poet? Why yes, 'tis pretended that there is a Fragment of an Ode, which was writ by him, remaining in *Athenæus*. But is that sufficient to denominate him a Poet? Did he ever write either Tragedy or Epick Poem? And yet how freely did he censure both Tragick and Epick Poets? *Dionysius Halicarnassæus*, and *Dionysius Longinus* among the *Greeks*, and *Quintilian* among the *Romans* were free Censurers, yet no Poets. And so are *Bossu* and *Dacier* at present among the *French*. And what is still more remarkable, is, that this young Author forgets himself to that degree, as to commend *Longinus* and *Quintilian* for accomplish'd Criticks contrary to his own Precept.

Another Instance which I shall give of his being a Slave to Authority and Opinion, is the servile Deference which he pays to the Ancients. P. 13.

> *Still Green with Bays each ancient Altar stands*
> *Above the reach of sacrilegious Hands,*
> *Secure from Flames, from Envy's fiercer Rage,*
> *Destructive War, and all devouring Age.*
> *See from each Clime the Learn'd their Incense bring,*
> *Hear in all Tongues triumphant Pæans ring!*
> *In Praise so just let ev'ry Voice be join'd,*
> *And fill the general Chorus of Mankind.*

Which is just the opposite Extravagance and Extreme to that of Monsieur *Perrault*.

For the *French*-man with an insolent Stupidity contemn'd and blasphem'd, even those Hero's of Antiquity, whose Writings are admirable and Divine: This Essayer deifies Authors, whose Writings are but tolerable and indifferent. *Boileau*, as a reasonable Man, took the Path that lay in the middle of the two Extremes, as we shall see by what follows.

"For what remains, says he, I would not have any one think, that in this number of ancient Writers approv'd of by all Ages, 'tis my Intention to comprehend some Authors, who indeed are ancient, but who have only acquir'd a moderate Esteem, as *Lycophron, Nonnus, Silius Italicus*, and the Author of the Tragedies which are attributed to *Seneca*, to whom in my mind we may not only boldly compare, but justly prefer several of the modern Writers. I only admit into that exalted Rank that small number of admirable Writers, whose Name alone is their Panegyrick, as *Homer, Plato, Cicero, Virgil, &c.* And I do not regulate the Esteem which I have for them, by that length of Time which their Works have lasted, but by the number of Years which they have been admir'd; of which 'tis convenient to advertise a great many People, who otherwise perhaps might indiscreetly believe, what Monsieur *Perrault* has a mind to insinuate, that we commend the Ancients for no other Reason, but because they are Ancients; and blame the Moderns for no other Reason, but because they are Moderns; which is utterly false; since there are several among the Ancients whom we do not admire, and several among the Moderns whom all the World extols. The Antiquity of a Writer is no certain proof of his Merit; but the ancient and constant Admiration which all the world has had for his Writings, is a certain and infallible proof that we ought to admire them." *Boileau* Reflect. the 7th on *Longinus*.[7]

Thus hath *Boileau* determin'd this matter like a dextrous Distinguisher, and a most rightful Judge. If I may be allow'd to speak my Sentiments after so great a Master, I must freely declare my Opinion, that of all the Poets among the *Grœcians*, I only admire *Homer, Sophocles, Pindar*, and *Euripides*, tho' I am very much pleas'd with some of the rest; and of all the Poets among the *Romans*, I admire only *Virgil* and *Horace*, and some parts of *Lucretius*; tho' I am very much pleas'd with *Catullus, Tibullus, Terence*, and others. For as for *Lycophron, Nonnus, Apollonius Rhodius, Valerius Flaccus, Silius Italicus, Statius*, I prefer the

Paradise lost of *Milton* before them all together: Nay I will go yet farther, and declare, that tho' I must freely own, that *Virgil* has infinitely the Advantage of *Milton*, in the wonderful Contrivance of his Poem, in the Harmony of his Versification, and in the constant Tenor of his Majesty, and his Elevation; yet that *Milton* in some particular parts of his Poem has the Advantage of *Virgil*, and of Mankind. And tho' I can by no means believe *Shakespear* to be of equal Merit with *Sophocles* or *Euripides*, for which I shall give my Reasons in another place;[8] yet this I can say for the Honour of my Countryman, and of *Great Britain*, that there are several single Scenes in *Shakespear*, which I prefer to all the Tragedies put together of which *Seneca* is accounted the Author.

I shall give one more Instance, by which it will appear that while this Youngster is pretending to give Laws, he behaves himself like one who is still in awe of the Rod; that he admires the Ancients, because his Master tells him that they must be admir'd; and that if the Ancients were his Contemporaries, and produc'd the same Writings now which they did formerly, he would use them with the same Insolence with which he treats his Contemporaries. In the 8th Page of this Essay, he gives a verbose and indigested Encomium of the first *Grecian* Criticks, but forgets and contradicts himself before he comes to the bottom of that very Page. For, says he,

> The gen'rous Critick fann'd the Poet's Fire,
> And taught the World with Reason to admire;
> Then Criticism, the Muses Handmaid, proud[D]
> To dress her Charms, and make her more belov'd:
> But following Wits from that Intention stray'd,
> Who could not win the Mistress, woo'd the Maid,
> Set up themselves, and drove a sep'rate Trade. }

Never was any thing more obscure and confus'd than the foregoing Rhimes; but if there is any meaning in them, it must be that which follows.

At first Poets and Criticks were all one; and these Poets made use of their Criticism only to make their Poetry more charming, and more accomplish'd. But the Wits who immediately follow'd after them, deviated from the Design of their Predecessors; and not being able to attain to Poetry, took up a Resolution to drive a separate Trade, and to set up only for Criticks. If this is not his meaning, I should be glad to hear in Prose, and in plain *English* what his meaning is; for Rhime has been always a wicked Abettor and Concealer of Nonsense. But if this is his meaning, then I desire to make these two Remarks, First, that the ancientest Criticks among the *Grœcians* were not Poets, as we observ'd before; and Secondly, that if *Aristotle* and *Dionysius Halicarnassœus*, and others were now alive, and their excellent Criticisms were now first to appear, it would be objected to those great Men, in order to disqualify them for Criticks, that they were no Versifyers. And it is plain from the 2^{d10} Page that another Objection would be made to them: For when he comes there to speak of the Moderns, he tells us,

> *Some dryly plain, without Invention's Aid,*
> *Write dull Receipts how Poems may be made.*

Now it being evident, that the Criticisms of *Aristotle* and of *Dionysius Halicarnassœus* are writ with a great deal of Simplicity, 'tis manifest that if those two Criticks had writ but yesterday, they would be accus'd to day of being drily plain, and of writing dull Receipts.

But a third infallible mark of a young Author, is, that he hath done in this Essay what School-boys do by their Exercises, he hath borrow'd both from Living and Dead, and particularly from the Authors of the two famous Essays upon Poetry and Translated Verse;[11] but so borrow'd, that he seems to have the very Reverse of *Midas*'s noble Faculty. For as the coursest and the dullest Metals, were upon the touch of that *Lydian* Monarch immediately chang'd into fine Gold; so the finest Gold upon this Author's handling it, in a moment loses both its lustre and its weight, and is immediately turn'd to Lead.

A fourth thing that shews him a young man, is the not knowing his own mind, and his frequent Contradictions of himself. His Title seems to promise an Essay upon Criticism in general, which afterwards dwindles to an Essay upon Criticism in Poetry. And after all, he is all along giving Rules, such as they are, for writing rather than Judging. In the beginning of the 8th Page the Rules are nothing but Nature.

> *These Rules of old discover'd, not devis'd,*
> *Are Nature still, but Nature methodiz'd.*

But no sooner is he come to the 10th Page, but the Rules and Nature are two different things.

> *When first great* Maro, *in his boundless mind,*
> *A Work t' outlast immortal* Rome *design'd,*
> *Perhaps he seem'd above the Critick's Law,*
> *And but from Nature's Fountains scorn'd to draw.*[12]

But in the last Line of this very Paragraph they are the same things again.

> *Learn hence for ancient Rules a just Esteem,*
> *To copy Nature is to copy them.*

But to this he will answer, That he is guilty of no Contradiction, that he is only shewing that *Virgil* was guilty of Error and Ignorance; who first absurdly began to write his *Æneis*, and afterwards sate down to learn the Rules of Writing; which when he began to write that Poem, he took to be things distinct from Nature; but that after he had wrote part of it, he fell to the reading of *Homer*, and that undeceiv'd him. That while he is talking of *Virgil's* Error and Ignorance, he is making a Parade of his own incomparable Wisdom and Knowledge; and not contradicting himself, but *Virgil*, or rather making him appear inconsistent with and contradicting himself: for that tho' *Virgil* took the Rules and Nature to be distinct from each other, for his own part he is wiser, and knows better things. Now is not this a very modest and a very judicious Gentleman?

A fifth Sign of his being a young Author is his being almost perpetually in the wrong. And here in relation to the foregoing passage, I might desire to ask him one or two civil Questions. First, who acquainted him with that noble Particularity of *Virgil's* Life, that he designed to write his *Æneis* without Art? Had he it from ancient or modern Authors, or does he owe it to a noble Effort of his own sagacious Soul? If *Virgil* had so little Knowledge of the Rules of his own Art, and so very little true Judgment within him, as to be capable of such an Extravagance, an Extravagance which, says this Essayer, nothing but the reading of *Homer* was able to correct, how comes he so far to have surpass'd his Master in the admirable Contrivance of his Poem? But secondly, what does he mean by *Maro*'s designing a Work to outlast immortal *Rome*? Does he pretend to put that Figure, call'd a Bull[13] upon *Virgil*? Or would he ambitiously have it pass for his own? 'Tis no wonder that one who is capable of imputing so great an Extravagance to *Virgil*, should be capable of writing himself without any manner of meaning.

Whenever we find a Simile, the first Line of it is like a Warning-piece, to give us notice that something extraordinary false or foolish is to follow. We have one in the 6th Page, where the former and the latter part have not the least relation, and bear not the least proportion to one another.

> *As on the Land while here the Ocean gains,*
> *In other Parts it leaves wide sandy Plains:*
> *Thus in the Soul while Memory prevails,*
> *The solid Power of Understanding fails;*
> *Where Beams of warm Imagination play,*
> *The Memory's soft Figures melt away.*

Here the Soul in the third Verse is made to answer to Land in the first, and Memory to Ocean, which in the fourth Verse is chang'd for Understanding; tho' in this Simile the Author shews neither Memory nor Understanding; for there are as many Absurdities in it as there are Lines. At this rate a man may make a thousand Similes in an hour! Any thing may become like to any thing. *Jungentur jam Gryphes Equis.*[14] But what a thoughtless Creature is this Essayer, to deny in these very Rhimes, by which he pretends to shew both Poetry and Criticism, the co-existence of those Qualities, without which 'tis impossible to be both Poet and Critick? Besides, how wrong is this; and how many Persons have I known who have had all these Qualities at the same time in a very great degree? What follows is more wrong and more absurd:

> *One Science only will one Genius fit,*
> *So vast is Art, so narrow Human Wit.*

Is not this a rare Pretender to Poetry and Criticism, who talks at this rate, when all the World knows that 'tis impossible for a Man with only one Science to be either Poet or Critick? Which is so much the more unlucky, because the very Fathers of Poetry and Criticism *Homer* and *Aristotle*, whom he mentions so often in this Essay, are believed to have had all the Sciences. 'Tis now between Two and three thousand Years since *Aristotle* wrote his Morals, his Politicks, his Rhetorick, and his Poetick; and three of these are the very best in their kinds to this very day, and have infinitely the Advantage of all those several thousand Treatises that have been writ since. What follows is still more false and more abominable.

> *Not only bounded to peculiar Arts,*
> *But ev'n in those confin'd to single Parts.*

What a wretched narrow Soul hath this Essayer? And what a thoughtless one – when *Homer*, whom he mentions so often in this Essay, had as admirable a Talent for Pleasantry, as he had a Genius equal to the most exalted Poetry? To come to the *Romans*, Horace is famous both for Elevation and Pleasantry. *Virgil* succeeded in his *Bucolicks* and *Georgicks*, as well as he did in his *Æneis*. To descend to the *Moderns*, *Shakespear* had a very good Genius for Tragedy, and a very good Talent for Comedy. And since him *Otway* had likewise a Talent for both.

But in the next Page there is likewise a Simile; and therefore we may be sure, as we observ'd above, that most of that Page is one continued Absurdity. P. 7.

> *First follow Nature, and your Judgment frame*
> *By her just Standard, which is still the same;*
> *Unerring Nature still divinely bright,*
> *One clear, unchang'd, and universal Light,*
> *Life, Force and Beauty next to all impart,*
> *At once the Source, and End, and Test of Art:*

Now here wou'd I fain ask one or two Questions. Is he giving Rules here for Judging or for Writing? And is he prescribing those Rules to the Knowing or the Ignorant? If he says to the Knowing, what is it that he tells them here? That they must judge according to Nature, or write according to Nature. Now does he tell them any thing in this that they did not know before? Well, but he says, he is laying down these Rules for the Ignorant; why then I humbly conceive that he ought to have told them what he means by Nature, and what it is to write or to judge according to Nature. For by expressing himself at the rate that he does, he neither says any thing to the Learned which they did not know before, nor any thing to the Ignorant which they can possibly understand. *Horace* proceeded in a very different Method from this, when he was to acquaint the *Piso*'s what was the principal Source of good Writing, he not only told them that it was moral Philosophy,

> *Scribendi recte, sapere est & principium & Fons,*

But pointed to the very Books where they might find that moral Philosophy,

> *Rem tibi Socraticæ poterunt ostendere Chartæ.*[15]

So that in one we have a clear and perspicuous Precept, and in the other an obscure and unintelligible Jargon. But let us go on.

> *That Art is best which most resembles her,*
> *Which still presides, yet never does appear.*

That is as much as to say, *Artis est celare artem,*[16] the common Subject that Pedants give their Boys to make Themes and Declamations upon. Is not this a noble Discovery? Well but now for the Simile;

> *In some fair Body thus the sprightly Soul*
> *With Spirit feeds, with Vigor fills the whole,*
> *Each motion guides, and ev'ry nerve sustains,*
> *It self unseen but in th' effects remains.*

This Youngster has not memory enough to know what he said six Lines before;

> *Thus in a Soul where memory ne'r prevails,*
> *The solid Power of understanding fails.*

In the fifth Line of this Page it was Nature that

Life, force and beauty must to all impart.

And here in the 10th we are told that 'tis Art that

With Spirit feeds, with Vigor fills the whole.

But how absurdly is Art compar'd to the Soul, to which only Genius can be justly compar'd, according to the Observation in the Essay upon Poetry.[17] But let us go on, and we shall find that as all that went before this Simile is unintelligible, so all is mighty absurd that follows it.

There are whom Heav'n hath bless'd with store of Wit,
Yet want as much again to manage it.

By the way what rare Numbers are here? Would not one swear that this Youngster had espous'd some antiquated Muse, who had sued out a Divorce upon the account of Impotence from some superannuated Sinner; and who having been pox'd by her former Spouse, has got the Gout in her decrepit Age, which makes her hobble so damnably – Why, this is more dismal than the *Italian* Opera, both that and the Essay are but sounds; but that is Harmony, and this is Discord.

But now, my dear Friend, if I had young Mr. *Bays* here, I would desire that I might ask him one Question, and he not be angry. And that is, what he means by

There are whom Heav'n has bless'd with store of Wit,
Yet want as much again to manage it.

But let us go on, and see if 'tis possible to find it out without him.

For Wit and Judgment ever are at strife,
Tho' meant each others, are like Man and Wife.

That is as much as to say, there are People who have that which they call Wit, without one dram of Judgment. Is not this another wonderful Discovery? But I fancy that Mr. *Bays* has the Misfortune to be wrong in the first Verse of the foresaid Couplet.

For Wit and Judgment ever are at strife.

What a Devil, Mr. *Bays*, they cannot be at strife sure, after they are parted, after Wit has made an Elopement, or has been barbarously forsaken by Judgment, or turn'd to separate maintenance! Much less can they be at strife where they never came together, which is the Case in the Essay. But now we talk of Man and Wife, let us consider the Yoke-fellow to the former Rhime.

> *Tho' meant each others, and like Man and Wife.*

Now cannot I for my Soul conceive the reciprocal *Aid* that there is between Wit and Judgment. For tho' I can easily conceive how Judgment may keep Wit in her Senses, yet cannot I possibly understand how Wit can controul, or redress, or be a help to Judgment.

If Mr. *Bays* in that Couplet

> *There are whom Heav'n has bless'd with store of Wit,*
> *Yet want as much agen to manage it.*

Intended to say that People have sometimes store of false Wit without Judgment to manage it, he intended nothing but what all the World knew before. But if he meant to say this of true Wit, nothing can be more mistaken; for I cannot conceive how any one can have store of Wit without Judgment. I believe that Father *Bouheurs* has given a tolerable Description of Wit in his Treatise upon that Subject, *C'est un solide qui brille*: "Tis a shining Solid, like a Diamond, which the more solid it is, is always the more glittering; and derives its height of Lustre from its perfect Solidity."[18] Now how any thing in the Works of the Mind can be solid without Judgment, I leave Mr. *Bays* to consider.

But let us pass to the 18th Page, at the bottom of which we shall find another Simile, and consequently another Absurdity.

> *Poets, like Painters, thus unskill'd to trace*
> *The naked Nature and the living Grace,*
> *With Gold and Jewels cover ev'ry part,*
> *And hide with Ornament their want of Art.*

Which in Prose and plain *English* runs thus:

Poets like Painters not having the Skill to draw Nature without Art, hide their want of Art with a super-abundance of Art.

In the 20th Page we have another Simile, and consequently another Absurdity.

> *But true Expression, like th' unchanging Sun,*
> *Clears and improves whate'er it shines upon.*

Which is borrow'd from the Essay on Poetry.

> *True Wit is everlasting like the Sun.*[19]

But awkardly borrow'd, and utterly spoil'd in the removal. For what can Expression be properly said to shine upon? True Wit, or Genius; for that the noble Author means, as is plain from several parts of his Poem, shines thro' and discovers it self by the Expression; but Expression, at the very best, can but shine with a borrow'd Light, like the Moon and the rest of the Planets, whereas Genius shines and flames with its own Celestial Fire.

His Instructions, his Assertions, his Commendations, his Censures, his Advice, wherever they are his own, are either false or trivial, or both. Such is that in the beginning of the twelfth Page.

> *And tho' the Ancients thus their Rules invade,*
> *As Kings dispense with Laws themselves have made,*
> *Moderns beware.*

Thus is this Essayer for a double Dispensing Power in Kings and ancient Authors, and is for making the Moderns doubly Slaves, Slaves in their Actions, and Slaves in their Writings. But as we boldly deny that Kings have either Power to make Laws, or to dispense with them after they are made; so those Laws of Writing were neither made by the Ancients, nor can those Ancients dispense with them. As they are the Laws of Nature, and not of Men, as he has himself hinted in the beginning of the 8th Page.

> *Those Rules of old discover'd, not devis'd,*
> *Are Nature still, but Nature methodiz'd.*

They are eternal and irrevocable, and never to be dispens'd with but by Nature that made them; and the only Rule for that Dispensation is this, that a less Law may be violated to avoid the infringing of a greater; and 'tis equally the Duty both of Ancients and Moderns, to break thro' a less important Rule, when without that Infringement a greater must be violated, or the great End of all the Rules neglected. The great End of all the Rules is to instruct, and the subordinate End is to please, by moving of Passion, and particularly that kind of Passion which ought chiefly to reign in that sort of Poetry in which the Poet writes. Now 'tis a Rule in Poetry, that the notorious Events of History are not to be falsifyed, nor the Periods of Time transpos'd or confounded. And yet *Virgil* in the fourth of his *Æneis*, broke thro' this Rule at once by a bold and a judicious Anachronism; in order to make his Poem more admirable, and the more to exalt the Glory of the *Roman* Name.[20] Whatever the Ancients justly did, the Moderns may justly do. 'Tis ridiculous and pedantick to imagine, that the natural Powers of the Soul were stronger or more excellent in the Ancients than they are in the Moderns. And as to Experience we have vastly the Advantage of them. When we consider Experience, as my Lord *Bacon* observes, we are properly the Ancients, who live in the elder Ages of the World, and have the Advantage of the Knowledge of Three thousand Years over the first Writers.[21] Not but that at the same time that I assert the Equality of Faculties in the Moderns, and the Advantage of their Experience, I freely acknowledge the actual Preheminence that several of the Ancients have over the Moderns; but I have sufficiently shewn in the *Advancement of Modern Poetry*,[22] that that actual Preheminence proceeded from accidental Causes, and not from any Superiority of Faculties in those ancient Authors.

At the bottom of the same Page 12. there is something asserted that is both false and impudent; where speaking of the Ancients, he tells us,

> *Those are but Stratagems which Errors seem,*
> *Nor is it* Homer *nods but we that dream.*

Which is a presumptuous Contradiction of *Horace*,

> *Aliquando bonus dormitat Homerus.*[23]

And of my Lord *Roscommon*.

> *His reeling Hero's and his wounded Gods*
> *Make some suspect he snores as well as nods.*[24]

And is in effect to declare that *Horace* was a Dreamer, and my Lord *Roscommon* a Dotard, and I, my Masters, only I, am *alerte* and *eueillè*, only I am the man of Importance.

In the beginning of the 21st Page there is something too very wrong.

> *In Words as Fashions the same Rule will hold,*
> *Alike fantastick if too new or old,*
> *Be not the first by whom the new are try'd,*
> *Nor yet the last to lay the old aside.*

This being directed to all without Exception, and deliver'd without Limitation or Restriction, is another flat Contradiction of *Horace.*

> *Si forte necesse est*
> *Indiciis monstrare recentibus abdita rerum:*
> *Fingere cinctutis non exaudita Cethegis*
> *Contiget, dabiturq; licentia sumpta pudenter.*
> *Et nova fictaq; nuper habebunt verba fidem, si*
> *Græco fonte cadant parce detorta.*[25]

This is likewise a Libel upon the memory of Mr. *Dryden* whom he pretends to admire; for never any one was a greater Coiner than he, and it is directly contrary to the Improvement of Languages; for if *Chaucer* and succeeding Authors had had this Advice given them, and had been weak enough to take it, how could our Language ever have improv'd in Purity, in Force, in Grace, or in Harmony? But if it was allow'd to *Chaucer*, and those who immediately follow'd him, why must it be deny'd to those who have liv'd since.

> *quid autem*
> *Cæcilio, Plautoq; dabit Romanus ademptum*
> *Virgilio, Varroque? Ego cur acquirere pauca*
> *Si possim, invideor? Quum lingua Catonis & Enni,*
> *Sermonem patrium ditaverit, & nova rerum*
> *Nomina protulerit, licuit semperq; licebit*
> *Signatum præsente nota producere nomen.*[26]

I must confess if we speak with relation to the constant and general Practice of a Writer, he ought to take what the *French* call the best Use, for the Mistress of the Language in which he writes; but a great Poet if he writes in the Language which he was born to speak, may be allow'd the Privilege sometimes to coin new words, and sometimes to revive the old, which last succeeded so well to *Milton*.

About the middle of the 22^d Page he gives Advice, which shews him very inconsistent with himself.

> *And praise the easie Vigor of a Line,*
> *Where* Denham*'s Strength and* Waller*'s Sweetness join.*

How vastly different is this from what he pretends to advise at the bottom of the 9th Page.

> *Be* Homer*'s Works your Study day and night,*
> *Read them by day, and meditate by night;*
> *Thence form your Judgment, thence your Notions bring,*
> *And trace the Muses upward to their Spring;*
> *Still with it self compar'd, his Text peruse,*
> *And let your Comment be the* Mantuan *Muse.*

Now he who is familiar with *Homer*, and intimate with *Virgil*, will not be extremely affected either with the Sweetness of *Waller*, or the Force of *Denham*. He requires something that is far above the Level of modern Authors, something that is great and wonderful. If I were to recommend a *British* Poet to one who has been habituated to *Homer* and *Virgil*, I would for the Honour of my Country, and of my own Judgment advise him to read *Milton*; who very often equals both the *Græcian* and the *Roman* in their extraordinary Qualities, and sometimes surpasses them, is more lofty, more terrible, more vehement, more astonishing, and has more impetuous and more divine Raptures. I will not deny but that *Waller* has Sweetness, and *Denham* Force; but their good and their shining Qualities are so sophisticated and debauch'd with these modern Vices of Conceit, and Point, and Turn, and Epigram, that 'tis impossible they can affect in an extraordinary manner those who have been long acquainted with the Ancients.

There is in the 38th and the 39th Pages another Inconsistency, which

I desire to lay before the Reader. In the 38th Page he speaks of *Horace* thus:

> *He who supreme in Judgment as in wit,*
> *Might boldly censure as he boldly writ;*
> *Yet judg'd with Coolness, tho' he sung with Fire*
> *His Precepts teach but what his Works inspire.*
> *Our Criticks take a contrary Extreme,*
> *They judge with Fury, but they write with Flegm.*

Before he goes ten Lines farther, he forgets himself, and commends *Longinus* for the very contrary Quality for which he commended *Horace*, and for the very same thing for which he condemns his Contemporaries.

> *The Muses sure* Longinus *did inspire,*
> *And blest their Critick with a Poet's Fire:*
> *An ardent Judge that zealous in his Trust*
> *With warmth gives Judgment, yet is always just;*
> *Whose own Example strengthens all his Laws,*
> *And is himself that great Sublime he draws.*

He commends *Horace* for judging cooly in Verse, and extols *Longinus* for criticizing with Fire in Prose. What a miserable Slave is this Author to Opinion? Can any thing be more plain, than that he condemns his Contemporaries for no other reason but because they are his Contemporaries; and commends *Longinus* for no other reason but because he has been approv'd of by others. For why should not a modern Critick imitate the great Qualities of *Longinus*; and when he treats of a Subject which is sublime, treat of it sublimely? Now he who writes any thing with Sublimity, let it be Prose or Verse, let it be Criticism or Poetry, writes sometimes with Fury, as *Longinus* hath shewn both by his Doctrine and his Example in the first Chapter of his Treatise.

But pray who are these Moderns that judge with Fury, and write with Flegm? Who are they that have writ both Criticism and Poetry, who have not in their Poetry shewn a thousand times this Essayer's Fire? Who is there among them that is not above borrowing so openly and so awkwardly from the most known Authors? For what Reader is so unacquainted with our *English* Poetry, as not to know that he has taken this last Couplet, with a very little variation from the Essay on Translated Verse?

> *Thus make the proper Use of each Extreme,*
> *And write with Fury, but correct with Flegm.*[27]

But what is a perspicuous sensible Precept in my Lord *Roscommon*, as soon as this Essayer handles it, becomes a gross Absurdity and a palpable Contradiction.

In the 28th Page there are no less than two or three Absurdities in the compass of four Lines.

> *Now length of Fame our second Life is lost,*
> *And bare Threescore is all ev'n that can boast.*
> *Our Sons their Fathers failing Language see,*
> *And such as* Chaucer *is shall* Dryden *be.*

Now what does young Mr. *Bays* mean by *our second Life*, and by *bare Threescore*? If he speaks of himself, and means threescore Days, he means too much in Reason: But if he speaks of *Chaucer*, *Spencer*, and *Shakespear*, and means threescore Years, he means too little in Conscience. 'Tis now a hundred Years since *Shakespear* began to write, more since *Spencer* flourished, and above 300 Years since *Chaucer* died. And yet the Fame of none of these is extinguish'd. The Reason that he gives for this is false too.

> *Our Sons their Fathers failing Language see,*

Mr. *Waller* may suffice to shew the Falsity of this. 'Tis above threescore Years since that Gentleman began to write, and yet his Language is still good and new. Thus we find that the Assertion is false here, the Reason of it false; and we shall find anon that the Inference is false too.

> *And such as* Chaucer *is shall* Dryden *be;*

That is, shall grow obsolete and neglected, and be either forgot, or be read but by a few.

Whether the Language of Mr. *Dryden* will ever be as obsolete as is at present that of *Chaucer*, is what neither this Author nor any one else can tell. For ev'ry Language hath its particular period of Time to bring it to Perfection, I mean to all the Perfection of which that Language is capable. And they who are alive cannot possibly tell whether that period hath happen'd or not: If that period has not yet happen'd; yet 'tis not the Obsoleteness of Language which makes a Poet fall from the Reputation which he once enjoy'd, provided the Language in which that Poet wrote was at the Time of his Writing come to be capable of Harmony. For *Spencer* is obsolete, yet is still renown'd. That which makes an Author fall from his former Reputation, is, says *Boileau*, in his seventh Reflection upon *Longinus*, his not having attain'd to that Point of Solidity and Perfection, which are necessary to give a never dying Esteem to his Works. For example, says he, the Latin Tongue in which *Cicero* and *Virgil* wrote, was already very much alter'd in the Time of *Quintilian* and of *Aulus Gellius*; and yet *Cicero* and *Virgil* were more esteem'd when those Criticks wrote, than they were in their own Age, because they had as it were by their Writings fix'd the *Roman* Language, having attain'd to that Point of Solidity and Perfection which I have mention'd above.

If we reflect upon that miserable Tast which reigns now among our Readers, and that want of Genius which is so deplorable in our present Writers, and that Tast and Genius daily more and more decline, we may without being Prophets foretel, according to the foremention'd Observation of the Solidity and Perfection of Poems, that the Language is not like to alter to the Disadvantage of those Poets, whose Works are the only Remains of them here below. But be that as it will, yet this is certain, that Mr. *Dryden* had one Quality in his Language, which *Chaucer* had not, and which must always remain. For having acquir'd some Justness of Numbers, and some Truth of Harmony and of Versification, to which *Chaucer* thro' the Rudeness of the Language, or want of Ear, or want of Experience, or rather perhaps a mixture of all, could not possibly attain, that Justness of Numbers, and Truth of Harmony and of Versification can never be destroy'd by any alteration of Language; and therefore Mr. *Dryden* whatever alteration happens to the Language, can never be like to *Chaucer*.

Wherever this Gentleman talks of Wit, he is sure to say something that is very foolish, as Page 29.

> *What is this Wit that does our Cares employ,*
> *The Owner's Wife that other Men enjoy?*
> *The more his Trouble as the more admir'd,*
> *Where wanted scorn'd, and envy'd where acquir'd.*

Here again I desire leave to ask two or three Questions. First, how can Wit be scorn'd where it is not? Is not this a Figure frequently employ'd in *Hibernian* Land?[28] The Person who wants this Wit may indeed be scorn'd; but such a Contempt declares the Honour that the Contemner has for Wit. But secondly, what does he mean by acquir'd Wit? Does he mean Genius by the word Wit, or Conceit and Point? If he means Genius, that is certainly never to be acquir'd; and the Person who should pretend to acquire it, would be always secure from Envy. But if by Wit he means Conceit and Point, those are things that ought never to be in Poetry, unless by chance sometimes in the Epigram, or in Comedy, where it is proper to the Character and the Occasion; and ev'n in Comedy it ought always to give place to Humour, and ev'n to be lost and absorp'd in that, according to the Precept of the noble Author of the *Essay on Poetry*.

> *That silly thing Men call sheer Wit avoid,*
> *With which our Age so nauseously is cloy'd;*
> *Humour is all, Wit should be only brought*
> *To turn agreeably some proper Thought.*[29]

In the beginning of the 33[d] Page there is a Couplet of Advice, the first line of which is very impertinent, and the second very wrong.

> *Be silent always when you doubt your Sense.*

Now who are the Persons to whom he is giving Advice here? Why, to Poets or Criticks, or both; but the Persons to whom he ought to be speaking are Criticks, that is, People who pretend to instruct others. But can any man of common Sense want to be told, that he ought not to pretend to instruct others, as long as he doubts of the Truth of his own Precepts?

But what can be more wrong or more absurd than the latter Verse of the Couplet?

> *Speak when you're sure, yet speak with Diffidence.*[30]

Now I should think that when a man is sure, 'tis his Duty to speak with a modest Assurance; since in doing otherwise he betrays the Truth, especially when he speaks to those who are guided more by Imagination than they are by Judgment, which is the Case of three parts of the World, and three parts of the other Part.

He is so great a Lover of Falshood, that whenever he has a mind to calumniate his Contemporaries, he upbraids them with some Defect, which is just contrary to some good Quality for which all their Friends and their Acquaintance commend them. As for Example, if a Man is remarkable for the extraordinary Deference which he pays to the Opinions and the Remonstrances of his Friends, him he Libels for his Impatience under Reproof. On the contrary, if he has a mind to extol the Ancients, he passes by either thro' Envy or Ignorance all the great Qualities which they have, and extols them for some peculiar one, the very want of which is known to all the World to be their Infirmity and their Defect. Thus in the 37th Page he takes occasion to commend *Aristotle* for what he wrote in Physicks, a great deal of which is so justly censur'd and condemn'd ev'n by the same learned and judicious Men, who allow his *Æthicks*, his *Politicks*, his *Rhetorick*, and his *Poetick*, to be worthy of the greatest Philosopher. And here as the Commendation which he gives him is false, the manner of giving it is still more false. For, says he,

> *Not only Nature did his Laws obey,*
> *But Fancy's boundless Empire own'd his Sway.*[31]

The Expression in the first Verse is not only absurd, but blasphemous. The Laws of Nature are unalterable and indispensable but by God himself; and the greatest Excellence to which the wisest Philosopher can attain, is not to controul, but to obey Nature.

In the Libel upon King *Charles* the Second, he has not only endeavour'd to brand the Memory of that Prince for something which is utterly false, but for something which if it had been true had been an

Excellence in that Prince. For *Wits*, says he, in that Monarch's Reign had Pensions, when all the World knows that it was one of the Faults of that Reign that none of the politer Arts were then encourag'd. For of this we may be sure, that whenever we have a Prince and Ministers, who truly understand either their own Interest, or that of the Publick, Arts and Learning will be then encourag'd; I mean not speciously and pretendedly, but really and sincerely.

The King of *France* pretended to encourage Arts by allowing Pensions to some few Professors of them, whereas at the same time he was and is doing a thing, which has a natural Tendency to the driving them out of *Europe*. For by kindling and prosecuting an unjust War thro' so many different Nations, he has gone a very great way towards the barbarizing the Christian World; and the Arts would have been at a much greater height, than they are now, without any manner of Encouragement from him, if they had been suffer'd to have enjoy'd the Quiet of an universal Peace.[32] In the same manner some Persons of Quality in *Great Britain* have been kind to some particular Professors of Poetry; but at the very same time, by not only introducing the *Italian* Opera among us, but by continuing constant Encouragers of it to this very day, they are doing a thing which will drive the very Art it self out of the Kingdom, as it has been already driven out of every other Nation; and are depriving their Favourite Authors of more than ever they yet bestow'd upon them. Any great Minister would now have a glorious Opportunity of being a true Encourager of Poetry, and ev'ry other generous Art, by representing effectually to her Majesty the Mischief that the *Italians* do both to her Subjects, and to the Arts, and so driving those melodious Ballad-Singers out of the Nation.

But to return to the Reign of King *Charles* the Second, from which I may seem to have in some measure digress'd; there was then indeed a favourable regard shewn to Wit, but no real Encouragement. *Butler* was starv'd at the same time that the King had his Book in his Pocket. Another great Wit lay seven Years in Prison for an inconsiderable Debt,[33] and *Otway* dar'd not to shew his Head for fear of the same Fate. These are some of the Glories of that Reign according to this Author. For if it be a Vice in a Prince to encourage an Art, 'tis a

Vertue to neglect it. What a wretched Creature is this Pretender to Criticism and Poetry to keep such a pother about an Art, the Encouragement of which he imputes as Infamy to King *Charles* the Second?

Well! but he tells us that not only

> *The Wits had Pensions, but young Lords had Wit.*

Here in the compass of one poor Line are two devilish Bobs for the Court. But 'tis no easy matter to tell which way the latter squinting Reflection looks. For if he pretends to reflect upon that Prince, for receiving Persons of Quality who had Wit into his Court, can any thing be more impertinent than twice in one Line to libel a Monarch for being favourable to that very thing, which he takes so much pains in this very Book to recommend to the World? If he means that the young Lords of the Court who pretended to Wit had it not, can any thing be more arrogant than to fly in the Face of all Mankind, and to contradict almost the only thing in which all sorts of People agree, ev'n in this divided Age, *Britons* and Foreigners, Protestants and Papists, Whigs and Tories, Churchmen and Dissenters, and to pretend to reflect upon Persons whose very Names are their Panegyricks? The young Lords who had Wit in the Court of King *Charles* the Second, are these: The young former Duke of *Buckingham*,[34] the young Earl of *Mulgrave* now Duke of *Buckingham*, the young Lord *Buckhurst* afterwards Earl of *Dorset* and *Middlesex*, and the young Marquess of *Halifax*; the young Earl of *Rochester*, the young Lord *Vaughan* now Lord *Carbury*, and several others. If the looking favourably upon young Persons of Quality who had Wit, may be imputed as Scandal to the Court of King *Charles* the Second, that Court was certainly the most scandalous one in *Europe*. But if he says on the other side that 'tis dishonourable to a Prince to be mistaken in this Point, and to look with a favourable Eye on Pretenders instead of real Masters; to that all the World with one accord will answer that never Prince had a clearer Reputation in this Point.

Thus are his Assertions, and his Precepts frequently false or trivial, or both, his Thoughts very often crude and abortive, his Expressions absurd, his Numbers often harsh and unmusical, without Cadence and without Variety, his Rhimes trivial and common. He dictates perpetually, and pretends to give Law without any thing of the Simplicity or Majesty of a Legislator, and pronounces Sentence without any thing of the Plainness or Clearness, or Gravity of a Judge. Instead of Simplicity we have little Conceit and Epigram, and Affectation. Instead of Majesty we have something that is very mean, and instead of Gravity we have something that is very boyish. And instead of Perspicuity and lucid Order, we have but too often Obscurity and Confusion.

But what most shews him a very young Author, is, that with all these Faults and this Weakness he has the Insolence of a Hero, and is a downright Bully of *Parnassus*, who is ev'ry moment thund'ring out Fool, Sot, Fop, Coxcomb, Blockhead, and thinks to hide his want of Sense by his pretended Contempt of others, as a Hector does his want of Courage by his perpetual blustring and roaring; and is sagaciously of Opinion, that he arrogates so much Sense to himself as he imputes Folly to other People.

> *Thus a wild* Tartar *when he spies*
> *A Man that's handsome, valiant, wise,*
> *Thinks if he kills him to inherit*
> *His Wit, his Beauty, and his Spirit,*
> *As if just so much he enjoy'd*
> *As in another he destroy'd.*[35]

But what he says Page the 25th, and his returning to the Charge, Page 34, his particular Pique seems to be at People of Quality, for whom he appears to have a very great Contempt, I mean for the Authors of that Rank; as if a Man were to assert his Title to *Parnassus*, by proving himself a Plebeian in *Great Britain*; or as if an *English* Sovereign by making a Man honourable, made him dull. Good Gods, how absolute would our Princes be at that rate! when they would have the very Understandings of their Subjects at their disposal, and would need only to prefer the Disobedient to chastise them.

I hope, I may without offence, gently put young Mr. *Bays* in mind, that the Subordination which is absolutely necessary to the Government of the World requires that Respect should be paid to

Persons of Quality, ev'n where Esteem cannot be paid to them; but that in this case they both may and ought to have our Respect and Esteem together. For I know very few People of Quality who have applied themselves to Poetry, who have not succeeded; on the other side 'tis known to all the World that some of them have been admirable. For nothing is more certain than that supposing equal Talent and equal Application, a Man of Quality has great Advantages over the rest of Men. But can any thing be more stupidly impudent and impertinent, than that this little Gentleman should rail thus at the Writings of People of Quality in this very Essay, the one half of which he has borrow'd from two noble Authors, and appropriated it to himself, by the same Method by which a *Jack-pudding* engrosses a Sack-posset, *viz.* by mingling some Beastliness with it, which does not fail to render it nauseous to those who made it. This extraordinary Proceeding of borrowing and railing puts me in mind of a Passage in Mr. *Cowley.*

> 'Tis now become the frugal Fashion
> Rather to hide than pay the Obligation;
> Nay Wrongs and Outrages we do,
> Lest Men should think we Owe.[36]

But the Men of Quality, as they want not the Discernment, will have the Satisfaction to see, that as there is a great deal of Venom in this little Gentleman's Temper, Nature has very wisely corrected it with a great deal of Dulness.

> His rankest Libels lull asleep his Foes,
> As Vipers blood in Treacle makes us dose.[37]

As there is no Creature in Nature so venomous, there is nothing so stupid and so impotent as a hunch-back'd Toad; and a Man must be very quiet and very passive, and stand still to let him fasten his Teeth and his Claws, or be surpriz'd sleeping by him, before that Animal can have any power to hurt him.

Thus in order to find out his outward Person have we taken a Survey of his inward Man, in his several noble Talents and Vertues, his Poetry, his Criticism, his Modesty, his Humility, his Gratitude, and his good Breeding. Let us now take a Survey of his Politicks, and his Religion, not by any means by way of Reflection; for Poetry and Criticism are of no Party, and of no Religion, but only to find who he is.

I find then that in the compass of one Page, which is the thirty first, he has Libell'd two Monarchs and two Nations. The two Monarchs are King *Charles* and King *William*: The two Nations are the *Dutch* and our own. The *Dutch* we are told are a parcel of Sharpers, and we are downright Bubbles and Fools.³⁸ King *Charles* the Second was too much a Libertine, and too much an Encourager of Wit for him; King *William* the Third was too much a *Socinian*. But tho' he has without Mercy condemn'd the Reigns of the foremention'd Monarchs, he is graciously pleas'd to pass over in silence that which comes between them. In the beginning of the 12ᵗʰ Page, we find what that is which so happily reconcil'd him to it, and that was the Dispensing Pow'r, which was set on foot in order to introduce and to establish Popery, and to make it the National Religion. Now I humbly conceive that he who Libels our Confederates, must be by Politicks a *Jacobite*; and he who Libels all the Protestant Kings that we have had in this Island these threescore Years, and who justifies the Dispensing Pow'r so long after we are free'd from it, a Pow'r which as was hinted above was set on foot on purpose to introduce Popery: He who justifies this when he lyes under the Tye of no Necessity, nor ev'n Conveniency to approve of it, must, I humbly conceive, derive his Religion from St. *Omer*'s,³⁹ as he seems to have done his Humanity and his Criticism; and is, I suppose, politickly setting up for Poet-Laureat against the coming over of the Pretender, which by his Insolence he seems to believe approaching, as People of his Capacity are generally very sanguine.

Let us now see if we can find any thing in his Rhimes, which may direct us to his Coffee-house, or to his Booksellers. By his taking three Opportunities to commend Mr. *Dryden*, in so small a compass as p. 23, 27, 28, I fancy we may hear of him at *Shakespear*'s Head, or at *Will*'s, for to revive old Quarrels which have been long out of doors, and to renew the memory of Poetical Wars wag'd formerly between Sir *R.B.*, Mr. *L.M.*⁴⁰ and Mr. *Dryden*, can be agreeable to none but a very few of the Frequenters of those Places. This is to run counter to his own Direction; for he tells us Page 27. that formerly

> *Pride, Malice, Folly against* Dryden *rose*
> *In various shapes of Parsons, Criticks, Beaus.*

Upon which, Page 28, he gives this grave Advice,

> *Be thou the first true Merit to befriend,*
> *His Praise is lost who stays till all commend.*

The appearing in Mr. *Dryden*'s behalf now is too late. 'Tis like offering a Man's self for a Second, after the Principal has been whipp'd through the Lungs. Now Mr. *Dryden* is dead, he commends him with the rest of the World. But if this little Gentleman had been his Contemporary thirty Years ago, why then I can tell a very damn'd shape that Pride and Malice, and Folly would have appear'd in against Mr. *Dryden*.

For his Acquaintance he names Mr. *Walsh*. I had the good Fortune to know Mr. *Walsh* very well; who was a learned, candid, judicious Gentleman. But he had by no means the Qualification which this Author reckons absolutely necessary to a Critick; it being certain that Mr. *Walsh* was like this Essayer a very indifferent Poet; but he was a Man of a very good Understanding, in spight of his being a Beau. He lov'd to be well dress'd, as *Dorimant*[41] says, and thought it no Disparagement to his Understanding; and I remember a little young Gentleman, with all the Qualifications which we have found to be in this Author, whom Mr. *Walsh* us'd sometimes to take into his Company as a double Foil to his Person, and his Capacity. It has been observ'd that of late Years a certain Spectre exactly in the shape of that little Gentleman, has haunted a certain ancient Wit,[42] and has been by the People of *Covent-Garden* styl'd his evil Genius. For it hath been extremely remarkable, that while that Spectre hath haunted that ancient Wit, he has never been able to write or talk like himself: Which has by no means happen'd by any Decay of his natural Parts, but by the wonderful Pow'r of Magick. For as soon as the dumb Conjurer has been employ'd to lay the Spectre for three or four months, either in the midst of the *Red Sea*, or the middle of *Windsor-Forest*, the old Gentleman has strait been his own Man as perfectly as ever he was in his Life.

And now if you have a mind to enquire between *Sunning-Hill* and *Ockingham*, for a young, squab, short Gentleman, with the forementioned Qualifications, an eternal Writer of Amorous Pastoral Madrigals, and the very Bow of the God of Love, you will be soon directed to him. And pray as soon as you have taken a Survey of him, tell me whether he is a proper Author to make personal Reflections on others; and tell him if he does not like my Person, 'tis because he is an ungrateful Creature, since his Conscience tells him, that I have been always infinitely delighted with his: So delighted, that I have lately drawn a very graphical Picture of it; but I believe I shall keep the *Dutch* Piece from ever seeing the Light,[43] as a certain old Gentleman in *Windsor-Forest* would have done by the Original, if he durst have been half as impartial to his own Draught as I have been to mine. This little Author may extol the Ancients as much and as long as he pleases, but he has reason to thank the good Gods that he was born a Modern. For had he been born of *Grœcian* Parents, and his Father by consequence had by Law had the absolute Disposal of him, his Life had been no longer than that of one of his Poems, the Life of half a day. Instead of setting his Picture to show, I have taken a keener Revenge, and expos'd his Intellectuals, as duly considering that let the Person of a Gentleman of his Parts be never so contemptible, his inward Man is ten times more ridiculous; it being impossible that his outward Form, tho' it should be that of downright Monkey, should differ so much from human Shape, as his immaterial unthinking part does from human Understanding. How agreeable it is to be in a Libel with so much good Company as I have been, with two great Monarchs, two mighty Nations, and especially the People of Quality of *Great Britain*, and this Libel compos'd by a little Gentleman, who has writ a Panegyrick upon himself! Which Panegyrick if it was not writ with Judgment, yet was it publish'd with Discretion, for it was publish'd in Mr. *W—*'s Name;[44] so that by this wise Proceeding he had the Benefit of the Encomium, and Mr. *W—* had the Scandal of the Poetry; which it brought upon him to such a degree, that 'tis ten to one if ever he recovers the Reputation of a good Versifyer. And thus for the present I take my leave of you and of this little Critick and his Book; a Book throughout which Folly and Ignorance, those Brethren so lame and so impotent, do ridiculously at one and the same time look very big and very dull, and strut, and hobble cheek by jowl with their Arms on Kimbo, being led and supported, and Bully-back'd by that blind Hector Impudence. I am,

SIR,

Your, &c.

ANNOTATIONS.

1. *First follow Nature*, p. 7.

Horace has giv'n a Precept, which may be quoted by undistinguishing People to keep this in countenance.

> *Respicere exemplar vitæ, morumq; jubebo*
> *Doctum imitatorem & veras hinc Ducere voces.*[45]

For he bids the Person to whom this is directed consult Nature; but then he does three things, which vastly distinguish him from the Writer of the Essay: For first he makes it very plain what sort of Person this is to whom he directs himself, and that is *Doctus Imitator*, one who is both Poet and Critick, Dramatick Poet, and Dramatick Critick; one who writes Plays, and understands the Rules, and knows the Secrets of his Art; notwithstanding which, he may be ignorant of that important one, which *Horace* is about to discover to him; or in case he does already know it, he may want to be put in mind of it, because his Interest, as we shall find anon, is a strong Temptation to deviate from it. But secondly *Horace* tells us very intelligibly what he means by Nature here, and that is, human Life, and the manners of Men. Thirdly, he makes it as clear as the Sun, what it is to follow Nature in giving a draught of human Life, and of the manners of Men, and that is not to draw after particular Men, who are but Copies and imperfect Copies of the great universal Pattern; but to consult that innate Original, and that universal Idea, which the Creator has fix'd in the minds of ev'ry reasonable Creature, and so to make a true and a just Draught. For as ev'ry Copy deviates from the Original both in

Life and Grace, and Resemblance, a Poet who designs to give a true Draught of human Life and Manners, must consult the universal Idea, and not particular Persons. For Example, when a Poet would draw the Character of a covetous or a revengeful person, he is not to draw after *Lucius* or *Caius*; but to consult the universal pattern within him, and there to behold what Revenge or Covetousness would do in such and such Natures, upon such and such Occasions. For if he draws after *Lucius* or *Caius*, the workings of Revenge and Covetousness in these two, being but Copies and imperfect Copies of their workings according to the universal *Idea*, and the Poet degenerating in his Draught ev'n from those faint and imperfect Copies, whenever a just and discerning Judge comes to compare that Draught with the Original within him, he immediately finds that that Draught falls extremely short of the Truth of Nature, and immediately disapproves of it, as a second, ungraceful, faint, unresembling Copy. Agreeable to this is that passage of the most discerning Author of the Essay upon Poetry.

> *If once the Justness of each part is lost,*
> *Well may we laugh, but at the Poet's cost.*[46]

Thus *Horace* here speaks to the Knowing, yet tells them something that several of them want to be taught, and several to be put in mind of. For it has been a Complaint of Two thousand Years standing, that Poets have been us'd to violate their Subjects, and to force their Characters out of complaisance to their Actors, that is, to their Interest. Most of the Writers for the Stage in my time, have not only adapted their Characters to their Actors, but those Actors have as it were sate for them. For which reason the Lustre of the most shining of their Characters must decay with the Actors, while those of *Sophocles*, *Euripides*, *Terence*, and *Ben Johnson* will eternally remain.

2. *Still green with* Bays *each ancient Altar stands*, p. 13.

If Mr. *Bays* should say here that by each ancient Altar he does not mean ev'ry ancient Poet, but only those few who have been admir'd by all succeeding Ages; to this I answer, that besides that the Expression will by no means bear this Sense, it appears plainly from the two first lines of p. 12. that he speaks of the Ancients in general.

> *And tho' the Ancients thus their Rules invade,*
> *As Kings dispense with Laws themselves have made,*
> *Moderns beware.*   p. 12.

I think nothing can be more plain, than that here he prefers all the Ancients before all the Moderns, treating the former as so many Monarchs and Legislators at the same time in the Regions of Sense, and the latter as so many Slaves. Besides that these Verses manifestly relate rather to the indifferent Poets among the Ancients, than to those who are admirable; for the indifferent ones have most and oftnest invaded the Rules. Indeed they have scarce ever observ'd them; as *Homer* and *Virgil* have scarce ever transgressed them.

FINIS.

IV
Introducing Shakespeare,
1725–1744

Alexander Pope,
'Preface' to *The Works of Shakespear*
(1725)

IT is not my design to enter into a Criticism upon this Author; tho'
to do it effectually and not superficially, would be the best occasion
that any just Writer could take, to form the judgment and taste of our
nation. For of all *English* Poets *Shakespear* must be confessed to be the
fairest and fullest subject for Criticism, and to afford the most numerous, as well as most conspicuous instances, both of Beauties and Faults
of all sorts. But this far exceeds the bounds of a Preface, the business
of which is only to give an account of the fate of his Works, and the
disadvantages under which they have been transmitted to us. We shall
hereby extenuate many faults which are his, and clear him from the
imputation of many which are not: A design, which tho' it can be no
guide to future Criticks to do him justice in one way, will at least be
sufficient to prevent their doing him an injustice in the other.

I cannot however but mention some of his principal and characteristic Excellencies, for which (notwithstanding his defects) he is justly
and universally elevated above all other Dramatic Writers. Not that
this is the proper place of praising him, but because I would not omit
any occasion of doing it.

If ever any Author deserved the name of an *Original*, it was *Shakespear*.
Homer himself drew not his art so immediately from the fountains of
Nature, it proceeded thro' *Ægyptian* strainers and channels,[1] and came
to him not without some tincture of the learning, or some cast of the
models, of those before him. The Poetry of *Shakespear* was Inspiration
indeed: he is not so much an Imitator, as an Instrument, of Nature;
and 'tis not so just to say that he speaks from her, as that she speaks
thro' him.[2]

His *Characters* are so much Nature her self, that 'tis a sort of injury to call them by so distant a name as Copies of her. Those of other Poets have a constant resemblance, which shews that they receiv'd them from one another, and were but multiplyers of the same image: each picture like a mock-rainbow is but the reflexion of a reflexion. But every single character in *Shakespear* is as much an Individual, as those in Life itself; it is as impossible to find any two alike; and such as from their relation or affinity in any respect appear most to be Twins, will upon comparison be found remarkably distinct. To this life and variety of Character, we must add the wonderful Preservation of it; which is such throughout his plays, that had all the Speeches been printed without the very names of the Persons, I believe one might have apply'd them with certainty to every speaker.[3]

The *Power* over our *Passions* was never possess'd in a more eminent degree, or display'd in so different instances. Yet all along, there is seen no labour, no pains to raise them; no preparation to guide our guess to the effect, or be perceiv'd to lead toward it: But the heart swells, and the tears burst out, just at the proper places: We are surpriz'd, the moment we weep; and yet upon reflection find the passion so just, that we shou'd be surpriz'd if we had not wept, and wept at that very moment.

How astonishing is it again, that the passions directly opposite to these, Laughter and Spleen, are no less at his command! that he is not more a master of the *Great*, than of the *Ridiculous* in human nature; of our noblest tendernesses, than of our vainest foibles; of our strongest emotions, than of our idlest sensations!

Nor does he only excell in the Passions: In the coolness of Reflection and Reasoning he is full as admirable. His *Sentiments* are not only in general the most pertinent and judicious upon every subject; but by a talent very peculiar, something between Penetration and Felicity, he hits upon that particular point on which the bent of each argument turns, or the force of each motive depends. This is perfectly amazing, from a man of no education or experience in those great and publick scenes of life which are usually the subject of his thoughts:[4] So that he seems to have known the world by Intuition, to have look'd thro' humane nature at one glance, and to be the only Author that gives ground for a very new opinion, That the Philosopher and even the Man of the world, may be *Born*, as well as the Poet.

It must be own'd that with all these great excellencies, he has almost as great defects; and that as he has certainly written better, so he has perhaps written worse, than any other.[5] But I think I can in some measure account for these defects, from several causes and accidents; without which it is hard to imagine that so large and so enlighten'd a mind could ever have been susceptible of them. That all these Contingencies should unite to his disadvantage seems to me almost as singularly unlucky, as that so many various (nay contrary) Talents should meet in one man, was happy and extraordinary.

It must be allowed that Stage-Poetry of all other, is more particularly levell'd to please the *Populace*, and its success more immediately depending upon the *Common Suffrage*. One cannot therefore wonder, if *Shakespear* having at his first appearance no other aim in his writings than to procure a subsistance, directed his endeavours solely to hit the taste and humour that then prevailed. The Audience was generally composed of the meaner sort of people; and therefore the Images of Life were to be drawn from those of their own rank: accordingly we find, that not our Author's only but almost all the old Comedies have their Scene among *Tradesmen* and *Mechanicks*. And even their Historical Plays strictly follow the common *Old Stories* or *Vulgar Traditions* of that kind of people. In Tragedy, nothing was so sure to *Surprize* and cause *Admiration*, as the most strange, unexpected, and consequently most unnatural, Events and Incidents; the most exaggerated Thoughts; the most verbose and bombast Expression; the most pompous Rhymes, and thundering Versification. In Comedy, nothing was so sure to *please*, as mean buffoonry, vile ribaldry, and unmannerly jests of fools and clowns. Yet even in these our Author's Wit buoys up, and is born above his subject: his Genius in those low parts is like some Prince of a Romance in the disguise of a Shepherd or Peasant;[6] a certain Greatness and Spirit now and then break out, which manifest his higher extraction and qualities.

It may be added, that not only the common Audience had no notion of the rules of writing, but few even of the better sort piqu'd themselves upon any great degree of knowledge or nicety that way; till *Ben Johnson*

getting possession of the Stage, brought critical learning into vogue:[7]
And that this was not done without difficulty, may appear from those
frequent lessons (and indeed almost Declamations) which he was forced
to prefix to his first plays, and put into the mouth of his Actors, the
Grex, *Chorus*, &c. to remove the prejudices, and inform the judgment
of his hearers. Till then, our Authors had no thoughts of writing on
the model of the Ancients: their Tragedies were only Histories in
Dialogue; and their Comedies follow'd the thread of any Novel as
they found it, no less implicitly than if it had been true History.

To judge therefore of *Shakespear* by *Aristotle*'s rules, is like trying a
man by the Laws of one Country, who acted under those of another.[8]
He writ to the *People*; and writ at first without patronage from the
better sort, and therefore without aims of pleasing them: without
assistance or advice from the Learned, as without the advantage of
education or acquaintance among them: without that knowledge of
the best models, the Ancients, to inspire him with an emulation of them;
in a word, without any views of Reputation, and of what Poets are
pleas'd to call Immortality: Some or all of which have encourag'd the
vanity, or animated the ambition, of other writers.

Yet it must be observ'd, that when his performances had merited
the protection of his Prince, and when the encouragement of the
Court had succeeded to that of the Town, the works of his riper years
are manifestly raised above those of his former. The Dates of his plays
sufficiently evidence that his productions improved, in proportion to
the respect he had for his auditors. And I make no doubt this observation would be found true in every instance, were but Editions extant
from which we might learn the exact time when every piece was
composed, and whether writ for the Town, or the Court.

Another Cause (and no less strong than the former) may be deduced
from our Author's being a *Player*, and forming himself first upon the
judgments of that body of men whereof he was a member. They have
ever had a Standard to themselves, upon other principles than those
of *Aristotle*. As they live by the Majority, they know no rule but that of
pleasing the present humour, and complying with the wit in fashion;
a consideration which brings all their judgment to a short point.
Players are just such judges of what is *right*, as Taylors are of what is

graceful. And in this view it will be but fair to allow, that most of our Author's faults are less to be ascribed to his wrong judgment as a Poet, than to his right judgment as a Player.

By these men it was thought a praise to *Shakespear*, that he scarce ever *blotted a line*. This they industriously propagated, as appears from what we are told by *Ben Johnson* in his *Discoveries*, and from the preface of *Heminges* and *Condell* to the first folio Edition. But in reality (however it has prevailed) there never was a more groundless report, or to the contrary of which there are more undeniable evidences.[9] As, the Comedy of the *Merry Wives* of *Windsor*, which he entirely new writ; the *History of* Henry *the 6th*, which was first published under the Title of the *Contention of* York *and* Lancaster; and that of *Henry the 5th*, extreamly improved; that of *Hamlet* enlarged to almost as much again as at first, and many others. I believe the common opinion of his want of Learning proceeded from no better ground. This too might be thought a Praise by some; and to this his Errors have as injudiciously been ascribed by others. For 'tis certain, were it true, it would concern but a small part of them; the most are such as are not properly Defects, but Superfœtations: and arise not from want of learning or reading, but from want of thinking or judging: or rather (to be more just to our Author) from a compliance to those wants in others. As to a wrong choice of the subject, a wrong conduct of the incidents, false thoughts, forc'd expressions, *&c.* if these are not to be ascrib'd to the foresaid accidental reasons, they must be charg'd upon the Poet himself, and there is no help for it. But I think the two Disadvantages which I have mentioned (to be obliged to please the lowest of people, and to keep the worst of company) if the consideration be extended as far as it reasonably may, will appear sufficient to mis-lead and depress the greatest Genius upon earth. Nay the more modesty with which such a one is endued, the more he is in danger of submitting and conforming to others, against his own better judgment.

But as to his *Want of Learning*, it may be necessary to say something more: There is certainly a vast difference between *Learning* and *Languages*. How far he was ignorant of the latter, I cannot determine; but 'tis plain he had much Reading at least, if they will not call it Learning. Nor is it any great matter, if a man has Knowledge, whether he has it from one language or from another. Nothing is more evident than that he had a taste of natural Philosophy, Mechanicks, ancient and modern History, Poetical learning and Mythology: We find him very knowing in the customs, rites, and manners of Antiquity. In *Coriolanus* and *Julius Cæsar*, not only the Spirit, but Manners, of the *Romans* are exactly drawn;[10] and still a nicer distinction is shown, between the manners of the *Romans* in the time of the former, and of the latter. His reading in the ancient Historians is no less conspicuous, in many references to particular passages: and the speeches copy'd from *Plutarch* in *Coriolanus* may, I think, as well be made an instance of his learning, as those copy'd from *Cicero* in *Catiline*, of *Ben Johnson*'s. The manners of other nations in general, the *Egyptians*, *Venetians*, *French*, &c. are drawn with equal propriety. Whatever object of nature, or branch of science, he either speaks of or describes; it is always with competent, if not extensive knowledge: his descriptions are still exact; all his metaphors appropriated, and remarkably drawn from the true nature and inherent qualities of each subject. When he treats of Ethic or Politic, we may constantly observe a wonderful justness of distinction, as well as extent of comprehension. No one is more a master of the Poetical story,[11] or has more frequent allusions to the various parts of it: Mr. *Waller* (who has been celebrated for this last particular) has not shown more learning this way than *Shakespear*. We have Translations from *Ovid* published in his name, among those Poems which pass for his,[12] and for some of which we have undoubted authority, (being published by himself, and dedicated to his noble Patron the Earl of *Southampton*:) He appears also to have been conversant in *Plautus*, from whom he has taken the plot of one of his plays:[13] he follows the *Greek* Authors, and particularly *Dares Phrygius*, in another:[14] (altho' I will not pretend to say in what language he read them.) The modern *Italian* writers of Novels he was manifestly acquainted with;[15] and we may conclude him to be no less conversant with the Ancients of his own country, from the use he has made of *Chaucer* in *Troilus* and *Cressida*, and in the *Two Noble Kinsmen*, if that Play be his, as there goes a Tradition it was, (and indeed it has little resemblance of *Fletcher*, and more of our Author[16] than some of those which have been received as genuine.)

I am inclined to think, this opinion proceeded originally from the zeal of the Partizans of our Author and *Ben Johnson*; as they endeavoured to exalt the one at the expence of the other. It is ever the nature of Parties to be in extremes; and nothing is so probable, as that because *Ben Johnson* had much the most learning, it was said on the one hand that *Shakespear* had none at all; and because *Shakespear* had much the most wit and fancy, it was retorted on the other, that *Johnson* wanted both. Because *Shakespear* borrowed nothing, it was said that *Ben Johnson* borrowed every thing. Because *Johnson* did not write extempore, he was reproached with being a year about every piece; and because *Shakespear* wrote with ease and rapidity, they cryed, he never once made a blot. Nay the spirit of opposition ran so high, that whatever those of the one side objected to the other, was taken at the rebound, and turned into Praises; as injudiciously, as their antagonists before had made them Objections.

Poets are always afraid of Envy; but sure they have as much reason to be afraid of Admiration. They are the *Scylla* and *Charybdis* of Authors; those who escape one, often fall by the other. *Pessimum genus inimicorum Laudantes*,[17] says *Tacitus*: and *Virgil* desires to wear a charm against those who praise a Poet without rule or reason.

> — *Si ultra placitum laudarit, baccare frontem*
> *Cingite, ne Vati noceat* —[18]

But however this contention might be carried on by the Partizans on either side, I cannot help thinking these two great Poets were good friends, and lived on amicable terms and in offices of society with each other. It is an acknowledged fact, that *Ben Johnson* was introduced upon the Stage, and his first works encouraged, by *Shakespear*. And after his death, that Author writes *To the memory of his beloved Mr.* William Shakespear, which shows as if the friendship had continued thro' life. I cannot for my own part find any thing *Invidious* or *Sparing* in those verses, but wonder Mr. *Dryden* was of that opinion.[19] He exalts him not only above all his Contemporaries, but above *Chaucer* and *Spenser*, whom he will not allow to be great enough to be rank'd with him; and challenges the names of *Sophocles, Euripides*, and *Æschylus*, nay all *Greece* and *Rome* at once, to equal him. And (which is very particular)

271

expresly vindicates him from the imputation of wanting *Art*, not enduring that all his excellencies shou'd be attributed to *Nature*. It is remarkable too, that the praise he gives him in his *Discoveries* seems to proceed from a *personal kindness*; he tells us that he lov'd the man, as well as honoured his memory; celebrates the honesty, openness, and frankness of his temper; and only distinguishes, as he reasonably ought, between the real merit of the Author, and the silly and derogatory applauses of the Players. *Ben Johnson* might indeed be sparing in his Commendations (tho' certainly he is not so in this instance) partly from his own nature, and partly from judgment. For men of judgment think they do any man more service in praising him justly, than lavishly. I say, I would fain believe they were Friends, tho' the violence and ill-breeding of their Followers and Flatterers were enough to give rise to the contrary report. I would hope that it may be with *Parties*, both in Wit and State, as with those Monsters described by the Poets; and that their *Heads* at least may have something humane, tho' their *Bodies* and *Tails* are wild beasts and serpents.

As I believe that what I have mentioned gave rise to the opinion of *Shakespear*'s want of learning; so what has continued it down to us may have been the many blunders and illiteracies of the first Publishers of his works. In these Editions their ignorance shines almost in every page; nothing is more common than *Actus tertia. Exit Omnes. Enter three Witches solus*. Their *French* is as bad as their *Latin*, both in construction and spelling: Their very *Welsh* is false. Nothing is more likely than that those palpable blunders of *Hector*'s quoting *Aristotle*,[20] with others of that gross kind, sprung from the same root. It not being at all credible that these could be the errors of any man who had the least tincture of a School, or at least conversation with such as had. *Ben Johnson* (whom they will not think partial to him) allows him at least to have had *some Latin*; which is utterly inconsistent with mistakes like these. Nay the constant blunders in proper names of persons and places, are such as must have proceeded from a man, who had not so much as read any history, in any language: so could not be *Shakespear*'s.

I shall now lay before the reader some of those almost innumerable Errors, which have risen from one source, the ignorance of the Players, both as his actors, and as his editors. When the nature and kinds of these are enumerated and considered, I dare to say that not *Shakespear* only, but *Aristotle* or *Cicero*, had their works undergone the same fate, might have appear'd to want sense as well as learning.

It is not certain that any one of his Plays was published by himself. During the time of his employment in the Theatre, several of his pieces were printed separately in Quarto. What makes me think that most of these were not publish'd by him, is the excessive carelessness of the press: every page is so scandalously false spelled, and almost all the learned or unusual words so intolerably mangled, that it's plain there either was no Corrector to the press at all, or one totally illiterate. If any were supervised by himself, I should fancy the two parts of *Henry the 4th*, and *Midsummer-Night's Dream* might have been so: because I find no other printed with any exactness; and (contrary to the rest) there is very little variation in all the subsequent editions of them. There are extant two Prefaces, to the first quarto edition of *Troilus and Cressida* in 1609, and to that of *Othello*; by which it appears, that the first was publish'd without his knowledge or consent, and even before it was acted, so late as seven or eight years before he died: and that the latter was not printed till after his death. The whole number of genuine plays which we have been able to find printed in his life-time, amounts but to eleven. And of some of these, we meet with two or more editions by different printers, each of which has whole heaps of trash different from the other: which I should fancy was occasion'd, by their being taken from different copies, belonging to different Play-houses.

The folio edition (in which all the plays we now receive as his were first collected) was published by two Players, *Heming* and *Condell*, in 1623, seven years after his decease. They declare, that all the other editions were stolen and surreptitious, and affirm theirs to be purged from the errors of the former. This is true as to the literal errors, and no other; for in all respects else it is far worse than the Quarto's:

First, because the additions of trifling and bombast passages are in this edition far more numerous. For whatever had been added, since those Quarto's, by the actors, or had stolen from their mouths into the written parts, were from thence conveyed into the printed text, and all stand charged upon the Author. He himself complained of this usage in *Hamlet*, where he wishes that *those who play the Clowns wou'd speak no more than is set down for them.* (Act 3. Sc. 4.)[21] But as a proof that he could not escape it, in the old editions of *Romeo* and *Juliet* there is no hint of a great number of the mean conceits and ribaldries now to be found there. In others, the low scenes of Mobs, Plebeians and Clowns, are vastly shorter than at present: And I have seen one in particular (which seems to have belonged to the playhouse, by having the parts divided with lines, and the Actors names in the margin) where several of those very passages were added in a written hand, which are since to be found in the folio.

In the next place, a number of beautiful passages which are extant in the first single editions, are omitted in this: as it seems, without any other reason than their willingness to shorten some scenes: These men (as it was said of *Procrustes*)[22] either lopping, or stretching an Author, to make him just fit for their Stage.

This edition is said to be printed from the *Original Copies*; I believe they meant those which had lain ever since the Author's days in the play-house, and had from time to time been cut, or added to, arbitrarily. It appears that this edition, as well as the Quarto's, was printed (at least partly) from no better copies than the *Prompter*'s *Book*, or *Piece-meal Parts* written out for the use of the actors: For in some places their very* names are thro' carelessness set down instead of the *Personæ Dramatis*: And in others the notes of direction to the *Property-men* for their *Moveables*, and to the *Players* for their *Entries*,† are inserted into the Text, thro' the ignorance of the Transcribers.

The Plays not having been before so much as distinguish'd by *Acts* and *Scenes*, they are in this edition divided according as they play'd them; often when there is no pause in the action, or where they thought fit to make a breach in it, for the sake of Musick, Masques, or Monsters.

---

* Much ado about nothing, *Act* 2. *Enter Prince* Leonato, Claudio, *and Jack Wilson, instead of* Balthasar. *And in Act* 4. Cowley, *and* Kemp, *constantly thro' a whole Scene.* Edit. Fol. of 1623, and 1632.

† *Such as,*

    — My Queen is murder'd! *Ring the little Bell* —

    — His nose grew as sharp as a pen, and *a table of Greenfield's*, &c.

Sometimes the scenes are transposed and shuffled backward and forward; a thing which could no otherwise happen, but by their being taken from seperate and piece-meal-written parts.

Many verses are omitted intirely, and others transposed; from whence invincible obscurities have arisen, past the guess of any Commentator to clear up, but just where the accidental glympse of an old edition enlightens us.

Some Characters were confounded and mix'd, or two put into one, for want of a competent number of actors. Thus in the Quarto edition of *Midsummer-Night's Dream*, Act. 5. *Shakespear* introduces a kind of Master of the Revels called *Philostratus*: all whose part is given to another character (that of *Ægeus*) in the subsequent editions: So also in *Hamlet* and *King Lear*. This too makes it probable that the Prompter's Books were what they call'd the Original Copies.

From liberties of this kind, many speeches also were put into the mouths of wrong persons, where the Author now seems chargeable with making them speak out of character: Or sometimes perhaps for no better reason, than that a governing Player, to have the mouthing of some favourite speech himself, would snatch it from the unworthy lips of an Underling.

Prose from verse they did not know, and they accordingly printed one for the other throughout the volume.

Having been forced to say so much of the Players, I think I ought in justice to remark, that the Judgment, as well as Condition, of that class of people was then far inferior to what it is in our days. As then the best Playhouses were Inns and Taverns (the *Globe*, the *Hope*, the *Red Bull*, the *Fortune*, &c.) so the top of the profession were then meer Players, not Gentlemen of the stage: They were led into the Buttery by the Steward, not plac'd at the Lord's table, or Lady's toilette: and consequently were intirely depriv'd of those advantages they now enjoy, in the familiar conversation of our Nobility, and an intimacy (not to say dearness) with people of the first condition.

From what has been said, there can be no question but had *Shakespear* published his works himself (especially in his latter time, and after his retreat from the stage) we should not only be certain which are genuine; but should find in those that are, the errors lessened by some thousands.

If I may judge from all the distinguishing marks of his style, and his manner of thinking and writing, I make no doubt to declare that those wretched plays, *Pericles, Locrine, Sir John Oldcastle, Yorkshire Tragedy, Lord Cromwell, The Puritan,* and *London Prodigal,* cannot be admitted as his. And I should conjecture of some of the others (particularly *Love's Labour Lost, The Winter's Tale,* and *Titus Andronicus*) that only some characters, single scenes, or perhaps a few particular passages, were of his hand. It is very probable what occasion'd some Plays to be supposed *Shakespear*'s was only this; that they were pieces produced by unknown authors, or fitted up for the Theatre while it was under his administration: and no owner claiming them, they were adjudged to him, as they give Strays to the Lord of the Manor. A mistake which (one may also observe) it was not for the interest of the House to remove. Yet the Players themselves, *Hemings* and *Condell,* afterwards did *Shakespear* the justice to reject those eight plays in their edition; tho' they were then printed in his name, in every body's hands, and acted with some applause; (as we learn from what *Ben Johnson* says of *Pericles* in his Ode on the *New Inn.*) That *Titus Andronicus* is one of this class I am the rather induced to believe, by finding the same Author openly express his contempt of it in the *Induction* to *Bartholomew-Fair,* in the year 1614, when *Shakespear* was yet living. And there is no better authority for these latter sort, than for the former, which were equally published in his life-time.

If we give into this opinion, how many low and vicious parts and passages might no longer reflect upon this great Genius, but appear unworthily charged upon him? And even in those which are really his, how many faults may have been unjustly laid to his account from arbitrary Additions, Expunctions, Transpositions of scenes and lines, confusion of Characters and Persons, wrong application of Speeches, corruptions of innumerable Passages by the Ignorance, and wrong Corrections of 'em again by the Impertinence, of his first Editors? From one or other of these considerations, I am verily perswaded, that the greatest and the grossest part of what are thought his errors would vanish, and leave his character in a light very different from that disadvantageous one, in which it now appears to us.

This is the state in which *Shakespear*'s writings lye at present; for since the above-mentioned Folio Edition, all the rest have implicitly followed it, without having recourse to any of the former, or ever making the comparison between them. It is impossible to repair the Injuries already done him; too much time has elaps'd, and the materials are too few. In what I have done I have rather given a proof of my willingness and desire, than of my ability, to do him justice. I have discharg'd the dull duty of an Editor,[23] to my best judgment, with more labour than I expect thanks, with a religious abhorrence of all Innovation, and without any indulgence to my private sense or conjecture. The method taken in this Edition will show it self. The various Readings are fairly put in the margin, so that every one may compare 'em; and those I have prefer'd into the Text are constantly *ex fide Codicum*, upon authority. The Alterations or Additions which *Shakespear* himself made, are taken notice of as they occur. Some suspected passages which are excessively bad, (and which seem Interpolations by being so inserted that one can intirely omit them without any chasm, or deficience in the context) are degraded to the bottom of the page; with an Asterisk referring to the places of their insertion. The Scenes are mark'd so distinctly that every removal of place is specify'd; which is more necessary in this Author than any other, since he shifts them more frequently: and sometimes without attending to this particular, the reader would have met with obscurities. The more obsolete or unusual words are explained. Some of the most shining passages are distinguish'd by comma's in the margin; and where the beauty lay not in particulars but in the whole, a star is prefix'd to the scene. This seems to me a shorter and less ostentatious method of performing the better half of Criticism (namely the pointing out an Author's excellencies) than to fill a whole paper with citations of fine passages, with *general Applauses*, or *empty Exclamations* at the tail of them. There is also subjoin'd a Catalogue of those first Editions by which the greater part of the various readings and of the corrected passages are authorised, (most of which are such as carry their own evidence along with them.) These Editions now hold the place of Originals, and are the only materials left to repair the deficiences or restore the corrupted sense of the Author: I can only wish that a greater number of them (if a greater were ever published) may yet be found, by a search more successful than mine, for the better accomplishment of this end.

I will conclude by saying of *Shakespear*, that with all his faults, and with all the irregularity of his *Drama*, one may look upon his works, in comparison of those that are more finish'd and regular, as upon an ancient majestick piece of *Gothick* Architecture, compar'd with a neat Modern building: The latter is more elegant and glaring, but the former is more strong and more solemn. It must be allow'd, that in one of these there are materials enough to make many of the other. It has much the greater variety, and much the nobler apartments; tho' we are often conducted to them by dark, odd, and uncouth passages. Nor does the Whole fail to strike us with greater reverence, tho' many of the Parts are childish, ill-plac'd, and unequal to its grandeur.

Lewis Theobald,
'Preface' to *The Works of Shakespeare*
(1733/1740)

THE Attempt to write upon SHAKESPEARE is like going into a large, a spacious, and a splendid Dome thro' the Conveyance of a narrow and obscure Entry. A Glare of Light suddenly breaks upon you, beyond what the Avenue at first promis'd: and a thousand Beauties of Genius and Character, like so many gaudy Apartments pouring at once upon the Eye, diffuse and throw themselves out to the Mind. The Prospect is too wide to come within the Compass of a single View: 'tis a gay Confusion of pleasing Objects, too various to be enjoyed but in a general Admiration; and they must be separated, and ey'd distinctly, in order to give the proper Entertainment.[1]

And as in great Piles of Building, some Parts are often finish'd up to hit the Taste of the *Connoisseur*; others more negligently put together, to strike the Fancy of a common and unlearned Beholder: Some Parts are made stupendiously magnificent and grand, to surprize with the vast Design and Execution of the Architect; others are contracted, to amuse you with his Neatness and Elegance in little. So, in *Shakespeare*, we may find *Traits* that will stand the Test of the severest Judgment; and Strokes as carelesly hit off, to the Level of the more ordinary Capacities: Some Descriptions rais'd to that Pitch of Grandeur, as to astonish you with the Compass and Elevation of his Thought: and others copying Nature within so narrow, so confined a Circle, as if the Author's Talent lay only at drawing in Miniature.

In how many Points of Light must we be oblig'd to gaze at this great Poet! In how many Branches of Excellence to consider, and admire him! Whether we view him on the Side of Art or Nature, he ought equally to engage our Attention: Whether we respect the Force and Greatness of his Genius, the Extent of his Knowledge and Reading, the Power and Address with which he throws out and applies either Nature, or Learning, there is ample Scope both for our Wonder and Pleasure. If his Diction, and the cloathing of his Thoughts attract us, how much more must we be charm'd with the Richness, and Variety, of his Images and Ideas! If his Images and Ideas steal into our Souls, and strike upon our Fancy, how much are they improv'd in Price, when we come to reflect with what Propriety and Justness they are apply'd to Character! If we look into his Characters, and how they are furnish'd and proportion'd to the Employment he cuts out for them, how are we taken up with the Mastery of his Portraits! What Draughts of Nature! What Variety of Originals, and how differing each from the other! How are they dress'd from the Stores of his own luxurious Imagination; without being the Apes of Mode, or borrowing from any foreign Wardrobe! Each of them are the Standards of Fashion for themselves: like Gentlemen that are above the Direction of their Tailors,[2] and can adorn themselves without the Aid of Imitation. If other Poets draw more than one Fool or Coxcomb, there is the same Resemblance in them, as in that Painter's Draughts, who was happy only at forming a Rose: you find them all younger Brothers of the same Family, and all of them have a Pretence to give the same Crest: But *Shakespeare*'s Clowns and Fops come all of a different House: they are no farther allied to one another than as Man to Man, Members of the same Species: but as different in Features and Lineaments of Character, as we are from one another in Face, or Complexion. But I am unawares launching into his Character as a Writer, before I have said what I intended of him as a private Member of the Republick.

Mr. *Rowe* has very justly observ'd, that People are fond of discovering any little personal Story of the Great Men of Antiquity: and that the common Accidents of their Lives naturally become the Subject of our critical Enquiries: That however trifling such a Curiosity at the first View may appear, yet, as for what relates to Men of Letters, the Knowledge of an Author may, perhaps, sometimes conduce to the better understanding his Works: And, indeed, this Author's Works, from the bad Treatment he has met with from Copyists and Editors, have so long wanted a Comment, that one would zealously embrace every Method of Information, that could contribute to recover them from the Injuries with which they have so long lain o'erwhelm'd.

'Tis certain, that if we have first admir'd the Man in his Writings, his Case is so circumstanc'd, that we must naturally admire the Writings in the Man: That if we go back to take a View of his Education, and the Employment in Life which Fortune had cut out for him, we shall retain the stronger Ideas of his extensive Genius.

His Father, we are told, was a considerable Dealer in Wool; but having no fewer than ten Children, of whom our *Shakespeare* was the eldest, the best Education he could afford him was no better than to qualify him for his own Business and Employment. I cannot affirm with any Certainty how long his Father liv'd; but I take him to be the same Mr. *John Shakespeare* who was living in the Year 1599, and who then, in Honour of his Son, took out an Extract of his Family-Arms from the Herald's Office; by which it appears, that he had been Officer and Bailiff of *Stratford* upon *Avon* in *Warwickshire*; and that he enjoy'd some hereditary Lands and Tenements, the Reward of his Great Grandfather's faithful and approved Service to King *Henry* VII.

Be this as it will, our *Shakespeare*, it seems, was bred for some Time at a Free-School; the very Free-School, I presume, founded at *Stratford*: where, we are told, he acquired what *Latin* he was Master of: but, that his Father being oblig'd, thro' Narrowness of Circumstance, to withdraw him too soon from thence, he was thereby unhappily prevented from making any Proficiency in the Dead Languages: A Point, that will deserve some little Discussion in the Sequel of this Dissertation.

How long he continued in his Father's Way of Business, either as an Assistant to him, or on his own proper Account, no Notices are left to inform us: nor have I been able to learn precisely at what Period of Life he quitted his native *Stratford*, and began his Acquaintance with *London*, and the *Stage*.

In order to settle in the World after a Family-manner, he thought fit, Mr. *Rowe* acquaints us, to marry while he was yet very young. It is certain, he did so: for by the Monument, in *Stratford* Church, erected to the Memory of his Daughter *Susanna*, the Wife of *John Hall*,

Gentleman, it appears, that she died on the 2d Day of *July*, in the Year 1649, aged 66. So that she was born in 1583, when her Father could not be full 19 Years old; who was himself born in the Year 1564. Nor was she his eldest Child, for he had another Daughter, *Judith*,[3] who was born before her, and who was married to one Mr. *Thomas Quiney*. So that *Shakespeare* must have entred into Wedlock, by that time he was turn'd of seventeen Years.[4]

Whether the Force of Inclination merely, or some concurring Circumstances of Convenience in the Match, prompted him to marry so early, is not easy to be determin'd at this Distance: but 'tis probable, a View of Interest might partly sway his Conduct in this Point: for he married the Daughter of one *Hathaway*, a substantial Yeoman in his Neighbourhood, and she had the Start of him in Age no less than 8 years. She surviv'd him, notwithstanding, seven Seasons, and dy'd that very Year in which the *Players* publish'd the first Edition of his Works in *Folio*, Anno Dom. 1623, at the Age of 67 Years, as we likewise learn from her Monument in *Stratford*-Church.

How long he continued in this kind of Settlement, upon his own Native Spot, is not more easily to be determin'd. But if the Tradition be true, of that Extravagance which forc'd him both to quit his Country and Way of Living; to wit, his being engag'd, with a Knot of young Deer-stealers, to rob the Park of Sir *Thomas Lucy* of *Cherlecot* near *Stratford*: the Enterprize savours so much of Youth and Levity, we may reasonably suppose it was before he could write full Man. Besides, considering he has left us six and thirty Plays, at least, avow'd to be genuine; and considering too, that he had retir'd from the Stage, to spend the latter Part of his Days at his own Native *Stratford*; the Interval of Time, necessarily required for the finishing so many Dramatic Pieces, obliges us to suppose he threw himself very early upon the Play-house. And as he could, probably, contract no Acquaintance with the Drama, while he was driving on the Affair of Wool at home; some Time must be lost, even after he had commenc'd Player, before he could attain Knowledge enough in the Science to qualify himself for turning Author.

It has been observ'd by Mr. *Rowe*, that, amongst other Extravagances which our Author has given to his Sir *John Falstaffe*, in the *Merry Wives* of *Windsor*, he has made him a Deer-stealer; and that he might at the same time remember his *Warwickshire* Prosecutor, under the Name of *Justice Shallow*, he has given him very near the same Coat of Arms, which *Dugdale*, in his Antiquities of that County, describes for a Family there. There are two Coats, I observe, in *Dugdale*, where three Silver Fishes are borne in the Name of *Lucy*; and another Coat, to the Monument of *Thomas Lucy*, Son of Sir *William Lucy*, in which are quarter'd in four several Divisions, twelve little Fishes, three in each Division, probably *Luces*. This very Coat, indeed, seems alluded to in *Shallow*'s giving the *dozen* White *Luces*, and in *Slender* saying, *he may quarter*.[5] When I consider the exceeding Candour and Good-nature of our Author, (which inclin'd all the gentler Part of the World to love him; as the Power of his Wit obliged the Men of the most delicate Knowledge and polite Learning to admire him;) and that he should throw this humorous Piece of Satire at his Prosecutor, at least twenty Years after the Provocation given; I am confidently persuaded it must be owing to an unforgiving Rancour on the Prosecutor's Side: and if This was the Case, it were Pity but the Disgrace of such an Inveteracy should remain as a lasting Reproach, and *Shallow* stand as a Mark of Ridicule to stigmatize his Malice.

It is said, our Author spent some Years before his Death, in Ease, Retirement, and the Conversation of his Friends, at his Native *Stratford*. I could never pick up any certain Intelligence, when He relinquish'd the Stage. I know, it has been mistakenly thought by some, that *Spenser*'s *Thalia*, in his *Tears of his Muses*, where she laments that Loss of her *Willy* in the Comic Scene,[6] has been apply'd to our Author's quitting the Stage. But *Spenser* himself, 'tis well known, quitted the Stage of Life in the Year 1598; and, five Years after this, we find *Shakespeare*'s Name among the Actors in *Ben Jonson*'s *Sejanus*, which first made its Appearance in the Year 1603. Nor, surely, could he then have any Thoughts of retiring, since, that very Year, a Licence under the Privy-Seal was granted by K. *James* I. to him and *Fletcher*, *Burbage*, *Phillippes*, *Hemings*, *Condel*, &c. authorizing them to exercise the Art of playing Comedies, Tragedies, &c. as well at their usual House call'd the *Globe* on the other Side of the Water, as in any other Parts of the Kingdom, during his Majesty's Pleasure: (A Copy of which Licence is preserv'd in *Rymer*'s *Fœdera*.)[7] Again, 'tis certain, that *Shakespeare* did not exhibit his *Macbeth*, till after the Union was brought about, and till after K. *James* I. had begun to touch for the *Evil*: for 'tis plain, he has inserted Compliments, on both those Accounts, upon his Royal Master in that Tragedy. Nor, indeed, could the Number of the Dramatic Pieces, he produced, admit of his retiring near so early as that Period. So that what *Spenser* there says, if it relate at all to *Shakespeare*, must hint at some occasional Recess he made for a time upon a Disgust taken: or the *Willy*, there mention'd, must relate to some other favourite Poet. I believe, we may safely determine that he had not quitted in the Year 1610. For in his *Tempest*, our Author makes mention of the *Bermuda* Islands, which were unknown to the *English*, till, in 1609, Sir *John Summers* made a Voyage to *North-America*, and discover'd them: and afterwards invited some of his Countrymen to settle a Plantation there. That he became the private Gentleman, at least three Years before his Decease, is pretty obvious from another Circumstance: I mean, from that remarkable and well-known Story, which Mr. *Rowe* has given us of our Author's Intimacy with Mr. *John Combe*, an old Gentleman noted thereabouts for his Wealth and Usury: and upon whom *Shakespeare* made the following facetious Epitaph.

> *Ten in the hundred lies here ingrav'd,*
> *'Tis a hundred to ten his Soul is not sav'd;*
> *If any Man ask who lies in this Tomb,*
> *Oh! oh! quoth the Devil, 'tis my* John-a-Combe.

This sarcastical Piece of Wit was, at the Gentleman's own Request, thrown out extemporally in his Company. And this Mr. *John Combe* I take to be the same, who, by *Dugdale* in his Antiquities of *Warwickshire*, is said to have dy'd in the Year 1614, and for whom at the upper end of the Quire, of the Guild of the Holy Cross at *Stratford*, a fair Monument is erected, having a Statue thereon cut in Alabaster, and in a Gown, with this Epitaph. "Here lyeth enterr'd the Body of *John Combe* Esq; who dy'd the 10th of *July*, 1614, who bequeathed several Annual Charities to the Parish of *Stratford*, and 100l. to be lent to fifteen poor Tradesmen from three years to three years, changing the Parties every third Year, at the Rate of fifty Shillings *per Annum*, the Increase to be

distributed to the Almes-poor there." – The Donation has all the Air
of a rich and sagacious Usurer.

Shakespeare himself did not survive Mr. *Combe* long, for he dy'd in
the Year 1616, the 53d of his Age. He lies buried on the North Side
of the Chancel in the great Church at *Stratford*; where a Monument,
decent enough for the Time, is erected to him, and plac'd against the
Wall. He is represented under an Arch in a sitting Posture, a Cushion
spread before him, with a Pen in his Right Hand, and his Left rested
on a Scrowl of Paper. The *Latin* Distich, which is placed under
the Cushion, has been given us by Mr. *Pope*, or his Graver, in this
Manner.

> *INGENIO* Pylium, *Genio* Socratem, *Arte* Maronem,
> *Terra tegit, Populus mæret, Olympus habet.*

I confess I don't conceive the Difference betwixt *Ingeniô* and *Geniô*
in the first Verse. They seem to me intirely synonomous Terms; nor
was the *Pylian* Sage *Nestor* celebrated for his Ingenuity, but for an
Experience and Judgment owing to his long Age. *Dugdale*, in his
Antiquities of *Warwickshire*, has copied this Distich with a Distinction
which Mr. *Rowe* has follow'd, and which certainly restores us the true
Meaning of the Epitaph.

> *JUDICIO Pylium,* Genio *Socratem,* &c.[8]

In 1614, the greater part of the Town of *Stratford* was consumed by
Fire; but our *Shakespeare*'s House, among some others, escap'd the
Flames. This House was first built by Sir *Hugh Clopton*, a younger
Brother of an ancient Family in that Neighbourhood, who took their
Name from the Manor of *Clopton*. Sir *Hugh* was Sheriff of *London* in
the Reign of *Richard* III, and Lord Mayor in the Reign of King *Henry*
VII. To this Gentleman the Town of *Stratford* is indebted for the fine
Stone-bridge, consisting of fourteen Arches, which at an extraordinary
Expence he built over the *Avon*, together with a Cause-way running
at the West-end thereof; as also for rebuilding the Chapel adjoining
to his House, and the Cross-Isle in the Church there. It is remarkable
of him, that, tho' he liv'd and dy'd a Batchelor, among the other
extensive Charities which he left both to the City of *London* and Town

of *Stratford*, he bequeath'd considerable Legacies for the Marriage of poor Maidens of good Name and Fame both in *London* and at *Stratford*. Notwithstanding which large Donations in his Life, and Bequests at his Death, as he had purchased the Manor of *Clopton*, and all the Estate of the Family, so he left the same again to his Elder Brother's Son with a very great Addition: (a Proof, how well Beneficence and Oeconomy may walk hand in hand in wise Families:) Good part of which Estate is yet in the Possession of *Edward Clopton*, Esq; and Sir *Hugh Clopton*, Knt. lineally descended from the Elder Brother of the first Sir *Hugh*: Who particularly bequeathed to his Nephew, by his Will, his House, by the Name of his *Great-House* in *Stratford*.

The Estate had now been sold out of the *Clopton* Family for above a Century, at the Time when *Shakespeare* became the Purchaser: who, having repair'd and modell'd it to his own Mind, chang'd the Name to *New-place*; which the Mansion-house, since erected upon the same Spot, at this day retains. The House and Lands, which attended it, continued in *Shakespeare*'s Descendants to the Time of the *Restoration*: when they were repurchased by the *Clopton* Family, and the Mansion now belongs to Sir *Hugh Clopton*, Knt. To the Favour of this worthy Gentleman I owe the Knowledge of one Particular, in Honour of our Poet's once Dwelling-house, of which, I presume, Mr. ROWE never was appriz'd. When the Civil War raged in *England*, and K. *Charles* the *First's* Queen was driven by the Necessity of Affairs to make a Recess in *Warwickshire*, She kept her Court for three Weeks in *New-place*.[9] We may reasonably suppose it then the best private House in the Town; and her Majesty preferr'd it to the *College*, which was in the Possession of the *Combe*-Family, who did not so strongly favour the King's Party.

How much our Author employ'd himself in Poetry, after his Retirement from the Stage, does not so evidently appear: Very few posthumous Sketches of his Pen have been recover'd to ascertain that Point. We have been told, indeed, in Print, but not till very lately, That two large Chests full of this Great Man's loose Papers and Manuscripts,[10] in the Hands of an ignorant Baker of *Warwick*, (who married one of the Descendants from our *Shakespeare*) were carelessly scatter'd and thrown about, as Garret-Lumber, and Litter, to the particular Knowledge of the late Sir *William Bishop*, till they were all consumed in the general Fire and Destruction of that Town. I cannot help being a little apt to distrust the Authority of this Tradition; because his Wife surviv'd him seven Years, and as his Favourite Daughter *Susanna* surviv'd her twenty six Years, 'tis very improbable, they should suffer such a Treasure to be remov'd, and translated into a remoter Branch of the Family, without a Scrutiny first made into the Value of it. This, I say, inclines me to distrust the Authority of the Relation: but, notwithstanding such an apparent Improbability, if we really lost such a Treasure, by whatever Fatality or Caprice of Fortune they came into such ignorant and neglectful Hands, I agree with the *Relater*, the Misfortune is wholly irreparable.

To these Particulars, which regard his Person and private Life, some few more are to be glean'd from Mr. ROWE's Account of his *Life* and *Writings*: Let us now take a short View of him in his publick Capacity, as a *Writer*: and, from thence, the Transition will be easy to the *State* in which his *Writings* have been handed down to us.

No Age, perhaps, can produce an Author more various from himself, than *Shakespeare* has been universally acknowledg'd to be. The Diversity in Stile, and other Parts of Composition, so obvious in him, is as variously to be accounted for. His Education, we find, was at best but begun: and he started early into a Science from the Force of Genius, unequally assisted by acquir'd Improvements. His Fire, Spirit, and Exuberance of Imagination gave an Impetuosity to his Pen: His Ideas flow'd from him in a Stream rapid, but not turbulent; copious, but not ever overbearing its Shores. The Ease and Sweetness of his Temper might not a little contribute to his Facility in Writing: as his Employment, as a *Player*, gave him an Advantage and Habit of fancying himself the very Character he meant to delineate. He used the Helps of his Function in forming himself to create and express that *Sublime*, which other Actors can only copy, and throw out, in Action and graceful Attitude. But *Nullum sine Veniâ placuit Ingenium*, says *Seneca*.[11] The Genius, that gives us the greatest Pleasure, sometimes stands in Need of our Indulgence. Whenever this happens with regard to *Shakespeare* I would willingly impute it to a Vice of *his Times*. We see Complaisance enough, in our Days, paid to a *bad Taste*. So that his

Clinches, false Wit, and descending beneath himself, may have proceeded from a Deference paid to the then *reigning Barbarism.*

I have not thought it out of my Province, whenever Occasion offer'd, to take notice of some of our Poet's grand Touches of Nature: Some, that do not appear superficially such; but in which he seems the most deeply instructed; and to which, no doubt, he has so much ow'd that happy Preservation of his *Characters,* for which he is justly celebrated.[12] Great Genius's, like his, naturally unambitious, are satisfy'd to conceal their Art in these Points. 'Tis the Foible of your worser Poets to make a Parade and Ostentation of that little Science they have; and to throw it out in the most ambitious Colours. And whenever a Writer of this Class shall attempt to copy these artful Concealments of our Author, and shall either think them easy, or practised by a Writer for his Ease, he will soon be convinced of his Mistake by the Difficulty of reaching the Imitation of them.

> *Speret idem, sudet multùm; frustráq; laboret,*
> *Ausus idem:* —[13]

Indeed, to point out, and exclaim upon, all the Beauties of *Shakespeare,* as they come singly in Review, would be as insipid, as endless; as tedious, as unnecessary: But the Explanation of those Beauties, that are less obvious to common Readers, and whose Illustration depends on the Rules of just Criticism, and an exact Knowledge of human Life, should deservedly have a Share in a general Critic upon the Author. But, to pass over at once to another Subject: –

It has been allow'd on all hands, how far our Author was indebted to *Nature;*[14] it is not so well agreed, how much he ow'd to *Languages* and acquir'd *Learning.* The Decisions on this Subject were certainly set on Foot by the Hint from *Ben Jonson,* that he had small *Latin* and less *Greek:* And from this Tradition, as it were, Mr. *Rowe* has thought fit peremptorily to declare, that "It is without Controversy, he had no Knowledge of the Writings of the ancient Poets, for that in his Works we find no Traces of any thing which looks like an Imitation of the Ancients. For the Delicacy of his Taste (*continues He,*) and the natural Bent of his own great Genius (equal, if not superior, to some of the Best of theirs;) would certainly have led him to read and study them with so much Pleasure, that some of their fine Images would naturally have insinuated themselves into, and been mix'd with, his own Writings: and so his not copying, at least, something from them, may be an Argument of his never having read them."[15] I shall leave it to the Determination of my Learned Readers, from the numerous Passages, which I have occasionally quoted in my Notes, in which our Poet seems closely to have imitated the Classics, whether Mr. *Rowe*'s Assertion be so absolutely to be depended on. The Result of the Controversy must certainly, either way, terminate to our Author's Honour: how happily he could imitate them, if that Point be allow'd; or how gloriously he could think like them, without owing any thing to Imitation.

Tho' I should be very unwilling to allow *Shakespeare* so poor a Scholar, as Many have labour'd to represent him, yet I shall be very cautious of declaring too positively on the other side of the Question: that is, with regard to my Opinion of his Knowledge in the dead Languages. And therefore the Passages, that I occasionally quote from the *Classics*, shall not be urged as Proofs that he knowingly imitated those Originals; but brought to shew how happily he has express'd himself upon the same Topicks. A very learned Critick of our own Nation has declar'd, that a Sameness of Thought and Sameness of Expression too, in Two Writers of a different Age, can hardly happen, without a violent Suspicion of the Latter copying from his Predecessor.[16] I shall not therefore run any great Risque of a Censure, tho' I should venture to hint, that the Resemblance, in Thought and Expression, of our Author and an Ancient (which we should allow to be Imitation in One, whose Learning was not question'd) may sometimes take its Rise from Strength of Memory, and those Impressions which he ow'd to the School. And if we may allow a Possibility of This, considering that, when he quitted the School, he gave into his Father's Profession and way of Living, and had, 'tis likely, but a slender Library of Classical Learning; and considering what a Number of Translations, Romances, and Legends, started about his Time, and a little before; (most of which, 'tis very evident, he read;) I think, it may easily be reconcil'd why he rather schemed his *Plots* and *Characters* from these more latter Informations, than went back to those Fountains, for which he might entertain a sincere Veneration, but to which he could not have so ready a Recourse.

In touching on another Part of his Learning, as it related to the Knowledge of *History*, and *Books*, I shall advance something, that, at first sight, will very much wear the Appearance of a Paradox. For I shall find it no hard Matter to prove, that, from the grossest Blunders in History, we are not to infer his real Ignorance of it: Nor from a greater Use of *Latin* Words, than ever any other *English* Author used, must we infer his intimate Acquaintance with that Language.

A Reader of Taste may easily observe, that tho' *Shakespeare*, almost in every Scene of his historical Plays, commits the grossest Offences against Chronology, History, and Ancient Politicks; yet This was not thro' Ignorance, as is generally supposed, but thro' the too powerful Blaze of his Imagination; which, when once raised, made all acquired Knowledge vanish and disappear before it. But this Licence in him, as I have said, must not be imputed to Ignorance: since as often we may find him, when Occasion serves, reasoning up to the Truth of History; and throwing out Sentiments as justly adapted to the Circumstances of his Subject, as to the Dignity of his Characters, or Dictates of Nature in general.

Then, to come to his Knowledge of the *Latin* Tongue, 'tis certain, there is a surprising Effusion of *Latin* Words made *English*, far more than in any one *English* Author I have seen; but we must be cautious to imagine, this was of his own doing. For the *English* Tongue, in his Age, began extremely to suffer by an Inundation of *Latin*: And this, to be sure, was occasion'd by the Pedantry of those two Monarchs, *Elizabeth* and *James*, Both great *Latinists*. For it is not to be wonder'd at, if both the Court and Schools, equal Flatterers of Power, should adapt themselves to the Royal Taste.

But now I am touching on the Question, (which has been so frequently agitated, yet so entirely undecided) of his Learning and Acquaintance with the Languages; an additional Word or two naturally falls in here upon the Genius of our Author, as compared with that of *Jonson* his Contemporary. They are confessedly the greatest Writers our Nation could ever boast of in the *Drama*. The first, we say, owed all to his prodigious natural Genius; and the other a great deal to his

Art and Learning. This, if attended to, will explain a very remarkable Appearance in their Writings. Besides those wonderful Masterpieces of Art and Genius, which each has given Us; They are the Authors of other Works very unworthy of them: But with this Difference; that in *Jonson*'s bad Pieces we don't discover one single Trace of the Author of the *Fox* and *Alchemist*: but in the wild extravagant Notes of *Shakespeare*, you every now and then encounter Strains that recognize the divine Composer. This Difference may be thus accounted for. *Jonson*, as we said before, owing all his Excellence to his Art, by which he sometimes strain'd himself to an uncommon Pitch, when at other times he unbent and play'd with his Subject, having nothing then to support him, it is no wonder he wrote so far beneath himself. But *Shakespeare*, indebted more largely to Nature, than the Other to acquired Talents, in his most negligent Hours could never so totally divest himself of his Genius, but that it would frequently break out with astonishing Force and Splendor.[17]

As I have never propos'd to dilate farther on the Character of my Author, than was necessary to explain the Nature and Use of this Edition, I shall proceed to consider him as a Genius in Possession of an everlasting Name. And how great that Merit must be, which could gain it against all the Disadvantages of the horrid Condition in which he has hitherto appear'd! Had *Homer*, or any other admir'd Author, first started into Publick so maim'd and deform'd, we cannot determine whether they had not sunk for ever under the Ignominy of such an ill Appearance. The mangled Condition of *Shakespeare* has been acknowledg'd by Mr. *Rowe*, who publish'd him indeed, but neither corrected his Text, nor collated the old Copies. This Gentleman had Abilities, and a sufficient Knowledge of his Author, had but his Industry been equal to his Talents. The same mangled Condition has been acknowledg'd too by Mr. *Pope*, who publish'd him likewise, pretended to have collated the old Copies, and yet seldom has corrected the Text but to its Injury. I congratulate with the *Manes* of our Poet, that this Gentleman has been sparing in *indulging his private Sense*, as he phrases it;[18] for He, who tampers with an Author whom he does not understand, must do it at the Expence of his Subject. I have made it evident throughout my Remarks, that he has frequently inflicted a Wound where he intended a Cure. He has acted with regard to our Author, as an Editor, whom LIPSIUS mentions, did with regard to MARTIAL; *Inventus est nescio quis* Popa, *qui non* vitia *ejus, sed* ipsum *excîdit.*[19] He has attack'd him like an unhandy *Slaughterman*; and not lopp'd off the *Errors*, but the *Poet*.

When this is found to be the Fact, how absurd must appear the Praises of such an Editor? It seems a moot Point, whether Mr. *Pope* has done most Injury to *Shakespeare* as his Editor and Encomiast; or Mr. *Rymer* done him Service as his Rival and Censurer.[20] They have Both shewn themselves in an equal *Impuissance* of suspecting, or amending, the corrupted Passages: and tho' it be neither Prudence to censure, or commend, what one does not understand; yet if a man must do one when he plays the Critick, the latter is the more ridiculous Office: And by That *Shakespeare* suffers most. For the natural Veneration, which we have for him, makes us apt to swallow whatever is given us as *his*, and set off with Encomiums; and hence we quit all Suspicions of Depravity: On the contrary, the Censure of so divine an Author sets us upon his Defence; and this produces an exact Scrutiny and Examination, which ends in finding out and discriminating the true from the spurious.

It is not with any secret Pleasure, that I so frequently animadvert on Mr. *Pope* as a Critick; but there are Provocations, which a Man can never quite forget. His Libels have been thrown out with so much Inveteracy, that, not to dispute whether they *should* come from a *Christian*, they leave it a Question whether they *could* come from a *Man*. I should be loth to doubt, as *Quintus Serenus* did in a like Case,

> *Sive homo, seu similis turpissima bestia nobis,*
> *Vulnera dente dedit.*[21]

The Indignation, perhaps, for being represented a *Blockhead*, may be as strong in us as it is in the Ladies for a Reflexion on their *Beauties*. It is certain, I am indebted to Him for some *flagrant Civilities*; and I shall willingly devote a part of my Life to the honest Endeavour of quitting Scores: with this Exception however, that I will not return those Civilities in his *peculiar* Strain, but confine myself, at least, to the Limits of *common Decency*. I shall ever think it better to want *Wit*, than to want *Humanity*: and impartial Posterity may, perhaps, be of my Opinion.

But, to return to my Subject; which now calls upon me to inquire into those Causes, to which the Depravations of my Author originally may be assign'd. We are to consider him as a Writer, of whom no authentic Manuscript was left extant; as a Writer, whose Pieces were dispersedly perform'd on the several *Stages* then in Being. And it was the Custom of those Days for the Poets to take a Price of the *Players* for the Pieces They from time to time furnish'd; and thereupon it was suppos'd, they had no farther Right to print them without the Consent of the *Players*. As it was the Interest of the *Companies* to keep their Plays unpublish'd, when any one succeeded, there was a Contest betwixt the Curiosity of the Town, who demanded to see it in Print, and the Policy of the *Stagers*, who wish'd to secrete it within their own Walls. Hence, many Pieces were taken down in Short-hand, and imperfectly copied by Ear, from a *Representation*: Others were printed from piece-meal Parts surreptitiously obtain'd from the Theatres, uncorrect, and without the Poet's Knowledge. To some of these Causes we owe the Train of Blemishes, that deform those Pieces which stole singly into the World in our Author's Life-time.

There are still other Reasons, which may be suppos'd to have affected the whole Set. When the *Players* took upon them to publish his Works intire, every Theatre was ransack'd to supply the Copy; and *Parts* collected, which had gone thro' as many Changes as Performers, either from Mutilations or Additions made to them. Hence we derive many Chasms and Incoherences in the Sense and Matter. Scenes were frequently transposed, and shuffled out of their true Place, to humour the Caprice, or suppos'd Convenience, of some particular Actor. Hence much Confusion and Impropriety has attended, and embarras'd, the Business and Fable. To these obvious Causes of Corruption it must be added, that our Author has lain under the Disadvantage of having his Errors propagated and multiplied by Time: because, for near a Century, his Works were republish'd from the faulty Copies, without the Assistance of any intelligent Editor: which has been the Case likewise of many a *Classic* Writer.

The Nature of any Distemper once found has generally been the immediate Step to a Cure. *Shakespeare*'s Case has in a great measure resembled That of a corrupt *Classic*; and, consequently, the Method of Cure was likewise to bear a Resemblance. By what Means, and with what Success, this Cure has been effected on ancient Writers, is too well known, and needs no formal Illustration. The Reputation, consequent on Tasks of that nature, invited me to attempt the Method here; with this View, the Hopes of restoring to the Publick their greatest Poet in his Original Purity: after having so long lain in a Condition that was a Disgrace to common Sense. To this end I have ventur'd on a Labour, that is the first Assay of the kind on any modern Author whatsoever. For the late Edition of *Milton* by the Learned Dr. *Bentley*[22] is, in the main, a Performance of another Species. It is plain, it was the Intention of that Great Man rather to correct and pare off the Excrescencies of the *Paradise Lost*, in the manner that *Tucca* and *Varius* were employ'd to criticize the *Æneis* of *Virgil*,[23] than to restore corrupted Passages. Hence, therefore, may be seen either the Iniquity or Ignorance of his Censurers, who, from some Expressions, would make us believe, the *Doctor* every where gives us his Corrections as the Original Text of the Author; whereas the chief Turn of his Criticism is plainly to shew the World, that if *Milton* did not write as He would have him, he ought to have wrote so.

I thought proper to premise this Observation to the Readers, as it will shew that the Critic on *Shakespeare* is of a quite different Kind. His genuine Text is for the most part religiously adher'd to, and the numerous Faults and Blemishes, purely his own, are left as they were found. Nothing is alter'd, but what by the clearest Reasoning can be proved a Corruption of the true Text; and the Alteration, a real Restoration of the genuine Reading. Nay, so strictly have I strove to give the true Reading, tho' sometimes not to the Advantage of my Author, that I have been ridiculously ridicul'd for it by Those, who either were iniquitously for turning every thing to my Disadvantage; or else were totally ignorant of the true Duty of an Editor.

The Science of Criticism, as far as it affects an Editor, seems to be reduced to these three Classes; the Emendation of corrupt Passages; the Explanation of obscure and difficult ones; and an Inquiry into the Beauties and Defects of Composition. This Work is principally confin'd to the two former Parts: tho' there are some Specimens interspers'd of the latter Kind, as several of the Emendations were best supported, and several of the Difficulties best explain'd, by taking notice of the Beauties and Defects of the Composition peculiar to this Immortal Poet. But This was but occasional, and for the sake only of perfecting the two other Parts, which were the proper Objects of the Editor's Labour. The third lies open for every willing Undertaker: and I shall be pleas'd to see it the Employment of a masterly Pen.

It must necessarily happen, as I have formerly observ'd,[24] that where the Assistance of Manuscripts is wanting to set an Author's Meaning right, and rescue him from those Errors which have been transmitted down thro' a Series of incorrect Editions, and a long Intervention of Time, many Passages must be desperate, and past a Cure; and their true Sense irretrievable either to Care or the Sagacity of Conjecture. But is there any Reason therefore to say, That because All cannot be retriev'd, All ought to be left desperate? We should shew very little Honesty, or Wisdom, to play the Tyrants with an Author's Text; to raze, alter, innovate, and overturn, at all Adventures, and to the utter Detriment of his Sense and Meaning: But to be so very reserved and cautious, as to interpose no Relief or Conjecture, where it manifestly labours and cries out for Assistance, seems, on the other hand, an indolent Absurdity.

As there are very few Pages in *Shakespeare*, upon which some Suspicions of Depravity do not reasonably arise; I have thought it my Duty, in the first place, by a diligent and laborious Collation to take in the Assistances of all the older Copies.

In his *Historical Plays*, whenever our *English* Chronicles, and in his Tragedies when *Greek* or *Roman* Story, could give any Light; no Pains have been omitted to set Passages right by comparing my Author with his Originals: for, as I have frequently observed, he was a close and accurate Copier where-ever his *Fable* was founded on *History*.

Where-ever the Author's Sense is clear and discoverable, (tho', perchance, low and trivial;) I have not by any Innovation tamper'd with his Text; out of an Ostentation of endeavouring to make him speak better than the old Copies have done.

Where, thro' all the former Editions, a Passage has labour'd under flat Nonsense and invincible Darkness, if, by the Addition or Alteration of a Letter or two, or a Transposition in the Pointing, I have restored to Him both Sense and Sentiment; such Corrections, I am persuaded, will need no Indulgence.

And whenever I have taken a greater Latitude and Liberty in amending, I have constantly endeavour'd to support my Corrections and Conjectures by parallel Passages and Authorities from himself, the surest Means of expounding any Author whatsoever. *Cette voie d'interpreter un Autheur par lui-même est plus sure que tous les Commentaires*, says a very learned *French* Critick.[25]

As to my *Notes*, (from which the common and learned Readers of our Author, I hope, will derive some Satisfaction;) I have endeavour'd to give them a Variety in some Proportion to their Number. Where-ever I have ventur'd at an Emendation, a *Note* is constantly subjoin'd to justify and assert the Reason of it. Where I only offer a Conjecture, and do not disturb the Text, I fairly set forth my Grounds for such Conjecture, and submit it to Judgment. Some Remarks are spent in explaining Passages, where the Wit or Satire depends on an obscure Point of History: Others, where Allusions are to Divinity, Philosophy, or other Branches of Science. Some are added to shew, where there is a Suspicion of our Author having borrow'd from the Ancients: Others, to shew where he is rallying his Contemporaries; or where He himself is rallied by them. And some are necessarily thrown in, to explain an obscure and obsolete *Term*, *Phrase*, or *Idea*. I once intended to have added a complete and copious *Glossary*; but as I have been importun'd, and am prepar'd, to give a correct Edition of our Author's POEMS,[26] (in which many Terms occur that are not to be met with in his *Plays*,) I thought a *Glossary* to all *Shakespeare*'s Works more proper to attend that Volume.

In reforming an infinite Number of Passages in the *Pointing*, where the Sense was before quite lost, I have frequently subjoin'd Notes to shew the *deprav'd*, and to prove the *reform'd*, Pointing: a Part of Labour in this Work which I could very willingly have spar'd myself. May it not be objected, why then have you burthen'd us with these Notes? The Answer is obvious, and, if I mistake not, very material. Without such Notes, these Passages in subsequent Editions would be liable, thro' the Ignorance of Printers and Correctors, to fall into the old Confusion: Whereas, a Note on every one hinders all possible Return to Depravity; and for ever secures them in a State of Purity and Integrity not to be lost or forfeited.

Again, as some Notes have been necessary to point out the Detection of the corrupted Text, and establish the Restoration of the genuine Readings; some others have been as necessary for the Explanation of Passages obscure and difficult. To understand the Necessity and Use of this Part of my Task, some Particulars of my Author's Character are previously to be explain'd. There are *Obscurities* in him, which are common to him with all Poets of the same Species; there are Others, the Issue of the Times he liv'd in; and there are Others, again, peculiar to himself. The Nature of Comic Poetry being entirely satirical, it busies itself more in exposing what we call Caprice and Humour, than Vices cognizable to the Laws. The *English*, from the Happiness of a free Constitution, and a Turn of Mind peculiarly speculative and inquisitive, are observ'd to produce more *Humourists* and a greater Variety of original *Characters*, than any other People whatsoever:[27] And These owing their immediate Birth to the peculiar Genius of each Age, an infinite Number of Things alluded to, glanced at, and expos'd, must needs become obscure, as the *Characters* themselves are antiquated, and disused. An Editor therefore should be well vers'd in the History and Manners of his Author's Age, if he aims at doing him a Service in this Respect.

Besides, *Wit* lying mostly in the Assemblage of *Ideas*, and in the putting Those together with Quickness and Variety, wherein can be found any Resemblance, or Congruity, to make up pleasant Pictures, and agreeable Visions in the Fancy;[28] the Writer, who aims at Wit, must of course range far and wide for Materials. Now, the Age, in which *Shakespeare* liv'd, having, above all others, a wonderful Affection to appear Learned, They declined vulgar Images, such as are immediately fetch'd from Nature, and rang'd thro' the Circle of the Sciences to fetch their Ideas from thence. But as the Resemblances of such Ideas to the Subject must necessarily lie very much out of the common Way, and every Piece of Wit appear a Riddle to the Vulgar; This, that should have taught them the forced, quaint, unnatural Tract they were in, (and induce them to follow a more natural One,) was the very Thing that kept them attach'd to it. The ostentatious Affectation of abstruse Learning, peculiar to that Time, the Love that Men naturally have to every Thing that looks like Mystery, fixed them down to this Habit of Obscurity. Thus became the Poetry of DONNE (tho' the wittiest Man of that Age,) nothing but a continued Heap of Riddles. And our *Shakespeare*, with all his easy Nature about him, for want of the Knowledge of the true Rules of Art, falls frequently into this vicious Manner.

The third Species of *Obscurities*, which deform our Author, as the Effects of his own Genius and Character, are Those that proceed from his peculiar Manner of *Thinking*, and as peculiar a Manner of *cloathing* those *Thoughts*. With regard to his *Thinking*, it is certain, that he had a general Knowledge of all the Sciences: But his Acquaintance was rather That of a Traveller, than a Native. Nothing in Philosophy was unknown to him; but every Thing in it had the Grace and Force of Novelty. And as Novelty is one main Source of Admiration, we are not to wonder that He has perpetual Allusions to the most recondite Parts of the Sciences: and This was done not so much out of Affectation, as the Effect of Admiration begot by Novelty. Then, as to his *Style* and *Diction*, we may much more justly apply to SHAKESPEARE, what a celebrated Writer has said of MILTON; *Our Language sunk under him, and was unequal to that Greatness of Soul which furnish'd him with such glorious Conceptions.*[29] He therefore frequently uses old Words, to give his Diction an Air of Solemnity; as he coins others, to express the Novelty and Variety of his Ideas.

Upon every distinct Species of these *Obscurities* I have thought it my Province to employ a Note, for the Service of my Author, and the Entertainment of my Readers. A few transient Remarks too I have not scrupled to intermix, upon the Poet's *Negligences* and *Omissions* in point of Art; but I have done it always in such a Manner, as will testify my Deference and Veneration for the Immortal Author. Some Censurers of *Shakespeare*, and particularly Mr. *Rymer*, have taught me to distinguish betwixt the *Railer* and *Critick*. The Outrage of his Quotations is so remarkably violent, so push'd beyond all Bounds of

Decency and sober Reasoning, that it quite carries over the Mark at which it was levell'd. Extravagant Abuse throws off the Edge of the intended Disparagement, and turns the Madman's Weapon into his own Bosom. In short, as to *Rymer*, This is my Opinion of him from his *Criticisms* on the *Tragedies* of the Last Age. He writes with great Vivacity, and appears to have been a Scholar: but, as for his Knowledge of the Art of Poetry, I can't perceive it was any deeper than his Acquaintance with *Bossu* and *Dacier*, from whom he has transcrib'd many of his best Reflexions. The late Mr. *Gildon* was one attached to *Rymer* by a similar Way of Thinking and Studies. They were Both of that Species of Criticks, who are desirous of displaying their Powers rather in finding Faults, than in consulting the Improvement of the World: the *hypercritical* Part of the Science of *Criticism*.

I had not mentioned the modest Liberty I have here and there taken of animadverting on my Author, but that I was willing to obviate in time the splenetick Exaggerations of my Adversaries on this Head. From past Experiments I have reason to be conscious, in what Light this Attempt may be placed: and that what I call a *modest Liberty*, will, by a little of their Dexterity, be inverted into downright *Impudence*. From a hundred mean and dishonest Artifices employ'd to discredit this Edition, and to cry down its Editor, I have all the Grounds in Nature to beware of Attacks. But tho' the Malice of Wit, join'd to the Smoothness of Versification, may furnish some Ridicule; Fact, I hope, will be able to stand its Ground against Banter and Gaiety.

It has been my Fate, it seems, as I thought it my Duty, to discover some *Anachronisms*[30] in our Author; which might have slept in Obscurity but for *this Restorer*, as Mr. *Pope* is pleas'd affectionately to stile me; as, for Instance, where *Aristotle* is mentioned by *Hector* in *Troilus* and *Cressida*: and *Galen*, *Cato*, and *Alexander* the Great, in *Coriolanus*. These, in Mr. *Pope*'s Opinion, are Blunders, which, the Illiteracy of the first Publishers of his Works has father'd upon the Poet's Memory: *it not being at all credible, that These could be the Errors of any Man who had the least Tincture of a School, or the least Conversation with Such as had.* But I have sufficiently proved, in the course of my *Notes*, that such *Anachronisms* were the Effect of Poetic Licence, rather than of Ignorance in our Poet. And if I may be permitted to ask a modest Question by the way,

Why may not I restore an *Anachronism* really made by our Author, as well as Mr. *Pope* take the Privilege to fix others upon him, which he never had it in his Head to make; as I may venture to affirm He had not, in the Instance of Sir *Francis Drake*,[31] to which I have spoke in the proper Place?

But who shall dare make any Words about this Freedom of Mr. *Pope*'s towards *Shakespeare*, if it can be prov'd, that, in his Fits of Criticism, he makes no more Ceremony with good *Homer* himself? To try, then, a Criticism of his own advancing; In the 8th Book of the *Odyssey*, where *Demodocus* sings the Episode of the Loves of *Mars* and *Venus*; and that, upon their being taken in the Net by *Vulcan*,

> — *"The God of Arms*
> *Must pay the Penalty for lawless Charms;"*

Mr. *Pope* is so kind gravely to inform us, "That *Homer* in This, as in many other Places, seems to allude to the Laws of *Athens*, where Death was the Punishment of Adultery." But how is this significant Observation made out? Why, who can possibly object any Thing to the contrary? – *Does not* Pausanias *relate, that* Draco *the Lawgiver to the* Athenians *granted Impunity to any Person that took Revenge upon an Adulterer? And was it not also the Institution of* Solon, *that if Any One took an Adulterer in the Fact, be might use him as he pleas'd?* These Things are very true: and to see What a good Memory, and sound Judgment in Conjunction can atchieve! Tho' *Homer*'s Date is not determin'd down to a single Year, yet 'tis pretty generally agreed that he liv'd above 300 Years before *Draco* and *Solon*: And That, it seems, has made him *seem* to allude to the very Laws, which these Two Legislators propounded above 300 Years after. If this Inference be not sometimes like an *Anachronism* or *Prolepsis*, I'll look once more into my Lexicons for the true Meaning of the Words. It appears to me, that somebody besides *Mars* and *Venus* has been caught in a Net by this Episode: and I could call in other Instances to confirm what treacherous Tackle this Net-work is, if not cautiously handled.

How just, notwithstanding, I have been in detecting the *Anachronisms* of my Author, and in defending him for the Use of them, Our late Editor seems to think, They should rather have slept in Obscurity:

and the having discovered them is sneer'd at, as a sort of wrong-headed Sagacity.

The numerous Corrections, which I made of the Poet's Text in my SHAKESPEARE *Restor'd*, and which the Publick have been so kind to think well of, are, in the Appendix of Mr. *Pope*'s last Edition, slightingly call'd *Various Readings, Guesses,* &c. He confesses to have inserted as many of them as he judg'd of any the least Advantage to the Poet; but says, that the Whole amounted to about 25 Words: and pretends to have annexed a compleat List of the Rest, which were not worth his embracing. Whoever has read my Book will at one Glance see, how in both these Points Veracity is strain'd, so an Injury might but be done. *Malus, etsi obesse non pote, tamen cogitat.*[32]

Another Expedient, to make my Work appear of a trifling Nature, has been an Attempt to depreciate *Literal Criticism*. To this end, and to pay a servile Compliment to Mr. *Pope*, an *Anonymous* Writer has, like a *Scotch* Pedlar in Wit, unbraced his Pack on the Subject.[33] But, that his Virulence might not seem to be levelled singly at Me, he has done Me the Honour to join Dr. *Bentley* in the Libel. I was in hopes, We should have been Both abused with Smartness of Satire, at least; tho' not with Solidity of Argument: that it might have been worth some Reply in Defence of the Science attacked. But I may fairly say of this Author, as *Falstaffe* does of *Poins; – Hang him, Baboon! his Wit is as thick as* Tewksbury *Mustard; there is no more Conceit in him, than is in a* MALLET.[34] If it be not Prophanation to set the Opinion of the divine *Longinus* against such a Scribler, he tells us expresly, "That to make a Judgment upon *Words* (and *Writings*) is the most consummate Fruit of much Experience." ἡ γὰρ τῶν λόγων κρίσις πολλῆς ἐστὶ πείρας τελευταῖον ἐπιγέννημα.[35] Whenever Words are depraved, the Sense of course must be corrupted; and thence the Readers betray'd into a false Meaning.

If the *Latin* and *Greek* Languages have receiv'd the greatest Advantages imaginable from the Labours of the Editors and Criticks of the two last Ages; by whose Aid and Assistance the Grammarians have been enabled to write infinitely better in that Art than even the preceding Grammarians, who wrote when those Tongues flourish'd as living Languages: I should account it a peculiar Happiness, that, by the faint Assay I have made in this Work, a Path might be chalk'd out, for abler Hands, by which to derive the same Advantages to our own Tongue: a Tongue, which, tho' it wants none of the fundamental Qualities of an universal Language, yet, as a *noble Writer* says,[36] lisps and stammers as in its Cradle; and has produced little more towards its polishing than Complaints of its Barbarity.

Having now run thro' all those Points, which I intended should make any Part of this Dissertation, and having in my *former* Edition made publick Acknowledgments of the Assistances lent me, I shall conclude with a brief Account of the Methods taken in *This*.

It was thought proper, in order to reduce the Bulk and Price of the Impression, that the Notes, where-ever they would admit of it, might be abridg'd: for which Reason I have curtail'd a great Quantity of Such, in which Explanations were too prolix, or Authorities in Support of an Emendation too numerous: and Many I have entirely expung'd, which were judg'd rather Verbose and Declamatory, (and, so, Notes merely of Ostentation;) than necessary, or instructive.

The few literal Errors, which had escaped Notice, for want of Revisals, in the former Edition, are here reform'd: and the Pointing of innumerable Passages is regulated, with all the Accuracy I am capable of.

I shall decline making any farther Declaration of the Pains I have taken upon my Author, because it was my Duty, as his Editor, to publish him with my best Care and Judgment: and because, I am sensible, all such Declarations are construed to be laying a sort of a Debt on the Publick. As the former Edition has been received with much Indulgence, I ought to make my Acknowledgements to the Town for their favourable Opinion of it: and I shall always be proud to think That Encouragement the best Payment I can hope to receive from my poor Studies.

Sir Thomas Hanmer,
'Preface' to *The Works of Shakespear*
(1744)

WHAT the Publick is here to expect is a true and correct Edition of *Shakespear*'s works cleared from the corruptions with which they have hitherto abounded. One of the great Admirers of this incomparable Author hath made it the amusement of his leisure hours for many years past to look over his writings with a careful eye, to note the obscurities and absurdities introduced into the text, and according to the best of his judgment to restore the genuine sense and purity of it. In this he proposed nothing to himself but his private satisfaction in making his own copy as perfect as he could: but as the emendations multiplied upon his hands, other Gentlemen[1] equally fond of the Author desired to see them, and some were so kind as to give their assistance by communicating their observations and conjectures upon difficult passages which had occurred to them. Thus by degrees the work growing more considerable than was at first expected, they who had the opportunity of looking into it, too partial perhaps in their judgment, thought it worth being made publick; and he, who hath with difficulty yielded to their perswasions, is far from desiring to reflect upon the late Editors for the omissions and defects which they left to be supplied by others who should follow them in the same province. On the contrary, he thinks the world much obliged to them for the progress they made in weeding out so great a number of blunders and mistakes as they have done, and probably he who hath carried on the work might never have thought of such an undertaking if he had not found a considerable part so done to his hands.

From what causes it proceeded that the works of this Author in the first publication of them were more injured and abused than perhaps any than ever pass'd the Press, hath been sufficiently explained in the Preface to Mr. *Pope*'s Edition which is here subjoined, and there needs no more to be said upon that subject. This only the Reader is desired to bear in mind, that as the corruptions are more numerous and of a grosser kind than can well be conceived but by those who have looked nearly into them; so in the correcting them this rule hath been most strictly observed, not to give a loose to fancy, or indulge a licentious spirit of criticism, as if it were fit for any one to presume to judge what *Shakespear* ought to have written, instead of endeavouring to discover truly and retrieve what he did write: and so great caution hath been used in this respect, that no alterations have been made but what the sense necessarily required, what the measure of the verse often helped to point out, and what the similitude of words in the false reading and in the true, generally speaking, appeared very well to justify.

Most of those passages are here thrown to the bottom of the page and rejected as spurious, which were stigmatized as such in Mr. *Pope*'s Edition; and it were to be wished that more had then undergone the same sentence. The promoter of the present Edition hath ventured to discard but few more upon his own judgment, the most considerable of which is that wretched piece of ribaldry in King *Henry V.* put into the mouths of the *French* Princess and an old Gentlewoman,[2] improper enough as it is all in *French* and not intelligible to an *English* audience, and yet that perhaps is the best thing that can be said of it. There can be no doubt but a great deal more of that low stuff which disgraces the works of this great Author, was foisted in by the Players after his death, to please the vulgar audiences by which they subsisted: and though some of the poor witticisms and conceits must be supposed to have fallen from his pen, yet as he hath put them generally into the mouths of low and ignorant people, so it is to be remember'd that he wrote for the Stage, rude and unpolished as it then was; and the vicious taste of the age must stand condemned for them, since he hath left upon record a signal proof how much he despised them. In his Play of *The Merchant of Venice* a Clown is introduced quibbling in a miserable manner, upon which one who bears the character of a man of sense makes the following reflection; *How every fool can play upon a word! I think the best grace of wit will shortly turn into silence, and discourse grow commendable in none but parrots.*[3] He could hardly have found stronger words to express his indignation at those false pretences to wit then in vogue; and therefore though such trash is frequently interspersed in his writings, it would be unjust to cast it as an imputation upon his taste and judgment and character as a Writer.

There being many words in *Shakespear* which are grown out of use and obsolete, and many borrowed from other languages which are not enough naturalized or known among us, a Glossary is added at the end of the work, for the explanation of all those terms which have hitherto been so many stumbling-blocks to the generality of Readers; and where there is any obscurity in the text not arising from the words but from a reference to some antiquated customs now forgotten, or other causes of that kind, a note is put at the bottom of the page to clear up the difficulty.

With these several helps if that rich vein of sense which runs through the works of this Author can be retrieved in every part and brought to appear in its true light, and if it may be hoped without presumption that this is here effected; they who love and admire him will receive a new pleasure, and all probably will be more ready to join in doing him justice, who does great honour to his country as a rare and perhaps a singular Genius: one who hath attained an high degree of perfection in those two great branches of Poetry, Tragedy and Comedy, different as they are in their natures from each other; and who may be said without partiality to have equalled, if not excelled, in both kinds, the best writers of any age or country who have thought it glory enough to distinguish themselves in either.

Since therefore other nations have taken care to dignify the works of their most celebrated Poets with the fairest impressions beautified with the ornaments of sculpture, well may our *Shakespear* be thought to deserve no less consideration: and as a fresh acknowledgment hath lately been paid to his merit, and a high regard to his name and memory, by erecting his Statue at a publick expence;[4] so it is desired that this new Edition of his works, which hath cost some attention and care, may be looked upon as another small monument designed and dedicated to his honour.

V
Editing Milton,
1732−1734

Richard Bentley,
'Preface' to *Milton's Paradise Lost.*
A New Edition
(1732)

THE PREFACE, BY DR. *BENTLEY.*

'Tis but common Justice, to let the Purchaser know what he is to expect in this new Edition of *Paradise Lost.*

Our celebrated Author, when he compos'd this Poem, being obnoxious to the Government, poor, friendless, and what is worse of all, blind with a *Gutta Serena*, could only dictate his Verses to be writ by another.[1] Whence it necessarily follows, That any Errors in Spelling, Pointing, nay even in whole words of a like or near Sound in Pronunciation, are not to be charg'd upon the Poet, but on the Amanuensis.

The Faults therefore in Orthography, Distinction by Points, and Capital Letters, all which swarm in the prior Editions, are here very carefully, and it's hop'd, judiciously corrected: though no mention is made in the Notes of that little but useful Improvement.

Our Poet, in thousands of Places, melts down the Vowel at the end of a Word, if the following Word begins with a Vowel. This Poetical Liberty he took from the *Greeks* and *Latins*: but he followed not the former, who strike the Vowels quite out of the Text; but the latter, who retain them in the Line, though they are absorp'd in the Speaking; as,

Monstrum horrendum, informe, ingens:

Which in the *Greek* way would be writ thus;

Mostr' horrend' inform' ingens.

In this Innovation our Poet has shewn both his Judgment and

Resolution; who durst do Right against Custom, having no body to precede him, nor any yet to follow him. By this, he in some measure amended the Hollowness and Emptiness of our *English* Verses, which in Cases of Nouns, and Moods and Tenses of Verbs must cram in *of*, *to*, *from*, &c. and *have*, *will*, *may*, &c. where *Greek* and *Latin* only change the last Syllable, as *numeri*, *numero*; *legit*, *leget*, *legat*: which generally makes one *Latin* Verse aequiponderant to two *English*: as, let any one try in a Translation of this in *Virgil*.

> *Tuque ô, cui prima frementem*
> *Fudit equum magno Tellus percussa tridenti.*[2]

But then this Excellency in *Milton*'s Verse brought one Inconvenience with it, That his Numbers seem embarass'd to such Readers, as know not, or not readily know, where such Elision of Vowels is to take place. To remedy which, through this whole Edition such Vowels are mark'd by an Apostrophe; as *II.1021*.

> *So He with difficulty' and labour hard*
> *Mov'd on, with difficulty' and labour He.*

As also, where he gives a Tone to some Words, different from the present Use; those are mark'd here with an Accent, as *Aspéct*, *Obdúrate*, *Féalty*, &c.

These small Improvements will be found in the present Text, which challenges to be the Truest and Correctest that has yet appear'd: not ONE Word being alter'd in it; but all the Conjectures, that attempt a Restoration of the Genuine *Milton*, cast into the Margin and explan'd in the Notes. So that every Reader has his free Choice, whether he will accept or reject what is here offer'd him; and this without the least Disgust or Discontent in the Offerer.

But more Calamities, than are yet mention'd, have happen'd to our Poem: for the Friend or Acquaintance, whoever he was, to whom *Milton* committed his Copy and the Overseeing of the Press, did so vilely execute that Trust, that *Paradise* under his Ignorance and Audaciousness may be said to be *twice lost*. A poor Bookseller,[3] then living near *Aldersgate*, purchas'd our Author's Copy for ten Pounds, and (if a Second Edition follow'd) for five Pounds more: as appears by the original Bond, yet in being. This Bookseller, and that Acquaintance who seems to have been the sole Corrector of the Press, brought forth their First Edition, polluted with such monstrous Faults, as are beyond Example in any other printed Book. Such as among many Hundreds are these following:

Book Line		
I.91	Into what pit *for*	To what depth
259	Not built	No Butt
590	Gesture	Stature
662	Understood	Underhand
II.352	An Oath	A Nod
517	Alchymie	Orichalc
683	Front	Form
801	Vex	Hem
III.96	Faithless	Hapless
131	First	Fraud
534	And his Eye	As his Eyes
664	Favour, him	Favourite
IV.293	Severe	Serene
555	Ev'n	Heaven
879	Transgressions	Transcursions
945	Distances	Discipline
V.172	Thy greater	Creator
173	Eternal	Diurnal
215	Embraces	Branches
711	Eye	He
VI.162	Destruction	Instruction
332	Nectarous	Icharous
356	Ensigns	Onset
513	Subtle Art	Sooty Chark
VII.15	Thy temp'ring	Thee tempting
160	Chang'd	Chain'd
373	Longitude	Long Career
451	Fowl	Soul
VIII.158	Light	Nought

417	In degree	Indigent
559	Loveliest	Forehead
591	Is judicious	Unlibidinous
IX.5	Venial	Mensal
318	Domestic	Pathetic
458	Angelic	Adamic
815	Forbidder safe	Forbidder's Eye
X.329	Rose	Rode
647	To the Ages	Out of Ashes
728	Eat or drink	Act or think
805	Dust	Just
XI.51	Gross	Dross
212	Fear	Film
276	Tender	Tending
299	Wound	Stound
XII.53	Spirit	Speech
177	Fill	Foul
554	End	Extent
601	For	Come.

But these Typographical Faults, occasion'd by the Negligence of this Acquaintance, (if all may be imputed to That, and not several wilfully made) were not the worst Blemishes brought upon our Poem. For, this suppos'd Friend, (call'd in these Notes *the Editor*) knowing *Milton*'s bad Circumstances; *who, VII.26,*

> *Was faln on evil days and evil tongues,*
> *With* Darkness *and with* Dangers *compass'd round*
> *And* Solitude;

thought he had a fit Opportunity to foist into the Book several of his own Verses, without the blind Poet's Discovery. This Trick has been too frequently plaid; but especially in Works publish'd after an Author's Death. And poor Milton in that Condition, with Three-score Years Weight upon his Shoulders, might be reckoned more than half Dead. See Instances of such spurious Verses; which the Poet, had he known of them, *vel furcâ ejecisset,*[4] *would have thrown out with a Fork; I.197, 251,*

306, 357, 486, 575, 580, 717, 763. II.530, 609, 635, 659, 670, 1019, 1023. III.35, 381, 444, 535, 574, 597. IV.250, 256, 267, 294, 323, 499, 705, 714, 983. V.574, 826. VII.391, 463, 481, 490. VIII.24, 575, 628. IX.15, 77, 167, 386, 439, 504, 522, 1058. X.16, 524, 559, 578, 731, 818, 840. XI.8, 130, 387.

And yet a farther Misfortune befell this noble Poem, which must be laid to the Author's Charge, though he may fairly plead *Not Guilty*, and had he had his Eye-sight, he would have prevented all Complaints. There are some Inconsistences in the System and Plan of his Poem, for want of his Revisal of the Whole before its Publication. These are all first discover'd in this Edition; as *I.39, 170, 326. II.78, 456, 969, 997, 1001, 1052. III.556. IV.177, 381. V.176, 200. VI.55. X.601.* But though the Printer's Faults are corrigible by retrieving the Poet's own Words, not from a Manuscript, (for none exists) but by Sagacity, and happy Conjecture: and though the Editor's Interpolations are detected by their own Silliness and Unfitness; and easily cured by printing them in the *Italic* Letter, and inclosing them between two Hooks; yet *Milton*'s own Slips and Inadvertencies cannot be redress'd without a Change both of the Words and Sense. Such Changes are here suggested, but not obtruded, to the Reader: they are generally in this Stile; *It MAY be adjusted thus; Among several ways of Change this MAY be one.* And if any Person will substitute better, he will deserve every Reader's Thanks: though, it's hoped, even These will not be found absurd, or disagreeing from the *Miltonian* Character:

Sunt & mihi carmina; me quoque dicunt
Vatem pastores: sed non ego credulus illis.[5]

Upon the View of what has here been said, such Reflexions, as these following, must necessarily arise in an attentive Reader.

First, he'll be throughly convinc'd, That the Proof-sheets of the First Edition were never read to *Milton*: who, unless he was as deaf as blind, could not possibly let pass such gross and palpable Faults. Nay, the Edition, when publish'd, was never read to him in seven Years time. The First came out in *1667*, and a Second in *1674*;[6] in which all the Faults of the Former are continued, with the Addition of some New ones.

If any one fancy this *Persona* of an Editor to be a mere Fantom, a Fiction, an Artifice to skreen *Milton* himself; let him consider these four and sole Changes made in the second Edition, *I.505. V.638. XI.485, 551*. These are prov'd here in the Notes, every one of them to be manifestly for the worse. And whoever allows them to be worse, and yet will contend they are the Poet's own, betrays his Ill Judgment, as well as Ill Nature. But now if the Editor durst insert his Forgeries, even in the second Edition, when the Poem and its Author had slowly grown to a vast Reputation; what durst he not do in the First, under the Poet's Poverty, Infamy, and an universal Odium from the Royal and triumphant Party? Add to this a farther Confirmation; That when *Milton* afterwards publish'd his *Paradise Regain'd* and *Samson Agonistes*; that Edition is without Faults; because He was then in high Credit, and had chang'd his old Printer and Supervisor.[7]

There's another Reflexion, which the Reader must needs make. What a wonderful Performance, will he say, was this *Paradise Lost?* that under all these Disadvantages could gradually arise and soar to a national Applause and Admiration? How many Thousands would depress and vilify the Poem, out of Hatred and Detestation of the Poet; who they thought deserv'd Hanging on a Gibbet? What native, unextinguishable Beauty must be impress'd and instincted through the Whole, which the Defoedation of so many Parts by a bad Printer and a worse Editor could not hinder from shining forth? It seems to have been in the Condition of *Terence*'s beautiful Virgin, who in spite of Neglect, Sorrow, and beggarly Habit, did yet appear so very Amiable:

> Virgo pulchra: &, quo magis diceres,
> Nihil aderat adjumenti ad pulchritudinem:
> Capillus passus, nudus pes, ipsa horrida,
> Lacrimae, vestitus turpis: ut, ni VIS BONI
> In ipsa inesset Forma, hæc Formam extinguerent.[8]

But I wonder not so much at the Poem it self, though worthy of all Wonder; as that the Author could so abstract his Thoughts from his own Troubles, as to be able to make it; that confin'd in a narrow and to Him a dark Chamber, surrounded with Cares and Fears, he could spatiate at large through the Compass of the whole Universe, and through all Heaven beyond it; could survey all Periods of Time from before the Creation to the Consummation of all Things. This Theory, no doubt, was a great Solace to him in his Affliction; but it shews in him a greater Strength of Spirit, that made him capable of such a Solace. And it would almost seem to me to be peculiar to Him; had not Experience by others taught me, That there is that Power in the Human Mind, supported with Innocence and *Conscia virtus*;[9] that can make it quite shake off all outward Uneasinesses, and involve it self secure and pleas'd in its own Integrity and Entertainment.

Nor can the Reader miss another Reflexion; How it could happen, that for above *60* Years time this Poem with such miserable Deformity of the Press, and not seldom flat Nonsense, could pass upon the whole Nation for a perfect, absolute, faultless Composition: The best Pens in the Kingdom contending in its Praises, as eclipsing all modern Essays whatever; and rivaling, if not excelling, both *Homer* and *Virgil*.[10] And it's likely, he'll resolve it into This Cause; That its Readers first accede to it, possess'd with Awe and Veneration from its universal Esteem; and have been deterr'd by That from trusting to their Judgments; and even in Places displeasing rather suspecting their own Capacity, than that any thing in the Book could possibly be amiss. Who durst oppose the universal Vogue? and risque his own Character, while he labour'd to exalt *Milton*'s? I wonder rather, that it's done even now. Had these very Notes, been written forty Years ago; it would then have been Prudence to have suppress'd them, for fear of injuring one's rising Fortune. But now when Seventy Years *jamdudum memorem monuerunt*, and spoke loudly in my Ears.

Mitte leves spes & certamina divitiarium;[11]

I made the Notes *extempore*, and put them to the Press as soon as made; without any Apprehension of growing leaner by Censures, or plumper by Commendations.

Anon.,
Milton Restor'd and Bentley Depos'd
(1732)

ADDRESSED TO DR. *BENTLEY*.

THE Liberties you have taken with MILTON, and his admirable *Work*, notwithstanding your own Confession of its having met with universal Approbation and Applause; nay, and *that even the best Pens in the Kingdom have contended in its Praises*, will sufficiently justify me in examining your Emendations and Notes, let the Reputation of Dr. *Bentley*, as a Critick, be ever so great, or well established.[1] This with respect to the World. – As to yourself, Sir, you cannot surely take it ill, that I venture on remarking on your Remarks, when You Yourself have ventured on attacking the Reputation of a Piece, which, as you say, hath been hitherto taken for perfect and faultless; and to censure the labour of so many Years, by many Observations, made as you acknowledge, *extempore,* and sent to the Press as fast as they were made.

To begin regularly, Doctor, with your Preface. In the second Paragraph you say, *Our celebrated Author, when he composed this Poem, being obnoxious to the Government, poor, friendless, and what is worst of all, blind with Gutta Serena,* &c. One would have imagined you would not have entred thus far into the Circumstances of Mr. *Milton*, without some Assurance of the Facts you mention; whether, after what I have to say, you had, or no, the World will be able to judge.

First, As to his being obnoxious to the Government, I confess, his having defended the King's Murder, and his being *Oliver*'s *Latin* Secretary, were Things not likely to recommend him to Favour on the Restoration: Yet, though he absconded at first, after the Act of Oblivion, he appeared as freely as ever; nay, when he had even composed this Work, it could not have been published without Leave, the Press being then under the Restraint of a Licenser;[2] and, if he did meet with some Difficulty in obtaining it, might it not have been occasioned by some Passages in the Book itself? As for Example, the Verses you yourself quote, *viz*.

Was fal'n on evil Days and evil Tongues, &c.

are, as I take it, no Compliment to the Administration; and yet you know a Licence was obtained.

As to his Poverty, he had been *Latin* Secretary to both the Protectors, and to the Parliament, in which Capacity, though he did not endeavour to amass a large Fortune *per fas & nefas;*[3] yet none who have pretended to give us his Memoirs, say, that he was poor or indigent; nay, were it required, I can from Circumstances prove that he lived and died without feeling any Necessities, such as are usually suffered by those the World calls poor.[4]

But, to say MILTON was friendless, Doctor, is, I venture to assert, against all Authority. We know *his Friends procured him a Pardon*; and, as the Author of his Life informs us, *having now obtained a full Protection from the Government, (which was, in Truth, more than he could reasonably hope for) he appeared as much in publick as formerly he used to do; and employing his Friend Dr.* PAGET *to make choice of a third Consort, on his Recommendation, married* Elizabeth, *the daughter of Mr.* Minshul, *a* Cheshire *Gentleman.*[5]

A Pardon from a powerful Intercession, sure Protection, publickly appearing, and marrying a Gentleman's daughter on Dr. *Paget's* recommending her; how suits this with being obnoxious to the Government, poor, and friendless? good Doctor, explain it: nay, as to the *Gutta serena*, there is some Mistake too, as I shall shew on a more proper Occasion. But, to go on with the *Preface*.

From the Poverty of the Author you next come to that of his Bookseller, who, you say, lived then near *Aldersgate*, and purchased the Copy for Ten Pounds, and Five more, if it bore a second Edition. But this poor Bookseller was Mr. *Simmons*, a Citizen of *London*, Common Council-man of his Ward, and died worth some Thousands.[6] As to the Price, that I admit, because you for once refer to Authority, *viz*. of the original Bond, and the small Sum paid by way of Copy-Money was, I suppose, the Reason you fancied both Mr. *Milton* and Mr. *Simmonds*, in so ill Circumstances. Yet sure, had you reflected on the distance of Time, which in the next Paragraph you assign from the first to the second Edition, *viz.* from 1667 to 1674; (tho' in these Dates too you are certainly mistaken)[7] you could not have thought Ten Pounds so poor a Price for a Book of this Bulk, which in seven Years had but one Impression.

As if your Preface were intended continually to surprize us, you by and by tell us *Milton* could not have so much as heard his Poem read over during this space of seven Years: And why? Because the second Edition hath all the Faults of the first, with the addition of some new ones: So that, if it had been read to him, he must have been deaf as well as blind, if he had left them to the correcting of *Doctor Bentley*. Now, whether he was so deaf, the Publick may be Judges; for, certain it is, that in the second Edition he increased the number of Books from Ten to Twelve: which, by your leave, Doctor, is somewhat against your Supposition.

Upon the reading your Preface, some, who are not better acquainted with the History of *Milton*, will certainly be led into very great Mistakes, as to the times of publishing this Poem, and its several Editions. For example, you plainly say, that the *Paradise Regain'd* and *Sampson Agonistes* were printed after the second Edition of the *Paradise Lost*; and this second Edition in express words you place, *A.D.* 1674, the very Year that Milton died: whereas, with respect to *Paradise Regained* and *Sampson Agonistes*, they were licensed the second of *July*, 1670, and published the Year following.[8] To speak ingenuously, Doctor, there are Passages enough in your Preface, to prove that whatever you may understand of the Poem, you know very little of its Author, or even of the Editions of his Work; for, 'tis certain, *Paradise Lost* was published in 1669,[9] (tho' you would have it two Years before) as you may see in the Life of *Milton* prefixed to the common Edition.

As to the vast Amendments which this celebrated Piece has received from your Hand; for my Part, I think those the most valuable which you least esteem, *viz.* your correcting the Faults in Orthography, Distinction by Points and capital Letters: these are, I confess, Services done to the Author and to the Publick; and, would to Heaven, Doctor, you had stuck here, and gone no farther. But, when you talk of rectifying Mistakes not from Manuscripts, (for of those you confess there are none existing) but by Sagacity and happy guessing, I own I pity *Milton*, and every other Author who runs the same Fate; and by falling into the Hands of a Critick, loses his own Beauties thro' the Corrector's want of Taste: who, because at first Sight, his purblind Genius finds not out his Author's Meaning, substitutes a new Reading, and by an *extempore* Rectification, blots out Beauties which have cost so much Pain and Time. As a common Dawber, when he ventures at retouching the Pictures of some eminent Master, destroyes those Excellencies which he wants Skill to know; and when he has busied his Pencil awhile about them, leaves, through his Folly, the Pieces blurr'd, which he, thro' Self-Conceit, had tried to varnish. Such Usage hath some of the most valued Classicks met with, which so hurt the Sense and Elegancy of the Writers, that the first Editions are become highly valuable, from their want of Corrections; or, as Mr. *Dryden* says,

> *Are least deformed, because reform'd the least.*
> Hind *and* Panth.[10]

Yet I believe *Milton* alone has had the hard Fate of being murder'd by an Editor in sixty Years space, and his Numbers sullied by a Grammarian, whose Trade lies in Genders, Moods, and Tenses, who cannot dispense with Excellence beyond a Rule, nor suffer a Grace to remain which is not obedient to Construction. Will not this damp the Poet's Fire? Who that reflects on the Fate of *Paradise Lost*, would venture to publish the sublimest Work for fear some future Critick should rise up, and prove a second *Bentley*?

The same Liberty may be assumed by every Reader, as by you, Doctor; and so the whole of *Milton*'s, or any other Poem, extinguished by degrees, and a new one set forth by Editors, challenge the Title not of Notes, but of a Text *variorum*. To regulate the Work of a deceased Author from various Readings in Manuscripts or printed Copies is a laborious, but useful Undertaking: But this way of restoring, *i.e.* interpolating by Guess, is so sacralegious an Intrusion, that, as it had its rise, so it is to be hoped it will have its Fall with you.

As to the Wonder you express that no-body hitherto had attempted, thro'Awe and Reverence, as you suppose, the amending *Milton*; I confess 'tis no Wonder to me: but that, after having been for so long a space admired and applauded, so much read, and so often published, you should, at last, be able to discover innumerable Faults and Blemishes hitherto undiscern'd, is, I own, no less the Object of my Astonishment than it is of yours: However, thus much I will say for your Edition; that, comparing it with that in Twelves and the Annotations annexed, Mankind may reasonably decide between the candid Critick and the petulant Carper, and thereby do justice to Dr. *Bentley* and Mr. *Addison*.[11]

[There follows a list of all Bentley's amendments to Book I of *Paradise Lost*.]

DR. *BENTLEY*'S NOTES, WITH REMARKS THEREON.

> V.6. Sing Heav'nly Muse; that on the *secret* top
> 7. Of *Horeb* or of *Sinai* didst inspire
> 8. That Shepherd, &c.   MILTON.

NOTE I.

SECRET *Valleys*, secret *Caves*, (says BENTLEY) come frequently in Poetry; but *secret top of a mountain*, visible several Leagues *off*, is only met with here. Our Poet dictated it thus; *That on the* sacred *top* Of Horeb: from *Exod*. iii.5. *Moses came to the Mountain of God, Horeb. And God said, Put off thy shoes from off thy Feet; for the place whereon thou standest is* HOLY *ground*. So our Author, V.619. VI.25. *Sacred Hill*. And *Spenser*, in his *Fairy Queen*, I.10.54; and as frequently in the Classic Writers, *Mons sacer*. Some perhaps may prefer the present Reading, *secret top*, because in most Countries the high Mountains have against rainy Weather their Heads surrounded with Mists. True; but yet it's question-able whether, in the wide and dry *Desert of Arabia, Mount *Horeb* has

---

* *potius* Desart.

such a cloudy Cap. I have in my Youth read several Itineraries, where the Travellers went up to the Top of *Horeb*; and I remember not, that they took notice of its Cloudiness. And a just Presumption lies against it from Holy Writ, *Exod.* xvii; where the *Israelites*, encamped at the foot of *Horeb*, could find no Water which was provided *mriaculously**, when *Moses* smote the Rock with his sacred Rod: for all Natural History informs us, and Reason vouches it, That a Mountain, whose Head is cloudy, has always running Springs at its Foot. But allowing all, and granting that *Horeb* was like the *European* Hills; yet no Poet hitherto has on that account said *The Secret*; but the Cloudy; Misty, Hazy, Grey-Top. Nay, allow further†, That *secret Top* is a passable Epithet; yet it is common to all Mountains whatever: but *Horeb*, whose *Ground was Holy*, Horeb the *Mountain of God*, Exod. iii.1; I Kings xix.8. deserv'd a peculiar Epithet. If therefore, (which the best Poets have adjudg'd) a proper Epithet is always preferrable to a general one; and if *secret* and *sacred* are of a near sound in Pronunciation; I have such an esteem for our Poet; that which of the two Words is the better, That, I say, was dictated by *Milton*.

REMARKS.

Parturiunt Montes![12] Was there ever read a more flagrant Specimen of genuine, dull, *Dutch*[13] Commentatorship? Our *Cambridge* Critic, 1. affirms positively, that *Milton* dictated the Epithet *Sacred* to his *Amanuensis*, not *Secret*. 2. To prove this, he cites *Exod.* iii.5. a Passage from our Author; another from *Spenser*, and the *Mons Sacer* of the Classic Writers. 3. Tells a *Cock* and *Bull* Story of high Mountains, whose Heads are surrounded with Mists and *cloudy Caps*, but believes Mount *Horeb* to be *bald-pated*. 4. Informs us, that he was a mighty Reader of Books of *Travels*, *alias* Itineraries in his Youth; wherein he found that all Mountains, whose *Heads* were cloudy, had running Springs at their Feet. 4. He next gives us choice of Epithets for

---

* *potius* miraculously.
† *potius* farther.

Mountains, such as *Cloudy, Misty, Hazy* and *Grey*-topp'd ones; but never heard of *Secret Top* us'd by any poet but *Milton*: tho' he not only allows it to be a passable Epithet but common to all Mountains whatever. 5. He will have it, that Mount *Horeb*, deserves a peculiar Epithet, and that a *proper* one is preferrable to a *general* one. 6. He recants, and gives up his own Cause, confessing, that whichsoever of the two Epithets *Secret* and *Sacred* is the better, that he gives his *Ipse dixit* was dictated by *Milton*.

I join in the same Opinion with him, and declare Secret to be the best Epithet not only because I am sure *Milton* chose it, but for the Reason why he chose it, which did not any ways relate to the *Top* of Mount *Horeb*, but to the *Secret* Conference held between *God* and *Moses* on the Top of that Mountain.[14]

NOTE II.

V.13. *Invoke thy Aid to my adventurous Song.*

Some Aquaintance of our Poet's, entrusted with his Copy, took strange Liberties with it, unknown to the blind Author, as will further appear hereafter. 'Tis very odd, that in V.13. *viz.*

Things unattempted in Prose or Rime.

Milton should not put *Rime* here as equivalent to *Verse*, who had just declared against *Rime*, as *no true Ornament to good Verse, but the Invention of a barbarous Age, to set off wicked Matter and lame Metre*, I am persuaded, this Passage was given thus: (Ver. 13. 14. 15. 16.)

> *Invoke thy Aid to my adventurous* Wing,
> *That with no middle Flight intends to soar,*
> *Above th'Aonian Mount while I* pursue
> *Things unattempted yet in Prose or* Song.

Let's examine the particulars: WING, the properest here of all Metaphors, which is justified and prov'd by the following Words *Flight* and *Soar*.

So III.13.

> *Thee I revisit now with* bolder Wing.

And IX.45.

> *Damp my intended* Wing.

nor let it be objected; that in the IXth the Wing is *intended* by the Poet, but here the Wing itself *intends*. For that is an allow'd Figure, and frequent in the best Writers. So II.727.

> *O Father what* intends *thy* Hand, *she cried,*

And 738.

> *That my sudden* Hand
> *Prevented spares* to tell *thee yet by Deeds,*
> *What it* intends

B.I. V.15. *While it pursues.*] The Author I believe, gave it in the first Person. *While* I Pursue, as III.15.

> while *in my* Hight I sung of *Chaos*

V.16. In Prose or *Rime,*] The Author gave it.

> *Things unattempted yet in Prose or* SONG.

But the 13th Verse being once chang'd into *Adventrous* SONG, that Word could not be here repeated; and so for *Song* was substituted RIME. It may be said he took *Rime* from *Ariosto*, Cant. I.

> *Cosa, non detta in* PROSA *mai, ne in* RIMA.[15]

But *Ariosto*'s Poem is in *Rime*, *Milton*'s neither in *Rime* nor *Prose*: So that this Argument is even *yet unattempted* in either of them. But it's V.150.

> *Flow'd from their Lips* in Prose *or numerous* Verse:

and in the *Mask* one of his *Juvenile* Poems;

> *For I will tell you now*
> *What never yet was heard in* Tale *or* Song.[16]

REMARKS.

Risum teneatis Amici?[17] Here is a *Croud* of *Witnesses* with cloudy Caps on, as the Dr. observes of the Eastern Mountains, but not *one Evidence* to prove a single Fact. Our Philologist metes the same Measure to MILTON that he did to HORACE, *scripsit aut scripsisse debuit.*[18] He either *dictated* or *should have dictated*, thus – *aid my Adventrous* WING. It may be chang'd with equal propriety, *aid my Adventrous* LEG, because the Muse can no more soar without *Legs* than without *Wings*.

NOTE III.

V.28. *Nor the deep* Tract *of Hell.*] *Tract* is properly not a deep, to hide from view; but a plain expanded Surface, exposed to view;

> *Terrasque* tractusque maris, *coelumque profundum.*[19]

Better therefore, *Nor the deep* GULPH *of Hell.* So II.12.

> *For since no* Deep *within her* Gulph *can hold*
> *Immortal Vigour:*

And often besides.

REMARKS.

TRACT you say is not properly *Deep*. True, Doctor, but yet there may be *deep Tracts*; as if you travel into *Sussex*, you may find *deep roads*, tho' *Road* does not signify *deep* any more than *Tract*. I readily grant you, that *Gulph* may be read there; the Emendation (if it be one) is obvious, so obvious, that if *John Bunyan* had wrote this Poem, I am confident he would not have stood in need of half so many Corrections from you, learned Doctor, as *John Milton*, who, if he thought fit to dictate it so, it has certainly a Right to remain so, notwithstanding your *better therefore*; which, to shew you my Skill at Interpolation, I affirm may be *better'd thus*:

> *Say first, for Heaven, hides nothing from thy view,*
> *Nor the* vast Depth *of Hell:*

And at this rate may you and I go on to *better* and *better Milton*, till we make him *worse* and *worse*.

NOTE IV.

V.33. *Who first seduc'd them to that foul Revolt?*
The infernal Serpent:] This you say is a manifest imitation of *Homer.*[20] I confess I think the Passage you quote might occur to our Poet's Mind: had, therefore, your Notes been always like this, I should not have thought *Milton* stood in need of a Restorer.

NOTE V.

V.35. *Deceiv'd* The *Mother of Mankind.*] I believe the Author spoke it thus, in Address to *Eve*, which will raise the Sense;

> *Deceiv'd*
> Thee, *Mother of Mankind.*

REMARKS.

WHAT a prodigious Man is Dr. *Bentley*! He corrects the Numbers of *Horace*! and raises the Sense of *Milton*!

NOTE VI.

V.39. *To set himself in Glory above his Peers*] Our Poet had not at first so settled his whole Scheme, as to be uniform and self-consistent in all its Parts. *Satan*'s Crime was not to aim above *his Peers*: God himself had placed him above them, as *Abdiel* the good Angel says to Satan. V.812.

> *Ingrate,*
> *In Place thyself so high above thy* Peers.

His Ambition was to be above the *Messiah*, as it is at large shewn in the Sequel. Put it therefore thus:

> *Aspiring*
> *To Place and Glory above the Son of God.*

So V.662.

> Satan *fraught*
> *With Envy against the* Son, &c.

Aspiring to a Throne is a juster Phrase than *aspiring to set one's self on a Throne.*

REMARKS.

IT is, methinks, the highest Presumption in Dr. *Bentley* to affirm of *Milton*, That his whole Scheme was not uniform and self-consistent in its Parts. I am confident, that every attentive Reader will be able to understand the Poet's Meaning, when he says of SATAN, that

> with all his Host
> Of rebel Angels; by whose Aid aspiring
> *To set himself in Glory above his Peers,*
> He trusted to have equall'd the Most High,

Which, as I apprehend, means plainly aspiring to rise by Force to a

Dominion over *Spirits* in their Nature his *Peers*; and thereby equalling in Power God himself: who, should he oppose, his Ambition tempts him to raise an impious War against his Throne: As the Poet tells us he did in the very next Line.

NOTE VII.

V.46. *With hideous ruin and* combustion *down.*] Having said in Verse before, *Hurl'd headlong* FLAMING; he superfluously adds *Combustion*. But I doubt not, he gave it thus,

> *With hideous ruin and* CONFUSION *down.*

So II.995. spoken of the same Event;

> *With* ruin *upon ruin, rout on rout,*
> Confusion *worse confounded.*

REMARKS.

Whoever has read any thing relating to *Milton*, and this his admirable Performance, cannot but have heard, that, in order to preserve the Majesty of his Verse, our Poet had often Recourse to old and seldom used Words, instead of ordinary and vulgar Expressions; this alone will prove to a candid Reader, that *Milton* dictated as it is in the Text.

> *With hideous ruin and* COMBUSTION *down,*

especially if he reflect that this is much more nervous and poetick than *Bentley*'s mean creeping Epithet, in as much as it expresses *Burning* and *Confusion* too.

NOTE VIII.

V.52. *Lay vanquish'd.*] *Vanquish'd* is too low a Word for the Occasion. They were more than vanquish'd even while in Heaven, V.1.851.

> *Of their vigour drain'd,*
> *Exhausted, spiritless, afflicted, fallen.*

Our Author gave it Lay STONISH'D. *Stonish'd, stonied, stounded, stunn'd,* common in the Elder Poets. So here

> V.266.   *Lie thus* astonish'd *on th'oblivious Pool.*
> 281.   *As we erewhile* astounded *and amaz'd.*

And in the Argument: *Satan with his Angels lying* on *the burning Lake, Thunder-struck and* astonish'd.

REMARKS.

I Confess I am so stonish'd, stonied, and stunn'd with the Arrogance and Impertinence of the Doctor's Emendations, that I have scarce patience to read them. *Milton* the most elevated Writer our Nation boasts of, makes use of low Words, in the Opinion of this Critick; who, like a Corrector to the Press, never looks on his Author but to spy his Faults. Let us see if the Likeness holds any farther, that is, whether our Editor hath here mended a Fault, or made it. I am obliged to cite the Context, and then the Doctor's acute Genius in cavilling will easily be discerned.

> *he with his horrid crew*
> Lay vanquish'd, *rolling in the fiery Gulph,*
> Confounded, *tho' immortal.*

A Note before *Combustion* was to be struck out, because too near *flaming*; now *stonish'd* is to be put in, because 'tis the same with *confounded*. Are not these strain'd Corrections! I cannot, however, pass by the Doctor's Method here, and elsewhere, of citing *Milton's* Verses, to prove his use of the Epithet he would interpolate, but what does this prove? Nothing, but that he knew how to apply them properly; and makes not any way for the Doctor; unless, in Imitation of *Homer*'s *Cloud-compelling Jove*, he would have *Milton* invariable in his Epithets. But this 52d. is sure an unhappy Line; in seven Words two Notes and two Emendations.

NOTE IX.

Ibid. *Rolling in the fiery Gulph.*] The Poet gave it

Rolling on *the fiery Gulph.*

As it was twice quoted already. So V.195.

His other parts behind prone on *the Flood.*

V.210.   *Chain'd* on *the burning Lake.*
V.280.   *Groveling and prostrate* on *yon Lake of Fire.*

REMARKS.

I Confess I care not to dwell on such an Emendation as ON for IN. I shall, therefore, only say, that, considering the immense space thro' which Satan fell, he might easily be conceived to roll *in* the fiery Gulph, *i.e.* immers'd *in* it.

NOTE X.

V.54.   *But now the* thought
Both of lost Happiness and lasting Pain
Torments *him.*]

The Thought of *Happiness*, and then the Thought of *Pain*, are not One, but Two; so that it's probable *Milton* gave it in the Plural, *The Thoughts torment him.*

REMARKS.

So that it's probable *Milton* gave it, is a Prodigy of Modesty in Dr. *Bentley*; and therefore I shall only say, that, as it is more poetical to refer the Verb to each of the Nominatives; that is, as if it had been the *Thought of lost Happiness torments him, and the Thought of lasting Pain torments him.* To me, therefore, it seems more probable, that *Milton* gave it as it stands.

NOTE XI.

V.63. *No Light, but rather Darkness visible.*] *Darkness visible* and *Darkness palpable* are in due Place very good Expressions: but the next Line makes *visible* here a flat Contradiction. Darkness visible will not serve to *discover sights of Woe* thro' it, but to cover and hide them. Nothing is visible to the Eye but so far as it is opake, and not seer through; not by transmitting the Rays, but by reflecting them back. To come up to the Author's Idea, we may say thus,

No Light, but rather a TRANSPICUOUS GLOOM.

Gloom is equivalent to Darkness; yet so as to be in some measure *transparent.*

So here,

v.544.	*All in a Moment through the Gloom were seen.*
v.244.	*This mournful* Gloom
	For that cœlestial Light.
II.858.	*Into this* Gloom *of* Tartarus *profound.*
VIII.11.	*Through the wide* transpicuous *Air.*

REMARKS.

IF there were really any Darkness in this Passage, I am sure the Doctor has not rendred it visible by his Note upon it. What *Milton* says is this,

> A Dungeon horrible on all sides round
> As one great furnace, flam'd: yet from those flames
> No Light, but rather *Darkness visible*
> Serv'd only to discover sights of Woe.

I believe the Poet's Meaning, however bold his Expression may be, will be readily apprehended by his Readers. But for *transpicuous Gloom*, equivalent to Darkness, and yet *transparent*, I confess it is to me much more obscure than any thing I have met with in *Milton*.

NOTE XII.

V.72. *In* utter *Darkness, As far remov'd from God.*] *Utter Darkness* is absolute Darkness, and gives no notion of Place or Remoteness. The Poet, therefore, gave it OUTER *Darkness*, as in Scripture.

> So III.16, read,
> *Through* outer *and through* middle *Darkness born.*

REMARKS.

HERE is another dark Note upon *utter Darkness*, which, when the Doctor had Wit enough to know meant absolute Darkness, I am surprized he should want to substitute OUTER in its room. God is call'd the Spring of *Light*; the Scripture mentions the *Light* of his Countenance, *&c.* and therefore *utter Darkness* expresseth a vast Distance from the DEITY, in whose Presence it were not possible: so that the Expression of *Milton* is perfectly consistent, as it is also exceedingly bold and truly sublime.

David Mallet,

Of Verbal Criticism: An Epistle to Mr. Pope.
Occasioned by Theobald's Shakespear,
and Bentley's Milton.

(1733)

AMONG the numerous Fools, by fate design'd
Oft to disturb, and oft divert mankind,
The *Reading Coxcomb* is of special note,
By rule a Poet, and a Judge by rote;
Grave Son of idle Industry and Pride,
Whom learning but perverts, and books misguide.
    O fam'd for judging, as for writing well,[1]
That rarest science where so few excel;
Whose life, severely scan'd, transcends thy lays,
For wit supreme is but thy second Praise;
'Tis thine, O *POPE*, who chuse the better part,
To tell how false, how vain the *Scholiast*'s Art,
Which nor to taste, nor genius has pretence,
And if 'tis learning, is not common sense.[2]
    See, in the darkness of dull Authors bred,
With all their refuse lumber'd in his head,
Long years consum'd, large volumes daily turn'd,
And *Servius* read perhaps, while *Maro* burn'd,
In error obstinate, in wrangling loud,
Unbred, unsocial, positive, and proud;
Forth steps at last the self-applauding *Wight*,
Of points and letters, chaff and straws, to write:
Sagely resolv'd to swell each bulky piece
With venerable toys, from *Rome* and *Greece*;
How oft, in *Homer*, *Paris* curl'd his Hair;
If *Aristotle*'s Cap were round or square;

If in the Cave where *Dido* first was sped,
To *Tyre* she turn'd her Heels, to *Troy* her head.[3]
    Such the choice Anecdotes, profound and vain,
30   That store a *Bentley*'s and a *Burman*'s brain:
Hence *Plato* quoted, or the *Stagyrite*,[4]
To prove that flame ascends, and snow is white:
Hence much hard study without sense or breeding,
And all the grave impertinence of reading.
If *Shakespear* says, the noon-day sun is bright,
His *Scholiast* will *remark*, it then was light;
Turn *Caxton*, *Winkin*,[5] each old *Goth* and *Hun*,
To rectify the reading of a *pun*.
Thus, nicely trifling, accurately dull,
40   How one may toil, and toil – to be a fool!
    But is there then no honour due to age?
No Reverence to great *Shakespear*'s noble page?
And he, who half a life has read him o'er,
His mangled points and commas to restore,
Meets he such slight regard in nameless lays,
Whom *Bufo*[6] treats, and Lady *Wou'd be* pays?
    Shakespear each passion drew in every dress,
Bold to design, and powerful to express;
Great above rule, and imitating none;
50   Rich without borrowing, nature was his own.
Yet is his sense debas'd by gross allay:
As Gold in mines lyes mix'd with dirt and clay.
Now, eagle-wing'd, his heavenward flight he takes;
The big stage thunders, and the soul awakes:
Now, low on earth, a kindred reptile creeps;
Othello quibbles, and the hearer sleeps.
    Such was the Poet: Next the Scholiast view;
Faint tho' the coloring, yet the features true.
    Condemn'd to dig and dung a barren soil,
60   Where hardly tares will grow with care and toil,
He, with low industry, goes gleaning on
From good, from bad, from mean, neglecting none;

His brother book-worm so, in shelf or stall,
Will feed alike on *Woolston* and on *Paul*.
See him on *Shakespear* pore, intent to steal
Poor farce, by fragments, for a third-day meal.
Such that grave *Bird* in northern seas is found,
Whose name a *Dutchman* only knows to sound:
Where-e'er the King of fish moves on before,
70 This humble friend attends from shore to shore;
His eyes still earnest, and his Bill declin'd,
He picks up what his patron drops behind,
With those choice cates his palate to regale,
And is the careful *Tibbald*[7] of a whale.†

   Blest Genius! who bestows his oil and pains
On each dull passage, each dull book contains;
The toil more grateful, as the task more low:
So Carrion is the quarry of a Crow.
Where his fam'd Author's page is flat and poor,
80 There most exact the reading to restore;
By dint of plodding, and by sweat of face,
A bull[8] to change, a blunder to replace:
Whate'er is refuse critically gleaning,
And mending nonsense into doubtful meaning.
For this, dread *Dennis* (* and who can forbear,‡
Dunce or not dunce, relating it, to stare?)
His head tho' jealous, and his years fourscore,
Even *Dennis* praises, who ne'er prais'd before!§
For this, the Scholiast claims his share of fame,
90 And, modest, prints his own with *Shakespear*'s name.

---

† V.74. This remarkable bird is called the *Strundt-Jager*. Here you see how he purchases his *Food*: And the same Author, from whom this account is taken, tells us farther how he comes by his *Drink*. You may see him, adds the *Dutchman*, frequently pursuing a sort of seamew called *Kutge-Gehef*, whom he torments incessantly to make him void an Excrement; which being liquid, serves him, I imagine, for *Drink*. See *a Collection of Voyages to the North*.

‡ V.85. — * *Quis talia fando*
     Myrmidonum, Dolopumve, &c.[9] —   Virg.

§ V.88. See the Dedication of his Remarks on the *Dunciad* to Mr. *Lewis Theobald*.

How justly? POPE, in this short Story view,
Which may be dull, and therefore should be true.
A Prelate, fam'd for clearing each dark text,
Who sense with sound, and truth with rhetoric mixt,
Once, as his moving theme to rapture warm'd,
Inspir'd himself, his happy hearers charm'd.
The sermon o'er, the crowd remain'd behind,
And freely, man or woman, spoke their mind:
All said they lik'd the Lecture from their soul,
And each, remembring something, prais'd the whole.
At last an honest Sexton join'd the throng;
(For as the theme was large, their talk was long)
Neighbours, he cry'd, my Conscience bids me tell,
Tho' 'twas the Doctor preach'd, – I toll'd the bell.

   In this the Critic's folly most is shown;
Is there a Genius all unlike his own,[10]
With learning elegant, with wit well bred;[11]
Himself perplex'd, and dark, and thick of head:
That Writer he selects, in hobbling strain
His air to ape, his beauties to explain.
So *Florio* is a fop, with half a nose:
So fat West-Indian Planters mimic Beaus.
Thus gay *Petronius* was a *Dutchman*'s choice,†
And *Horace*, strange to say, tun'd *Bentley*'s voice.[12]

   Horace, who form'd in palaces to please,
Mix'd mirth with morals, eloquence with ease;
His genius social, as his judgment clear,
When frolic, prudent; smiling when severe;
Secure each temper, and each taste to hit,
His was the curious happiness of wit:
Skill'd in that noblest Science, *how to live*,
Which learning may direct, but heaven *must* give;
Grave with *Agrippa*, with *Mecenas* gay;
Among the Fair, but just as wise as they;

100

110

120

† V.114. See his Poem to my Lord *Hallifax* before his Edition of *Horace*.

First in the friendships of the Great enroll'd,
The *St. Johns*, *Talbots*, and the *Boyles*, of old.

　　While *Bentley*, long to wrangling schools confin'd,
And but by books acquainted with mankind,
Dares, in the fulness of the Pedant's pride,

130　Rhime tho' no genius, tho' no judge decide.
Yet he, prime pattern of the captious art,
Out-tibbalding poor *Tibbald*, tops his part;
Holds high the scourge o'er each fam'd Author's head,
Nor are their graves a refuge for the Dead.
To *Milton* lending sense, to *Horace* wit,
He makes 'em write what never Poet writ:[13]
The *Roman Muse* arraigns his mangling pen,
And *Paradise*, by him, is *lost* agen.†
Such was his doom impos'd by Heaven's decree,

140　With ears that hear not, eyes that shall not see,
The Low to raise, to level the Sublime,
To blast all Beauty, and beprose all Rhyme.
Great eldest born of Dulness, blind and bold!
Tyrant! more cruel than *Procrustes* old;[14]
Who to his iron bed, by torture fits
Their nobler part, the souls of suffering Wits.

　　Such is the Man, who heaps his head with bays,
And calls on human kind to sound his praise,
For points transplac'd with curious want of skill,

150　For alter'd sounds, and sense amended ill.
So wise *Caligula*, in days of yore,
His helmet fill'd with pebbles on the shore,
Swore he had rifled ocean's richest spoils,
And claim'd a trophy for his martial toils.[15]

---

† V.138. This sagacious Scholiast is pleased to create an imaginary Editor of *Milton*; who, he says, by his blunders, interpolations, and vile alterations, lost *Paradise* a second time. This is a *postulatum* which surely none of his readers can have the heart to deny him; because otherwise he would have wanted a fair opportunity of calling *Milton* himself, in the person of this phantom, fool, ignorant, ideot, and the like critical compellations, which he plentifully bestows on him.

Yet be his merits, with his faults, confest:
Fair-dealing, as the plainest, is the best.
Long lay the *Critic*'s work, with trifles stor'd,
Admir'd in *Latin*, but in *Greek* ador'd:
Men, so well read, who confidently wrote,
160   Their readers could have sworn, were Men of note.
To pass upon the croud for Great or Rare,
Aim not to make 'em knowing, make 'em stare.
For these blind Votaries good *Bentley* griev'd,
Writ *English* Notes – and mankind undeceiv'd:
In such clear light the serious Folly plac'd,
Lords, or their Ladies, now may see the jest.

But what can cure our vanity of mind,
Deaf to reproof, and to discovery blind?
Let *Cooke*, a Brother-Scholiast *Shakespear* call,
170   *Tibbald*, to *Hesiod-Cooke* returns the ball.
So runs the circle still: in this, we see
The Lackies of the Great, and Learn'd agree.
If *Britain*'s Nobles mix in high debate,
Whence *Europe* in suspense attends her fate;
In mimic Session their gay Footmen meet,
Reduce an Army, or equip a Fleet,
And rivaling the Critic's lofty stile,
Mere *Tom* and *Dick* are *Carteret* and *Argyll*.
Yet those, whom pride and dulness join to blind,
180   To narrow cares in narrow space confin'd,
Tho' with big titles each his fellow greets,
Are but to Wits, as Scavengers to streets:
The humble Black-guards of a *Pope* or *Gay*,
To brush off dust, and wipe their spots away.

Or if not trivial, harmful is their art;
Fume to the head, or poison to the heart.
Where antient Authors hint at things obscene,
The Scholiast speaks out broadly what they mean.
Disclosing each dark vice, well-lost to fame,
190   And adding fewel to redundant flame,

He, sober pimp to Lechery, explains
What *Capreæ*'s *Isle*,[16] or *'s *Alcove* contains;
Why *Paulus*, for his sordid temper known,
Was lavish to a Stepmother alone;
Why those fond female Visits duly paid
To tuneful *Incuba*; and what her *Trade*;
How modern Love has made so many martyrs,
And which *keeps* oftenest, Lady *, or *Chartres*.[17]
    But who their various follies can explain?

200 The tale is infinite, the task were vain.
'Twere to read New-year Odes in search of thought;
To sum the Libels *O**** has wrote;
To guess, ere *One Epistle* saw the light,†
How many brother-dunces club'd their mite;
To vouch for truth what *W*** prints of *Pope*,
Or from *C****'s pleadings steal a Trope.
That be the Part of persevering *W**,‡
With Pen of lead; or, *A***, thine of brass;
A Text for *H***, or a Gloss for *H**,

210 Who loves to teach, what no man cares to learn.[18]
    How little Knowledge reaps from toils like these!
Too doubtful to direct, too poor to please,
Yet, Critics, would your tribe deserve a name,
And nobly useful, rise to honest fame;
First, from the head, a load of lumber move,
And from the Volume, all yourselves approve;
For patch'd and pilfer'd Fragments, give us Sense,
Or Learning, clear from learn'd Impertinence,
Where moral meaning or where taste presides,

220 And Wit enlivens but what Reason guides:

---

† V.203. See a Poem published some time ago under that title, said to be the production of several ingenious and prolific heads; One contributing a simile, Another a character, and a certain Gentleman four shrewd lines wholly made up of Asterisks.

‡ V.207. See the preface to his edition of *Sallust*; and read, if you are able, the Scholia of sixteen Annotators by him collected, besides his own.

Great without swelling, without meanness plain,
Serious, not simple, sportive but not vain;
On Trifles slight, on things of use profound,
In quoting sober, and in judging sound.

The END.

Jonathan Richardson,
Selections from *Explanatory Notes and Remarks on Milton's Paradise Lost*
(1734)

If I can give a more Exact, and a more Just Idea of *Milton*, and of *Paradise Lost* than the Publick has yet had of Either, I am Assur'd it will be Acceptable to all Honest and Ingenuous Minds of What Party Soever. This is All I Intend; not a Panegyrick, not to give my Own Sense of What a Man should be, but what This Man Really was. Not to Plead for the Poet, or the Poem, but for Truth, by giving Light into What hath Hitherto lain in Obscurity, and by Dispelling Mistakes which have Injur'd the Memory of a Deserving Man, Debas'd a Work Worthy of the Highest Estimation, and Robb'd the World of the Pleasure and Advantage it Might have Receiv'd, and I presume to Hope Will Hereafter Receive. This is My Aim in the Present Undertaking [p. i].

Some of his most Particular and Distinguish'd Good Qualities I have Noted, but a General Love of Vertue appears throughout the whole Course of his Life. . . . What *Milton* meant by Vertue is what All should mean by it, a Constant, Uniform, Universal Regularity of Manners. *Vertue that Wavers is not Vertue, but Vice Revolted from it self, and after a While returning.*[1] These are his own Words. but of This More hereafter. for I fear it will be to little Purpose if I proceed on *Milton*'s Moral or Religious, 'till I have quenched or abated the Prejudices of Most of my Readers with Regard to his Political Character. 'tis Certain he was a Republican: So was *Cato*, So was *Brutus*, So was *Phocion*, *Aristides*. – Such were by Much the Most of the Greatest Names of Roman and Greek Antiquity. We have none of These Prejudices against Them, but Admire, and are Delighted with their Abilities and Vertues; and, if we are Wise and Good Our Selves, will become Wiser and Better by their Example notwithstanding they were Republicans, and Did, or Encourag'd the Doing, what We who happen to possess Other Notions of Government would Abhor to Think of. in Judging of a particular Man, let us Consider him as an Individual of the Species, as a Rational Creature, not as of any Particular Country, or as having had his small Portion of Being in whatsoever Point of the Vast Circle of Eternity. We all judge Thus when we Read *Plutarch*; Reading Mee alters not the Case in That; or if we cannot Intirely divest our Selves of all Kind of Prejudices; if we find a Byas towards a Greek or Roman upon Account of the Great Idea we have of Those People, let our own Country-man have a Share of our Partiality; and Consider *Milton* as a *Briton, and a Brave One too*, and One who sacrific'd More than Most of us will Care to do, and Ventur'd Still More in the Cause of Civil and Religious Liberty, as He thought, though upon Principles, and in a Manner, as You and I are Far from Approving. be That to God and his Own Conscience [pp. xvi–xix].

a Man that Practises Severity on Himself in an Exact Observation of Vertue's Commands, finds himself Obliged by those very Laws to Exact a like Obedience from All under his Care. I have Heard, and do Believe, and Allow, *Milton*'s Family was a Well Order'd Government; Licentiousness was not Permitted by Him: he could be a Rigid Monarch Here with a good Grace; he could require Vertue, Frugality, and Strict Discipline (which Women and Children fail not to call Severity) as he Bravely Led the Way, by being an Example, and Able moreover to Stand a Retrospect into his Own Behaviour when Young, and through all the Stages of Life. and Happy would it be if in these little Patriarchal Monarchies the Subjects would Obey Such Laws, Rigid though they may Seem to be to Green Years, or Green Minds; it would be Happiness to Themselves More than to their Governors, Otherwise than as *Rejoycing in Their Joy*[2] [pp. xxx–xxxi].

My Other Delightful Task [i.e. in addition to relating the life and character of Milton] remains; 'tis to give the History of *Paradise Lost*, and Some Idea of it [p. cvi].

Whatever preparations he had made, it seems Probable, he set not about the Work in good Earnest 'till after the Restauration. the

Beginning of the IXth Book gives Grounds for This Conjecture. the Subject he was *Long Choosing and Beginning Late*: he Apprehends his Vigour is Decay'd by Years, or that the Cold Climate may Affect him too much, So Entring on his VIIth Book, he Complains he is *fall'n on Evil Dayes and Evil Tongues, compast round with Dangers*,[3] &c. an Exact Description of This time according to Him, though So Gay and Happy to the Nation in General. . . .

How had that Man, *Milton*, the Courage to Undertake, and the Resolution to Persist in Such a Work with the Load of Such Difficulties upon his Shoulders! Ill Health, Blindness; Uneasy in his Mind, no doubt, on Occasion of the publick Affairs, and of his Own; not in Circumstances to maintain an Amanuensis, but Himself Oblig'd to teach a Couple of Girls (or as Some say One) to Read Several Languages, and to Pronounce them, so as not to be Grievous to an Ear as Delicate as His, or even to be Intelligible. to be perpetually Asking One Friend or Another who Visited him to Write a Quantity of Verses he had ready in his Mind, or what should Then occur. . . . He Undertook the Work, and was Equal to it.

For the truth is, though he was in Some respects in a Disadvantageous Situation for Such an Enterprize, in Others he had Peculiar Encouragements. That Inexhaustible Fund of Learning in all the Languages in which Science is deposited, particularly what relates to Poetry; a most Intimate Knowledge of All the Poets worthy his Notice, Ancient or Modern; Chiefly the Best, and above All *Homer*; nor will I forbear to say the Scripture,[4] Infinitely Superiour to *Homer*, as in Other respects, so in its being a Treasure of the Sublimest Poetry. More even than All This, and without Which All his Other Great Talents had been of no Avail on This Occasion, he Possess'd the Soul of Poetry, the Soul of a Poet of the First and Purest Ages, with the Additional Advantages of Later Times; Chiefly of Christianity. And yet to All This the vast Amusement and Pleasure it must be to Him Amidst his Difficulties and Distresses to have the Noblest Ideas continually making his Imagination a Scene of Happiness; the Hope of Fame, in the Accomplishment of what had been from his Youth Resolv'd on as the Great Work of his Whole Life, that Great Fruit of all his Laborious

Studies; which Work Compar'd with all that he did Else, all Those however Esteem'd by All Men of Taste at Home and Abroad, were but as if done with his *Left hand*; 'tis his own Expression[5] [pp. cx–cxiii].

Thus, what by One means, what by Another, and Those Complicated and Manag'd as Providence well Can, This Poem, this *Waste Paper*, (like an Acorn Hid and Lost) has, by its Inherent Life, and a Little Cultivation, Sprung Out of the Earth, Lifted up its Head and Spread its Branches, a Noble Oak; has become a Richer Treasure to the World than it has receiv'd from Most of Those Names which Glitter in the Records of Time.

Who would have Imagin'd Now that *Milton*'s *Paradise Lost* was not Yet Safe! 'tis in our Possession indeed in Many Editions, but *Milton*'s Blindness and Other Disadvantages has Occasion'd Suggestions and Assertions that we have it not as the Author *gave* it, but as Corrupted by Presumption, Folly, Carelessness, and I know not What. Presumption, Folly, or Somthing Worse, has been at Work, in Suggesting, or Believing Such things, which is the more Dangerous because founded on a Specious Probability, which Commonly Cheats Us, Few having the Opportunity, or the Skill to Distinguish between Probability and Truth; and Fewer yet that are not too Lazy to Examine with that Degree of Care and Pains which Truth will Demand. Persuasion is Cheaper come at by Probability [pp. cxxi–cxxii].

What has been alledg'd as probabilities, appears in Fact to be Certain. That the Original MS. was of the Hand-Writing of Several is Agreed, but does That appear by the Printed Book? Nothing Less; 'tis Uniform Throughout: it must have Then been Revis'd and Corrected by Some One, Directed at least. and that This was *Milton* himself is Evident by its Exact Conformity with his Spelling and Pointing in What he Publish'd when he had his Sight; as also with his Other Works after That was gone. for full Satisfaction, Those that please may have recourse to Those Works, the Original Editions, for They are to be had. in the Mean time if they will give Me Credit, they will be Assured, that not only the Printing is Equally Accurate with what is to be found in Any of them, but 'tis rather More So than in most of the rest. as indeed 'tis of more Importance, that it should be Just Here than in Any of his Other Works, as 'tis his Principal One, and That in which even the Points Direct and Determine the Sense most Often and most Remarkably. We have found, in Several Instances, that what seem'd at first Sight to be the True One, was far Inferiour to what was indeed So, but would not have been Discover'd, unless by following Those Guides, Almost Universally Faithful [p. cxxix].

And not only we have the Genuine Work as much as can be Hop'd for from Printing, Why not as from Any Manuscript can be Expected? since such a Number of Verses, Written and Corrected by a very Careful Man, with his own Hand, will go off with Some Faults, and I think Rarely without as Many, and as Material as in the Edition I am speaking of; I know of None, but Here and There a Point, and perhaps I am Somtimes Mistaken in Those I think are Wrong, . . . how Easily These Faults might be Committed by the Printer, and the most Exact Authors with *Lynxes* Eyes, I leave the Reader to judge; and then Whether This Book affords any Pretence or Excuse to a New Editor, who shall Dare to Change though it were with the Utmost Deliberation, and Taste. He may indeed Honestly Say Thus and Thus the Author Should have Thought or Said, but let him not Palm Himself upon us as a Genuine *Milton* [p. cxxxv].

Every Author has a Right to say What a Lady said to a Painter (not to Me upon my Word) when She Observ'd him, under Pretence of Complimenting her, making a Face for her which She had not been Acquainted with. *Sir,* (says She) *I see what you are about, You don't like my Face, and are for giving me a Better in the Stead of it. I'd have you to know My Face is as Good as Any You will make, let me have That if you Can, but I will have no Other, nor Other do my Friends Desire.* If any Author could put his Head out of his Grave, and say Thus to an Editor, *Milton* might, and he may say it as justly as the most Beautiful Woman Alive, were She Sitting for her Picture to the Best Painter in the World. But when conceited Daubers, though they have seen All that *Italy* is Adorn'd with, when Such as have neither *Pittoresque* Eyes, nor Hands, Pretending to Excel Beauty, show us a Monster instead of an Angel, who can have Patience? if a Like Attempt is made upon an Admir'd Poetical Work, Who can forbear saying, *Pray you Sir, no more of your Patches in a*

Poem quite Elevated above Your Reach and Imitation? Such Kind of People as These were in Ancient times as Now, and are well Describ'd by Him who says, *As a Madman who casteth Firebrands, Arrows, and Death, So is the Man that Deceiveth his Neighbour, and saith, Am I not in Sport?*[6]

in a word, as *Milton*'s Care in This Matter is not to be doubted, nor his Ability and Opportunity to Prevent the Corruption Pretended, or to Detect any Such, had it been Attempted (for Fact, as well as Probability is on Our Side) Whatsoever Suggestion or Assertion, in Jest or in Earnest, concerning Some Unknown, Pragmatical, or Rascally Editor has been flung out, 'tis spilt on the Ground, and Stinks in the Nostrils of all who have a right Sense of the Veneration due to the Ashes of an Excellent Writer and a Good Man, and to Good Nature, Good Manners, Truth and Justice. but they shall not hurt the Book, That, and its Author are safe. So – *Go thy Ways, the Flour and Quintessence of all Editors.* the Edition of 1674 is the Finish'd, the Genuine, the Uncorrupted Work of *John Milton* [pp. cxxxvii–cxxxviii].

It will seem Strange to Those who do Me the Honour to Entertain themselves with what I Offer them, when they find Me remarking on the Greek and Latin Writers, whose Languages I have Acknowledg'd my Self not to Understand. My Time of Learning was Employ'd in Business. but after All, I Have the Greek and Latin Tongues, I have them because a Part of Me Possesses them to Whom I can recur at Pleasure, just as I have a Hand when I would Write or Paint, Feet to Walk, and Eyes to See. My Son[7] is my Learning, as I am That to Him which He has Not; We make One Man; and Such a Compound Man (what Sort of One Soever He is whom We make) May Probably, produce what no Single Man Can. When therefore I, in my Own Person talk of Things which in my Separate Capacity I am known to be a Stranger to, let Me be Understood as the Complicated *Richardson*. 'Twas Necessary to Say This as having Engag'd in a Work I am, Singly, as Unqualify'd for as the Ear is to Write; but when I want to do That I make use of my Hand; so if I would see the Satellites of *Jupiter*, or those of *Saturn*, or the Belts of One, or the Ring of the Other, I know well enough my Naked Eye is no Eye at all on This Occasion; I then apply to my Telescope: In what depends on the Knowledge of the Learned Languages my Son is my Telescope. 'tis by the help of

This I have seen That in *Milton* which to Me Otherwise had been Invisible; though before I had my Instrument I saw a Sky of shining Stars, How much more Throng'd and Bright soever That Sky Now appears.

Milton's Language is English, but 'tis *Milton*'s English; 'tis Latin, 'tis Greek English; not only the Words, the Phraseology, the Transpositions, but the Ancient Idiom is seen in All he Writes, So that a Learned Foreigner will think *Milton* the Easiest to be Understood of All the English Writers. This Peculiar English is most Conspicuously seen in *Paradise Lost*, for This is the Work which he Long before Intended should Enrich and Adorn his Native Tongue – *not caring to be once Nam'd Abroad though Perhaps I could Attaine to That, but Content with these British Ilands as My World, whose Fortune hath Hitherto bin, that if the* Athenians, *as Some say, made their Small Deeds Great and Renown'd by their Eloquent Writers,* England *hath had her Noble Atchievements made Small by the Unskillfull Handling of Monks and Mechanicks.*[8] See More to the Present Purpose in the Preface (Cited more than Once already) to his second Book *of Church-Government.*

to this *Miltonick* English may be apply'd what Himself Says of the New-Testament Greek – *He therefore who thinks to* Scholiaze *upon the Gospel, though Greek, according to his Greek Analogies, and hath not been Auditor to the Oriental Dialects, shall want in the heat of his Analysis no Accommodation to Stumble.* Tetrachord. Tol. Ed. 365.[9]

Poetry pretends to a Language of its Own. That of the Italian Poetry is so remarkably peculiar that a Man may Well understand a Prose Writer, and not a Poet. Words, Tours of Expression, the Order of them, All has Somthing not Prosaic. This is Observable particularly in *Shakespear*. *Milton* has Apply'd it to that Sublimity of Subject in which he perpetually Engages his Readers, above what *Shakespear* ever Aim'd at and where This is Peculiarly Necessary.

Nor does he want Abundant Instances of what All Good Poets Have. the Sound of the Words, their Harshness, Smoothness, or Other Properties, and the Ranging, and Mixing them, all help to Express aswell as their Signification. We have Noted This Occasionally, in Particular on VII.303.[10]

As his Mind was Rich in Ideas, and in Words of Various Languages to Cloathe them with, and as he had a Vast Fire, Vigour and Zeal of Imagination, his Style must Necessarily Distinguish it Self; it Did So; and even in his Younger days, his Juvenile Poems, English, Latin, and Italian, have a Brilliant not Easily found Elsewhere; Nor is it not seen in his Controversial Prose Works; *Paradise Lost* wants it not, in which there are Specimens of All his Kinds of Styles, the Tender, the Fierce, the Narrative, the Reasoning, the Lofty, &c. So Early as when he Wrote for Divorce,[11] though he Conceal'd his Name his Hand was known . . . There is Somthing in Every Man's whereby he is Known, as by his Voice Face, Gait, &c. in *Milton* there is a certain Vigour, whether *Versing or Prosing*, which will Awaken Attention be She never so Drowsy, and then Persuade her to be Thankful though She was Disturb'd.

a Reader of *Milton* must be Always upon Duty; he is Surrounded with Sense, it rises in every Line, every Word is to the Purpose; There are no Lazy Intervals, All has been Consider'd, and Demands, and Merits Observation. Even in the Best Writers you Somtimes find Words and Sentences which hang on so Loosely you may Blow 'em off; *Milton*'s are all Substance and Weight; Fewer would not have Serv'd the Turn, and More would have been Superfluous.

His Silence has the Same Effect, not only that he leaves Work for the Imagination when he has Entertain'd it, and Furnish'd it with Noble Materials; but he Expresses himself So Concisely, Employs Words So Sparingly, that whoever will Possess His Ideas must Dig for them, and Oftentimes pretty far below the Surface. if This is Call'd Obscurity let it be remembred 'tis Such a One as is Complaisant to the Reader, not Mistrusting his Ability, Care, Diligence, or the Candidness of his Temper; not That Vicious Obscurity which proceeds from a Muddled Inaccurate Head, not Accustomed to Clear, Well Separated and Regularly Order'd Ideas, or from want of Words and Method and Skill to Convey them to Another, from whence Always Arises Uncertainty, Ambiguity, and a Sort of a Moon-Light Prospect over a Landscape at Best not Beautiful; whereas if a Good Writer is not Understood 'tis because his Reader is Unacquainted with, or Incapable of the Subject, or will not Submit to do the Duty of a Reader, which is to Attend Carefully to what he Reads.

What *Macrobius* says of *Virgil* is Applicable to *Milton*. "He keeps his Eye Fix'd and Intent upon *Homer*, and emulates Alike his Greatness and Simplicity; his Readiness of Speech and Silent Majesty." by *Silent Majesty*, he seems to mean with *Longinus*: "His Leaving more to the Imagination than is Express'd."[12] [pp. cxl–cxlv].

if the Sublimity and Peculiarity of the Matter of this Poem, if its Superiority in That Respect has rais'd it above Some of the Rules given by *Aristotle*, or Whatever Other Criticks, and Gather'd From, or Founded on the *Iliad*, *Odyssey*, or *Æneid*, it has Distinguish'd it to its greater Glory; 'tis not only an Heroic Poem, but the Most So that Ever was Wrote. *Milton* did not despise Rules, Such as were Built upon Reason, So far as those Establish'd Reach'd; but as his Free and Exalted Genius Aspir'd Beyond what had Yet been Attempted in the Choice of his Subject, Himself was his Own Rule when in Heights where None had gone before, and Higher than Which None Can Ever go.

Milton's true Character as a Writer is that he is an Ancient, but born two Thousand years after his Time. his Language indeed is Modern, but the Best, next to Greek and Latin, to Convey those Images Himself Conceiv'd; and That moreover Greek'd and Latiniz'd, and made as Uncommon and Expressive as our Tongue could be, and yet Intelligible to us for whom he Wrote. But All his Images are Pure Antique. So that We read *Homer* and *Virgil* in reading Him. We hear Them in our Own Tongue, as we See What They Conceiv'd when *Milton* Speaks; Yes, and We find Our Selves amongst Persons and Things of a more Exalted Character. *Connoisseurs* in Painting and Sculpture can Best tell what is the Difference of Taste in Ancient and Modern Work, and can therefore Best Understand what I am Now Saying; it must Suffice that I tell Others that there is a Certain Grace, Majesty and Simplicity in the Antique which is its Distinguishing Character. the Same Kind of Taste is Seen in Writing; and *Milton* has it, I think, to a Degree beyond what We have ever found in Any Modern Painter or Sculptor, not Excepting *Rafaelle* Himself [pp. cxlvii–cxlviii].

But whatever *Milton* has Woven into his Poem of Others, still his Sublimest Passages are More So than could enter the Heart of *Orpheus*,

Hesiod, Homer, Pindar, Callimachus, &c. Such as the Heathen World Were Incapable of by Infinite Degrees, Such as None but the Noblest Genius could attain to, and That Assisted by a Religion Reveal'd by God Himself. We have then in *Paradise Lost* a Collection, the Quintessence of All that is Excellent in Writing; Frequently Improv'd and Explain'd Better than by the Best of their Profess'd Commentators, but Never Debas'd; and a Sublimity which All other Human Writings put Together have not. to Compleat All, He has made Use of All These, so as to be subservient to the Great End of Poetry, which is to Please and Inrich the Imagination, and to Mend the Heart, and make the Man Happy.

that This was His Idea of the Use of Poetry, and his Intention in This his Principal Work; This, for the Production of Which All his Study, Learning, Capacity, and Genius; his Whole Life was Mainly given to, will appear by what he Says, though Much more, by what he has Done. . . .

Were I call'd upon to Define Poetry in General, which *Milton* has not done in the Passages I have Cited [from the preface to the second book of *The Reason of Church Government* and from *Of Education*], nor any where Else that I know of, I would do it by saying 'tis ORNAMENT. This Implies Fiction, for Dress, Lace, Gold, Jewels, &c. is not the Body. Poetry therefore is not Truth, but Somthing More Agreeable, at least than Meer Truth.

and its Business is, Consequently, to Awaken, to Please, to Allure; 'tis Address'd to the Imagination, to the Passions, and This Supposes Energy as well as Beauty.

Verse and Prose are Opposites, but Verse may be Destitute of Poetry, as Prose may be Poetick, by having All the Beauties of Poetry Except the Numbers. Verse, With, or Without Rime, is but One of the Advantages Poetry makes Use of, 'tis not Alone Worthy of That Name. 'tis Prosaick Verse.

Argument, History, even Oratory it Self is not Allow'd the Gaudiness and Splendour which Poetry demands; but should an Orator Deck Himself with the Utmost of These, without the Musick of *Numerous Verse*[13] he would not be a Poet; for tho' Verse Alone is not Poetry, 'tis, strictly speaking, Essential to it.

as We are Most Easily Led, or Intic'd by Pleasure, Poetry has Proportionable Influence on the Mind, Whether to carry it to Good or Evil; Whether 'tis made Subservient to One, or the Other, 'tis no Less, or More Poetry Still. if you Ask What is the Most Excellent, the most Amiable Poetry, the Answer is Easy; 'tis That Whose Elevation of Language, Arrangement of Words, its Sentiments and Images are Directed, and made Subservient to, not Only the Delight, but the Improvement of Mankind. and This after All Terminates in Pleasure, as True Wisdom and Goodness has the Greatest Tendency to our Happiness. in This Use of Poetry, and not its Power over Us, consists its Real, its most Important Dignity. . . .

'tis of no Small Consequence towards the Happiness of Life to have a Lively, Inventive, a Great and Beautiful Imagination, 'twill Always furnish Us with Delight, Fill up all the Chasms in Time, and Intervals of Business, and Sweeten even Those, which Most People seem to consider but as the Offals, if not the Incumbrance of Life; but the Happiest in This particular may be made Happier by Assistance from Abroad, by Conversation and Reading.

Paradise Lost is Such a Fountain in This Case as the Sun, VII.364. Whence even These may in their *Golden Urns* draw Light. Here the *Morning Planet* may *Gild its Horns*; Those too who are not So Expert at this Poetical Imagery may Richly *Augment their Small Peculiar* here.[14] All may Gather Somthing that will Adorn and Delight their Minds.

if Ever any Book was Truly Poetical, if Ever Any Abounded with Poetry, 'tis *Paradise Lost*. What an Expansion of Facts from a Small Seed of History! What Worlds are Invented, What Embellishments of Nature upon what Our Senses Present Us with? Divine things are More Nobly, more Divinely Represented to the Imagination than by Any Other Poem, a More Beautiful Idea is given of Nature than any Poet has Pretended to; Nature as just come out of the Hand of God, in its Virgin Loveliness, Glory, and Purity; and the Human Race is Shown, not as *Homer*'s, More Gigantick, more Robust, more Valiant, but without Comparison more Truly Amiable, more So than by the Pictures and Statues of the Greatest Masters. and all These Sublime Ideas are Convey'd to Us in the most Effectual and Engaging Manner.

the Mind of the Reader is Tempered, and Prepar'd, by Pleasure, 'tis Drawn, and Allured, 'tis Awaken'd and Invigorated to receive Such Impressions as the Poet intended to give it: it Opens the Fountains of Knowledge, Piety and Virtue, and pours Along Full Streams of Peace, Comfort and Joy to Such as can Penetrate the true Sense of the Writer, and Obediently Listen to his Song. . . .

Paradise Lost not only Aims at a More Noble and More Extensive Moral, not only leads the Mind towards it by the Way of Pleasantness, All the Flowers in that Way are not only Fragrant, but Wholesom and Balsamick; All is Interesting, All not only Delight the Mind, but Contribute to make it Better,

> *"What's* Hecuba *to Him, or He to* Hecuba?"[15]

what does the War of *Troy*, or the Original of the *Roman* Name, say it was That of *Britain*, Concern You and Me? the Original of Things, the First Happy, but Precarious Condition of Mankind, his Deviation from Rectitude, his Lost State, his Restoration to the Favour of God by Repentance, and Imputed Righteousness; and That upon a Foundation which Cannot be Shaken. the Great Doctrines of the Christian Religion, Regeneration, Adoption and Glorification, Happiness Here, and For Ever; These Concern Us All Equally, and Equally with our First Parents, whose Story, and That of the Whole Church of God, this Poem sets before us; that is, These things are of the Utmost Importance, Such Importance as that what all the World calls Great are Comparatively Trifles, and Known to be So upon the least Serious Reflection. Without a Solid Establishment of Mind in These Sublime Truths, All Comprehended in a Just Idea of God, (So far as we are Enabled to Conceive of Him, and He has Sufficiently Reveal'd Himself to Us for That Purpose, More we Need not) whatever Happiness Any One may Seem to Enjoy, 'tis a Cheat, Precarious, and Will Fail, when the Mind is it Self, when Awaken'd by its Own Vigour, or by Some Adventitious Circumstance: Whereas Whoever profits, as he May, by This Poem will, as *Adam* in the Garden, Enjoy the Pleasures of Sense to the Utmost, with Temperance, and Purity of Heart, and Truest and fullest Enjoyment of them; and will Moreover perceive his Happiness is Establish'd upon a Better Foundation than That of his

Own Impeccability, and Thus possess a Paradise Within Far more Happy than that of *Eden*.[16]

O *Milton* thou hast employ'd all thy Vast Treasure of Wit, Learning and Ability, all the Beauty, Energy, and Propriety of Words Our Language was Capable of, all the Sweetness and Harmony of Numbers thy Musical and Judicious Ear furnish'd thee with, All the Fire and Beauty and Sublimity of Imagination Peculiar to thy Self, Added to what could be Supply'd by Those who have most Excell'd in That Angelical Faculty, in whatever Ages or Languages, All the Firmness, Force and Dignity of Mind thy Vertue and Piety Excited in thee, or Rewarded thee with; and together with All These a Genius Perfectly Poetical, if Ever any Man's was, and That Regulated by a most Solid Judgment. All These thou hast Consecrated to Produce a Poem, more Instrumental than any Other Human Composition, to Calm and Purify the Mind, and through the Delightful Regions of Poetry, to Exalt and Fix it to the Mysteries, Sublimities and Practice of Religion; to a State of Tranquility and Happiness, the Utmost Mortality is Capable of [pp. clii–clxiii].

it will be Expected Somthing should be said Concerning our NOTES and REMARKS; and indeed 'tis Necessary for our Own Sakes, as well as the Reader's.

though after all, Every Book is Obscure to Him who brings not with Him good Sense, Candour, Modesty and Application, which are the Same in All Languages; and if a Poem is to be Read They will best Understand it, whether in the Original, or Translated or Explain'd and Remark'd upon, who have Most of the Poetical Genius by which it was Wrote, and which Those may be possess'd of who have not, or are not Known to have Attempted *to build the Lofty Rhyme*.[17]

Learning is Unquestionably Necessary to a Thorough Understanding of *Milton*: but is That Sufficient? As Unquestionably No. 'tis Here as in the Case of being a *Connoisseur* in Painting; Seeing the Finest Works in *Italy*, is a Very Proper Qualification, but With That a Man must have Several Others, or he may be Very Ridiculous, Pretending to Understand a Picture. I will go on to say, that the Knowledge of Books in a Certain View, or Learning in a Certain Branch of it, though Useful in Some Respects, may in Others be not only Useless, but a

Hindrance, but may lead us Out of the Way; and Particularly as 'tis too Apt to Occasion a Self-Sufficiency and Arrogance upon Account of What is Quite Beside the Purpose in Hand; and where Another Kind of Reading, or perhaps Only Good Sense is Requisite; as This last is Always without Comparison Preferable to All the Learning of the World, how Pertinent Soever. in our Judgments of Men, as well as when We Apply to Theirs as Guides, These Observations are Evermore to be Carefully remember'd; and the Rather as the Not doing So has Commonly Pernicious Effects [pp. clxiv–clxvi].

it has been Our Good Fortune and the World's, that we have not been put to Conjecture what were the Genuine Thoughts of our Author from a Corrupted Text, or Even from an Incorrect One. We have Prov'd That of 74 to be Neither One, nor the Other. There are Several Careful Editions, I mean Those in which That has been follow'd without Pretending to make a Better, but This we are to consider as That which the Author bequeath'd as his Legacy to the World, and 'tis As much His as if his Own Manuscript, He having his Sight, had been in Our Hands; and Probably more Exact than Such would have been; Unless Revis'd Sheet by Sheet with the Same Care and Diligence, and by as many Eyes as a Well Printed Book is. We have Therefore Consider'd This Edition as bearing the Image and Superscription of *Milton*; and that to Mutilate or Alter any thing in it, (except the Error of the Printer, or Oversight is Apparent,) is Clipping or Coining, and Capitally Criminal in the Republick of Letters. . . .

We have Reverenc'd our Text, have handled it as Somthing which it would be a Sort of Prophaneness, as well as a Ridiculous Presumption in Us to Aim at Improving, by Adding or Diminishing. If any Man Could do it, 'tis not his Business; 'tis his Author's Thoughts, not his Own, which the Publick Expects from an Expositor, and Such Only We pretend to be. if in Any thing we may Seem to have done Otherwise it has been in That View, That is Our End in All we have done [pp. clxxi–clxxiv].

If, though not so Perfectly as Others Might, We have made This Admirable *Sallie* of Human Nature of more Universal Use than it has Yet been, we shall to Such who are Assisted by it, in Proportion as That Assistance happens to be, do for Them what *Milton* Himself did

Not. What he gave to Others of a Superiour Class we have Handed down to Them. With respect to Them *Paradise Lost* is So far Our Gift. We found This Book, as a Picture of the Greatest Master, Obscur'd for want of a Proper Light; We hold it Up to Them in Such a One; but we Abhor to do what is Too Often done by the Best Pictures, We dare not Scour, much Less Retouch it. I must give my Reader an *a-propos* Story which I had from a Friend of Mine, well Acquainted with These Matters, and who, as I remember, told it of his Own Knowledge. a Gentleman visited an Old Painter who Understood Pencils, Cloath, and Colours Extreamly well, but was Absolutely Void of a *Pittoresque* Genius; This Creature was found very Busy with a Fine Picture of *Van-Dyke*;[18] there were Two Hands in the Picture, One of which was in Shadow. What are you doing Here! says the Gentleman; Doing, says That Beast; See here your Great *Van-Dyke*, as you call him; Was there ever Such a Blunderer! he has made a Man with a pair of Hands, a White One and a Black One; *Outrageous Nonsense!* then with great Triumph show'd Both his Own Hands as being Both White; and to work he went to Mend *Van-Dyke*. and did So as He thought, but the Picture would have been Utterly Ruin'd had not that Wretch's Colours been got off while they were Yet Wet.

I have from my Infancy Lov'd and Practic'd Painting and Poetry; One I Possess'd as a Wife, the Other I Kept Privately, and shall Continue to do So whilst I Live. I have Already Endeavour'd to be Serviceable to the Lovers of Painting in what has been Publish'd by My Self First, and Afterward in Conjunction with My Son; Particularly having on All Occasions Strove to give an Idea of the Dignity and Usefulness of the Art as Understood and Practic'd in its Best Times and Where it was Most Esteem'd. an Idea Always Necessary to be Inculcated, but Never More So than at Present, when the Miserable Low Taste of our Ancestors Seems to be Returning upon us every day More and More. Now I have Try'd to be Useful in the Other Way. Both these Arts have Contributed to the Greatest Happiness of My Life, and I wish with all my Soul I may be Instrumental in making Them Greatly Serviceable to Ingenious Minds: they are by All Acknowledg'd to be Noble, and Sure they are Well Worthy the Most Exalted Abilities of Human Nature. I could not with More

Delight to my Self, though with Vast Labour and Application, have Employ'd That Leisure which the Industry in Business of Much More than Half a Century (besides That of my most Juvenile days) has Entitled me to, than in doing My part in Remarking upon, and Explaining a Poem which for Threescore years has been Consider'd as a "*Perfect, Absolute, Faultless Composition; the Best Pens in the Kingdom Contending in its Praises, as Eclipsing all Modern Essays whatsoever; and Rivalling, if not Excelling, both* Homer *and* Virgil."[19]

a Poem, whose Subject is the most Advantageous Imaginable; All whose Persons are Superiour by many Degrees to Those of any Other; All whose Images of Things are More Great and Beautiful than any Human Poet has given Us; and whose Design is to make its Readers Better and More Happy than Any Other Can pretend to have Aim'd at; and a Poem whence may be learnt the Whole Art of Poetry, as being Written with the Utmost degree of Genius, Spirit, Accuracy and Judgment; but withal a Poem Partly Hid, not by Clouds, but its Own Lustre. if Now I have Contributed to Assist the General Eye in Contemplating this Noble Luminary; Or (to descend to a more Familiar Allusion) if I have had Some Share in giving my Country a *Paradise Lost* Written in a Plain, Fair Character, instead of One in a Hand Oftentimes Scarce Legible; and have Thus been Instrumental in making the Best Poem in the World (All things Consider'd) of More Extensive Use, More Understood, More Delightful, More Instructive, and More Edifying than it Was, or Could have been made by the Poet without Somwhat Debasing his Own Work: if Moreover I have Help'd to Demolish that too Common Notion that how Excellent and Sublime Soever 'twas in *Milton*'s Mind, and on his Tongue, in Our Hands the Poem is, at least, Imperfect for want of His Eyes to Watch over the Editor and the Printer: if besides All This I have done Justice to One to Whom I am Infinitely Oblig'd; if I have shown a Man who has done More Honour to Our Species than most of Those we have been Accustom'd to be Dazzled with and Abused by; a Character where is found Honesty, Vertue, Piety; a Mind like that of the most Celebrated Philosophers when Suppos'd to be blest with the Improvements of Christianity, together with an Heroical and Poetical Greatness; and This instead of a Man who, upon Account of One Mistake in Opinion, has Hitherto, by Most people, been Worse thought of, as a Man, however he has been Honour'd as a Poet, than many a Worthless Profligate: if, Lastly, by What has been done I have in any Degree been Serviceable to the Interest of Religion and Vertue, which I am Sure Was, and Is, and Ever Shall be My Sincere Intention, I shall Rejoice in it More than in Any thing my most Sanguine Expectations have Yet in Store for Me whilst I am Continu'd on the Present Stage of Being.

in This Consciousness, and the Hopes of a Candid Acceptance from Those I have Endeavour'd to Serve, and of Somthing of Success, I do Already Rejoice; and withal that I have Finish'd This Work, which though Very Delightful and Edifying, has been Long, Difficult, and Laborious; it has require'd great Intenseness, Variety and Compass of Thought; and That many times from one thing to Another of Very Different Kinds with Sudden Transitions. Not that I Now Purpose to be Idle: I have indeed no further Design upon the Publick, (Unless perhaps Somthing may come to them after Men shall *see my Face no more*)[20] but as from my Infancy I have Always known How to Crowd every Particle of Time with Somthing not to be Blush'd at upon a Retrospect, (if Purity of Intention Secures Thought, Word, and Action; with the Supream Judge I Trust it will) I Resolve to go On in the Old Track as Vigorously as I Can; Thought, Books, the Pencil, the Pen, Enough will be Ready Fully to Employ my Many Beloved Retir'd Hours, as doing what Good Offices of Benevolence and Friendship I am able, Conversation, Exercise and Refreshment will be Sufficient to Fill All the Rest, Except what Higher Obligations Demand; and This till the time shall Come, which Now cannot be at any great Distance, it Cannot be Long before Health, Vigour, Hands and Eyes shall Begin to Decay; it cannot Now be Long *before he cause Darkness, and before* my *Feet Stumble upon the Dark Mountains.*[21]

Reader, be so Good to Forgive Me, I fear I have Talk'd Too much of My Self, and am Sure I have Not Said as Well as I should what More Concerns You; Chiefly have the Wisdom Your Selves to make Your Utmost Advantage of My Best Intention; That's Your Principal Affair; as it was Mine, How Unequal Soever to the Undertaking. Adieu [pp. clxxvi–clxxxii].

NOTES

Richard Fleckno, *A Short Discourse of the English Stage* (1664)

RICHARD FLECKNO (*c.* 1620–78). Reputedly a Roman Catholic priest. Critic, poet and composer of operas.

TEXT: Taken from *Love's Kingdom, a Pastoral Trage-Comedy* (1664).

1. *Dol Common*: Character in Ben Jonson's *The Alchemist* (1610).
2. *The Italians . . . the greatest masters*: On Italian stage machinery, see Nicola Sabbatini, *Pratica di Fabricar Scene e Machine ne' Teatri* (1638).

Sir Robert Howard, 'Preface' to *Four New Plays* (1665)

SIR ROBERT HOWARD (1626–98). Dramatist and politician; Auditor of the Exchequer, 1677–98; Privy Councillor, 1688–9; author of the *Reign of King Richard II* (1681), *Account of the State of his Majesties Revenue* (1681) and the anti-deistical *History of Religion, by a Person of Quality* (1694); brother-in-law to Dryden; according to John Evelyn, 'not ill-natured, but insufferably boasting'.

TEXT: Taken from *Four New Plays* (1665).

1. *non tamen . . . odi*: 'Yet you will not show unsuitable material upon the stage, and you will keep much out of sight which may with ease and speed be narrated before us. So Medea is not to butcher her boys in the face of the people, nor should the abominable Atreus openly cook human flesh. Procne should not be turned into a bird, nor Cadmus into a snake. Whatever you show to me of this nature, I disbelieve and reject': Horace, *De Arte Poetica*, ll. 182–8 (*ALC*, p. 284).
2. *Aut . . . spectator*: 'An event is either acted on the stage, or the action is narrated. A man's mind is stirred more sluggishly by what he hears than by

what is presented to his faithful eyes, by what the spectator can see for himself': Horace, *De Arte Poetica*, ll. 179–82 (*ALC*, p. 284).

3. *Si modo . . . dicto*: 'If only you and I know how to separate the elegant from the crude': Horace, *De Arte Poetica*, ll. 272–3 (*ALC*, p. 286).

4. *Whether Verse in Rhime . . . is to be preferr'd?*: Cf. Dryden's defence of rhymed drama in the dedication of *The Rival Ladies* (1664).

5. *my Lord of Orory*: Roger Boyle, Earl of Orrery.

John Dryden, *Of Dramatick Poesie, An Essay* (1668)

JOHN DRYDEN (1631–1700); the greatest poet, translator, critic and playwright of the late seventeenth century; Poet Laureate (1668) and Historiographer Royal (1670).

TEXT: Taken from the first edition of 1668; italic and roman reversed in the text of the prefatory material. Some slips have been silently corrected, where appropriate after comparison with the wording of the second edition of 1684. The second edition embodied for the most part only stylistic revisions, and the handful of readings representing substantive changes are noted below, identified by *1684*.

1. *Fungar . . . secandi*: 'I shall play the part of a whetstone, which, though it cannot cut, can give an edge': Horace, *De Arte Poetica*, ll. 304–5 (*ALC*, p. 287).

2. *BUCKHURST*: Although Charles Sackville, Lord Buckhurst, was present at the battle which serves as the backdrop to the *Essay*, he has traditionally been identified with one of the speakers in the dialogue, Eugenius. Dryden also dedicated his *Original and Progress of Satire* (1693) to Sackville.

3. *Plague had driven me from the Town*: The Great Plague of 1665 closed the theatres from May to November in 1666.

4. *a little alter'd*: not a little altered *1684*.

5. *Pompey . . . in its defence*: Corneille's *La Mort de Pompée* (1644), translated in 1664 by Buckhurst, Sedley, Waller and Godolphin.

6. *Spurina . . . the lookers on*: Cf. Valerius Maximus, *De Verecundia*, IV.5.

7. *better part of Writers*: better part of Poets *1684*.

8. *Pars . . . cubilia*: 'The part superior to the ineducable herd; let the weak and hopeless keep to their luckless beds!': Horace, *Epodes*, XVI.37–8.

9. *the French Poet*: Untraced.

10. *As Nature . . . sing*: Sir William Davenant, *Poem to the King's Most Sacred Majesty* (1663).

11. *Homer tells us . . . fighting Men*: Cf. *Iliad*, XVI.46ff.

12. *which were first made publick*: Dryden here refers to the letter to Roger Boyle, first Earl of Orrery, which he had prefixed to *The Rival Ladies* (1664), and in which he had argued for the use of rhymed verse in drama, rather than blank verse.

13. *Even Tully . . . Senate*: Cicero, *De Legibus*.

14. *Tully to Atticus . . . to praise Cicero*: Cicero, *Ad Atticum*, XII.40; Plutarch, *Julius Cæsar*, LIV.

15. *Sine studio partium aut ira*: A misquotation of Tacitus's *Annals* I.i, in which the historian explained the spirit in which he intended to examine the early principate: 'sine ira et studio, quorum causas procul habeo' ('without anger and party-spirit, from the causes of which I am far removed').

16. *the second part . . . impartially imitated*: This promised sequel was never written.

17. *day . . . when our Navy ingag'd the Dutch*: 3 June 1665.

18. *his Royal Highness*: James, Duke of York; later James II.

19. *we knew was then deciding*: they knew was then deciding *1684*.

20. *the Park*: St James's Park.

21. *Eugenius, Crites, Lisideius and Neander*: These four characters are traditionally understood to be versions of, respectively, Sackville, Dryden's brother-in-law Sir Robert Howard, Sir Charles Sedley and Dryden himself.

22. *Quem . . . scriberet*: 'We have seen Sulla at a public meeting, when a bad poet in the crowd handed up an epigram on himself, slackly written in unmetrical elegiacs. Sulla at once ordered that the poetaster be rewarded from the proceeds of the sale, on condition that he never write again': Cicero, *Pro Archia Poeta*, X.25.

23. *whom you intend*: Probably Robert Wild and Richard Fleckno, both of whom had already written on the battle.

24. *Catecresis or Clevelandism*: Catacresis is the rhetorical term of art for the improper use of a word. John Cleveland was the most exuberant follower of Donne's metaphysical style.

25. *that he spares*: that he intends at least, to spare *1684*.

26. *he creeps along . . . behind it*: Compare Pope's compression of Crites's portrait of the dull poet in *An Essay on Criticism*, ll. 347–50 (above, p. 218).

27. *Pauper . . . pauper*: 'Cinna wishes to seem poor, and therefore is indeed poor': Martial, *Epigrams*, VIII.19.

28. *the very Withers of the City*: A reference to George Wither.

29. *famous Poem . . . 1660*: Possibly a reference to Robert Wild's *Iter Boreale* of April 1660, which commemorated General Monck's march on London.

30. *qui Bavium non odit, &c.*: 'Let him, who does not hate Bavius, love your poems, Maevius': Virgil, *Eclogues*, III.90.

31. *Nam . . . contemnimus*: 'For we despise those who praise the objects of our contempt': untraced.

32. *Pace . . . perdidistis*: 'Forgive me if I say that you teachers have ruined true eloquence': Petronius, *Satyricon*, 2.

33. *Indignor . . . annus*: 'I lose my patience, and I own it too, / When works are censur'd, not as bad, but new' (Pope's version): 'If poems, like wine, improve with age, I ask; how many years are needed to mature a poem?': Horace, *Epistles*, II.i.76–7 and 34–5 (*ALC*, pp. 274 and 273).

34. *a wide dispute . . . on either side*: On this indeed 'wide dispute' of the Ancients and Moderns, see most recently J. M. Levine, *The Battle of the Books: History and Literature in the Augustan Age* (Ithaca: Cornell University Press, 1991).

35. *a genere & fine . . . perfect*: 'by type and purpose'. It is imperfect because it does not include a definition by difference (*a differentia*); a point made later by Neander, when he notes that Lisideius's definition might equally apply to epic (above, p. 73).

36. *Alit . . . accendit*: Paterculus, *Historia Romana*, I.17.

37. *monstrous and disfigur'd*: For Pope's similar assertion of an especial intimacy between ancient poetry and Nature, see *An Essay on Criticism*, ll. 131–9 (above, p. 212).

38. περί ῖῆς Ποιητικῆς: i.e. the *Poetics*. Aristotle's discussions of epic and comedy have not come down to us; the surviving copies of the *Poetics* contain only his discussion of tragedy.

39. *Time, Place, and Action*: In the *Poetics* Aristotle is silent concerning place, and nowhere in that work does he formulate explicit rules (*ALC*, pp. 85–132). Castelvetro was the first to regularize Aristotle, in his 1570 translation of the *Poetics*.

40. *are to*: are (as near as they may be) to *1684*.

41. *Johnson . . . Discoveries*: For Jonson's defence of plurality in dramatic plot, see the section headed 'Of the magnitude, and compasse of any Fable, Epicke, or Dramatick' in *Discoveries* (1640) (*Jonson*, viii, 645–9).

42. *sayes Corneile*: See Corneille's *Discours des trois unités* (1660).

43. *call'd by . . . Paterculus*: For these classical evaluations, see respectively: Suetonius, *Vita Terentii*; Horace, *Odes*, I.6, *Satires*, I.ix.23 and I.x.44, *De Arte Poetica*, l. 55; Martial, *Epigrams*, VIII.xviii.7. I have traced no references to Velleius Paterculus.

44. *Macrobius . . . Virgil*: Dryden alludes here to Macrobius's *Conviviorum Saturnaliorum libri septem*, bk IV.

45. *Audita . . . credimus*: 'We more readily praise what we have heard than what we have seen. Admiring the past, we disparage the present and believe that the former benefits us with instruction while we are obscured by the latter': Velleius Paterculus, *Historia Romana*, II.92 ('*admiratione*' should read '*veneratione*').

46. *into four*: In this division of the play into four parts, Dryden is relying more on the *Poetices* (1561) of J. C. Scaliger than on Aristotle.

47. *Catastasis, or Counterturn*: *Catastasis*, call'd by the Romans, *Status*, the heighth, and full growth of the Play: we may properly call it the Counterturn, *1684*.

48. *Neu . . . actu*: 'Let no play contain more or fewer than five acts': Horace, *De Arte Poetica*, l. 189 (*ALC*, p. 284). Dryden seems to be quoting from memory; the line should read 'Neve minor neu sit quinto productior actu.' Horace's advice is offered for all plays, not just comedies.

49. *but three acts*: A custom of the Spanish stage established by Lope de Vega.

50. *observ'd by a late Writer*: Cf. Sir Robert Howard (above, p. 10).

51. *Chapon Bouillé*: Boiled capon.

52. *Juno Lucina fer opem*: 'Goddess of childbirth, help me!': Terence, *Andria*, III.i.15.

53. *the French Poet*: Untraced.

54. *Sock and Buskin*: The sock was a light shoe or slipper worn by actors in comedy, the buskin was a thick-soled boot worn by actors in tragedy. Hence the sock and buskin became the emblems of, respectively, comedy and tragedy.

55. *Tandem . . . triduum*: 'But can't I do without her, if need be, for three days running?' 'Well! three whole days!': Terence, *Eunuch*, II.i.17–18.

56. *Sed Proavi . . . loquendi*: 'But our forebears relished Plautus's verse, and even his wit. In this they were forebearing to the point of stupidity.' 'Many obsolete terms will come back into favour, and many which are now prized will fall away, if usage so wills it – usage, in whose hands lies the judgement, rule and law of speech': Horace, *De Arte Poetica*, ll. 270–72 and 70–72 (*ALC*, pp. 286 and 281). Once again Dryden's quotations are slightly inaccurate.

57. *Mistaque . . . carinas*: 'The Egyptian bean, mixed with the laughing acanthus, will flourish.' 'The waves and the woods marvel, shocked by the flashing shields of the warriors and the painted ships': Virgil, *Eclogues*, IV.20 and *Æneid*, VIII.91–3.

58. *Si verbo . . . pompas*: 'If I may be so bold, I would not shrink from styling it Heaven's palace.' 'And Capitols witness long processions': Ovid, *Metamorphoses*, I.175–6 and 561.

59. *most easily digested*: Compare Pope, *An Essay on Criticism*, ll. 300–307 (above, pp. 216–17).

60. *Had Cain . . . home*: John Cleveland, *The Rebel Scot*, ll. 63–4.

61. *Si sic, omnia dixisset!*: 'If only he had always spoken like this!': Juvenal, *Satires*, X.123–4.

62. *For Beauty . . . destroyes*: John Cleveland, 'To P. Rupert', ll. 39–40. 'White powder' may be either arsenic, or a kind of gunpowder.

63. *Omne . . . vincit*: 'Tragedy exceeds all other kinds of writing in gravity': Ovid, *Tristia*, II.381.

64. *that Scene . . . to kill him*: Seneca, *Troades*, ll. 524ff.

65. *anima . . .* Ψυχη: 'My life and my soul': Juvenal, *Satires*, VI.195.

66. *Sum . . . votus*: 'I am the faithful Aeneas, renowned even in heaven': Virgil, *Æneid*, I.378–9. Dryden has erroneously linked the first half of l. 378 to the second half of l. 379.

67. *Si . . . Lucilius)*: 'Yet had he chanced by fate to be born in our day': Horace, *Satires*, I.x.68.

68. *Quos libitina sacravit*: 'Whom the goddess of funerals has hallowed': Horace, *Epistles*, II.i.49.

69. *reform'd their Theatre*: The Académie française was founded in 1635 by Armand Jean du Plessis, Cardinal and duc de Richelieu, Louis XIII's Prime Minister since 1624. The Académie was charged with regulating French literature and the French language, and its values were emphatically neo-classical.

70. *confounding of the Audience*: Compare Sir Robert Howard's similar sentiments in the 'Preface' to *Four New Plays*; above, p. 11.

71. *Atque . . . poscunt*: 'And they [the vulgar] call for a bear or for boxers in the middle of the performance': Horace, *Epistles*, II.i.185–6 (*ALC*, p. 277). The Red Bull was a theatre in Clerkenwell with a reputation as a focus of unruly behaviour.

72. *Ex . . . sequar*: 'I aim at poetry fashioned from familiar materials': Horace, *De Arte Poetica*, l. 240 (*ALC*, p. 285).

73. *Atque . . . imum*: 'And he [Homer] employs such artifice, confusing truths with fictions, that the beginning harmonizes with the middle, and the middle with the end': Horace, *De Arte Poetica*, ll. 151–2 (*ALC*, p. 283).

74. *Whom Justin . . . old age*: Justinus, I.8; Xenophon, *Cyropædia*, VIII.7.

75. *Quodcunque . . . odi*: 'Whatever of this kind you show me, I disbelieve and loathe': Horace, *De Arte Poetica*, l. 177 (*ALC*, p. 284).

76. τὰ ετυηα . . . *express'd it*: If not 'the truth', yet 'resembling the truth': Hesiod, *Theogony*, l. 27 and Homer, *Odyssey*, XIX.203.

77. *Rollo . . . in Herodian*: Dryden is referring to *The Bloody Brother. A Tragedy*, first published in 1639, which in its second edition of 1640 was retitled *The Tragoedy of Rollo, Duke of Normandy*. The play's main source is Herodian, bks III and IV.

78. *Golias*: A comic character in medieval literature.

79. *In Sejanus . . . the rest*: *Sejanus*, II.i; *Catiline*, III.iii and II.i.

80. *ingenious person*: Possibly Thomas Sprat, in his *Observations on M. de Sorbier's Voyage into England* (1665).

81. *protatick persons*: Characters who serve only to introduce the subject of the play. Dryden has borrowed the phrase from Corneille.

82. *can perswade us to*: can insinuate into us, *1684*.

83. *Philosophers . . . stop put to it*: René Descartes, *Principia Philosophiae* (1644), II.37.

84. *Corneille . . . by narration*: *Discours des trois unités* (1660).

85. *Segnius . . . anguem, &c.*: 'The mind is less vigorously moved by what it hears than by what is presented to the loyal eyes . . . however, don't act out what should be kept off-stage, and hide from us much which an actor will soon and conveniently narrate. Medea must not butcher her boys in the face of the people . . . nor should Procne be turned into a bird, or Cadmus into a snake': Horace, *De Arte Poetica*, ll. 180–87 (*ALC*, p. 284).

86. *We find . . . entertainment*: *Magnetick Lady*, III.ii; *Eunuch*, IV.iii.

87. *The relations . . . believ'd*: *Sejanus*, V.x.

88. *Scornful Lady*: In Beaumont and Fletcher's *The Scornful Lady* (1616) the astonishing conversion of Morecraft, the usurer, occurs in V.i.

89. *sayes Corneille*: *Discours des trois unités* (1660).

90. *spoke against it*: An allusion to Sir Robert Howard's opposition to the use of rhyme on the stage as unnatural in the 'Preface' to *Four New Plays* (above, pp. 11–13). Dryden had already declared himself a supporter of the use of rhyme in plays in the dedication to *The Rival Ladies* (1664).

91. *Sed . . . conquirimus*: 'But, as when we set out we are on fire to overtake those whom we regard as leaders, so when we despair of either overtaking or even equalling them, our zeal weakens along with our hope – it ceases to pursue what it cannot surpass; . . . turning aside from a field in which we cannot be pre-eminent, we search out some new object for our efforts': Velleius Paterculus, *Historia Romana*, I.17. Dryden is again quoting inaccurately. The ellipsis indicates the omission of seven words from the Latin.

92. *the Lier*: Corneille's *Le Menteur* (1643) was translated and put on in London in 1661 as *The Mistaken Beauty: or the Liar*.

93. *clear it up*: clear it, and reconcile them. *1684*.

94. *Quinault*: Dryden had adapted Quinault's *Les Rivales* (1653) when writing his own *The Rival Ladies* (1664).

95. *the Adventures*: Sir Samuel Tuke, *Adventures of Five Hours* (1663); a translation of Antonio Coello's *Los Empeños de Seis Horas* (*c.* 1641).

96. *contraries . . . set off each other*: 'Opposita juxta se posita, magis elucescunt'; 'Opposites, when juxtaposed, shine more brightly' (F. Burgersdijck, *Institutionem logicarum libri duo* (1626), I.xxii).

97. *Eugenius*: A slip for 'Crites'.

98. *Co-ordination*: i.e. the absence of subordination.

99. *Cinna ... Pompey ... Polieucte*: All plays by Corneille from the early 1640s: *Cinna* (1640), *La Mort de Pompée* (1644) and *Polyeucte* (1641).

100. *of an hundred or two hundred lines*: of an hundred lines *1684*.

101. *can arrive at*: can, reasonably, hope to reach *1684*.

102. *the Maids Tragedy*: Beaumont and Fletcher, *The Maid's Tragedy* (1619).

103. *the Fox*: i.e. Jonson, *Volpone* (1607).

104. *Andromede*: A spectacle-play of 1650.

105. *one of their newest Playes*: Thomas Corneille, *L'Amour à la mode* (1651).

106. *Sad Shepherd*: *The Sad Shepherd* (*c.* 1635); Jonson's last, unfinished, play.

107. *Faithful Shepherdess*: *The Faithful Shepherdess* (1609).

108. *the Merry Wives of Windsor, and the Scornful Lady*: Both *The Merry Wives of Windsor* (1602) and *The Scornful Lady* (1616) have action occupying two days.

109. *The Silent Woman*: i.e. *Epicæne, or The Silent Woman* (acted 1609; published 1616).

110. *found her there*: For other, later, identifications of Shakespeare with Nature, see above, pp. 265–6, 288 and 291.

111. *Quantum ... cupressi*: 'As cypresses do amongst the bending osiers': Virgil, *Eclogues*, I.25.

112. *Verses he writ to him*: Jonson, Epigram 55.

113. *Philaster ... Every Man in his Humour*: *Philaster, or Love Lies a-Bleeding* (1608–10; published, 1620); *Every Man in his Humour* was first acted in September 1598.

114. *no Poet can ever paint as they have done*: no Poet before them, could paint as they have done *1684*.

115. *in his serious Playes;*: in his Comedies especially: *1684*.

116. *five hours ... wonder*: Cf. n. 95 above.

117. *the latitude ... in one*: An overstatement; the play in fact requires at least four locations, although they are all in London.

118. τὸ γελοῖου: 'The ludicrous': Aristotle, *Poetics*, V (*ALC*, p. 96).

119. *Socrates brought upon the Stage ... Spectators*: Cf. Aristophanes, *Clouds*, ll. 218ff.

120. ἦθος ... πάθος *of Mankind*: 'Character' and 'emotion' respectively.

121. *Ex homine hunc natum dicas*: 'The one the exact image of the other': Terence, *Eunuch*, l. 460.

122. *Creditur ... minus*: 'Some think that Comedy, because it is based on common life, is easier work. But actually it is more exacting, because there is less margin for error': Horace, *Epistles*, II.i.168–70 (*ALC*, p. 276).

123. *Corneille has laid down ... depend*: *Discours des trois unités* (1660).

124. *Ubi . . . maculis*: 'When a poem teems with beauties, I will not quibble over a few faults': Horace, *De Arte Poetica*, ll. 351–2 (*ALC*, p. 289).

125. *an Ancient Writer . . . living*: Velleius Paterculus, *Historia Romana*, II.36.

126. *Etiam . . . Laberi*: 'Even with me on your side you have been bested, Laberius': Macrobius, *Saturnalia*, II.7.

127. *such reasons against Rhyme . . . way*: Compare Crites's argument with that of Sir Robert Howard in the 'Preface' to *Four New Plays* (above. pp. 11–13).

128. *sayes Aristotle . . . nearest Prose*: Aristotle, *Poetics*, IV (*ALC*, p. 95).

129. *Arcades . . . dicere*: 'All Arcadians are equally prepared both to sing and to reply'; 'whatever I tried to speak [was poetry]': Virgil, *Eclogues*, VIII.4–5; Ovid, *Tristia*, IV.x.26 (misquoted).

130. *Ars est celare artem*: 'Art is the concealment of art'; see p. 387, n. 16.

131. *Nescivit . . . Ponto*: 'He did not know when to leave well alone'; 'All was sea, and the sea had no shores': Marcus Seneca, *Controversiae*, IX.5 (misquoted); Ovid, *Metamorphoses*, I.292.

132. *I Heav'n invoke . . . make*: Untraced: not in Beaumont and Fletcher.

133. *perpetuo tenore fluere*: Cicero, *Orator*, VI.21 (misquoted).

134. *Nations*: Nations: at least we are able to prove, that the Eastern people have us'd it from all Antiquity, *Vid, Dan.*, his *Defence of Rhyme 1684*. Samuel Daniel's *Defence of Ryme* (1603) was an answer to Thomas Campion's *Art of English Poesie* (1602), in which it was argued that English metres should be based on quantity, as had been those of classical poetry.

135. *the Siege of Rhodes*: Sir William D'Avenant, *The Siege of Rhodes* (1656); traditionally regarded as the first English opera.

136. *Tentanda . . . humo*: 'I must venture on a path which will raise me, too, from the earth': Virgil, *Georgics*, III.8–9.

137. *the Faithful Shepherdess, and Sad Shepherd*: See above, nn. 107 and 106.

138. *Est . . . peccat*: 'Sometimes the mob are right; sometimes they're wrong': Horace, *Epistles*, II.i.63 (misquoted) (*ALC*, p. 274).

139. *the Siege of Rhodes . . . Emperour*: Siege of Rhodes, see above, n. 135; Roger Boyle, *The Tragedy of Mustapha, Son of Solyman the Magnificent* (acted 1665; published 1668); John Dryden, *The Indian Queen* (1664) and *The Indian Emperour* (1665).

140. *Indignatur . . . versus*: 'For the feast of Thyestes disdains to be related in the idiom of common life, which is more suited to comedy'; 'Tragedy is above babbling trivial verses': Horace, *De Arte Poetica*, ll. 90–91 and 231 (*ALC*, pp. 281 and 295).

141. *ranck'd above it*: Aristotle, *Poetics*, XXVI (*ALC*, p. 132).

142. *quidlibet audendi*: 'Daring anything': Horace, *De Arte Poetica*, l. 10 (*ALC*, p. 279).

143. *Musas colere severiores*: 'To cultivate the more demanding Muses': Martial, *Epigrams*, IX.xi.17.

144. *the Water Poet's Rhymes*: A reference to John Taylor.

145. *Delectus . . . Eloquentiæ*: 'The choice of language is the foundation of eloquence': Cicero, *Brutus*, LXXII.253 (misquoted).

146. *Reserate . . . Laris*: 'Unbar the closed portals of the royal house': *Hippolytus*, l. 863.

147. *may excuse them*: At this point *1684* inserts an additional sentence: 'For if they are little and mean in Rhyme, they are of consequence such in Blank Verse.'

148. *a most acute person*: i.e. Sir Robert Howard.

149. *Piazze*: i.e. Covent Garden.

Sir Robert Howard, 'Preface' to *The Great Favourite* (1668)

SIR ROBERT HOWARD (1626–98); see above, p. 357.
TEXT: Taken from *The Great Favourite* (1668).

1. *The Duke of Lerma*: the author of this earlier version is unknown.

2. *Ubi . . . Triumphos*: 'Where there is no possibility of triumph': Lucan, *Pharsalia*, I.12.

3. *Sancho Pancos Doctor*: Cf. Cervantes, *Don Quixote*, pt 2, ch. 47.

4. *Reserate . . . Laris*: See above, p. 76 and p. 366, n. 146.

5. *To shew . . . not at all*: Compare Howard's attack on the dramatic unities with that of Samuel Johnson in the 'Preface' to his edition of Shakespeare (*Johnson on Shakespeare*, ed. H. R. Woudhuysen (Harmondsworth: Penguin, 1989), pp. 133–7).

6. *others to afford to me*: Dryden answered Howard in the *Defence of an Essay of Dramatick Poesie*, published in 1668 as the preface to the second edition of his *Indian Emperour*.

Thomas Shadwell, 'Preface' to *The Humorists* (1671)

THOMAS SHADWELL (?1642–92); dramatist and Whig; political and literary opponent of Dryden.
TEXT: Taken from *The Humorists* (1671).

1. *She would if she could*: By Sir George Etherege (1668). Samuel Pepys, present at the first performance on 6 February, criticized it as 'a silly, dull thing, though there was something very roguish and witty; but the design of the play, and end, mighty insipid.'

2. *without correction or instruction*: Cf. the position taken up by Dryden in the preface to *An Evening's Love, or the Mock Astrologer* (1671). Shadwell continued his argument with Dryden in the dedication, prologue and epilogue to *The Virtuoso* (1676).

3. *Pectus . . . Exemplis*: 'He moulds the heart with kindly precepts; he is the corrector of crudeness, envy and anger. He relates noble deeds, and instructs the rising generation with famous examples': Horace, *Epistles*, II.i.128–31 (*ALC*, p. 275).

4. *Simul . . . vitæ*: 'To utter words at once pleasing and useful': Horace, *De Arte Poetica*, l. 334 (*ALC*, p. 288).

5. *Odi . . . Arceo*: 'I hate and shun the vulgar throng': Horace, *Odes*, III.i.1.

6. *Garganum . . . ergo*: 'You might take it for the roaring of the Garganian forest or the Tuscan sea. The play is watched in the midst of such clamour! And when, overladen with works of art and foreign finery, the actor makes his entrance, the right hand clashes with the left. 'Has he said anything yet?' 'Not a word.' 'Then what pleases them so?': Horace, *Epistles*, II.i.202–6 (*ALC*, p. 277).

7. *Mr. Johnson . . . particular men*: For Jonson's reply to the imputations of 'supercilious politiques', see the dedication of *Volpone* to the universities of Oxford and Cambridge (*Jonson*, v, 18).

8. *my particular friend*: Dryden.

9. *Cui . . . debacchatur*: 'Which poet was ever more wont to take fire in sudden frenzy? When he was warmed, he raged more strongly and with more felicity.' Untraced.

10. σώφρουα μαυίαυ: 'Wise madness': cf. Plato, *Phædrus*, 244 d 4.

11. *Inter . . . Poema*: 'Perhaps in their midst a fitting word will attract attention, or one or two lines which are slightly better turned. But then these unfairly carry and recommend the whole poem': Horace, *Epistles*, II.i.73–5 (*ALC*, p. 274).

12. *Sir John Dawe and Sir Amorous la Foole*: Characters in Jonson's *Epicœne, or The Silent Woman* (acted 1609, published 1616).

13. *Creditur . . . minus*: 'It is thought that comedy takes less effort because its subject matter is common life. But in fact it is harder work, because you have less latitude': Horace, *Epistles*, II.i.168–70 (*ALC*, p. 276).

Buckingham, *An Essay Upon Poetry* (1682)

JOHN SHEFFIELD (1648–1721), third Earl of Mulgrave and later first Duke of Buckingham and Normanby; patron of Dryden and friend of Pope.

TEXT: Taken from the first edition (1682).

1. *the late Convert*: The Earl of Rochester, who on his deathbed in 1680 had been converted by Bishop Burnet.

2. *Panegyrick ... Coopers-Hill*: Edmund Waller, *A Panegyrick to My Lord Protector* (1655). Sir John Denham, *Cooper's Hill* (1642).

3. *another's Rimes*: Dryden had been assaulted at the instigation of the Earl of Rochester, who attributed to Dryden's influence the attack on him in Sheffield's *Essay on Satire* (1680).

4. *Bellario*: A character in Beaumont and Fletcher's *Philaster* (?1609).

5. *humane sence*: Cf. René Rapin, *Réflexions sur la poétique* (1674). Here, as elsewhere, Sheffield reveals the influence upon him of seventeenth-century French criticism; much of the *Essay* is in dialogue with Nicolas Boileau's *L'Art poétique* (1673).

6. *Torquato*: i.e. Tasso.

Roscommon, *An Essay On Translated Verse* (1685)

WENTWORTH DILLON (?1633–85), fourth Earl of Roscommon; poet, politician, gambler and duellist; founder of an informal literary academy, which included Charles Montagu, Earl of Halifax, Lord Maitland, the Earl of Dorset and Dryden; alleged to be the first to praise *Paradise Lost* in print. See Carl Niemeyer, 'The Earl of Roscommon's Academy', *Modern Language Notes*, 49 (1934), pp. 432–7.

TEXT: Taken from the 'second edition, corrected and enlarged' of 1685 (an error in l. 35 of *1685* suggests that it was set from a corrected text of *1684*). The most substantial variant readings from the first edition of 1684 (*1684*) are given in the notes. Charles Gildon published a commentary on this poem in his *Laws of Poetry* (1721).

1. *correct Essay*: The allusion is to Buckingham's *Essay upon Poetry* (above, pp. 97–107).

2. ll. 3–6, *1684*:   And happy those, who, (if concurring Stars
                            Prædestinate them to Poetick Wars)

> With Pains, and leisure, by such Precepts write;
> And learn to use their arms before they fight.

3. ll. 8–9, *1684*:   Joyn all their forces, to invade our Age,
> Provok'd, and urg'd, we, resolutely must

4. l. 35, *1684*:   And *Europe* must acknowledge, that she gains,

5. *not . . . in Prose*: Cf. André Dacier's prose translation of Horace, first published in 1681.

6. ll. 49–50, *1684*:   'Tis *copious, florid*, pleasing to your *Ear*;
> With softness, more perhaps, then *Ours* can bear.

7. *Pierian*: Pieria is a district on the northern slopes of Mount Olympus associated with the Muses.

8. *Baralipton*: A term of art in scholastic philosophy; here epitomizing pedantry.

9. *Examine . . . your Mind*: Cf. Pope, *Epistles to Several Persons*, i. 174ff. and *An Essay on Man*, ii, 131–60.

10. ll. 106–7, *1684*:   As 'tis the *deepest*, ought to be the *Best*:
> No rigid *Awe* shou'd breed a servile *Fear*,

11. ll. 111–12, *1684*:   *Habitual Innocence* adorns each *Thought*,
> And 'tis *your Crime* if *She* commit a *Fau't*.

12. ll. 113–14, *1684*:   *Immodest words* (whatever the Pretence)
> *Always* want *Decency*, and *often, Sense*.

13. *Oxymel of Squils*: Medicine concocted from vinegar and honey.

14. *Snores, as well as Nods*: On the seventeenth- and eighteenth-century debate on Homer, particularly in France, see most recently Howard Weinbrot, *Britannia's Issue* (Cambridge: Cambridge University Press, 1993), pp. 193–236.

15. l. 146, *1684*:   And with inviting *Majesty* surprise,

16. *Ferry-man of Hell*: Charon: cf. Virgil, *Æneid*, Book VI.

17. l. 162, *1684*:   Proceeds from *Ignorance*, and want of *Thought*,

18. *religious Fear*: Cf. Pope, *An Essay on Criticism*, ll. 184–203 (above, pp. 213–14).

19. l. 170, *1684*:   No *petty Deity* inhabits *there*:

20. *Mantuan God*: i.e. Virgil.

21. l. 184, *1684*:   Which has been, and *is* often in the *Wrong*.

22. After l. 192, *1684* has four lines deleted in *1685*:

> Yet if one shadow of a *Scruple* stay,
> Sure the most *beaten* is the *safest* way.
> *Fear* is the base Companion of a *Slave*,
> But *Prudence* the Perfection of the *Brave*.

23. l. 201, *1684*: They, who too formally on *Names* insist,

24. ll. 205–8, *1684*: Judicious *Horace* us'd a *Parthian* Name,
> (*Rome* was no Stranger to *Monæse*'s Fame,)
> Yet since the *Victor* is but little *known*,
> But *Crassus* more for being *overthrown*.
> The *Roman* for the *Parthian* Name will be,
> A Tedious Comment's True *Epitome*.

25. *And some . . . Clime*: Cf. William Coward, *Licentia Poetica* (1709).

26. ll. 216–24, *1684*: Be not too fond of a Sonorous Line;
> *Good Sence* will through a *plain expression* shine.
> *Few Painters* can such *Master strokes* command,
> As are the noblest in a *skilful Hand*.
> In This, your Author will the best advise,

27. ll. 230–31, *1684*: Tho all imaginable *Faults* abound,
> Will never want the *Pageantry of Sound*.

28. ll. 232–5 are omitted in *1684*.

29. *As Archimedes . . . Camp*: Cf. Plutarch's life of Marcellus, XVII.3.

30. l. 271, *1684*: In such Distress what could our *Vermin* do?

31. *Shews . . . ought to Thrive*: Cf. Nicolas Boileau, *L'Art poétique* (1673), IV.1ff.

32. *Pompilian*: A term of contempt.

33. *transport then when they write*: Cf. Horace, *De Arte Poetica*, ll. 102–3 (*ALC*, p. 282), and Boileau, *L'Art poétique*, III.142.

34. *Impatient Maid Divinely Rave*: An allusion to the Sybil, whose grotto ('antrum immane') was at Cumæ; cf. Virgil, *Æneid*, Book VI.

35. *sound . . . Sense*: An aesthetic commonplace since Dionysius of Halicarnassus, and widespread in European criticism of the early modern period. Cf. Pope, *An Essay on Criticism*, ll. 365–74 (above, p. 219).

36. *1684* omits ll. 376–402.

37. l. 403, *1684*: O may I Live to see that glorious Day,

38. ll. 407–8, *1684*: And in that *Roman Majesty* appear,
> Which none knows better and none *Comes* so near.

Francis Atterbury, 'Preface' to the
Second Part of Waller's *Poems* (1690)

FRANCIS ATTERBURY (1662–1732), Bishop of Rochester; Jacobite and contro-versialist.

TEXT: Taken from *The Second Part of Mr. Waller's Poems* (1690).

1. *Tu ... vita*: 'You are our father, the discoverer of truths. You furnish us with fatherly precepts and from your pages, O great man, as the bees in the flowery glades sip freely, so we too are nourished by your golden words: golden, because most worthy of life everlasting': Lucretius, *De Rerum Natura*, III.9–13.

2. *Augustan Age*: For the idea of an Augustan age and what it might mean, see in the first place Howard Erskine-Hill, *The Augustan Idea in English Literature* (London: Edward Arnold, 1983), and for a contrasting view, Howard Weinbrot, *Augustus Cæsar in 'Augustan' England* (Princeton: Princeton University Press, 1978).

3. *Menstruums*: A term of art used in alchemy to denote solvents.

4. *Their Poetry ... World*: Cf. Pope, *An Essay on Criticism*, l. 350 (above, p. 218).

5. *hook't Attoms ... Des Cartes*: An allusion to René Descartes's mechanistic philosophy, outlined in *Principia Philosophiae* (1644).

6. *Sense was cloy'd ... returning upon it*: Cf. Pope, *An Essay on Criticism*, ll. 351–2 (above, p. 218).

7. *Quæ ... fastidiosissimum*: 'Thus the grand and beautiful can give pleasure for a long time, but the neat and graceful quickly sate the hearing, the most fastidious of the senses': Cicero, *Ad Herennium*, IV.xxiii.32.

8. *the living Glory of our English Poetry*: Dryden.

9. *troublesome bondage of Rhyming*: Cf. Milton's note on 'The Verse' prefacing *Paradise Lost*.

10. *Jam ... Senectus*: 'Now aged – but the old age of gods is vigorous and green': Virgil, *Æneid*, IV.304.

11. *a neat Tomb ... Rubbish, &c.*: In the 'Preface' to his *Works* (1668), Cowley reflected on the unwisdom of inflating posthumous publications with sub-standard poems, a practice arising from the 'indiscretion of their [i.e. poets'] Friends, who think a vast *heap* of Stones or Rubbish a better *Monument*, then a little *Tomb of Marble*'.

12. *mille anni*: Literally, 'thousand years'.

Lansdowne, *Concerning Unnatural Flights in Poetry* (1701)

GEORGE GRANVILLE (1667–1735), Lord Lansdowne; statesman, poet and dramatist; suspected Jacobite; early patron of Pope.

TEXT: Taken from Charles Gildon's *A New Miscellany of Original Poems on Several Occasions* (1701). Cf. also the remarks on the poem in Gildon's *Laws of Poetry* (1721), and the work to which Granville is principally indebted, Dominique Bouhours's *La Manière de bien penser dans les ouvrages d'esprit* (1687). Granville later revised the poem and its notes substantially. The most significant variant readings from his *Genuine Works in Verse and Prose*, 2 vols. (1732) are given below, identified by *1732*.

1. *bright resemblance*: just resemblance *1732*.

2. *Nature is their Object*: Nature sits, the Object *1732*.

3. *just proportions*: due Proportions *1732*.

4. *bold Hyperboles*: rash Hyperboles *1732*.

5. *Hero, in the War*: Hero slain and dead: *1732* (the last word of the previous line being revised to 'read' from 'bear').

6. As J. E. Spingarn points out (*Critical Essays of the Seventeenth Century*, 3 vols. (Oxford: Clarendon Press, 1908–9), iii, 337), not in fact from Ariosto, but from Berni's *rifacimento* of Boiardo's *Orlando Innamorato*, LIII.60:

> Così colui, del colpo non accorto,
> Andava combattendo ed era morto.

1732 quotes a different instance of extravagance:

> Kill'd as he was, insensible of Death,
> He still fights on, and scorns to yield his Breath.

7. *1732* inserts a long passage at this point:

> The captive Canibal weigh'd down with Chains,
> Yet braves his Foes, reviles, provokes, disdains,
> Of Nature fierce, untameable, and proud,
> He grins Defiance at the gaping Croud,
> And spent at last, and speechless as he lies,
> With Looks still threatning, mocks their Rage, and dies.
> This is the utmost Stretch that Nature can,
> And all beyond is fulsom, false, and vain.

Beauty's the theme; some Nymph divinely fair
Excites the Muse: Let Truth be even there:
As Painters flatter, so may Poets too,
But to Resemblance must be ever true.

> "The *Day that she was born, the CYPRIAN Queen
> Had like t'have dy'd thro' Envy and thro' Spleen;
> The Graces in a hurry left the Skies
> To have the Honour to attend her Eyes;
> And Love, despairing in her Heart a Place,
> Would needs take up his Lodging in her Face."

Tho' wrote by great CORNEILLE, such Lines as these,
Such civil Nonsense sure could never please.
WALLER, the best of all th'inspir'd Train,
To melt the Fair, instructs the dying Swain.

*Corneille

8. *Roman Wit . . . sides*: Lucan.

9. *Almanzor's . . . Maximin*: Almanzor is a character in Dryden's heroic play *The Conquest of Granada* (1672), Maximin in his *Tyrannic Love* (1670).

10. *The Stagyrite*: Aristotle.

11. *Explanatory Annotations . . . Poem*: The first three notes are lifted from Bouhours, *La Manière*, pp. 13–14, 21–2 and 31–2.

12. *Homer . . . Beauty it self*: *Iliad*, II.673.

13. *Martial . . . Lewdness it self*: *Epigrams*, XI.92.

14. *Seneca . . . credibility*: *De Beneficiis*, VII.23.

15. *Quodcunq . . . Odi*: 'Whatever you thus show me, I discredit and abhor': Horace, *De Arte Poetica*, l. 188 (*ALC*, p. 284).

16. *These lines . . . &c.*: In *1732* this note is greatly expanded, to cover two pages.

17. *Victrix . . . Catoni*: 'The gods smile on the cause of the victors, Cato on that of the losers': Lucan, *Pharsalia*, I.128.

18. *He's bound . . . Cloaths*: From the prologue to *The Rival Ladies* (1664).

19. *third day*: The profits of the performance on each third day were by tradition the perquisite of the playwright.

20. *I remember . . . proper*: From the dedication of *The Spanish Friar* (1681) to John, Lord Haughton.

John Dennis, selections from *The Grounds of Criticism in Poetry* (1704)

JOHN DENNIS (1657–1734); Whig poet, critic and playwright; adversary of Pope.

TEXT: The 'Preface', the 'Proposal' and the 'Specimen' are taken from the first edition of 1704, the remainder from the corrected, but substantively unrevised, version printed in the second volume of Dennis's *Select Works* (1718). This version did not include the 'Preface', 'Proposal' and 'Specimen'.

1. *Churchmen against Divine Inspiration*: An allusion to Jeremy Collier, whose *A Short View of the Immorality and Profaneness of the English Stage* had been published in 1698. Nahum Tate had also drawn up in 1699 a *Proposal for Regulating the Stage and Stage-Players*. Cf. J. W. Krutch, 'Governmental Attempts to Regulate the Stage after the Jeremy Collier Controversy', *Publications of the Modern Language Association*, 38 (1923), pp. 161–2.

2. *Evil Communications . . . Menander*: In fact I Corinthians 15:33. Cf. Grotius's *Annotations in Libros Evangeliorum Compendiatæ*.

3. *Dramatick . . . Solitary*: *De Augmentis Scientiarum*, ii, 13.

4. *That Discerning Princess . . . Manners*: For Anne's support of the stage, see Allardyce Nicoll, *A History of English Drama 1660–1900*, 6 vols. (Cambridge: Cambridge University Press, 1923–59), vol. ii, 'Early Eighteenth-Century Drama', p. 282.

5. *in another place*: *A Large Account of the Taste in Poetry, and the Causes of the Degeneracy of It* (1702).

6. *Vatis . . . ridet*: 'The poet's mind is not easily made avaricious. He loves verses – that is his whole study. Financial losses, absconding slaves, fires: these he laughs at': Horace, *Epistles*, II.i.119–21 (*ALC*, p. 275).

7. *as Aristotle . . . affirm of it*: Aristotle, *Poetics*, 1451b (*ALC*, p. 102).

8. *Is . . . sour*: Milton, *The Reason of Church Government* (1642), Book II (*Prose Works*, i, 816–18).

9. *what Monsieur Dacier has taken*: André Dacier, *Poétique d'Aristote* (1692), ch. xv, rem. 13, pp. 225–6.

10. *Conviction . . . Obligation*: Cf. Basil Kennett, *Lives and Characters of the Ancient Greek Poets* (1697), pp. 83–4.

11. *the little Treatise . . . a sublime Art*: *Of Education* (1644) (*Prose Works*, ii, 404).

12. *Treatise of Education to Mr. Hartlip*: See n. 11 above.

13. *in another place*: In *The Advancement and Reformation of Modern Poetry* (1701), pt II, ch. 1.

14. *prefer Tragedy to Epick Poetry*: Aristotle, *Poetics* (*ALC*, pp. 123–32).

15. *are not great*: Longinus, *On Sublimity*, sect. 7 (*ALC*, pp. 466–7).

16. *any other Passion*: At this point the detailed discussion of a series of sublime passages from Milton and Tasso has been omitted.

17. *The First . . . attain'd*: *On Sublimity*, 'Preface' (*ALC*, p. 462).

18. *Loftiness . . . nature of it*: *On Sublimity*, sect. 8 (*ALC*, pp. 467–8).

19. *Sublime . . . persuading*: *On Sublimity*, 'Preface' (*ALC*, p. 462).

20. *Marks . . . Definition*: For these 'marks' as given, slightly differently, by Longinus, see *On Sublimity*, sect. 7 (*ALC*, pp. 466–7).

21. *most delightful*: Aristotle, *Poetics*, 1462b (*ALC*, p. 132).

22. *Strabo . . . Geography*: Strabo, *Geography*, I.ii.6.

23. *Well sounding Verses . . . persuades*: Edmund Waller, 'Upon the Earl of Roscommon's Translation of Horace, "De Arte Poetica;" and Of the Use of Poetry', ll. 22–8.

24. *In boundless Verse . . . place*: Edmund Waller, 'Of Divine Poesy', Canto I, ll. 21–6.

25. *to God*: At this point a comparison of Scriptural with Homeric sublimity, to the advantage of the former, has been omitted.

26. *Rule of Horace . . . Strength*: Horace, *De Arte Poetica*, ll. 38–40 (*ALC*, p. 280).

27. *Mr. Mede . . . as follow*: Joseph Mede, *Diatribæ* (1642), Discourse xvi on I. Cor. 15.5, 'Every woman praying or prophecying with her head uncovered, dishonoureth her head', pp. 246–61, this passage pp. 251–2.

28. *As . . . has said*: Titus 1:12.

Sir Richard Blackmore, *Advice to the Poets* (1706)

SIR RICHARD BLACKMORE (1654–1729); physician to William III and Queen Anne; epic poet and staunch Whig.

TEXT: Taken from the first edition of 1706.

1. The organizing conceit of the poem is that of offering advice to poets on how best to commemorate the Duke of Marlborough's victory over the French at Ramillies in May 1706. The poem therefore has points of contact with the 'Instructions' poems popular during the Restoration, and of which the best-known examples are Edmund Waller's *Instructions to a Painter* (1665) and Andrew Marvell's *Last Instructions to a Painter* (1667): see M. T. Osborne, *Advice-to-a-Painter Poems, 1638–1856* (Austin, Texas: University of Texas Press, 1949). For a later comparison, see Aaron Hill's *Advice to the Poets* (1731). The most readable account of Ramillies and the campaign of which it was a part is still that offered by G. M. Trevelyan in *England Under Queen Anne: Ramillies and the Union with Scotland* (London: Longmans, Green, 1932), ch. 6, 'Ramillies', pp. 100–120.

2. *Blenheim's glorious Toil*: Marlborough had also defeated the French two years earlier at Blenheim. The most famous of the many poems written to celebrate this victory was Addison's *The Campaign* (1705).

3. *delightful Seat on Isis found*: Blenheim Palace, at Woodstock.

4. *decline the proffer'd War*: Marlborough had complained to his wife that 'the French will not venture in this country.'

5. *Louvania*: Louvain.

6. *Paster-Fido's Strain*: Guarini's pastoral tragicomedy *Il Pastor Fido* (1589) had been translated into English in 1647 by Sir Richard Fanshawe as *The Faithfull Shepherd*.

7. *Mantua*: Traditionally (although with slight inaccuracy) deemed the birthplace of Virgil.

8. *Summers*: John, Lord Somers.

9. *fam'd Grecian's . . . Sphere of Sense*: Aristotle, *Metaphysics* Λ.

10. *Angelo*: Michelangelo Buonarroti.

11. *Dyle . . . Scamander's Flood*: The Dyle is a river to the north and west of Ramillies. The Scamander is a river to the south of the site of Troy.

12. *from the raging Fire*: Cf. Virgil, *Æneid*, II.707ff.

13. *Boian Fields*: Boia was a town in ancient Gaul (Cæsar, *De Bello Gallico*, VII.14); Blackmore uses Boian as a classical synonym for 'French'.

14. *In Raphael's famous Piece . . . pursue*: The reference is to Raphael's Vatican mural, *The Victory of Constantine at the Milvian Bridge*: 'such another Briton' refers to Constantine; Maxentius was his opponent.

15. *Vill'roy*: Marshal François de Neufville, duc de Villeroi.

16. *Gaul's proud Statue . . . demands*: An allusion to the results of the so-called 'statue campaign' of 1685–6.

17. *Moses crown*: Exodus 34:29–35.

18. *Mechlinia's Tow'rs*: Mechlinia was the medieval name of Mechelen (in French, Malines), a town a few miles north-east of Brussels.

19. *Lutetia*: The name of the Gallic city which occupied the present site of Paris.

Samuel Cobb, *A Discourse on Criticism and the Liberty of Writing* (1707)

SAMUEL COBB (1675–1713); poet and translator; composer of Whig panegyric; master at Christ's Hospital.

TEXT: Taken from Cobb's *Poems on Several Occasions* (1707).

1. *Daughters of Memory*: In Greek mythology the Muses were the daughters of Mnemosyne, a Titaness and the personification of memory.

2. *done on This*: For the political context to which Cobb alludes, see above, pp. xix–xxii.

3. *Congreve . . . Pindaric Verse*: William Congreve's 'A Discourse on the Pindaric Ode' was published as a preface to his own, intensely classical, poem on the victory at Ramillies, *A Pindarique Ode, Humbly Offer'd to the Queen, on the Victorious Progress of Her MAJESTY's Arms, under the Conduct of the Duke of Marlborough* (1706). Congreve argues vigorously for the strict regularity of the Pindaric ode, and takes issue with what he sees as the mistaken notion, derived from Cowley, that Pindaric odes lack form. For a recent discussion of the Pindaric ode in Augustan England, see Howard Weinbrot, *Britannia's Issue* (Cambridge: Cambridge University Press, 1993), pp. 329–401.

4. *Mr. Prior*: Cobb refers to Prior's loose imitation of Horace's fourth ode of the fourth book, written in Spenserian stanzas to celebrate the victory at Ramillies: *An Ode, Humbly Inscrib'd to the Queen. On the Glorious Success of Her Majesty's Arms. Written in Imitation of Spencer's Style* (1706).

5. *ex pede Herculem*: Literally, 'Hercules by his foot', i.e. '[you may judge] the size of Hercules from that of his footprint'; therefore, 'you may judge of the whole by the part'.

6. *Lynceus*: In Greek mythology, the son of Aphareus, and an Argonaut possessed of sight so keen that he could see through the earth.

7. *Juvenal . . . Scripture*: 'Sed facilis cuivis rigidi censura cachinni' ('We all find it easy to censure with a cutting laugh'): Juvenal, X.31. 'For as the crackling of thorns under a pot, so is the laughter of the fool': Ecclesiastes VII:6.

8. *In vitium . . . arte*: 'Shunning a fault may lead to error, if art is wanting': Horace, *De Arte Poetica*, l. 31 (*ALC*, p. 280).

9. *Homer . . . Best of Judges*: For an account of the contemporary disputes over the status of Homer (to which Saint-Évremond contributed as a detractor), see Weinbrot, *Britannia's Issue*, pp. 193–236.

10. *Longinus . . . himself*: An allusion to section 33 of *On Sublimity*, where Longinus contrasts the occasional irregularity of genius with the uniform correctness of mediocrity: 'I have myself cited not a few mistakes in Homer and other great writers, not because I take pleasure in their slips, but because I consider them not so much voluntary mistakes as oversights let fall at random through inattention and with the negligence of genius' (*ALC*, p. 492).

11. *Sub pedibusq . . . sydera*: 'And beneath his feet he sees the clouds and the stars': Virgil, *Eclogues*, V.57.

12. *Alcibiades . . . Goddesses*: Cobb alludes to Alcibiades's praise of Socrates in Plato's *Symposium*: 'he is exactly like the busts of Silenus, which are set up in the statuaries' shops, holding pipes or flutes in their mouths; and they are made to open in the middle, and have images of gods inside them' (215 a–b). In Greek mythology Silenus was an elderly, drunken satyr, the companion of Dionysius.

13. *Bocalin . . . Advertisement*: Boccalini's *Ragguagli di Parnaso* ('Reports from Parnassus') were translated into English by Henry Carey, second Earl of Monmouth, as *Advertisements from Parnassus* (1656). The episode to which Cobb alludes is to be found on pp. 45–6.

14. *Nec . . . deserere*: 'Nor has least honour been earned when they [Latin poets] have dared to leave the footsteps of the Greeks': Horace, *De Arte Poetica*, ll. 286–7 (*ALC*, p. 287).

15. *Dryden's Pers.*: Dryden's translation of the first satire of Persius, ll. 119–20.

16. *Mentiri . . . poscere*: 'I cannot lie: if a book is bad, I cannot praise it and ask for a copy': Juvenal, III.41–2.

17. *Corrige . . . hoc*: 'Prithee, correct this and this, he would say': Horace, *De Arte Poetica*, ll. 438–9 (*ALC*, p. 291). 'Fastus' is haughtiness or arrogance.

18. *Insistere . . . petere*: Cobb is slightly misremembering André Dacier's 'Præfatio in Horatii Satiras', where Dacier says, referring to earlier traditions of commentary, 'Substiterunt in ipso cortice, verbisque interpretandis intenti nihil ultrà petiere . . .' ('They halted at the very surface [*lit.* "outer rind"], and, concentrating on verbal criticism, sought for nothing beyond . . .'). The essay was much reprinted, but see e.g. *Q. Horatii Flacci Opera* (1699), sig. Aa6^r.

19. *err with Mr. Cowley*: For Cowley's views on the Pindaric and how it was to be rendered in English, see the 'Preface' to *Pindarique Odes* (1656).

20. *Mr. Congreve . . . Lines*: See above, n. 3.

Alexander Pope, *An Essay on Criticism* (1711)

ALEXANDER POPE (1688–1744); the most accomplished poet, critic and translator of the early Hanoverian period; Roman Catholic in religion, and of Jacobite inclinations.

TEXT: Taken from the first edition of 1711. The most important of the many variants introduced in later editions are given below. They show that Pope continued to refine this poem until his death.

1. *in Writing or in Judging ill*: Cf. Buckingham, *An Essay upon Poetry*, ll. 1–2 (above, p. 97).

2. *De Pictore . . . potest*: 'Only a craftsman can judge of the fine arts': Pliny, *Epistles*, I.x.4.

3. *Omnes . . . dijudicant*: 'For everybody is able to distinguish what is sound from what is bad in matters of art and proportion by a kind of instinctive sense, without being equipped with any theory of art or proportion of their own': Cicero, *De Oratore*, III.50.

4. *Those hate . . . Lovers.*: In the *Miscellany Poems* of 1732 and thereafter this couplet was changed to: 'Each burns alike, who can, or cannot write, / Or with a *Rival's*, or an *Eunuch's* spite.'

5. *Fools at last*: Allegedly taken by John Dennis to be a hit at him.

6. *One science . . . fit*: Cf. Buckingham, *An Essay upon Poetry*, l. 342 (above, p. 107).

7. *follow NATURE*: For the injunction to follow Nature, cf. Cicero, *De Officiis*, I.xxviii.10.

8. *Universal Light*: Cf. Roscommon, *An Essay on Translated Verse*, ll. 193–4 (above, p. 114).

9. *That Art . . . Appear;*: In the *Works* of 1717 and thereafter this couplet was changed to: '*Art* from that Fund each *just Supply* provides, / Works *without Show*, and *without Pomp* presides:'.

10. *sprightly*: Pope worried over this word: in the *Works* of 1717 it was changed to 'the secret'; in the *Works* of 1736 and thereafter, it reads 'th'informing'.

11. *There are . . . manage it*: In the quarto edition of 1744 and thereafter this couplet was changed to: 'Some, to whom Heav'n in Wit has been profuse, / Want as much more, to turn it to its use;'.

12. *ever*: In the quarto edition of 1744 Pope softened 'ever' to 'often'.

13. *The winged Courser . . . check his Course*: Cf. Edmund Waller, 'Upon the Earl of Roscommon's Translation of Horace, "De Arte Poetica;" and Of the Use of Poetry', ll. 11–12: 'Direct us how to back the winged Horse, / Favour his flight, and moderate his force.'

14. *Monarchy*: In the quarto edition of 1744 'Monarchy' was replaced, perhaps at the suggestion of William Warburton, by 'Liberty'.

15. *First learned Greece . . . Flight:*: In the *Works* of 1717 and thereafter this couplet was altered to read, 'Hear how learn'd *Greece* her useful Rules indites, / When to repress, and when indulge our Flights:'.

16. *From great Examples . . . giv'n;*: In the *Works* of 1717 and thereafter this line was altered to read, 'Just *Precepts* thus from great *Examples* giv'n'.

17. *Set up . . . Trade*: In the *Works* of 1736 and thereafter this line was deleted, and the triplet thus became a couplet.

18. *so modern Pothecaries . . . Fools*: An allusion to the late seventeenth-century conflict between physicians and apothecaries commemorated in Samuel Garth's *The Dispensary* (1699). The apothecaries, although without formal training, wished to retain the whole lucrative business of the supply of drugs in their own hands, and vigorously resisted moves by the physicians to sell drugs at cost.

19. *You may . . . Criticize.*: In the second edition of 1713 and thereafter this line was revised to read: '*Cavil* you may, but never *Criticize*.' In its original form the line alluded to Roscommon's *An Essay on Translated Verse*, ll. 195–6 (above, p. 114).

20. *meditate by Night*: Cf. Horace, *De Arte Poetica*, ll. 268–9 (*ALC*, p. 286).

21. *Notions*: In the quarto edition of 1744 'Notions' was altered to 'Maxims'.

22. *Still . . . peruse*: Cf. Roscommon, *An Essay on Translated Verse*, l. 186 (above, p. 113).

23. *the Mantuan Muse*: Virgil.

24. *great*: In the second edition of 1713 and thereafter 'great' was altered to 'young'.

25. *When first . . . design'd,*: From the second edition of 1713 until the *Works* of 1743 this couplet read, 'When first young *Maro* sung of *Kings* and *Wars*, / Ere warning Phœbus touch'd his trembling Ears,'.

26. *And did . . . confine,*: In the *Works* of 1717 and thereafter this line was revised to read, 'And Rules as strict his labour'd Work confine,'.

27. *the Stagyrite*: Aristotle.

28. *Neque . . . sequemur*: 'Nor are these rules so sacred: but they are the product of expediency. I will not deny that it is in general expedient to adopt them; but if expediency suggests some other course to us, we shall follow it and abandon the authority of the professors': Quintilian, *Institutio Oratoria*, II.xiii. 6–7.

29. *But Care . . . Mad*: This couplet was deleted in the quarto edition of 1744 and thereafter.

30. *Oft hide*: In the second edition of 1713 and thereafter 'Oft *hide*' became 'Conceal'.

31. *are but*: In the second edition of 1713 and thereafter 'are but' became 'oft are'.

32. *all-devouring*: In the quarto edition of 1744 'all-devouring' became 'all-involving'.

33. *Triumphant*: In the second edition of 1713 and thereafter 'Triumphant' became 'consenting'.

34. *Oh may . . . inspire*: Cf. Roscommon, *An Essay on Translated Verse*, ll. 173–6 (above, p. 113).

35. *Pride . . . Sense*: Cf. Roscommon, *An Essay on Translated Verse*, ll. 161–2 (above, p. 113).

36. *Pierian Spring*: The cult of the Muses was said to have been brought from Pieria to Helicon, and the Muses are sometimes referred to as Pierian. The '*Pierian* Spring' is therefore a spring sacred to the Muses.

37. *Fir'd . . . Art;*: In the *Works* of 1717 and thereafter this couplet reads, 'Fir'd at first Sight with what the *Muse* imparts, / In *fearless Youth* we tempt the Heights of Arts,'.

38. *survey*: In the second edition of 1713 and thereafter 'survey' became 'behold'.

39. *Alps on Alps arise*: A celebrated image, probably drawn originally from Silius Italicus, *Punica*, III.528–35.

40. *regularly low*: Cf. Horace, *De Arte Poetica*, ll. 267–8 (*ALC*, p. 286).

41. *nor e'er shall be*: Cf. Buckingham, *Essay upon Poetry*, ll. 232–5 (above, p. 104).

42. *oft the*: In the *Works* of 1717 and thereafter 'oft the' was replaced by 'sometimes'.

43. *Diligenter . . . resumendus*: 'One must read diligently, and with almost as much care as one would write. Everything is to be scrutinized, not just a little at a time. One should read a book right through, and then start again at the beginning': Quintilian, *Institutio Oratoria*, X.i.20 (*ALC*, p. 383).

44. *Parts they*: In the *Works* of 1717 and thereafter 'Parts they' was replaced by 'Notions'.

45. *La Mancha's Knight, they say*: Pope found this episode in bk III, ch. x of John Stevens's 1705 translation of Avellaneda's *Continuation of the Comical History of . . . Don Quixote de la Mancha*.

46. *D—s, of the Laws o' th' Stage*: In the *Works* of 1717 and thereafter Dennis's name is spelt out. In the *Miscellany Poems* of 1727 and 1732 'of the Laws o' th' Stage' temporarily became 'of *th'Athenian* Stage', then reverted to the first form in subsequent printings before becoming 'of the *Grecian* Stage' in the quarto edition of 1744.

47. *Concluding . . . Rules*: For Dennis's devotion to regularity and his admiration for the theatre of antiquity, see *The Grounds of Criticism in Poetry* (above, pp. 149–50).

48. *The Stage . . . contain.*: In the quarto edition of 1744 this line was rearranged to read, 'So vast a Throng the Stage can ne'er contain.'

49. *before Exprest*: In the second edition of 1713 and thereafter 'before' was amended to 'so well'.

50. *Naturam . . . agnoscunt*: 'Fix your eyes on Nature and follow her. The mind is always most receptive to what it recognizes as natural': Quintilian, *Institutio Oratoria*, VIII.iii.71.

51. *Plainness . . . Wit*: Cf. Roscommon, *An Essay on Translated Verse*, l. 219 (above, p. 114).

52. *true Expression . . . Sun*: Cf. Buckingham, *An Essay upon Poetry*, l. 12 (above, p. 97).

53. *Abolita . . . nova*: 'But to retain the obsolete and extinct is impertinence and the sheerest pedantry': Quintilian, *Institutio Oratoria*, I.vi.20. 'But such archaisms must be used sparingly and without ostentation, since there is nothing more tiring than affectation, nor above all must they be drawn from remote and forgotten ages. But what a faulty thing is speech, whose prime virtue is clarity, if it requires an interpreter? Therefore in the case of old words the best will be the newest, just as in the case of new words the best will be the oldest': ibid., 39–41.

54. *Equal Syllables . . . require*: Cf. Roscommon, *An Essay on Translated Verse*, ll. 226ff. (above, p. 115).

55. *one dull Line*: Cf. Dryden, *Of Dramatick Poesie, An Essay* (above, p. 21).

56. *expected Rhymes*: Cf. Atterbury, 'Preface' to Waller (above, p. 123).

57. *Every Man in his Humour*: Fungoso in fact appears in Jonson's *Every Man Out of His Humour* (1599).

58. *Quis . . . uno*: ' "What says the public?" Well, what? – if not that poetry now has at last a soft and rhythmic flow. Its smooth joins shrug off the relentless probe. "He can draw out a verse like someone positioning the builder's mark with one eye closed" ': Persius, *Satires*, I.63–6. Persius draws his metaphors here from building.

59. *Fugiemus . . . reddunt*: 'We shall avoid the frequent collision of vowels, which make style harsh and gaping': Cicero, *Ad Herennium*, IV.12. The passage in Quintilian to which Pope draws the reader's attention is *Institutio Oratoria*, IX.iv.33, and translates as follows: 'There are some blemishes so obvious that even the uneducated hold them worthy of censure . . . as when vowels clash. When this happens, the language is broken by gaps and interruptions and seems to labour.'

60. *Sweetness join*: In the *Works* of 1717 and thereafter Pope inserted the following, celebrated, couplet: 'True Ease in Writing comes from Art, not Chance, / As those move easiest who have learn'd to dance.' Given the frequency with which this couplet is cited as an expression of Pope's aesthetic, both in this poem and elsewhere, it is important to recognize that it originally formed no part of the poem.

61. *an Eccho to the Sense*: Cf. Roscommon, *An Essay on Translated Verse*, l. 345 (above, p. 118).

62. *various*: In the *Works* of 1736 and thereafter 'various' was changed to 'vary'd'.

63. *Men of Sense Approve*: Cf. Horace, *De Arte Poetica*, ll. 455–6 (*ALC*, p. 291).

64. *Dulness . . . Magnify*: Cf. Sir Robert Howard, 'Preface' to *The Great Favourite* (above, p. 84).

65. *the French*: In the quarto edition of 1744 'the *French*' became '*foreign*'.

66. *damn*: In the *Works* of 1717 and thereafter 'damn' was replaced by 'blame'.

67. *teems with Thought*: Cf. Horace, *De Arte Poetica*, ll. 382–4 (*ALC*, p. 289).

68. *dull*: In the second edition of 1713 and thereafter '*dull*' was amended to '*plain*'.

69. *Scotists and Thomists*: Followers of, respectively, the medieval philosophers Duns Scotus (1265 or 1275–1308) and Thomas Aquinas (*c.* 1227–74).

70. *Duck-Lane*: In Pope's words, 'A place where old and second-hand books were sold formerly, near *Smithfield*.'

71. *Bl—s . . . M—s*: Sir Richard Blackmore and Luke Milbourne. In editions published between 1713 and 1716 Blackmore's name was replaced with that of Thomas Shadwell.

72. *Zoilus*: A grammarian of late antiquity famous for his strictures on Homer.

73. *too*: In the *Works* of 1717 and thereafter 'too;' was replaced by 'true;'.

74. *Sun . . . the Day*: Cf. Buckingham, *An Essay upon Poetry*, ll. 12–14 (above, p. 97).

75. *fair*: In the *Works* of 1717 and thereafter '*fair*' was replaced by '*bright*'.

76. *When . . . give,*: In the *Works* of 1717 and thereafter this line was rewritten as 'When mellowing Years their full Perfection give,'.

77. *The treach'rous . . . decay,*: In the *Works* of 1717 and thereafter this line was rewritten as 'The *treach'rous Colours* the fair Art betray,'.

78. *Repays . . . brings:*: In the second edition of 1713 and thereafter this line was rewritten as 'Attones not for that *Envy* which it brings.'

79. *Like . . . rise*: In the *Works* of 1717 and thereafter this line was rewritten as 'Like some fair *Flow'r* the early *Spring* supplies,'.

80. *The more . . . with Ease;*: These three lines were vigorously attacked by Dennis (see above, p. 251), and Pope revised them repeatedly until his death. In their final form, they read, 'Then most our *Trouble* still when most *admir'd*, / And still the more we *give*, the more *requir'd*; / Whose Fame with *Pains* we guard, but lose with *Ease*,'.

81. *Too much . . . undergo,*: In the *Works* of 1717 and thereafter this line was rewritten as: 'If *Wit* so much from *Ign'rance* undergo,'.

82. *Obscenity should find*: Cf. Buckingham, *An Essay upon Poetry*, ll. 80ff., and Roscommon, *An Essay on Translated Verse*, ll. 113–14 (above, pp. 99 and 111).

83. *rank Weed*: Cf. *Hamlet*, I.v.32 and Roscommon, *An Essay on Translated Verse*, l. 66 (above, p. 110).

84. *Monarch's*: i.e. Charles II, who reigned between 1660 and 1685.

85. *Jilts*: kept mistresses.

86. *Statesmen Farces writ*: Perhaps an allusion to Buckingham's *The Rehearsal* (1671), a burlesque play mocking Dryden's heroic dramas.

87. *Mask*: A woman wearing a mask, a play-house fashion of Charles II's reign. 'Mask' eventually became a synonym for 'whore'.

88. *Foreign Reign*: The reign of William III (1689–1702).

89. *Socinus*: Socinus denied the divinity of Christ, and hence questioned the efficacy of Christ's atonement for men's sins. But 'Socinianism' could refer more generally to the use of reason in matters of religion.

90. *Then first . . . gold*: This couplet was deleted from the *Works* of 1736 and was not reinstated thereafter. Pope drew attention to the deletion by inserting the following note in all subsequent editions: '*The Author has omitted two lines which stood here, as containing a* National Reflection, *which in his stricter judgment he could not but disapprove, on any People whatever.*'

91. *more Pleasant . . . Salvation*: Allegedly a hit at the sermon preached by White Kennett at the funeral of the Duke of Devonshire in 1708, where he argued that men of condition found deathbed repentance easier than did those of lesser birth.

92. *too Absolute*: Pope here implies a connection between a doctrinally corrupt priesthood and Whiggish politics.

93. *Licenc'd Blasphemies*: An allusion to the Commons' refusal in 1694 to renew the Licensing Act of 1663. The case against renewing the Act had been prepared by John Locke, who had argued that the Act had been ineffective, not that its purpose of controlling the output of the press was improper.

94. *'Tis not . . . join;*: In the quarto edition of 1744 this line was rewritten as ' 'Tis not enough, Taste, Judgment, Learning, join;'.

95. *Judgment's*: In the quarto edition of 1744 '*Judgment*'s' was replaced by '*Sense* is'.

96. *Speak . . . with Diffidence;*: In the second edition of 1713 and thereafter this line was rewritten as 'And *speak*, tho' *sure*, with *seeming Diffidence*:'. Dennis had attacked this line as 'absurd' (see above, p. 252), and Pope's revision deferred to the criticism.

97. *ne'er known*: In the *Works* of 1717 and thereafter '*ne'er known*' was replaced with '*unknown*'.

98. *not approv'd*: In the *Works* of 1717 and thereafter 'not approv'd' was replaced with 'disapprov'd'.

99. *Appius*: A stab at Dennis, whose *Appius and Virginia* had been performed at Drury Lane in February 1709. In the quarto of 1744 Pope inserted the following note to this line (italics reversed): 'This picture was taken to himself by *John Dennis*, a furious old Critic by profession, who, upon no other provocation, wrote against this Essay and its author, in a manner perfectly lunatic: For, as to the mention made of him in ver. 270. he took it as a Compliment, and said it was treacherously meant to cause him to overlook this *Abuse* of his *Person*.'

100. *dull Fools*: In the second edition of 1713 and thereafter 'dull Fools' was changed to 'the Dull'.

101. *For who . . . write*: Cf. Buckingham, *Essay upon Satire*, l. 71: 'But who can rail as long as he can sleep?'

102. *old dull*: In the second edition of 1713 and thereafter 'old dull' was changed to 'drowzy'.

103. *D—y's*: In the *Miscellany Poems* of 1727 Durfey's name was spelt out.

104. *Garth . . . Dispensary*: See above, n. 18.

105. *tho' well-bred, sincere*: Cf. Roscommon, *An Essay on Translated Verse*, ll. 69–70 (above, p. 110).

106. *Nihil . . . perdocent*: 'There are none worse than those who, as soon as they have gone beyond a knowledge of the alphabet, delude themselves that they are really knowledgeable. For they disdain to stoop to the drudgery of teaching, and believing that they have acquired authority (a frequent source of vanity in such people) they become imperious or even brutal in instilling a thorough dose of their own stupidity': Quintilian, *Institutio Oratoria*, I.i.8.

107. *Mæonian Star*: Homer, who was supposed to have been born in Maeonia.

108. *Not only . . . Sway*: In the second edition of 1713 and thereafter this couplet was omitted.

109. *Does*: In the *Works* of 1717 and thereafter 'Does' was replaced by 'Will'.

110. *Our Criticks . . . Fle'me*: Cf. Roscommon, *An Essay on Translated Verse*, ll. 300–301 (above, p. 117): an allusion noted by Dennis in his strictures on Pope's *Essay* (above, pp. 248–9).

111. *Quotations*: In the second edition of 1713 and thereafter the following couplet was inserted at this point, set out as a separate verse paragraph: 'See *Dionysius Homer*'s Thoughts refine, / And call new Beauties forth from ev'ry Line!'

112. *and*: In the second edition of 1713 and thereafter 'and' was replaced by 'with'.

113. *Nor thus . . . with Ease.*: In the quarto edition of 1744 this couplet was rewritten as: 'But less to please the Eye, than arm the Hand, / Still fit for Use, and ready at Command.'

114. *The Muses . . . inspire,*: In the second edition of 1713 and thereafter this line was rewritten as: 'Thee, bold Longinus! all the Nine inspire,'. As Joseph

Warton commented, this abrupt direct address is 'more suitable to the character of the person addressed'.

115. *All . . . understood,*: In the second edition of 1713 and thereafter this line was softened to read: 'Much was *Believ'd*, but little *understood*'. In its original form it had been construed by Pope's co-religionists as a slight on their faith.

116. *Leo's Golden Day's*: A reference to Leo X, who reigned as Pope from 1513 to 1521, and who acted as patron to artists such as Raphael and Michelangelo.

117. *Vida sung*: Pope had made a careful study of Vida's *Poetica*, and its influence is discernible throughout *An Essay on Criticism*.

118. *from Latium chas'd*: An allusion to the sack of Rome in 1527 by the troops of Charles V.

119. *Fundamental Laws*: In the *Works* of 1717 and thereafter the following compliment to John Sheffield, Duke of Buckingham, was inserted: 'Such was the Muse, whose rules and Practice tell, / *Nature's chief Master-piece is writing well*.' The allusion is to his *An Essay upon Poetry*, l. 2 (above, p. 97).

John Dennis, *Reflections . . . Upon . . . An Essay Upon Criticism* (1711)

JOHN DENNIS (1657–1734); see above, p. 374.

TEXT: Taken from the first edition of 1711; italic and roman reversed in the text of 'The Preface'.

1. *Italian Opera . . . happen'd*: For an example of Dennis's hostility to Italian opera, see his *An Essay on the Opera's after the Italian Manner . . . with some Reflection on the Damage which they may Bring to the Publick* (1706). This hostility was a point of contact with Pope: see *The Dunciad*, IV.45–70.

2. *Fit . . . miror*: 'He becomes another Choerilus, whose one or two good lines cause laughter and surprise': Horace, *De Arte Poetica*, ll. 357–8 (*ALC*, p. 289).

3. *Provocation . . . Fortune*: Pope indeed appears to have attacked Dennis for no other reason than that he was the butt of Pope's friends (Sherburn, i, 69–70). In a letter to Caryll of 25 June 1711 Pope protested that he was unaware of the adversity – indigence – against which Dennis was struggling (ibid., i, 120–23).

4. *Happy . . . Horatian way*: Roscommon's *An Essay on Translated Verse* (1684) begins with this praise of Buckingham's *An Essay upon Poetry* (1682) (above, p. 108).

5. *De Pictore . . . potest*: Pliny, *Epistles*, I.x.4 (above, p. 379, n. 2).

6. *living noble Author*: John Sheffield, Earl of Mulgrave and Duke of Buckingham.

7. *Boileau . . . Longinus*: *Réflexions Critiques sur quelques Passages du Rhéteur Longin*, 'Réflexion VII', in *Oeuvres de Nicolas Boileau*, 'Nouvelle Édition' (1713), pp. 542–3.

8. *in another place*: Dennis here alludes to his *Essay on the Genius and Writings of Shakespeare*, which was to be published in November 1711.

9. *proud*: This should read 'prov'd' (above, p. 211, l. 102).

10. 2^d: A slip for '8th'.

11. *Authors . . . Verse*: i.e. Buckingham and Roscommon (above, pp. 97–107 and 108–20).

12. *When first . . . draw*: Pope amended the first couplet of this passage in response to Dennis's criticism (above, p. 380, n. 25).

13. *that Figure, call'd a Bull*: i.e. a statement which unconsciously implies an absurdity.

14. *Jungentur . . . Equis*: 'Griffins now shall mate with mares': Virgil, *Eclogues*, VIII.27.

15. *Scribendi . . . Chartæ*: 'The source and fount of good writing is wisdom. Your subject the Socratic pages can show you': Horace, *De Arte Poetica*, ll. 309–10 (*ALC*, p. 288).

16. *Artis est celare artem*: 'Art is the concealment of art': a proverbial tag, not to be found in classical Latin literature, although the thought that artifice should be concealed is a commonplace among ancient rhetorical writers. See also Ovid, *Ars Amatoria*, II.313.

17. *Essay upon Poetry*: Dennis alludes to l. 20 of Buckingham's *An Essay upon Poetry* (above, p. 97).

18. *Tis . . . Solidity*: The quotation (slightly misremembered) is from Dominique Bouhours's *La Manière de bien penser dans les ouvrages d'esprit* (1687: Nouvelle Édition, 1709), Dialogue IV: 'Les pensées ingénieuses sont comme les diamans, qui tirent leur prix de ce qu'ils ont encore plus de solidité que d'éclat . . .' (p. 299).

19. *True Wit . . . Sun*: Buckingham, *An Essay upon Poetry*, l. 12 (above, p. 97).

20. *Glory of the Roman Name*: Dennis is perhaps referring to the foreshadowing of the later conflicts between Rome and Carthage which Virgil inserts into Book IV of the *Æneid*.

21. *Bacon . . . first Writers*: Bacon, *Advancement of Learning*, I.v.1.

22. *in the Advancement of Modern Poetry*: i.e. in *The Advancement and Reformation of Modern Poetry* (1701).

23. *Aliquando . . . Homerus*: 'Sometimes even good Homer nods': Horace, *De Arte Poetica*, l. 359 (*ALC*, p. 289).

24. *His reeling . . . nods*: Roscommon, *An Essay on Translated Verse*, ll. 139–40 (above, p. 112).

25. *Si forte . . . detorta*: 'If by chance you have to suggest outlandish things in neologisms, you will be able to forge words never heard of by the kilted Cethegi, and licence will be granted if they are used with modesty; while words, though new and of recent make, will be accepted if they are Greek in origin and used sparingly': Horace, *De Arte Poetica*, ll. 48–53 (*ALC*, pp. 280–81).

26. *quid autem . . . nomen*: 'Why indeed shall Romans grant this licence to Caecilius and Plautus, and refuse it to Virgil and Varius? And why should I be grudged the right to add, if I can, my little store? When the language of Cato and Ennius has enriched our mother-tongue and brought to light new terms for things, it has been, and always will be permitted to issue words stamped with the current mark': Horace, *De Arte Poetica*, ll. 53–9: (*ALC*, p. 281). The punctuation of Dennis's text does not accord with that of modern editions.

27. *Thus . . . Flegm*: Roscommon, *An Essay on Translated Verse*, ll. 300–301 (above, p. 117).

28. *a Figure . . . Hibernian Land*: i.e. a bull (see above, n. 13), to which the Irish were supposed to be especially prone.

29. *That silly thing . . . Thought*: Buckingham, *An Essay Upon Poetry*, ll. 269–72 (above, p. 105); but Dennis is clearly using a later edition of the poem.

30. *speak . . . with Diffidence*: Once again, Pope here amended his wording in response to Dennis's criticism (above, p. 384, n. 96).

31. *Not only . . . Sway*: This couplet was deleted from later editions of the *Essay on Criticism* (above, p. 227 and p. 385, n. 108).

32. *The King of France . . . Peace*: For a similar animadversion on the harmful consequences of Louis XIV's drive to establish a universal monarchy, see William Coward, *Licentia Poetica* (1709).

33. *Another great Wit . . . Debt*: i.e. William Wycherley.

34. *former Duke of Buckingham*: George Villiers.

35. *Thus . . . destroy'd*: Samuel Butler, *Hudibras* (1663), I.ii.23–8; slightly misquoted.

36. *'Tis now . . . Owe*: Abraham Cowley, 'The Second Olympique Ode of Pindar', stanza 11, misquoted. The passage should read: ' 'Tis now the *cheap* and *frugal* fashion, / Rather to *Hide* than *Pay* the *Obligation*. / Nay 'tis much worse than so, / It now an *Artifice* does grow, / *Wrongs* and *outrages* to do, / Lest men should think we *ow*.'

37. *His rankest . . . dose*: Untraced.

38. *The Dutch . . . Fools*: The allusion is to the couplet reflecting on Belgian irreligion and graspingness which Pope eventually removed, although so late that its deletion cannot be construed as deference to Dennis (above, p. 384, n. 90).

39. *St. Omer's*: A reference to the college founded by English Jesuits in 1592 in the town of St Omer. It later became a military hospital.

40. *Sir R.B., Mr. L.M.*: Sir Richard Blackmore; Luke Milbourne.

41. *Dorimant*: The rakish hero of Sir George Etherege's *The Man of Mode* (1676).

42. *a certain ancient Wit*: i.e. Wycherley; cf. Charles Gildon, *Memoirs of the Life of William Wycherley* (1718), pp. 16–17.

43. *from ever seeing the Light*: But see Dennis's *True Character of Mr. Pope* (1716).

44. *Panegyrick . . . in Mr. W—'s Name*: Here Dennis alludes to the poem 'To my friend Mr. Pope, on his Pastorals', published under William Wycherley's name in Jacob Tonson's *Miscellany*. Charles Gildon alleged in his *Memoirs of the Life of William Wycherley* (1718) that Pope had confessed to writing this poem himself.

45. *Respicere . . . voces*: 'I recommend that the skilled imitator attends to the model of life and manners, and draws from them true words': Horace, *De Arte Poetica*, ll. 317–18: modern editions read 'vivas', living, for 'veras', true (*ALC*, p. 288).

46. *If once . . . cost*: Buckingham, *An Essay upon Poetry*, ll. 267–8 (above, p. 105).

Alexander Pope, 'Preface' to *The Works of Shakespear* (1725)

ALEXANDER POPE (1688–1744); see above, p. 378.
TEXT: Taken from the first edition of *The Works of Shakespear* (1725).

1. *Ægyptian . . . channels*: There was a general belief in the early modern period that Homer had travelled in Egypt, and had there acquired his knowledge of arts and sciences. See, for example, Sir Richard Blackmore, 'An Essay Upon Epick Poetry', in *Essays Upon Several Subjects*, vol. 1 (1716), p. 27.

2. *Nature . . . thro' him*: For the identification of Shakespeare and Nature, see e.g. Dryden, *Of Dramatick Poesie, An Essay* (above, p. 57) and Theobald (above, pp. 288 and 291).

3. *every speaker*: The distinctiveness of Shakespeare's characters had been previously praised by Charles Gildon in his *Essays on the Stage* (1710), p. li. Addison later praised Homer in similar terms; *The Spectator*, no. 273 (12 January 1712).

4. *of no education . . . thoughts*: The unschooled nature of Shakespeare's talent was a familiar point in criticism of his works: see, e.g., Dryden, *Of Dramatick Poesie, An Essay* (above, p. 57).

5. *worse, than any other*: Compare Dryden, *Of Dramatick Poesie, An Essay* (above, p. 57).

6. *Prince . . . Peasant*: Pope is here likening Shakespeare to Florizel in *The Winter's Tale*.

7. *Johnson . . . into vogue*: Compare Dryden's very similar understanding of the significance of the changes to the drama effected by Jonson; *Of Dramatick Poesie, An Essay* (above, pp. 58–9).

8. *Shakespear by Aristotle's rules . . . another*: On Shakespeare's freedom from Aristotle's rules, compare Nicholas Rowe, 'Some Account of the Life, etc., of Mr. William Shakespear' (1709) and George Farquhar, 'A Discourse Upon Comedy' (1701).

9. *groundless report . . . evidences*: In fact in 1737 Pope himself would choose to accept the tradition: cf. *Epistle to Augustus*, ll. 279–81; 'And fluent Shakespear scarce effac'd a line. / Ev'n copious Dryden wanted, or forgot, / The last and greatest art, the art to blot.'

10. *exactly drawn*: Pope is here taking issue with John Dennis, who in his 'Essay on the Genius and Writings of Shakespeare' (1711) had attacked *Julius Cæsar* and *Coriolanus* for the ignorance of antiquity they evinced.

11. *Poetical story*: i.e. ancient mythology.

12. *pass for his*: The seventh volume of Pope's edition of Shakespeare contained, as had the seventh volume of Rowe's edition, miscellaneous poetic apocrypha, together with *Venus and Adonis* and *The Rape of Lucrece*, but excluding the *Sonnets*.

13. *one of his plays*: *The Comedy of Errors*.

14. *Dares Phrygius, in another*: Since Dares Phrygius was the supposed author of an account of the destruction of Troy, Pope presumably has in mind *Troilus and Cressida*.

15. *Italian writers . . . acquainted with*: Pope may here be thinking of Cinthio, whose *Gli Hecatomithi* furnished the source for *Othello*.

16. *more of our Author*: The second edition reads, 'more of the Author's worse sort'.

17. *Pessimum . . . Laudantes*: 'The worst enemies are those who praise': Tacitus, *Agricola*, 41.

18. *Si . . . noceat*: 'If Codrus should overpraise me, bind my brow with foxglove, lest he harm the poet': Virgil, *Eclogues*, VII.27–8.

19. *Mr. Dryden was of that opinion*: In his 'Discourse Concerning the Original and Progress of Satire' (1693).

20. *Hector's quoting Aristotle*: A blunder, of course, because Aristotle was born long after the Trojan war. It occurs in *Troilus and Cressida*, II.ii.166.

21. *(Act 3. Sc. 4.)*: Now III.ii.

22. *Procrustes*: A brigand who placed travellers on a bed; if they were too long for it, he would trim their limbs; if too short, he would stretch them.

23. *the dull duty of an Editor*: 'I . . . am become, by due gradation of dulness, from a poet a translator, and from a translator, a meer editor' (Sherburn, ii, 140: Pope to John Caryll, 16 October 1722).

Lewis Theobald, 'Preface' to *The Works of Shakespeare* (1733/1740)

LEWIS THEOBALD (1688–1744); poet, essayist and playwright; Shakespearean scholar, and one of the first to understand the importance of source-study for the appreciation of Shakespeare's art.

TEXT: Taken from the second edition of *The Works of Shakespeare* (1740: first edition, 1733).

1. *THE Attempt . . . Entertainment*: This architectural metaphor corrects and expands upon the final paragraph of the 'Preface' to Pope's edition of Shakespeare (above, p. 278).

2. *above the Direction of their Tailors*: Compare Pope's gibe that 'Players are just such judges of what is *right*, as Taylors are of what is *graceful*' (above, pp. 268–9).

3. *Judith*: Judith was Shakespeare's younger daughter, and the twin of Hamnet.

4. *seventeen Years*: Shakespeare was married by the end of 1582, the bond permitting him to marry Anne Hathaway being issued on 28 November of that year.

5. *Shallow's . . . he may quarter*: Merry Wives of Windsor, I.i.16 and 22.

6. *in the Comic Scene*: Spenser, *The Teares of the Muses*, l. 208.

7. *Rymer's Fœdera*: Thomas Rymer, *Foedera*, 10 vols. (The Hague, 3rd edn, 1745), vii. pt 2, p. 71.

8. *JUDICIO . . . &c.*: 'The earth covers, the people mourn, and Olympus holds a Nestor in wisdom, a Socrates in wit, and a Virgil in art.'

9. *three Weeks in New-place*: 11–13 July, 1643: three days, not three weeks.

10. *loose Papers and Manuscripts*: See John Roberts, *An Answer to Mr. Pope's Preface to Shakespear* (1729), p. 45.

11. *Nullum . . . Seneca*: 'No unblemished genius pleases': Seneca, *Epistles*, CXIV.12.

12. *Characters . . . celebrated*: Compare Pope's praise of Shakespeare's characterization (above, p. 266).

13. *Speret . . . idem*: 'Whoever hopes to achieve the same, may sweat much and toil in vain in making the attempt': Horace, *De Arte Poetica*, ll. 241–2 (*ALC*, p. 285).

14. *indebted to Nature*: For other identifications of Shakespeare with Nature, see Pope and Dryden, pp. 265–6 and 57 above.

15. *It is without Controversy . . . them*: Nicholas Rowe, 'Some Account of the Life, etc., of Mr. William Shakespear' (1709): Smith, p. 2.

16. *A very learned Critick . . . Predecessor*: William Warburton: see his letter to

Concanen of 2 January 1726, in Edmond Malone, *The Plays and Poems of William Shakespeare* (1821), xii, 157–60, esp. p. 158.

17. *break out . . . Splendor*: Compare Pope's evocation of the eruptive quality of Shakespeare's imagination; above, p. 267.

18. *indulging his private Sense, as he phrases it*: For Pope's use of this phrase, see above, p. 277.

19. *Inventus . . . excîdit*: Justus Lipsius, *Satyra Menippæa*, in his *Opera* (1611), p. 640.

20. *Mr. Rymer . . . Censurer*: Rymer's attacks on Shakespeare occur in *The Tragedies of the Last Age Considered* (1678) and *A Short View of Tragedy* (1692).

21. *Sive . . . dedit*: 'If a man, or the vilest beast in human form, wounds with its teeth . . .': Quintus Serenus, *De Medicina*, xlv, 'Hominis ac simiae morsui' (1533), sig. cii[v].

22. *Edition of Milton . . . Dr. Bentley*: For the Preface to Bentley's edition of *Paradise Lost*, see above, pp. 309–15.

23. *Tucca and Varius . . . Virgil*: Varius Rufus and Plotius Tucca were friends of Virgil, and edited the *Æneid* after his death.

24. *formerly observ'd*: Cf. Theobald, *Shakespeare Restored* (1726), pp. ii and iv.

25. *Cette voie . . . Critick*: 'This method of interpreting an author by himself is more sure than any commentary': untraced. For a similar sentiment, see Roscommon, *An Essay on Translated Verse*, ll. 185–8 (above, p. 113).

26. *Edition . . . Poems*: This edition of the poems was in fact never realized.

27. *The English . . . whatsoever*: On the English disposition to humour, see William Congreve, *Concerning Humour in Comedy* (1695) and George Farquhar, 'A Discourse on Comedy' (1701).

28. *Wit . . . Fancy*: For similar definitions of wit, see John Locke, *Essay Concerning Human Understanding* (1690), II.xi.2 and Joseph Addison, *The Spectator*, no. 62 (11 May 1711).

29. *Our Language . . . Conceptions*: Joseph Addison, *The Spectator*, no. 297 (9 February 1712).

30. *some Anachronisms*: See Theobald's *Shakespeare Restored*, pp. 134–5.

31. *Sir Francis Drake*: See Pope's conjectural emendation of *1 Henry VI*, I.i.56, which completed the metre by adding the phrase 'Francis Drake'.

32. *Malus . . . cogitat*: 'Though powerless to hurt, the evil man nevertheless meditates harm': Publilius Syrus M 39.

33. *Anonymous Writer . . . Subject*: The allusion is to David Mallet's *Of Verbal Criticism* (1733) (above, pp. 332–9).

34. *Hang him . . . MALLET*: *2 Henry IV*, II.iv.261.

35. ἡ . . . ἐπιγέυυημα: Longinus, *On the Sublime*, section 6 (*ALC*, p. 466).

36. *noble Writer says*: Shaftesbury, 'Advice to an Author', Part II, Sect. 1, in *Characteristicks*, 3 vols. (1711), i, 217.

Sir Thomas Hanmer, 'Preface' to *The Works of Shakespear* (1744)

SIR THOMAS HANMER (1677–1746); Speaker of the House, 1714–15; instrumental in bringing over George I on the death of Anne, though also a leading Hanoverian Tory.

TEXT: Taken from *The Works of Shakespear* (1744).

1. *other Gentlemen*: These 'other Gentlemen' included William Warburton, the 'reverend Mr. Smith of Harleston in Norfolk' and Thomas Cooke, the editor of Plautus: see Smith, p. 297.

2. *the French Princess and an old Gentlewoman*: *Henry V*, III.iv.

3. *How every fool . . . parrots*: *Merchant of Venice*, III.v.48.

4. *erecting his Statue at a publick expence*: Hanmer here refers to the erection in 1741 of the statue of Shakespeare in Poets' Corner in Westminster Abbey. Designed by William Kent and executed by Peter Scheemaker, it had been paid for by public subscription.

Richard Bentley, 'Preface' to *Milton's Paradise Lost. A New Edition* (1732)

RICHARD BENTLEY (1662–1742); the greatest English classical scholar of his day; editor of Horace and Manilius; Master of Trinity College, Cambridge from 1699.

TEXT: Taken from the first edition of *Milton's Paradise Lost. A New Edition* (1732).

1. *Our celebrated Author . . . writ by another*: For Milton's situation when writing *Paradise Lost*, see *Paradise Lost*, VII.1–39 and Parker, i, 567–605.

2. *Tuque . . . tridenti*: 'And thou [i.e. Neptune], for whom the earth, struck by thy great trident, first sent forth the neighing steed': Virgil, *Georgics*, I.12–13.

3. *A poor Bookseller*: Samuel Simmons, nephew of Milton's friend Matthew Simmons (Parker, i, 601–5).

4. *vel furcâ ejecisset*: This appears to be a phrase of Bentley's own coining. However, see Horace, *Epistles*, I.x.24: 'Naturam expelles furca, tamen usque recurret' ('You may drive out Nature with a pitchfork, but she will hurry back').

5. *Sunt . . . illis*: 'I too have songs; I too am called a poet by the shepherds. But I do not believe them': Virgil, *Eclogues*, IX.33–4.

6. *1667 . . . 1674*: Bentley gives the dates of the first and second editions of

Paradise Lost accurately, despite what his anonymous assailant contends (above, p. 318).

7. *chang'd his old Printer and Supervisor*: *Paradise Regained* and *Samson Agonistes* were published in 1671 by John Starkey (Parker, i, 614).

8. *Virgo . . . extinguerent*: 'A lovely girl, and you might have said so the more because her beauty had nothing to set it off: hair dishevelled, barefoot, unkempt, in tears, shabbily dressed. In fact, but for the force of goodness in her face, these blemishes would have overwhelmed her': Terence, *Phormio*, ll. 104–8.

9. *Conscia virtus*: Literally 'conscious virtue'.

10. *above 60 Years time . . . Virgil*: Praise of *Paradise Lost* begins with Roscommon's *An Essay on Translated Verse* of 1684 (see above, p. 119), so Bentley's sixty years is a slight exaggeration.

11. *jamdudum . . . divitiarum*: 'Have long since warned me to be mindful': a phrase which does not occur in classical Latin literature, and which therefore seems to be another coinage by Bentley. 'Dismiss light hopes and the struggle for wealth': Horace, *Epistles*, I.v.8.

Anon., *Milton Restor'd and Bentley Depos'd* (1732)

TEXT: Taken from the first and only edition of 1732. The title may have been influenced by the controversy surrounding Bentley's edition of Horace, in particular by *Horatius Reformatus: sive, Emendationes omnes quibus editio Bentleiana a vulgaribus distinguitur* (1712), a non-satirical compilation of Bentley's new readings.

1. *Reputation . . . well established*: Bentley's reputation as a critic and as a classical scholar began with his *Letter to Mill* (1691), on the subject of Greek drama. It was consolidated by his Boyle lectures, *The Folly and Unreasonableness of Atheism* (1693) and by his exposure of the *Epistles of Phalaris* (1695) as spurious. His later editions of Horace and Manilius, remarkable for their audacious corrections of the received text, established him as the greatest classical scholar of his or perhaps any day: Housman praised him as 'alone and supreme'.

2. *Licenser*: The Licenser of the Press had been done away with in 1694 when Parliament had refused to renew the Licensing Act, in force from 1662 to 1679, and from 1685 to 1694. The requirement that books should be licensed for printing by either the Privy Council or the crown's nominees goes back to 1538.

3. *per fas & nefas*: 'by fair means or foul'.

4. *poor*: For Milton's 'modest' financial resources at the end of his life, see Parker, i, 606–41.

5. *his Friends . . . Gentleman*: This is taken from the life of Milton by the poet Elijah Fenton (1683–1730), a short biography commonly prefixed to early-eighteenth-century editions of *Paradise Lost*. In the twelfth edition of 1725 the quoted passage occurs on p. xviii.

6. *Mr. Simmons . . . Thousands*: See Parker, i, 601–5.

7. *certainly mistaken*: Bentley is in fact correct in his dating of the first and second editions of *Paradise Lost*.

8. *the Year following*: *Paradise Regained* and *Samson Agonistes* were published in 1671 (Parker, i, 614).

9. *published in 1669*: This error concerning the date of the first edition of *Paradise Lost* also occurs in Fenton's life of Milton. It can be found on p. xxi of the twelfth edition of 1725.

10. *Are least deform'd . . . Panth.*: Dryden, *The Hind and the Panther*, i, l. 409.

11. *Twelves . . . Mr Addison*: Addison's *Notes Upon the Twelve Books of Paradise Lost. Collected from the Spectator* (1719) was commonly bound with duodecimo editions of *Paradise Lost*; for instance, the tenth edition of 1719.

12. *Parturiunt Montes*: 'The mountains will labour [to give birth to a risible mouse]': Horace, *De Arte Poetica*, l. 139 (*ALC*, p. 283). A proverbial expression for bathos.

13. *Dutch*: Bentley had assumed the persona of a Dutchman in his attack on Anthony Collins's *Remarks upon a Late Discourse of Free-Thinking* (1713).

14. *Secret Conference . . . Mountain*: Exodus 3–4.

15. *Cosa . . . RIMA*: 'What has never before been recounted in prose or rhyme': Ariosto, *Orlando Furioso*, I.ii.2.

16. *For . . . Song*: Milton, *A Masque Presented at Ludlow Castle* [*Comus*], ll. 43–4.

17. *Risum teneatis Amici?*: 'My friends, could you suppress your laughter?': Horace, *De Arte Poetica*, l. 5 (*ALC*, p. 279).

18. *scripsit . . . debuit*: 'This is what he wrote, or what he ought to have written.' Bentley set out the principles of his edition of Horace in the 'Praefatio' (i, sigs. c2ʳ–c4ᵛ). His imperious freedom with the text excited irreverent comment: see, for instance, *Five Extraordinary Letters Suppos'd to be Writ to Dr. B——y, upon his Edition of Horace* (1712), p. 7; 'With how much Assurance, and how little Reason, do you alter the Text of your Author, and then tell us, that *Horace* either did, or ought to have writ so.' The phrase in question became notorious, as its use by Theobald and Hanmer suggests (above, pp. 294 and 304).

19. *Terrasque . . . profundum*: 'Earth, and expanse of sea and heaven's depth': Virgil, *Eclogues*, IV.51 and *Georgics*, IV.222.

20. *imitation of Homer*: Bentley compares *Iliad* I.8.

David Mallet, *Of Verbal Criticism: An Epistle to Mr. Pope* (1733)

DAVID MALLET (?1705–1765); poet, playwright and miscellaneous writer; born into a Roman Catholic and Jacobite milieu in Scotland; friend of Pope and Thomson, protégé of Bolingbroke, active in the opposition to Walpole.

TEXT: Taken from the first edition of 1733.

1. *judging, as for writing well*: An allusion to the opening of Pope's *An Essay on Criticism*, ll. 1–2 (see above, p. 208).

2. *common sense*: A similar rhyme and sentiment occur in Dryden's *Mac Flecknoe* (1682), ll. 19–20.

3. *Cave . . . head*: In the *Aeneid*, Book IV, Aeneas and Dido take shelter in a cave and consummate their love (ll. 160–72).

4. *the Stagyrite*: Aristotle.

5. *Winkin*: Wynkyn de Worde. Cf. Alexander Pope, *The Dunciad*, I.129.

6. *Bufo*: Literally, 'toad'. For its use in a literary context, see Pope, *An Epistle to Dr. Arbuthnot* (written 1731–4; published 1735), ll. 231–48.

7. *Tibbald*: i.e. Theobald.

8. *a bull*: a statement which unconsciously implies an absurdity.

9. *Quis . . . &c.*: 'What Myrmidon or Dolopian could, in telling such a tale, [refrain from tears]': Virgil, *Aeneid*, II.6–7.

10. *In this . . . his own*: Compare Roscommon, *An Essay on Translated Verse*, ll. 93–6 (above, p. 111).

11. *With learning . . . bred*: Compare *An Essay on Criticism*, l. 638 (above, p. 226).

12. *Dutchman's choice . . . Bentley's voice*: Burmann had published his edition of Petronius in 1709. There is no poem to Charles Montagu, Earl of Halifax, in the first edition of Bentley's Horace (Cambridge, 1711), in the 'Editio Altera' (Amsterdam, 1713) or in the 'Editio Tertia' (Amsterdam, 1728). However, in *Dr. Bentley's Dedication of Horace Translated* (1712) a poem to Halifax is included. Halifax is urged to seize his lyre, and thereby improve the poetry of his contemporaries: 'Nos etenim viles, corvi picaeque, poëtae / Vix pennas madido (turpe) levamus humo.' These lines are there translated by: 'For we're vile Poets, and, the more's the Pity, / Whate'er we sing is Crowd and Magpies Ditty: / Cawing and chattering on wet Ground we lye, / And for our Bloods an Inch we cannot fly.'

13. *To Milton . . . writ*: For the principles on which Bentley edited Milton, see above, pp. 309–15.

14. *Procrustes old*: For Procrustes, see above, p. 390, n. 22. Mallet, like Pope, employs him as a metaphorical example of crude or insensitive criticism.

15. *So wise Caligula . . . toils*: Suetonius, *Caligula*, XLVI.

16. *Capreæ's Isle*: For the depraved excesses which took place at Capri, see Suetonius, *Tiberius*, XLIII–XLIV.

17. *Chartres*: Francis Chartres or Charteris.

18. *'Twere to read . . . learn*: The literary figures alluded to in these lines are, in order: John Oldmixon, Leonard Welsted, Matthew Concanen, Joseph Wasse, William Arnall, John Henley and Thomas Hearne. The '*One Epistle*' refers to *One Epistle to Mr. A. Pope* (1730), by Welsted and James Moore Smythe. Mallet revised these lines: in his three-volume *Works* (1759), they read: ' 'Twere to read new-year odes in search of thought; / To sum the libels PRYN and WITHERS wrote, / To guess, ere *one Epistle* saw the light, / How many dunces met, and club'd their mite; / To vouch for truth what WELSTED prints of POPE, / Or from the *brother Boobies* steal a trope. / That be the part of persevering WASSE, / With pen of lead; or, ARNALL, thine of brass; / A text for HENLEY, or a Gloss for HERNE, / Who loves to teach, what no man cares to learn.' I am indebted to Roger Lonsdale for alerting me to this revision.

Jonathan Richardson, selections from *Explanatory Notes and Remarks on Milton's Paradise Lost* (1734)

JONATHAN RICHARDSON THE ELDER (1665–1745); portrait painter; author of *Theory of Painting* (1715); friend of Pope, Gay and Prior.

TEXT: Taken from the first edition of 1734. Richardson's idiosyncratic way with capitals has been left untouched.

1. *Vertue . . . returning*: Milton, *Reason of Church Government* (1642) (*Prose Works*, i, 795).

2. *Rejoycing in Their Joy*: Possibly a mis-remembrance of Zephaniah 3:17. The phrase does not occur in Milton's works.

3. *Long Choosing . . . Dangers*: *Paradise Lost*, IX.26 and VII.25–6.

4. *Homer . . . the Scripture*: Cf. John Dennis, *Grounds of Criticism in Poetry* (above, pp. 166–76).

5. *his own Expression*: Milton, *Reason of Church Government* (*Prose Works*, i, 808).

6. *As a Madman . . . Sport*: Proverbs 26:18–19.

7. *My Son*: Jonathan Richardson the Younger (1694–1771).

8. *not caring . . . Mechanicks*: Milton, *Reason of Church Government* (*Prose Works*, i, 812).

9. *He therefore . . . 365*: John Milton, *Tetrachordon* (1645) (*Prose Works*, ii, 671).

10. *in Particular on VII.303*: After quoting *Paradise Lost*, VII.303–306, Richardson comments: 'the Earth was Now just Emerg'd from the Waters in which it had been Wrapt, 'twas Therefore all One great Washy Oose, Slime and Mud; in This Soft Earth Deep Channels were Easily Worn by the Streaming Water 'till 'twas dry every where but within the Banks, the Bounds set to the Rivers, where they Now Perpetually draw Along after them their Moist Train; The Rivers are imagin'd as Persons of Great Quality, the Length of their Robe Trailing after them. Let it be Noted, that the Words, the Pronunciation of them without the Sense describes the Course of a Gentle River. . . . You cannot Read it Otherwise than Slowly, and so as to give your Mind a Picture of the thing Describ'd. Many Examples of the Like Kind are to be found in Our Author, and all Good Poets' (pp. 319–20).

11. *Wrote for Divorce*: Milton's tracts on divorce were: *The Doctrine and Discipline of Divorce* (1643), *Colasterion* (1645) and *Tetrachordon* (1645). For an account of the circumstances surrounding their composition, see *Prose Works*, ii, 137–83.

12. *What Macrobius . . . Express'd*: Macrobius, *Saturnalia*, V.xiii.40. Longinus does not use this exact phrase, but 7.3 is a relevant passage; see also 35.3 for his comments on our appetite for the immense (*ALC*, pp. 467 and 494).

13. *Numerous Verse*: *Paradise Lost*, V.150.

14. *Golden Urns . . . Small Peculiar Here*: *Paradise Lost*, VII.365–6.

15. *What's . . . He to Hecuba?*: *Hamlet*, II.ii.553.

16. *a Paradise Within . . . Eden*: Compare *Paradise Lost*, XII.587.

17. *to build the Lofty Rhyme*: Milton, *Lycidas*, l. 11.

18. *Van-Dyke*: Sir Anthony Van Dyck.

19. *Perfect . . . Virgil*: The quotation is from the preface to Bentley's edition; see above, p. 315.

20. *see my Face no more*: Genesis 44:23.

21. *before . . . Dark Mountains*: Jeremiah 13:16.

BIOGRAPHICA

This Biographica aims to provide succinct factual information about actual personages referred to in the texts and notes. Further information can usually be found in standard works of reference such as the *DNB*.

ADDISON, Joseph (1672–1719): Whig statesman, poet and man of letters; together with Richard Steele, responsible for *The Spectator* (1711–12); an arbiter of taste in the early eighteenth century.

ADOLPHUS, Gustavus (1594–1632): King of Sweden 1611–32; celebrated military commander.

AESCHYLUS (525–456 BC): Greek playwright, seven of whose tragedies survive; the founder of Greek tragedy.

ALCIBIADES (b. *c.* 450 BC): Athenian nobleman of great physical beauty, the lover of Socrates.

AMBROSE, Saint (*c.* 340–97): Bishop of Milan; credited with developing the use of music in church services; alleged to be the composer of the *Te Deum*.

ARBUTHNOT, John (1667–1735): physician to Queen Anne; close friend of Swift, Gay and Pope; member of the Scriblerus Club; co-author (with Pope and Gay) of *Three Hours After Marriage* (1717).

ARCHIMEDES (*c.* 287–212 BC): one of the greatest mathematicians, astronomers, engineers and inventors of antiquity.

ARGYLL, *see* CAMPBELL, John.

ARIOSTO, Ludovico (1474–1535): poet and playwright; author of *Orlando Furioso* (1532), the greatest Italian romantic epic.

ARISTIDES (d. *c.* 468 BC): one of the democratic leaders at Athens; renowned for his rectitude.

ARISTOTLE (384–322 BC): Greek philosopher; born at Stageira, hence sometimes referred to as 'the Stagyrite'.

ARNALL, William (*c.* 1715–1741): political writer retained by Walpole to answer

Bolingbroke's *Craftsman* (1730–31); attacked by Pope in *The Dunciad* (1728) and the *Epilogue to the Satires* (1738).

ATTERBURY, Francis (1662–1732): Bishop of Rochester; Jacobite and controversialist.

AULUS GELLIUS (fl. 2nd century AD): author of miscellaneous essays, collected as *Noctes Atticae*.

BAVIUS, *see* MAEVIUS.

BEAUMONT, Francis (1584–1616): playwright, who frequently worked in collaboration with John Fletcher; their plays were very popular on the Restoration stage.

BENTLEY, Richard (1662–1742): the greatest English classical scholar; editor of Horace and Manilius; Master of Trinity College, Cambridge, from 1699.

BRENI, Francesco (1496/7–1535): composer of facetious and burlesque poetry; his *rifacimento* of Boiardo's *Orlando Innamorato* (1487) enjoyed great popularity and long currency.

BLACKMORE, Sir Richard (1654–1729): physician to William III and Queen Anne; epic poet and staunch Whig.

BOCCALINI, Traiano (1556–1613): Italian satirist and political writer.

BOIOARDO, Matteomaria (?1441–94): composer of chivalrous epics, drawing on the legends of Arthur and Charlemagne.

BOILEAU, Nicolas (1636–1711): French neoclassic critic and poet.

BOLINGBROKE, *see* ST JOHN, Henry.

BOSSU, *see* LE BOSSU.

BOUHOURS, Dominique (1628–1702): Jesuit; literary critic and writer on religion.

BOYLE, Charles, fourth Earl of Orrery (1676–1731): adversary of Bentley in the controversy surrounding the *Epistles of Phalaris* (1695); also involved in the Treaty of Utrecht negotiations.

BOYLE, Roger, first Earl of Orrery (1621–79): playwright and poet; author of *Parthenissa* (1654–65), a romance in the French style.

BRUTUS, Marcus Junius (?78–42 BC): the assassin of Julius Caesar.

BUCKHURST, *see* SACKVILLE, Charles.

BUCKINGHAM, *see* SHEFFIELD, John.

BURBAGE, Richard (?1567–1619): actor and painter; shareholder in the Blackfriars and Globe theatres.

BURMANN, Pieter, the Elder (1668–1741): Dutch classical scholar and editor, remarkable more for erudition than for taste; student of Graevius and Gronovius; like Richard Bentley, a formidable and enthusiastic polemicist.

BUTLER, Samuel (1613–80): author of the popular burlesque poem *Hudibras* (1663).

CAESAR, Gaius Julius (102–44 BC): consummate Roman military commander and politician.

CAMPBELL, John, second Duke of Argyll and Duke of Greenwich (1678–1743): soldier and statesman of maverick character and allegiances; admired by Pope, Swift and Thomson.

CAREW, Thomas (1594/5–1640): Cavalier poet; friend of Sir John Suckling.

CARTERET, John, first Earl Granville (1690–1763): scholar, diplomat and statesman; political foe of Sir Robert Walpole; friend of Jonathan Swift.

CASTELVETRO, Ludovico (1505–71): scholar and critic; author of a commentary (1570, 1576) on Aristotle's *Poetics*, in which he made the doctrine of the unities yet more stringent.

CATO, Marcus Porcius (95–46 BC): grandson of Cato the Censor; the chief opponent of Julius Cæsar and the triumvirate; his last stand and suicide at Utica in North Africa were the subject of Joseph Addison's *Cato* (1713).

CAXTON, William (?1422–91): the first English printer.

CHARTRES, or Charteris, Francis (1675–1732): colonel; legendary rake, cheat, usurer and criminal; according to Arbuthnot, incorrigibly devoted to 'every human vice excepting prodigality and hypocrisy'.

CHURCHILL, John, first Duke of Marlborough (1650–1722): Captain-General, 1702–11; statesman and soldier.

CICERO, Marcus Tullius (106–43 BC): Roman statesman, philosopher and rhetorician.

CINTHIO (Giambattista Giraldi) (1504–73): playwright, critic and author of the influential *Hecatomithi*, or 'hundred tales' (1566).

CLEVELAND, John (1613–58): Cavalier poet, notorious for the difficulty of his verse.

COBB, Samuel (1675–1713): poet and translator; composer of Whig panegyric; master at Christ's Hospital.

COBHAM, *see* TEMPLE, Sir Richard.

COLLINS, Anthony (1676–1729): freethinker; attacked by Richard Bentley.

CONCANEN, Matthew (1701–1749): miscellaneous writer; collaborator with Theobald; adversary of Pope.

CONDELL, Henry (d. 1627): together with John Heminges, the editor of the First Folio of Shakespeare's plays (1623).

CONGREVE, William (1670–1729): dramatist.

CONSTANTINE the Great (Flavius Valerius Constantinus Augustus) (274–337): Roman Emperor from 306; traditionally supposed to have been born in Britain; the emperor who established Christianity as the religion of the empire.

COOKE, Thomas (1703–1756), commonly called 'Hesiod Cooke' because of his translation of Hesiod (1728): poet and miscellaneous writer; published an attack on Pope's translation of the *Iliad*, and was attacked by Pope in his turn (*Epistle to Arbuthnot* (1735), l. 146).

COOPER, Anthony Ashley, third Earl of Shaftesbury (1671–1713): Whig statesman, and influential philosopher on questions of morals and aesthetics; author of *Characteristicks* (1711).

CORNEILLE, Pierre (1606–84): French dramatist, pre-eminently of tragedy cast in the classical mould.

COWARD, William (?1657–1725): physician, deist and Whig literary critic.

COWLEY, Abraham (1618–67): royalist poet.

CRASSUS, Marcus Licinius (d. 53 BC): Roman senator of great wealth; triumvir with Cæsar and Pompey in 60 BC; killed after the defeat of the Roman forces by the Parthians at Carrhae in 53 BC.

DACIER, André (?1651–1720): French translator and editor of classical texts.

DENHAM, Sir John (1615–69): poet, royalist soldier and politician.

DENNIS, John (1657–1734): Whig poet, critic and playwright; adversary of Pope.

DESCARTES, René (1596–1650): French philosopher and mathematician.

DILLON, Wentworth, fourth Earl of Roscommon (?1633–85): poet, politician, gambler and duellist; founder of an informal literary academy, which included Halifax (Charles Montagu), Maitland, Dorset and Dryden; alleged to be the first to praise Milton's *Paradise Lost* (1667) in print.

DIONYSIUS OF HALICARNASSUS (fl. 25 BC): literary critic and historian.

DORSET, *see* SACKVILLE, Charles.

DRYDEN, John (1631–1700): the greatest poet, translator, critic and playwright of the late seventeenth century; Poet Laureate (1668) and Historiographer Royal (1670).

DURFEY, Thomas (1653–1723): playwright, man of letters, collector of songs and ballads.

ESCHYLUS, *see* AESCHYLUS.

ETHEREGE, Sir George (?1634–91): dramatist and statesman.

EURIPIDES (*c.* 480–406 BC): Athenian playwright, eighteen of whose tragedies survive.

FANSHAWE, Sir Richard (1608–66): royalist statesman and ambassador; translator of Guarini's *Il Pastor Fido* (1647).

FARQUHAR, George (?1677–1707): dramatist.

FIELD, Nathan (1587–1619/20): actor and dramatist; author of *A Woman is a*

Weathercock (1609) and *Amends for Ladies* (1610); perhaps succeeded Shakespeare as actor and shareholder in the King's Men.

FLECKNO (or Flecknoe), Richard (*c.* 1620–78): reputedly a Roman Catholic priest. Critic, poet and composer of operas.

FLETCHER, John (1579–1625): dramatist; frequent collaborator with Francis Beaumont.

GALEN (129–199): a celebrated physician of antiquity.

GARTH, Sir Samuel (1661–1719): physician, freethinker and author of the burlesque *The Dispensary* (1699).

GAY, John (1685–1732): poet and playwright; member of the Scriblerus Club; friend of Pope, Swift and Arbuthnot.

GILDON, Charles (1662–1724): Whig playwright, poet and critic.

GODOLPHIN, Sidney (1610–43): poet and royalist.

GRAEVIUS (Johann Georg Greffe) (1632–1703): Dutch classical scholar and antiquary; friend of Richard Bentley.

GRANVILLE, George, Lord Lansdowne (1667–1735): statesman, poet and dramatist; suspected Jacobite; early patron of Pope.

GRONOVIUS, Johann Friedrich (1611–71): Dutch classical scholar.

GUARINI, Giovanni Battista (1538–1612): author of *Il Pastor Fido* (1589), tr. in 1647 by Sir Richard Fanshawe as *The Faithfull Shepherd*.

HALES, John (1584–1656): Fellow of Eton College from 1613.

HALIFAX, *see* MONTAGU, Charles, and SAVILE, George.

HANMER, Sir Thomas (1677–1746): Speaker of the House, 1714–15; instrumental in bringing over George I on the death of Anne, though also a leading Hanoverian Tory.

HARRINGTON, James (1611–77): English republican political theorist; author of *The Commonwealth of Oceana* (1656) and *A System of Politics* (1661; published, 1700); influenced by Machiavelli.

HART, Charles (d. 1683): actor, equally accomplished at tragedy and comedy; Shakespeare's great-nephew.

HARTLIB, Samuel (d. 1662): a promoter of science and of educational reform.

HEARNE, Thomas (1678–1735): antiquary mocked by Pope as 'Wormius' in *The Dunciad* (1728).

HEINSIUS, Daniel (1580–1655): Dutch poet and classical scholar, whose 1611 edition of Aristotle's *Poetics* greatly influenced the French stage during the seventeenth century.

HEMINGES (or Heming), John (1556–1630): with Henry Condell, the editor of the First Folio of Shakespeare's plays (1623).

HENLEY, John (1692–1756): commonly known as 'Orator' Henley, mocked repeatedly by Pope in *The Dunciad* (1728); retained by Walpole to answer Bolingbroke's *Craftsman* (1730–31).

HERMOGENES of Tarsus (b. *c.* 160): celebrated rhetorician; author of *On Types of Style* (*ALC*, pp. 561–79).

HERRINGMAN, Henry (?1630–1704): publisher of Sir Robert Howard's plays; publisher of Dryden until 1678.

HIPPOCRATES (fl. 430 BC): a celebrated physician of antiquity.

HOMER (fl. 9th century BC): earliest and greatest Greek epic poet; author of the *Iliad* and the *Odyssey*.

HOPKINS, John (d. 1570): collaborated with Thomas Sternhold and others on a metrical version of the Psalms first published in 1549 and reprinted many times thereafter. Rochester's uncomplimentary epigram on Hopkins is an amusing index to the waning of his reputation. Not to be confused with the John Hopkins (fl. 1700) who wrote Whig panegyric.

HORACE (Quintus Horatius Flaccus) (65–8 BC): Latin poet; intimate of Augustus and his chief minister Maecenas.

HOWARD, Sir Robert (1626–98): dramatist and politician; Auditor of the Exchequer, 1677–98; Privy Councillor, 1688–9.

HUGHES, John (1677–1720): poet and dramatist.

JONSON (or Johnson), Ben (1572/3–1637): dramatist, poet and scholar; the most influential English dramatist of the seventeenth century; often compared with Shakespeare as an exponent of art, rather than nature.

KENNETT, White (1660–1728): Bishop of Peterborough; antiquarian; supporter of the Glorious Revolution of 1688; opponent of Dr Sacheverell.

LABIENUS, Quintus (d. 39 BC): renegade Roman republican general; made common cause with the Parthians against Rome; defeated and killed by Publius Ventidius in 39 BC.

LANSDOWNE, *see* GRANVILLE, George.

LE BOSSU, René (1631–80): author of the influential *Traité du poème épique* (1675), of which English translations appeared in 1695 and 1719.

LE CLERC, Jean (1657–1736): French Protestant theologian and man of letters; suspected of Socinianism.

LOCKE, John (1632–1704): philosopher and Whig political theorist.

'LONGINUS' (fl. *c.* 1st century AD): the author of a treatise on the sublime, and for long confused with Cassius Longinus (*c.* 220–73), the Neoplatonist and author of a treatise on rhetoric.

LOPE DE VEGA, *see* VEGA CARPIO, Lope Felix de.

LUCAN (Marcus Annaeus Lucanus) (39–65): epic poet, author of the *Pharsalia*; commanded by Nero to take his own life.

LYCOPHRON of Chalcis (b. *c.* 325 BC): poet and playwright, none of whose tragedies have survived.

MACHIAVELLI, Niccolò (1469–1527): Florentine statesman and political theorist.

MAEVIUS: a poetaster satirically glanced at in Horace's tenth Epode and (this time in company with another poetaster, Bavius) Virgil's third Eclogue.

MAITLAND, Richard, fourth Earl of Lauderdale (1653–95): Jacobite statesman and man of letters; translator of Virgil.

MALLET (or Malloch), David (?1705–65): poet, playwright and miscellaneous writer; born into a Roman Catholic and Jacobite milieu in Scotland; friend of Pope and Thomson, protégé of Bolingbroke, active in the opposition to Walpole.

MARLBOROUGH, *see* CHURCHILL, John.

MARO, *see* VIRGIL.

MEDE (or Mead), Joseph (1586–1638): biblical scholar.

MICHELANGELO Buonarroti (1475–1564): Florentine painter, sculptor, architect and poet.

MILBOURNE, Luke (1649–1720): poet and clergyman of High Church sympathies; supporter of Dr Sacheverell.

MILO (fl. 6th century BC): a famous wrestler of Croton; killed by wolves when his hands became trapped in a tree which he was trying to split – hence proverbially a warning of the dangers of presumption.

MILTON, John (1608–74): poet, theologian, historian and pamphleteer; supporter of the parliamentary cause in the Civil War, and Latin secretary to the Council of State.

MONAESES (fl. 36 BC): Parthian noble; defected to Mark Anthony in 37 or 36 BC; cf. Horace, *Odes*, III.vi.9.

MONCK (or Monk), George, first Duke of Albemarle (1608–70): general; played a leading role in the restoration of the monarchy in 1660.

MONTAGU, Charles, first Earl of Halifax (1661–1715): one of the signatories of the letter of invitation to William of Orange; prime architect, with John Somers, of William III's financial policy in the 1690s; founder of the Bank of England.

MULGRAVE, *see* SHEFFIELD, John.

NEUFVILLE, François de, duc de Villeroi (1644–1730): maréchal de France; commander of the French forces at Ramillies.

OLDMIXON, John (?1673–1742): Whig historian and pamphleteer.

ORRERY, *see* BOYLE, Charles, *and* BOYLE, Roger.

OTWAY, Thomas (1652–85): playwright.

PACORUS (d. 38 BC): Parthian prince, son of Orodes II; ally of the renegade Roman republican general Quintus Labienus; cf. Horace, *Odes*, III.vi.9.

PERCY, Thomas (1729–1811): Bishop of Dromore; friend of Thomas Warton; antiquarian, and editor of the influential collection of early English poetry *Reliques of Ancient English Poetry* (1765).

PERRAULT, Charles (1628–1703): French poet, raconteur and administrator. His *Parallèle des Anciens et des Modernes* (1688–97) was an attack on the Ancients and a vindication of the Moderns.

PHOCION (d. 318 BC): Athenian general and statesman.

PLATO (*c.* 427/8–348/7 BC): Greek philosopher.

PLINY the Younger (Gaius Plinius Caecilius Secundus) (62–*c.* 112): Roman letter-writer and politician.

POPE, Alexander (1688–1744): the most accomplished poet, critic and translator of the early Hanoverian period; Roman Catholic in religion, and of Jacobite inclinations.

PORTA, Giambattista della (1535–1615): Italian playwright; author of *La Sorella* (1589), which influenced Middleton's *No Wit, No Help Like a Woman's* (?1613).

PRIOR, Matthew (1664–1721): poet, essayist and diplomat.

QUINAULT, Philippe (1635–88): French playwright.

QUINTILIAN (Marcus Fabius Quintilianus) (35–95): rhetorician and critic.

RAPHAEL (Raffaello Sanzio) (1483–1520): painter and architect of the Italian High Renaissance.

RAPIN, René (1621–87): prolific French critic and poet; author of *Observationes in Poëmata Homeri et Virgilii* (1684).

RICHARDSON, Jonathan, the Elder (1665–1745): portrait painter; author of *Theory of Painting* (1715); friend of Pope, Gay and Prior.

RICHARDSON, Jonathan, the Younger (1694–1771): painter; son of the above.

RICHELIEU, Armand Jean du Plessis, cardinal and duc de (1585–1642); statesman and founder of the Académie française.

ROCHESTER, *see* WILMOT, John.

ROSCOMMON, *see* DILLON, Wentworth.

ROWE, Nicholas (1674–1718): playwright and poet.

RYMER, Thomas (1641–1713): antiquarian, playwright and critic.

SACHEVERELL (or Sachaverell), Revd Dr Henry (1674–1724): High Church and Tory political preacher.

SACKVILLE, Charles, Lord Buckhurst and later sixth Earl of Dorset (1638–1706): Lord Chamberlain, 1689–97; patron of poets, and supposed to be 'Eugenius' in Dryden's *Of Dramatick Poesie* (1668).

SAINT-ÉVREMOND, Charles de Marguetel de Saint-Denis, sieur de (1613/

14–1703): French man of letters and ethical philosopher; an exile in London and Holland from 1659.

ST JOHN, Henry, first Viscount Bolingbroke (1678–1751): Tory and Jacobite statesman and man of letters; David Mallet's patron.

SANDYS, George (1578–1644): author of a *Paraphrase upon the Psalmes* (1636).

SAVILE, George, Marquess of Halifax (1633–95); politician and essayist; 'Jotham' in Dryden's *Absalom and Achitophel* (1681).

SCALIGER, Joseph Justus (1540–1609): Dutch philologist, historian and classical scholar.

SEDLEY, Sir Charles (?1639–1701): dramatist and poet; 'Lisideius' in Dryden's *Of Dramatick Poesie* (1668).

SERVIUS, Marius Honoratus (fl. 4th–5th century AD): a Latin grammarian; author of a commentary on Virgil.

SHADWELL, Thomas (?1642–92): dramatist and Whig; political and literary opponent of Dryden.

SHAFTESBURY, *see* COOPER, Anthony Ashley.

SHAKESPEARE, William (1564–1616): dramatist and poet; after 1700, generally recognized to be the pre-eminent English poet and dramatist.

SHEFFIELD, John, third Earl of Mulgrave and later first Duke of Buckingham and Normanby (1648–1721): patron of Dryden and friend of Pope.

SILIUS ITALICUS, Tiberius Catius Asconius (25/26–101): Silver Age Latin epic poet; author of the *Punica*, a narrative of the Second Punic War.

SOCINUS (Lelio Sozzini) (1525–62): theologian who held that Jesus was not God but a prophet.

SOMERS, John (1651–1716): Lord Chancellor of England; adviser to William III; head of the Whig Junto during the reign of Anne.

SOPHOCLES (496–406 BC): Athenian playwright, seven of whose tragedies are extant.

STEELE, Sir Richard (1672–1729): dramatist and essayist.

STEPNEY, George (1663–1707): poet; Whig diplomat; associate of Charles Montagu, Earl of Halifax, and Marlborough.

STERNHOLD, Thomas (d. 1549): with John Hopkins, the author of a metrical version of the Psalms.

STRABO (64 BC–AD 19): geographer and historian.

SUCKLING, Sir John (1609–42): Cavalier poet, and playwright.

SWIFT, Jonathan (1667–1745): poet and man of letters; member of the Scriblerus Club; friend of Pope, Gay and Arbuthnot.

TALBOT, Charles, twelfth Earl and only Duke of Shrewsbury (1660–1718): statesman; Roman Catholic by birth and Jacobite by inclination, but also a supporter of William III and the Protestant Succession; partner of Bolingbroke in the negotiations leading up to the Treaty of Utrecht (1712).

TASSO, Torquato (1544–95): epic poet; author of *Gerusalemme Liberata* (1580–81), tr. in 1600 by Edward Fairfax as *Jerusalem Delivered*.

TAYLOR, John (1578–1653): the 'water-poet', the popularity of whose doggerel was often cited as a sign of the depravity of public taste.

TEMPLE, Sir Richard, Viscount Cobham (?1669–1749): soldier and statesman; as one of the 'boy patriots', active in the opposition to Sir Robert Walpole after 1733; friend of Pope.

THEOBALD, Lewis (1688–1744): poet, essayist and playwright; Shakespearean scholar, and one of the first to understand the importance of source-study for the appreciation of Shakespeare's art.

THOMSON, James (1700–48): poet; author of *The Seasons* (1726–30); friend of David Mallet.

TULLY, *see* CICERO.

VAN DYCK, Sir Anthony (1599–1641): court painter to Charles I from 1632.

VAUGHAN, John, third Earl of Carbery (1640–1713): President of the Royal Society 1686–9; patron of Dryden; notorious for lewdness and servility.

VEGA CARPIO, Lope Felix de (1562–1635): prolific Spanish poet and playwright.

VIDA, Marco Girolamo (1485–1566): Renaissance Latin poet; author of *De Arte Poetica* (1527), ed. Basil Kennett (Oxford, 1701) and Thomas Tristram (Oxford, 1723), tr. Christopher Pitt (1725; 2nd edn 1742).

VILLIERS, George, second Duke of Buckingham (1628–87): author of *The Rehearsal* (1672) and lampooned as 'Zimri' in Dryden's *Absalom and Achitophel* (1681).

VIRGIL (Publius Vergilius Maro) (70–19 BC): poet.

WALLER, Edmund (1606–87): poet and turncoat.

WALPOLE, Sir Robert, first Earl of Orford (1676–1745): Whig politician; Prime Minister 1715–17 and 1721–42.

WALSH, William (1663–1708): minor poet; friend of, and mentor to, the young Alexander Pope.

WARBURTON, William (1698–1779): Bishop of Gloucester; polemicist and theologian; editor of Pope, whose friend and literary executor he was, and of Shakespeare.

WARTON, Joseph (1722–1800): headmaster of Winchester; poet and critic, now chiefly remembered for his *Essay on the Writings and Genius of Pope* (1756, 1782); brother of Thomas Warton.

WARTON, Thomas (1728–90): poet and scholar; Professor of Poetry at Oxford,

1757–67; Poet Laureate, 1785; author of *The History of English Poetry* (1774–81).

WASSE, Joseph (1672–1738): classical scholar admired by Bentley; editor of Sallust (1710).

WELSTED, Leonard (1688–1747): Whig poet; friend of 'Hesiod' Cooke; adversary of Pope.

WILD (or Wylde), Robert (1609–79): Puritan divine and poet, but also a supporter and celebrant of the restoration of the monarchy in 1660.

WILMOT, John, second Earl of Rochester (1647–80): rake, poet and satirist.

WITHER, George (1588–1667): poet and pamphleteer, whose work included pastoral, religious and satirical writing. Fought on the side of Parliament during the Civil War, and occupied positions of trust.

WOOLSTON, Thomas (1670–1733): religious enthusiast and freethinker; having questioned the reality of the resurrection and the virgin birth, he was successfully prosecuted for blasphemy in 1729.

WORDE, Wynkyn de (d. 1535): Caxton's assistant, and successor.

WYCHERLEY, William (1641–1715): dramatist, and friend of Pope.

READ MORE IN PENGUIN

In every corner of the world, on every subject under the sun, Penguin represents quality and variety – the very best in publishing today.

For complete information about books available from Penguin – including Puffins, Penguin Classics and Arkana – and how to order them, write to us at the appropriate address below. Please note that for copyright reasons the selection of books varies from country to country.

In the United Kingdom: Please write to *Dept. EP, Penguin Books Ltd, Bath Road, Harmondsworth, West Drayton, Middlesex UB7 0DA*

In the United States: Please write to *Consumer Sales, Penguin USA, P.O. Box 999, Dept. 17109, Bergenfield, New Jersey 07621-0120.* VISA and MasterCard holders call 1-800-253-6476 to order Penguin titles

In Canada: Please write to *Penguin Books Canada Ltd, 10 Alcorn Avenue, Suite 300, Toronto, Ontario M4V 3B2*

In Australia: Please write to *Penguin Books Australia Ltd, P.O. Box 257, Ringwood, Victoria 3134*

In New Zealand: Please write to *Penguin Books (NZ) Ltd, Private Bag 102902, North Shore Mail Centre, Auckland 10*

In India: Please write to *Penguin Books India Pvt Ltd, 706 Eros Apartments, 56 Nehru Place, New Delhi 110 019*

In the Netherlands: Please write to *Penguin Books Netherlands bv, Postbus 3507, NL-1001 AH Amsterdam*

In Germany: Please write to *Penguin Books Deutschland GmbH, Metzlerstrasse 26, 60594 Frankfurt am Main*

In Spain: Please write to *Penguin Books S. A., Bravo Murillo 19, 1° B, 28015 Madrid*

In Italy: Please write to *Penguin Italia s.r.l., Via Felice Casati 20, I–20124 Milano*

In France: Please write to *Penguin France S. A., 17 rue Lejeune, F–31000 Toulouse*

In Japan: Please write to *Penguin Books Japan, Ishikiribashi Building, 2–5–4, Suido, Bunkyo-ku, Tokyo 112*

In South Africa: Please write to *Longman Penguin Southern Africa (Pty) Ltd, Private Bag X08, Bertsham 2013*

PENGUIN AUDIOBOOKS

A Quality of Writing That Speaks for Itself

Penguin Books has always led the field in quality publishing. Now you can listen at leisure to your favourite books, read to you by familiar voices from radio, stage and screen. Penguin Audiobooks are produced to an excellent standard, and abridgements are always faithful to the original texts. From thrillers to classic literature, biography to humour, with a wealth of titles in between, Penguin Audiobooks offer you quality, entertainment and the chance to rediscover the pleasure of listening.

You can order Penguin Audiobooks through Penguin Direct by telephoning (0181) 899 4036. The lines are open 24 hours every day. Ask for Penguin Direct, quoting your credit card details.

A selection of Penguin Audiobooks, published or forthcoming:

Little Women by Louisa May Alcott, read by Kate Harper

Emma by Jane Austen, read by Fiona Shaw

Pride and Prejudice by Jane Austen, read by Geraldine McEwan

Beowulf translated by Michael Alexander, read by David Rintoul

Agnes Grey by Anne Brontë, read by Juliet Stevenson

Jane Eyre by Charlotte Brontë, read by Juliet Stevenson

The Professor by Charlotte Brontë, read by Juliet Stevenson

Wuthering Heights by Emily Brontë, read by Juliet Stevenson

The Woman in White by Wilkie Collins, read by Nigel Anthony and Susan Jameson

Nostromo by Joseph Conrad, read by Michael Pennington

Tales from the Thousand and One Nights, read by Souad Faress and Raad Rawi

Robinson Crusoe by Daniel Defoe, read by Tom Baker

David Copperfield by Charles Dickens, read by Nathaniel Parker

The Pickwick Papers by Charles Dickens, read by Dinsdale Landen

Bleak House by Charles Dickens, read by Beatie Edney and Ronald Pickup

PENGUIN AUDIOBOOKS

The Hound of the Baskervilles by Sir Arthur Conan Doyle, read by Freddie Jones

Middlemarch by George Eliot, read by Harriet Walter

Tom Jones by Henry Fielding, read by Robert Lindsay

The Great Gatsby by F. Scott Fitzgerald, read by Marcus D'Amico

Madame Bovary by Gustave Flaubert, read by Claire Bloom

Mary Barton by Elizabeth Gaskell, read by Clare Higgins

Jude the Obscure by Thomas Hardy, read by Samuel West

Far from the Madding Crowd by Thomas Hardy, read by Julie Christie

The Scarlet Letter by Nathaniel Hawthorne, read by Bob Sessions

Les Misérables by Victor Hugo, read by Nigel Anthony

A Passage to India by E. M. Forster, read by Tim Pigott-Smith

The Iliad by Homer, read by Derek Jacobi

The Dead and Other Stories by James Joyce, read by Gerard McSorley

On the Road by Jack Kerouac, read by David Carradine

Sons and Lovers by D. H. Lawrence, read by Paul Copley

The Prince by Niccolò Machiavelli, read by Fritz Weaver

Animal Farm by George Orwell, read by Timothy West

Rob Roy by Sir Walter Scott, read by Robbie Coltrane

Frankenstein by Mary Shelley, read by Richard Pasco

Of Mice and Men by John Steinbeck, read by Gary Sinise

Kidnapped by Robert Louis Stevenson, read by Robbie Coltrane

Dracula by Bram Stoker, read by Richard E. Grant

Gulliver's Travels by Jonathan Swift, read by Hugh Laurie

Vanity Fair by William Makepeace Thackeray, read by Robert Hardy

Lark Rise to Candleford by Flora Thompson, read by Judi Dench

The Invisible Man by H. G. Wells, read by Paul Shelley

Ethan Frome by Edith Wharton, read by Nathan Osgood

The Picture of Dorian Gray by Oscar Wilde, read by John Moffatt

Orlando by Virginia Woolf, read by Tilda Swinton

READ MORE IN PENGUIN

A CHOICE OF CLASSICS

ANTHOLOGIES AND ANONYMOUS WORKS

The Age of Bede
Alfred the Great
Beowulf
A Celtic Miscellany
The Cloud of Unknowing and Other Works
The Death of King Arthur
The Earliest English Poems
Early Irish Myths and Sagas
Egil's Saga
English Mystery Plays
Eyrbyggja Saga
Hrafnkel's Saga and Other Stories
The Letters of Abelard and Heloise
Medieval English Lyrics
Medieval English Verse
Njal's Saga
Roman Poets of the Early Empire
Seven Viking Romances
Sir Gawain and the Green Knight